THE

AUTOBIOGRAPHY AND CORRESPONDENCE

OF

MARY GRANVILLE,

MRS. DELANY.

Second Series.

VOL. II.

AMS PRESS
NEW YORK

Joseph Brown, sc.

ANN GRANVILLE,

Lady Stanley.

*From her Portrait by Huysman,
in the possession of Bernard Granville, Esq.*

London: Richard Bentley, 1862.

THE

AUTOBIOGRAPHY
AND CORRESPONDENCE

OF

MARY GRANVILLE,

MRS. DELANY:

WITH INTERESTING REMINISCENCES OF

KING GEORGE THE THIRD AND QUEEN CHARLOTTE.

EDITED

BY THE RIGHT HONOURABLE

LADY LLANOVER.

Second Series.

THREE VOLUMES,

VOL. II.

LONDON:
RICHARD BENTLEY, NEW BURLINGTON STREET,
Publisher in Ordinary to Her Majesty.
1862.

Library of Congress Cataloging in Publication Data

Delany, Mary, (Granville) Pendarves, 1700-1788.
  The autobiography and correspondence of Mary Granville, Mrs. Delany.

  1. Delany, Mary (Granville) Pendarves, 1700-1788.
  2. George III, King of Great Britain, 1738-1820.
  3. Charlotte, Queen consort of George III, 1744-1818.
  I. Llanover, Augusta (Waddington) Hall, Lady, d. 1896,
  ed. II. Title.
  DA483.D3A2 1974   942.07'3'0924 [B]   75-163683
  ISBN 0-404-02080-1

Reprinted from the edition of 1861-1862, London
First AMS edition published in 1974
Manufactured in the United States of America

International Standard Book Number:
Complete Set: 0-404-02080-1
Volume V: 0-404-02085-2

AMS PRESS INC.
NEW YORK, N. Y. 10003

LIST OF ILLUSTRATIONS.

THE

LIFE AND CORRESPONDENCE

OF

MARY GRANVILLE.

(MRS. DELANY.)

CHAPTER XXIV.

JUNE 1774—DECEMBER 1775.

Mrs. Delany to Mrs. Port, of Ilam.

I suppose you will be informed by the newspapers of all that passed at the Fête Champetre[1] last Thursday, the 9th of June, 1774, but as the authenticity of newspapers may sometimes be questioned, perhaps it may be more satisfactory to you to receive this, which came from one of the company, and when you have read it if you think it will be any amusement to my brother you may send it to Calwich; I think it a fairy scene that may equal any in Madame Dánois; nothing at least in modern days has been exhibited so perfectly magnificent—everybody in good humour, and agreed that it exceeded their expectation. The master of the entertainment (Lord Stanley),[2] was dressed like Reubens, and Lady Betty

---

[1] The Fête Champêtre was given at Lord Stanley's villa, the Oaks, near Epsom.

[2] Edward Stanley, eldest son of James, Lord Strange, and grandson of Edward, 11th Earl of Derby, whom he succeeded in the earldom, married first, 23rd June, 1774, Elizabeth, only daughter of James, 6th Duke of Hamilton.

Hamilton (for whom the feast was made), like Reubens' wife. The company were received in the lawn before the house, which is scattered with trees and opens to the downs. The company arriving, and partys of people of all ranks that came to admire, made the scene quite enchanting, which was greatly enlivened with a most beautiful setting sun breaking from a black cloud in its greatest glory. After half an hour's sauntering the company were called to the other side, to a more confined spot, where benches were placed in a semicircle, and a fortunate clump of trees in the centre of the small lawn hid a band of musick; a stage was (supposed to be formed) by a part being divided from the other part of the garden, with sticks entwined with natural flowers in wreaths and festoons joining each. A little dialogue between a Sheperd and Sheperdess, with a welcome to the company, was sung and said, and dancing by 16 men and 16 women *figuranti's* from the Opera lasted about half an hour; after which this party was employed in *swinging, jumping*, shooting with bows and arrows, and various country sports. The gentlemen and ladies danced on the green till it was dark, and then preceded the musick to the other side of the garden, the company following, where a magnificent saloon had been built, illuminated and decorated with the utmost elegance and proportion : here they danced till supper, when curtains were drawn up, which shewed the supper in a most convenient and elegant apartment, which was built quite round the saloon of a sufficient breadth and height to correspond with the saloon ; after the supper, (which was exceeding good, and everybody glad of it as the evening had begun so very early, all the company being assembled in the saloon,) an interlude, in which a Druid entered as an inhabitant of the *Oaks,* welcomed Lady Betty Hamilton, and described the happiness of Lord Stanley in having been so fortunate, and in a prophetic strain foretold the happiness that must follow so happy an union, which, with chorus's and singing and dancing by the Dryads, Cupid and Hymen attending and dancing also, it concluded with the happiness of *the Oak* making so considerable a part in the arms of Hamilton ; a piece of transparent painting was brought in, with the crest of Hamilton and Stanley, surrounded with all the emblems of Cupid and Hymen, who crowned it with wreaths of flowers. From the great room in the house a large portico was built, which was supported by transparent columns and a transparent architecture on which was written, "*To Propitious Venus.*" The pediment illuminated, and obelisks between the house and saloon. People in general very elegantly dressed : the very young as peasants ; the next as Polonise ; the matrons dominos ; the men principally dominos and many gardiners, as in the Opera dances.

The Dowager-Countess Gower to Mrs. Delany.

Pall Mall, 16th June, 74.

Just before I came hear I heard ye Dss Dr of Portland was indispos'd ; I very much desire to know how she does, and if ye sweet air of Bulstrode has restor'd her health, wch I expect it to do. How long I shall stay here I know not, by all accts Mrs. Leveson is so near out of all reckoning. I know not how to go, tho' I'm totally useless, and ignorant in all those affairs, yet on

B 2

ye aproaching hour I feel an anxiety ab^t her y^t makes me incapable of resolving one way or other; 'tis comfortable to see how tranquil she is.

I was told this day y^t ye old *hoyden* ye D^s of Bedford was not at Ld Stanley's[1] fête ; I sopose piqu'd at his recovering her niece's refusal so soon, for she w^d not let any of 'em go, tho' all ye Bloomsbury-gang was invited. Since she has heard how fine, charming, and elegant it was, she is silly enough to confess she repents ; c^d she have been silent, people might have thought she had comenc'd a descency suitable to her age. Geo. Selwin says, " ye fête apear'd to him as if Coll. Burgoyne[2] had *plan'd* it, and L—d Stanley had *paid* for it."

The Druids had L—d March[3] for their *speaker*, w^m ffame says was *not* very desent; and ye D^s of Argyle s^d "nothing but Betty c^d have stood it all." Perhaps y° have heard all this and a great deal more, but it being new to me I comunicate it.

I have wrote twice to Mr. Judson, ye apothecary at Uxbridge, for his bill; have rec^d no ans^r; sh^d be much oblig'd to you if y° w^d pay him, and trust me till I've ye pleasure of seeing you.

Adieu, d^r Mrs. Delany.

---

[1] Edward, who, at his grandfather's death in 1776, became 12th Earl of Derby. His father, James, Lord Strange, the Earl's eldest son, having died in 1771. Lord Stanley married first, in June, 1774, Elizabeth, only daughter of James, 6th Duke of Hamilton ; and secondly, in May, 1797, Miss Farren, the celebrated actress.

[2] The Right Hon. General John Burgoyne, who, in 1777, commanded the British army in America. He was the son of a younger brother of the Burgoynes of Sutton, Bedfordshire, and married Charlotte, daughter of Edward Stanley, 11th Earl of Derby. General Burgoyne wrote "The Lord of the Manor," and other dramas.

[3] William Douglas, 3rd Earl of March, succeeded, on his kinsman's death in 1778, to the Dukedom of Queensberry, and died unmarried in 1710.

The Hon. Mrs. Boscawen to Mrs. Delany.

Audley Street, Thursday, June 16th, 1774.

MY DEAR MADAM,

Do not think of *me* amidst dust, and heat, and stinks, and screams of (green hastings?) lest it make you hot and uncomfortable as I am now. *Hope* is my cordial, and the perfect good health of my dau^r ought to satisfy me, especially as my poor little soldier has had as good an outsetting as possible. He is gone in a man-of-war, the Capt. of wch wrote me: "He beg'd I would be easy about my son, for he should consider him as his own, and take the same care of him; that he should sleep in his own cabbin and fare as he did." George sail'd from Portsmouth under these auspices on ye 6th June and on ye 9th he wrote me from Plymouth on board the Albion (Capt. Leveson's ship), where he was visiting his brother-in-law, but is now, I trust, well on his way to Boston. God bless him. I ask y^r pardon, my dear madam, for this long article, especially as I cannot afford to scribble all my thoughts, for the letter must be single. I thought I *had* a frank, but I perceive I have none. I saw Lady Leicester and Lady Gower yesterday as well as Mrs. Montagu, whom I shall visit again now her friend has left her and is gone to Holkham, looking remarkably well; not so Lady Gower; she looks very ill, and, I find, has been extremely so, wch I am heartily sorry for. I hope she will take care of herself and recover. I thought Mrs. Montagu seem'd much the better for her excursion. The Duchess of Devonshire was to be presented to-day, but I have not seen any body that was at court. The Duke was at the levee yesterday; and at night at Ranelagh leaving his fair bride! Adieu, dear madam.

The Dowager-Countess Gower to Mrs. Delany, at Bulstrode.

Pall Mall, 23ᵈ June, 74.

Dʳ Mrs. Delany's letters are always welcome ; yᵉ last contain'd many pleasing lines, yᵉ good accᵗ of yᵉ Dˢ of Portland's health, wᶜʰ I wish long to continue, and wrote to you to enquire after 16ᵗʰ inst., imediately on my coming here. I find, by yᵉ date of yoʳ last, you had been so good as to tell me she was in a very improving way, unask'd, for yʳ letter travelled to B. Hill after I had left it ; you also give me hopes of seeing you at my cottage, wᶜʰ will be snug and clean, and ready for you, wⁿ ever it suits you to give me yᵗ pleasure, and I have no engagemᵗ either at home, or abroad, yᵗ can interfere ; Mag yᵉ great had two blooms almost ready to blow before I came away. I shall be much disapointed if her children do not inherit her blooming charms.

Mr. Montague [1] set forth for yᵉ North to-day, and Mr. Mason talks of going soon ; their visits to me were so short I fix'd no value upon 'em ; perhaps if you had been wᵗʰ me they might have prolong'd 'em ; yᵉ former seems to have had enough of yᵉ H. of Comons, and school-boy like rejoic'd at hollidays. His little mother goes on Monday next, *never* in a hurry to *leave* London. Mrs. Leveson told me wⁿ I came, her last reckon was out yˢ day ; now she says she may go on to yᵉ 8ᵗʰ July. I believe she knows nothing of yᵉ matter, however now I am here I'll stay (tho' of no use) till all's over, for I shall be anxious abᵗ her, *much more* yⁿ she is abᵗ herself !

---

[1] Of Papplewick, son of the Mrs. Montagu, so often called "*fat*" and "*good-natured*," and the friend of the Rev. William Mason the poet.

wch is a happiness ; her whimsical bro^r is going to Spa—
I believe a release to Mrs. Bos. on many acc^ts.

'Tis now s^d L—d Stanley's match is quite off, ye l—y
disliking him. Sure she sh^d have known her mind, *before
she accepted ye entertainm^t*?

All my best wishes attend ye D^s of Portland. Am ever,
d^r mad^m, yor most faithful

M. G.

The Hon. Mrs. Boscawen to Mrs. Delany.

Audley Street, ye 29th June, 1774.

When I had the pleasure of seeing y^r hand writing to-
day, my dear madam, I concluded it was the reproof I
deserv'd for not announcing your new cousin[1] to you, but
the truth is I really had not time. One good, however,
proceeds from it,—for now I can not only tell you of a
new cousin stout and strong, but also that she makes an
exceeding good nurse, and was obliged to-day to invite
another child to breakfast beside her own, who was under
suspicion of having *over eat* himself yesterday—but it is a
great addition of fatigue to the poor mother I perceive,
(for I *never* saw *till now* the beginning of this very natural
proceeding), and she is often rous'd when she seems
sleepy, but as she bears all with the greatest patience,
and never makes a complaint, I *hope* all will agree
with her, so as to leave none to make, were she so
inclin'd. Lady Gower staid for this event, and now
returns well satisfy'd to Bill Hill next Friday. I cannot
say I am perfectly so with her state of health, tho' I

---

[1] The birth of John Leveson, eldest son of Admiral the Hon. John Leveson,
and grandson of Mrs. Boscawen and the Dowager-Countess Gower.

hope and believe she is better for Dr. Warren's prescriptions. She is to be *let blood* to-morrow.[1] I have been sitting with her in Pall Mall, and now am going to my nursery, having had 13 letters by the post—besides congratulatory cards *not* a *few*—for my dear lady in the straw is well beloved and has many friends. I shall take the liberty with one very good one to end this abruptly, after assuring you, my dear madam, that I take the sincerest interest in the good account you give me of your health, and that my imagination is refresh'd with your charming picture of Bulstrode.

The allusions in this letter to Mrs. Leveson's being nurse to her child, and to Mrs. Boscawen's previous ignorance of such a proceeding, are a curious contrast to the violent outcry of the present day against wet nurses, which *if* there were not happily many parents in the higher ranks who have sufficient sense and natural affection to employ them, would insure even more disease, suffering and death than at present occur. It is a *sentiment* of this century, among the higher classes, that every mother (let her health and avocations be what they may) ought to nurse her own child. The way to view the question rationally is, what is the object to be attained ? the answer must be, the health of the child; but nobody ever thinks of inquiring what ladies' nursing *means ?* It is, like many other things in England, *a name* for what is *understood* to be done, but what *is never really done* by one gentlewoman in the higher ranks out of fifty, or perhaps not even by so large a proportion. If all these mothers actually supported their infants themselves, not a word could be said against it, but *they do not*, although perhaps out of each fifty, twenty-five assert that they do, and have the credit of doing so ! But the Editor must refrain from the temptation of writing a sermon on this text, and giving facts to prove that, unless the

---

[1] Lady Gower was then 73.

ladies of Great Britain can so alter their habits as to go to bed at nine o'clock and rise with the sun, walk about all day with their infant, and have it with them all night, and require neither " *tops* or *bottoms*,"[1] *bottles under pillows*, cookings or concoctions to assist in their maintenance, they had better not take the *name* of "nurses," but benefit the family of a *respectable* peasant by paying *very liberally* for a good wet nurse who *can* and *will* perform the duties she undertakes, night and day, for twelve or fifteen months, and who receives enough to pay another in her own class who can take two children, which is by no means impossible among peasants accustomed to be out of doors, with temperate habits.

The Dowager-Countess Gower to Mrs. Delany.

Pall Mall, 30th June, 74.

I this day rec̄ed kind congratulations from ye D^s of Portland, and from you, d^r mad^m, wch I've a thankfull sense of, and beg you'l tell her Grace so : and y^t I much rejoice to see it under her hand she was perfectly well. I believe ye painted glass at Ffairford[2] will ans^r any description she may have had of it; I liv'd some years there, at a house now in ye possession of a Mr. Lamb, which had great capabilities ; I peep'd at it some years ago, and it seem'd to me as if he had *marr'd* 'em well.

I propose going to Bill Hill to-morrow : w^never ye time

---

[1] " *Tops and bottoms*," the name of certain cakes with which many a poor infant is stuffed when his mother says " *I nurse myself*."

[2] Fairford, 4 miles from Lechlade, and 24 miles from Gloucester, is situated upon the river Colne. The town is famous for its church, which was built in the reign of King Henry VIII., by a merchant named John Tame, who having captured a vessel bound for Rome and laden with painted glass, of which the designs were drawn by Albert Durer, filled the 28 large windows of this church with it. These paintings are deemed very beautiful, and were greatly admired by Vandyke.

comes y^t you have promis'd to bestow on me, let me
know time enough to send my chaize to Bulstrode; I
never have anything for it to do.   Yo^r discription of y^e
demi-gentry is most just ; I have felt it in a small degree
how odious it is to be entangled wth 'em.

I have ye satisfaction to be able to say Mrs. Leveson
is as well as possible; I hope her good spirits won't run
away wth her, but keep herself properly quiet.   This I
preach perhaps too much, for Mrs. Bos. &c. seems to
want me gone.

I've heard no news, so take leave.

Mrs. Delany to Mrs. Port, of Ilam.

Bulstrode, 4th July, 1774.

My best thanks to you, my ever dear and kind Mary,
for your letters, and improving acct^s of your health ; this,
I suppose by the information of y^r last letter, dated the
25 of June, will salute you in y^r own sweet home, and
hope so well as not to regret the exchange.   Wherever
you are my tenderest wishes bear you company.   I am
glad you met with sociable people in y^r miscellaneous
assembly to make amends for the crowd.   A *crowd* in
such a scene as Matlock seems *most unnatural*, rather
calculated for solitude and contemplation, but as it tends
rather to melancholy in some of its gloomy parts, a
cheerfull beam is necessary now and then to give a
fillip to the spirits, like the sun darting thro' a wood
w^h enlivens without robbing you of ye shade.   Mrs.
Leveson is pure well, and happy in having a son.
Mrs. Bos. and dear L^y Gower no less so.   Mrs. Montague and her son gone to Papplewick ; and we, alas ! have

lost a pleasure that was plann'd before we came out of town, as Mr. Montⁿ and his two worthy friends Dr. Hurd and Mr. Mason, were to have spent 2 or 3 days at Bulstrode, but the dear Dss's illness delayed it till they c^d stay no longer in town, and we are deprived for this year of the pleasure and edification of such a matchless triumvirate! The Duchess's ramble, w^h was to have begun next Tuesday to Fairford, is put off till Monday 11th. The reviewers that were to have come here to inspect the road, w^h her Grace's *graceless* neighbours dispute with her about, is deferred to next week, and she goes to be out of the way; but I shall stand my ground secure and unmolested in my own delightful apartment. I have now not only the hares, the sheep, and the peacocks, &c., and their usual companions, but a thousand little pheasants running upon the lawn, and bred there to make them tame and used to the garden; one favorite gold pheasant of last year, just *coming into bloom,* feeds out of my hand almost every morn^g, and follows me round the American grove. I walk most mornings an hour before breakfast; a profusion of sweets, added to all its other charms, makes it charming indeed, tho' the recollections of *pains* and *pleasures* occupy my mind; but when the *cloud* prevails *too much* I try to disperse it by the consideration that this world is not designed for a place of permanent happiness, but a state of tryal, and that every pain and disappointment is meant to correct our faults, to check our too g^t attachment to the vanities of life, and to lead us into the path of peace and endless joy; I am then reconciled to all events, even with the insurmountable difficulties of making a visit *this* y^r to my darling Mary!

The D^e and Dss of Queensberry come here next Friday for a day or 2, *her Grace's* peculiarities may for a time do very well, but were they to last long w^d be too g^t a sacrifice of time in a place so endowed with every rational delight.

This letter was dated 4th July, 1774. On the 11th of that month the following memorandum was made in a pocket-book at Ilam—" *Dr. Johnson at Ilam.*" In speaking of Mrs. Delany, he said he had heard the great orator, Edmund Burke, say of her that " she was a *truly great* woman of fashion, that she was not only the woman of fashion of the *present age*, but she was the *highest bred woman in the world*, and the woman of fashion of all ages; that she *was* high bred, great in every instance, and *would continue* fashionable in *all ages.*"

The Hon. Mrs. Boscawen to Mrs. Delany.

Glan Villa, July 14th, 1774.

Right welcome were you to the caudle, dearest lady; and so indeed it happen'd, for tho' I had been *settled* here ever since Monday evening, yet on Wensday morning I set out pretty early and caught Mrs. Leveson in bed; by-and-by she treated me with caudle, w^{ch}, tho' I am oldfashioned enough to *like mightily*, yet the best part of the treat was to come from Audley Street, in the shape of a letter from Mrs. Delany. Before I thank you for it or tell any tale of mine, I must ask what of the viewers, for I am all impatience and eagerness to hear that they have decided for justice and the Duchess of Portland; I am persuaded they are both on one side, and I shall be very angry with my good friend Mr. Coles if he cannot persuade the jury to see this clearly, and decide accordingly. It is impossible not to have some little doubts of a Buckinghamshire jury, lest they should have taken any infection from their neighbour the Middlesex jury, who have long had the *Bostonian distemper* in a great degree, viz., an aversion to all superiority of rank or merit, or even right and law.

I must beg the earliest information you can give me upon this subject, for one cannot have enjoy'd les delices de Bulstrode, nor have any part of the respect and love wch I bear its noble mistress, not to be really and warmly interested in its success. We shall not be at Bill Hill sooner than the 2^d week in August I fancy, for Mad^m Leveson expects her husband in town as soon as he returns from his cruise, and as Lady Gower was so good to give her leave to chuse her own time, she thinks it best to wait Mr. Leveson's arrival. I am afraid Lady Gower is still very indifferent in her health. Her Grace *of Queens.* is in London, and likely to remain, as her porter told me one day last week, when I visited her, (door) in return for a civil congrat. I had receiv'd from her Grace.

Mrs. Chapone was here (with Mrs. Smith) last Tuesday, and to-morrow I am to drink tea with her at Mill Hill. I do not wonder you lik'd Mr. Cole, he is a great favourite of mine, still less do I wonder that he lik'd Bulstrode and the inhabitants thereof. My dear madam, I have let my son [1] go to Spa without leaving me any franks for Mrs. Delany! He has wrote me a very agreeable account of his journey, wch has been a long one, turn'd aside by a visit to his friend the Chev^r. Jerning-

---

[1] Edward Hugh Boscawen, Esq., M.P.

ham[1] at the head of his regiment at Valenciennes. There
he was exceedingly well entertain'd by himself and
other military gent*; describes ridiculously les Boues de
St. Amand, where *delicate* ladies bathe in *stinking mud.*

Adieu, my dear madam. Since Matlock agrees with
Mrs. Port she will be quite well, depend upon it. My
best wishes attend you.

Mrs. Delany to Bernard Granville, Esq.

Bulstrode, 17th July, 1774.

Great is my mortification that I dare not undertake
so long a journey as into Staffordshire, but it *w*^d *be* still
greater *if*, by going there, I c^d add any comfort or relief
to my dear brother! I have nothing to offer but my
constant wishes and prayers, and fly to that only true
consolation under all pain and sorrow, *that all things are
conducted by an all-wise and mercifull Providence*, and
that submission to His will is our sheet anchor. I thank
God *I am* much better in health than when I came to
Bulstrode, using constant gentle exercise, as much in the
air as the uncertainty of the weather will admit of; but
a little accident by the bite of a venemous fly on my
ancle, just above my shoe, has made me a prisoner for a
fortnight past—and very cautious of walking.

The Dss of Portland is quite well again. She went
last Monday to Fairford, and returned on Wednesday.

---

[1] Charles, a younger son of Sir George Jerningham, Bart., and brother of
William, 1st Baron Stafford. Charles Jerningham became a General Officer
in the French service, and a Knight of Malta and of the order of St. Louis. His
mother is often mentioned in the course of this correspondence, in connection
with her fine spinning and agreeable society.

Her usual good humour made her bear with some inconveniences of bad accommodation, and she thinks the windows more curious than beautiful, and was rather disappointed. Her cause with some of her perplexing, troublesome neighbours, who claim a common way thro' her park, comes on some day this week. I hope she will carry it, as they certainly can have no just claim to it. It w^d be vexatious to have her fine verdure at the mercy of wheels and scampering horses, and all her *happy creatures* disturbed in their quiet possessions. Her g^t civility to her neighbours is *ill requited*, but a gentleman (belonging to the law, too) s^d here the other day what is very true, that "*the law abominates all civility.*" I w^d have all my letters directed to me in St. James's Place. It is the surest way of my having them.

I am glad to hear that Mrs. Port found benefit from Matlock. I feel uncomfortable *not to be able* to come to her when she is under her confinement. I pray God preserve and support her. Adieu.

The Duchess's best wishes and comp^{ts}.

The Hon. Mrs. Boscawen to Mrs. Delany.

Glan Villa, 21st July, 1774.

I was quite pleas'd the other day to find dans le fond d'un livre a frank for my dear Mrs. Delany, and now I have occasion to use it, having had again the good luck to meet the excellent lady over my caudle in South Street. Yesterday I repair'd thither to visit my daughter, whom I found well, and very proud to have got so good a treat for me as a letter from Bulstrode. My dear madam, I shall not answer it en long and en large just now, because I am tongue-ty'd till that pretty word " *Victory* " makes me eloquent ; and besides I have been obeying your commands, which is better than prating.   I have wrote to Mr. Rashleigh (over and above the *sign manual* you mention, and wch I send you inclos'd,) an explanatory letter concerning Mr. Lightfoot, his purposes and the objects of his journey into Cornwall.   He will probably go from Mount Edgcumbe to Boconnoc, from thence to Lostwithiel, and there he will take directions to St. Austle, wch may possibly be rather out of the direct road to the Land's End ; but, beside that curious travellers are never out of their way, there is *a mine* near St. Austle better worth seeing than any, by reason of the resemblance it bears to the D. of Bridgewater's underground naviga-tion, &c., &c.   Mr. Rashleigh is nephew to Mr. Clayton of Harleyford, and a very worthy man, whose elder bro^{r}, Mr. Rashleigh of Menabilly, is mem^{r} of Parlia^{t}.   He is my steward, and as I have some farms pretty near the Land's End will be useful to Mr. Lightfoot in giving him passports to the farmers for lodging and good hos-pitality, for there is nothing of a town that way beyond Penzance.   In short, Mr. Rashleigh *can and will* be, I dare say, of great use to your ingenious friend, to whom I wish a good and pleasant journey, wch is all I can say just now, because the post is come in, whose *agreeable* property it is to be always in a hurry.   I shall write a dissertation some day on the torments of the penny post, but this minute can only say I am y^{rs}.

Direct to E. H. B.[1] without inclosing, for I know y^{r} hand so well I shall never doubt.

---

[1] Edward Hugh Boscawen, Esq., M.P., the eldest son of Mrs. Boscawen.

The Dowager-Countess Gower to Mrs. Delany.

Bill Hill, 21st July, 74.

I am much oblig'd to d^r M^rs. Delany for interesting herself ab^t my health; I've had a cough according to añual custom, hope ye fury of it is over.

It makes some amendm^t to here I shall soon have ye pleasure of seeing you; and ye choice you give me of ab^t ye 26th ins^t. or ten days later, gives me another hope y^t you have more time to bestow upon me y^n you have had in yor former vissits: I can aver wth ye strictest truth you can bestow yor time *on none* y^t will value it *higher.* I have no engagem^ts of any sort, a perfect free agent. Why is not my chaize to come to Bulstrode? ye stage from thence hither, is not too long to come wth out baiting.

I'm hapy to hear ye D^s of P. is so well, and y^t ye expedition to Ffairford agreed wth her; more y^n 30 years ago, *I thought* ye painted glass exquisitely fine; I conclude now, for *want of knowing finer!* I wish her health to make pleasant all her undertakings, and to you both a most faithfull hble serv^t.

———

Mrs. Delany to the Rev. John Dewes, at Calwich.

Bulstrode, 27 July, 1774.

I begin to think it very long since I heard from Calwich, as I am sure if you could give me satisfaction you would write when it is uneasy to my dear bro^r to do it.

I most earnestly pray God to support him, and cannot help lamenting my inability of giving him, in person, any consolation or support; for nothing alleviates the concern of a friend's sufferings but feeling oneself of some use to them, which I am sure you must be sensible of, and will always reflect with satisfaction on having done all in your power, by the utmost attention, to lessen the uneasy state of such a friend. All I can offer is a little amusement, and that will too often fail for want of materials, or perhaps coming at a time when it may be rather troublesome than amusing. I am sure my brother will be glad to hear of Lady Clanbrazill's recovery from the small-pox. She found Lord Clanb. *uneasy* about her *not* having had it, and took the resolution at once of being innoculated, which has succeeded very well, and I have this morning written my congratulations on the occasion. Nobody knew of her intention but her lord, Mrs. Granville, and Mrs. Tomlinson. Mr. Foley and family went out of town, thinking they were immediately going to Ireland but they set out, now, on Thursday se'night. It was goodnatured and attentive in Lady Clanbrasil *not* to let me know it *beforehand*, for knowing her excessive fears about it, I should have been anxious for the success; she was so low, after the operation was performed, as to alarm those about her very much, but as soon as it turned her spirits rose, and she is very well and happy.

Last Monday Princess Emily dined here, and three ladies with her—Lady Lothian, Lady Amelia Kerr,[1]

---

[1] Lady Emily Kerr, second daughter of William Henry, 4th Marquis of Lothian. She married, in 1783, Major-General John Macleod.

Lady Anne Howard,[1] the lady-in-waiting. She was gracious, good-humoured, and very comical, for she has a *great deal of humour*, and if my mind had been at ease I should have been very well entertained; and she seemed much pleased with her entertainment, which was suitable to the occasion. The Dss of Portland goes to Weymouth next Monday : I propose, please God, going with her as far as Maidenhead Bridge, and there Lady Gower's chaise will go on with me to Bill Hill; I shall stay a week there, and then go to town, and have some hopes of Mrs. Sandford's meeting me there. Our ingenious philosopher, Mr. Lightfoot, is going a progress to the Land's End in search of plants, and to explore its mines for curiosities. The Dss of P. has been setting in scientifick order all her ores and minerals, of which she has a most beautiful collection, and makes the best use of her treasures by considering them, as Milton does —*" These are thy glorious works,"* &c.

Lady Holland[2] has soon followed her lord, it is to be hoped, happily released from a miserable situation so rendered by the conduct and extravagance of her sons. The Dss of Kingston made a short visit in England; she came from Rome, where she was settled. She staid 24 hours at her house at Knight's bridge, and then set off for Russia—her sudden flight they say occasioned by Mr. Evelyn Meadows having gone to law with her, to prove her marriage with Mr. Hervey, which it is thought he will certainly do, having gained a certain evidence of

---

[1] Lady Anne Howard, daughter of Henry, 4th Earl of Carlisle.

[2] Henry Fox, 1st Lord Holland, died on the 1st of July, 1774, and his widow, Lady Georgina Fox, who had been created Baroness Holland, died on the 24th of the same month.

it—*a man* who the Dss of Kingston gave ten thousand pound for hush money, and *who* for the same sum from Mr. Evelyn Meadows is gained against her. So rogues betray rogues ; it is happy when innocence escapes their snares. Have you read Mr. Pennant's Voyage to the Hebrides ?[1] We have been very well amused with it ; his acc[ts] may be depended upon, which gives one satisfaction.

My affectionate compliments to your uncle.

Your most affect. aunt,

M. DELANY.

I have pretty good accounts from Ilam.

Mrs. Delany to Bernard Granville, Esq., at Calwich.

Bulstrode, 1st August, 1774.

It is always easy to find an excuse for doing what one likes, so I answer my dear brother's letter immediately, which I had the satisfaction of receiving this morning ; and if I delay[d] it, I might lose an opportunity of being serviceable to you whilst I am in London, whither I intend, please God, going on the 9th of Aug[t], and shall stay there a week or ten days at farthest.

I am glad to have it in my power to send you the Life of David ;[2] I *am sure* the *author* thought you had his works compleately. I have not yet heard a character of the remarks on L[d] Chesterfield's letters ; if worth your

---

[1] Tour in Scotland, a Voyage to the Hebrides, in 1772, by Thomas Pennant. Published in 1774.

[2] The Life of King David, by Dr. Delany.

having, I will send them to you, and pray recollect if
you want anything else, that I may have the pleasure of
doing it for you. I shall make my visit to Lady Gower
after my being in town, tho' the first plan was to have
gone first to Bill Hill; I will certainly make your proper
compliments there, and am sure she will agree in the
sentiments of the *present progeney* as *they* are going on
(to what number I can't tell.) Mr. Lewson (the sea
captain), bears a good character, as an honest man, and
no way profligate, and has more civility than tarrs are
generally blessed with. But a sad alloy of happiness
has clouded poor Mrs. Boscawen's situation occasioned
by the death of her eldest son,[1] who went about a month
ago to Spa for the recovery of his health ; we have
yet had no particulars about it, but that he died suddenly. This is the second son she has lost grown up to
man's estate, which beside the death of the admiral, have
been most severe strokes, and could only be supported
by religious considerations ; which as they have hitherto
supported her, I trust will not fail her now. Her
youngest (and *now only*) son had gone thro' Winchester
School with great credit, and she had promised herself
great satisfaction in his making a figure as a man of
learning in some profession, and was preparing him for
the University, when a frenzy of going into the army
seized him, and he would listen to no other occupation.
Mrs. Bos[n] thought it to no purpose to thwart an inclination that had taken such root, consented, and he sail'd
with the regiment he is in for America above a month

---

[1] " At the German Spa, Hugh Boscawen, Esq., son of the late Admiral,
nephew to Lord Falmouth, brother-in-law to the Duke of Beaufort, and Member
for Truro, in Cornwall, died July 17th, 1774."

ago ; so one may say she is deprived of all her sons. Indeed I am truly sorry for her ; *she felt for me* under *my great affliction,* and I should be very ungrateful not to do so for her. The Dss of Portland is much obliged to you for your kind congratulations on her gaining her lawsuit ; she does not go to Weymouth till the 9th ; she sends you her kind wishes and compliments ; she has now *added* to her usual assembly on the lawn under the windows of sheep, hares, &c., above 50 little pheasants of this year, part of which she hopes will be so familiar as to attend her in her garden, and make her amends for the loss of ye two past years. I have *made myself* a pair of *thin leathern stockings,* or rather boots, and dare not set abroad without them. I have this morning had a refreshing walk ; as I can't bear the heat of the day abroad, I make it a rule to walk an hour before breakfast, which is from 9 to 10, and I thank God I find it has strengthened me very much ; in the evenings I generally go in the chaise. As a *want of strength* is my chief complaint of *body* and *mind,* I avoid all fatigues for the one, and pray for the support of both to that gracious Being " *who is about our path and about our bed.*" *This* is my consolation on my dear brother's account, whose sufferings would be still more grievous to me were it not for that healing consideration. I apprehend you had another attack of your painful complaint, by my being longer than usual without a letter. You practise, while I fear I only speculate, and submit under your sufferings with resignation to that merciful Being who " *healeth those that are broken in heart, and giveth medicine to heal their sickness.*"

I wrote a few posts ago to John all the tattle I had

heard. I have heard a little anecdote since of Lady
Mary Cooke, quite in character. I don't know whether
you heard of her violent attachment to the Empress of
Germany, and of the marks of favour she had received;
upon the strength of which she made her another visit
last year, when the tables were turned, and she was refused admittance by all the royal family. She was
determined to make up for this disgrace, and went to
Berlin to pay her homage to the King of Prussia, who,
to avoid her, went to Potsdam; and she (*undaunted*)
followed him—in vain, the *many shifts* he made *to escape*
a rencontre are too numerous to tell! Piqued to the
quick, Lady M. left Prussia with the utmost indignation, but first sent a note written by her own hand, that
she had always had the highest admiration of him, but
found, tho' he might be equal to any of the antient
heroes in most respects, he *fell short of them in civility*.
Her ladyship is not a little mortified with receiving such
marks of royal contempt; perhaps it may do her good.
I find I am mistaken, it was only a *message*, and not a
note, that L^{dy} M. C.[1] sent to ye King of Prussia, but he
was a bold man that delivered the message!

Mrs. Delany to Mrs. Port, of Ilam.

Bulstrode, 5th Aug., 1774.

The Duchess of Portland is much obliged to you and
Mr. Port for your congratulations; her kindest compliments and wishes attend you both.

---

[1] Lady Mary Coke was the widow of Edward, Viscount Coke (only son
of Thomas, Earl of Leicester), and daughter of John, Duke of Argyll and
Greenwich.

The day for leaving Bulstrode is once more fixed, and please God, her Grace goes towards Weymouth on Monday next (the 8th), and I go to London, where I hope Mrs. Sandford will meet me, and then I propose going to Bill Hill; I believe the whole progress will not exceed three weeks.

I think you have managed very well about your *intended visitors*, and I think they love you too sincerely not to take it right; you should now keep yourself as free from all hurry as you can. As to the young woman that Mrs. Sandford recommended, I can give you no answer; I think she tried her herself and she did not do; when I see her I will ask about her.

I am sure you have been much concerned for poor *Mrs. Boscawen* and her daughters. I don't like to talk to you on dismal subjects, but I name this as I think it will be a satisfaction to you to know that that poor *unfortunate woman* has received this stroke with great composure and Xtian resignation; but the loss tho' great and sudden, I don't think (between ourselves) will be *as severe* a one as her son William's was, as she had not the same comfort and satisfaction and high expectation as she had from the other, nor indeed the same reason. She says Mrs. Leve^n has been a wonderfull support to her; she won't let the Duchess of Beaufort come to her yet; if she will see me I will make her a visit from London, but the sooner, I think, she sees those that she has a regard for the better; my intelligence has been from Mrs. Walsingham,[1] who spent the day here last Wednesday, came to breakfast, and brought her son with her,—a lad

---

[1] Charlotte, daughter of Sir Charles Hanbury Williams, and wife of Admiral the Hon. Robert Boyle Walsingham.

of twelve years old, and *the most agreeable boy* I know of
that age, so lively, sensible, and civil. Yesterday the
Duchess of Portland and your A.D. performed most
amazingly. It is well the day proved more temperate
than that that went before it. Soon after twelve we
sallied forth well attended, went to Old Windsor to Lady
Primrose, and found her tolerably well, Lady Bingham [1]
with her, modelling a statue in basrelievo very in-
geniously; as we passed by Dicky Bateman's, we moral-
ized on the vanities of human life; then went to
Frogmore, the habitation of Mrs. Anne Egerton [2] (you
have heard of Cousin Nan); she is sister to the Coll.
Egerton (and the Bishop of that name) that is so good
as to supply me with franks. We afterwards dined with
him and his family, consisting of a wife and three daughters. They have the lodgings in Windsor Castle that
were Lady Bateman's and Mrs. Granville's; *my spirits
sunk* when I went into them, and I recollected the many
pleasant days I had pass'd there. Thus life fluctuates,
and tho' tender regrets and sharp sorrow have their
turn, we *must dwell* upon *the blessings* that have been
graciously dealt to us, and *not* consider them as *lost,* but
only withdrawn from us till we are made *more worthy* of
enjoying them in a perfect state! Our dear Duchess
gives so much pleasure wherever she bestows herself,

---

[1] Lady Bingham, daughter and heiress of John Smith, of Canons Leigh,
co. Devon, and wife of Sir Charles Bingham, Bart.

[2] John, 5th and last Baron Berkeley, of Stratton, died in 1773. He left to
Miss Egerton, sister of the Bishop of Durham (his executrix), Berkeley Square
for her life, &c., to the amount of about 60,000*l.*; to Colonel Egerton, 1000*l.*;
to Major Egerton, 2000*l.*, &c., &c. After Miss Egerton's death, Berkeley
Square was to go to Earl Berkeley, a very distant relation, to whom he left
several estates, and all his plate, pictures, &c.

that it should recompence her for her day lost at Bulstrode. We came home before eight, and after solacing ourselves with tea and bread and butter, and talking over the adventures of the day, soon recovered our fatigue and both had a good night.

I have had a kind letter from my brother, but in a very trembling hand. He tells me he has had a very painfull return of his complaint. Pray God bless and support you all. Let me know immediately, by the hand of one of your secretaries, if you want any thing in London while I am there. I enclose you a rose-bud that was to have gone with the bag.

The Dowager-Countess Gower to Mrs. Delany.

Bill Hill, 1st Sept., 74.

Dr Mrs Delany is always kind to her friends and well-wishers, a fresh mark of wch I rec$\tilde{e}$d last post. All here were pleas'd and oblig'd by hearing she got well and in good time, according to her heart's desire, to Bulstrode, and y^e D^s of Portland in perfect health; long may it last, wth all y^t can contribute to hap̃iness. Yo^{rs} is so blended wth her Grace's, I need not be more particular.

Leveson's health I think mends, tho' I can't say he's quite clear of ye disorder; in his looks there still ap̃ears some remains. He desires his best complim^{ts} to you and ye D^s as do ye ladies.

I had a letter from L—y Hyde [1] wch we all club'd to

---

[1] Afterwards Countess of Clarendon.

read, wherein she says Sr P^s Mills, L—d Mansfeild's [1] nephew, is to marry Miss Moffatt, a great fortune and y^t his l^p is gone to Paris to see L—d Stormont.[2] Of y^s you may know more than I, being nearer ye great world. Adieu.

Mrs. Delany to Bernard Granville, Esq., at Calwich.

Bulstrode, Sept. 4th, 1774.

I began to grow uneasy at not hearing from Calwich, and should have written this post had I not received my dear brother's letter, and am sorry to find my conjectures were true. You were very good in writing to me when you can, but I cannot wish you to do it when it is uneasy to you. I am not at all surprised you should be entertained with Lord Chesterfield's letters, and approve of *many* of them; as a politician and what is called a man of the world, I suppose they are faultless, and his polishing precepts are useful and excellent, but I am afraid as you go on his *duplicity* and *immorality* will give you as much offence as his indiscriminate accusation does the ladies. Those who do not deserve his lash despise it, and conclude he kept very bad company. Those who are conscious they deserve his censure will be piqued but silent. The general opinion of these letters among the better sort of men is, that they are ingenious, usefull as to pollish of manners, but *very hurt-*

---

[1] The Hon. William Murray, third son of David, 5th Viscount Stormont, was made Lord Chief Justice of the King's Bench, Nov. 8th, 1756, and on the same day created Baron Mansfield. On Oct. 19th, 1776, he was created Earl of Mansfield.

[2] David, 7th Viscount Stormont, Lord Mansfield's nephew.

full in a *moral sense*. He mentions a decent regard to religion, at the same time recommends falsehood even to your most intimate acquaintance—and adultery as an accomplishment. *Les graces* are the sum total of his religion. The conclusion of his life showed how inferior his heart was to his head : unkind and ungrateful to an *excellent wife*, who had laid *great obligations on him* and the same to all his dependants.

Mrs. Eugenia Stanhope was a natural daughter of Mr. Dumville's, who used to visit Mrs. Donnellan, and whom he wanted to introduce into good society, but could never bring it about, tho' for some reason he did not acknowledge her at first as his daughter, but called her *his ward* (I forget now the name she went by). Mr. Stanhope met with her and engaged her as his mistress, and at last married her, which hurt Ld *Chesterf^d more* than any part of his behaviour. His false ambition about placing him in a high station, and making him a pattern for politeness and good breeding was sufficiently mortified by Mr. Stanhope's being as totally destitute of "*les graces*" as any fox-hunter in the nation. He did not want learning as to Greek, &c., &c., and knowledge of business, but he was *stupid* in conversation, and *wanting all manner of address* to the *last degree*. I don't recollect who his mother was, but some very mean person. Everybody condemns Mrs. E. Stanhope for publishing these letters without their having been gleaned of those that are meer repetitions, and above all those that are *censorious* against *living persons*, which, tho' a strange subject for letters to so young a man, he never could mean should be seen in publick. Till towards the year '50 I don't wonder you should in general be very much entertained, and they are certainly very usefull to young men, in point of *outward behaviour*; though his encouragement of gallantry in the French court was strange advice from a father to a son in whatever light it could be placed. If I have tired you on this subject it is your own fault : what follows will be my own. But I depend on your reading no more than what you like, and shall be happy if anything I write can give you a minute's amusement. I return'd hither from Bill Hill last Saturday was se'night; the Dss of Portland met me from Weymouth, I thank God in good health. She had fine weather for her expedition, and found great benefit from it. She brought some extraordinary *vegetable animals* from the sea-side of the polipus kind, and she has had some three years that she keeps in basins of sea-water (which she is supplied with from time to time), and they have increased since she had them. She has a green worm something like a centipede, but of a much greater length than any I ever saw, and not broader than a straw, and a little red animal about the size and shape of a shrimp, that has four branches, which it puts out at pleasure, of a fine scarlet ; and also throws out to a great length fine red strings with little roots at the end of each, so slender that you can but just discern them without a glass. These with some new sea plants has been this year's merchandise.

Mr. Lightfoot will soon return with his harvest from the west. He boasts of some new plants, but has been disappointed as to minerals, as there are no considerable mines at work at present. Sir Wm Musgrave has been here ever since Thursday : he always enquires after you, and desired me to add his best compliments, with

the Dss of Portland's.   I have recollected the name
Mrs. E. Stanhope went by, she was called *Miss Peters*.
The Dss of Port. has persuaded me to go with her to-
morrow to Luton, 30 miles from hence. Lady Bute has
often press'd me to come, and I hope I shall be able to
pick up something to amuse you in another letter, but
going out of my usual path seems formidable to me.
The account of the Dutchess of Leinster's marriage with
her son's tutor wants confirmation.   Her daughter,
Lady Em. Fitzgerald,[1] is at last married to Lord Bellamont. I fear she has made a wretched choice.

I pray God bless and support you.

The Hon. Mrs. Boscawen to Mrs. Delany.

Bill Hill, 11th Sept., 1774.

I have this moment received the favor of your kind
enquiry, my dear madam.   Last week I went to Badminton without saying a word to anybody there; but I
knew they had no company, and I believe it is natural
for affliction to be restless; besides, it is constantly
humour'd, so that if one proposes anything one's friends
on all sides encourage one to set about it.   This was my
case. I thought of it (when I could not sleep in the
night), I nam'd it in the morning, and was persuaded
to execute it the next morning; I did so, and got there
in 9 hours!   I staid till Wensday last, exceedingly
well paid for the trouble I had taken by finding the

---

[1] Lady Emilia-Maria Margaret Fitzgerald, eldest daughter of James,
1st Duke of Leinster, married, 20th Aug., 1774, Charles, Earl of Bellamont.

great and the small in most perfect health, and myself so welcome a guest, that they did nothing but study how to cheat my heavy hours. Among other kind devices to give me much air and exercise they carry'd me to Stinchcomb Hill, where you perhaps have been, my dear madam, and if so you still remember, I dare say, its superb beauties.

Wensday last I return'd hither, L^y Gower, with her usual kindness, sending her cavalry to meet me, so that I arriv'd before tea-time; Mr. Leveson determin'd to pursue his journey to Bath, having had a repeated exhortation from his doctor at Plymouth, and accordingly he went next day, but left his wife and son here to follow in due time. Y^r little cousin thrives. I am inclin'd to prolong my stay here, Lady Gower's kindness at the same time pressing me, partly, no doubt, out of compassion, lest home shou'd be painfull to me; indeed I cannot say enough of her indulgence. Yesterday being fine she wou'd carry me to see Caversham, tho' she has seen it twenty times. I think it a very fine place. I can easily believe, dear madam, that no eyes were more worthy to admire the curiosities of Luton than yours and the Duchess of Portland's. I am glad you have good accounts from Ilam. That all may long continue so is a very sincere wish of

My dear Mrs Delany's affectionate
Obliged friend,
F. Boscawen.

The letter from Mrs. Delany to the Viscountess Andover of the 14th Sept., 1774, which appears in page 541, Vol. I., ought to have appeared after the above letter.

Mrs. Delany to Bernard Granville, Esq., at Calwich.

Bulstrode, 16th Sept., 1774.

It is indeed an unspeakable pleasure to me to be able to give my dear brother one moment's relief, and should be most happy could I do more; but it is the will of God it should be otherwise, and his mercy will support those whom he chastiseth, and has graciously enlightened our minds with a blessed hope hereafter; which is our sheet-anchor.

I don't wonder *our* young men are entertained with Lord Chesterfield's letters, and I trust their principles are too well grounded to be hurt by his *immorality*. If you cast a veil over that *part,* there are many useful observations. The present Lord Chesterfield is gone to finish his travels. He came over on the death of the late lord, and is not yet of age. I don't hear him commended, and his behaviour to Lady Chesterfield was very unhandsome. He was a distant relation to the late lord, but nearest to the title, as Sir William Stanhope [1] had no children by the person he married. His father was a Mr. Abel Stanhope of Mansfield Woodhouse, in Nottinghamshire. Lord Chesterfield educated this boy, and had an attention to him; not out of kindness, but because he was to keep up the name and title, and left him near twenty thousand pound a year. Lady Chesterfield's income is £4000 a year, but chiefly her own money. It was hard, considering how good a wife she had been,

---

[1] Philip Stanhope, Esq., of Mansfield Woodhouse, co. Nottingham, a descendant of the fourth son of Philip, 1st Earl of Chesterfield; succeeded to the earldom on the death of the celebrated Lord Chesterfield in 1773.

Joseph Brown, sc.

MARY WORTLEY MONTAGUE.

Countess of Bute.

From a Miniature in the possession of
The Lady Anna Maria Dawson.

London: Richard Bentley, 1862.

and what a good fortune she was to him, *not* to leave her in *very* affluent circumstances for her own life. *He* even *left away* her jewels, which were *chiefly* purchased with her *own money*, and presents of the Duchess of Kendal's, but *the law* restored them to her as her own paraphanalia! I did not hear that he left anything considerable to his sister, Lady Gertrude Hotham,[1] with whom he always lived in friendship. So vanity, as you say, had taken possession of him, and drove out all gratitude and natural affection; and such is the case with human frailty if not well guarded against. Prejudice and passion are powerful enemies to struggle with if once indulged.

We put in practise our expedition to Luton on Monday, the 5th of this month, and returned the Thursday after. I thank God I performed my part tolerably well, and caught no cold, but was much amused, and most kindly received. *You* know *so much* of Lady Bute that I need say nothing of her agreeableness, her good sense, and good principles, which with great civility must be always pleasing. I don't know if you are acquainted with Lord B. but by publick character, which is little to be depended on—and seldom just in praise (or dispraise). I was surprised to see him in such good health. Nothing could be more polite, obliging, and entertaining than he was. He seemed happy in seeing the Dss of Portland at Luton, and *very pressing* to have us stay, and made the best use of our time in showing us everything that was worth attending to, and they were numerous. The situation you know. They have opened a

---

[1] Lady Gertrude Hotham, eldest daughter of Philip, 3rd Earl of Chesterfield and wife of Sir Charles Hotham, Bart.

view to the river, and the ground and plantations are
fine. It would be better if there was a greater command
of the river, and if MR. BROWN had not turn'd all the
deer *out of the park*; they are beautiful enliveners of
every scene, where there is range sufficient for them.
The house, tho' not entirely finished according to the
plan, is very handsome and convenient; but as part of
the old house still remains, it does not appear to advantage, nor is the best front compleated; and this makes it
very difficult to describe, as there is no regular entrance.
You go in at the hall of ye old house; from thence into
a parlour, and then into a large dining-room; all this
the old house. You then go up some steps, cross
a stone staircase, which leads you to a gallery, or
rather passage, from which you go into an antecham-
ber. On the left hand a large drawing room, with a
coved ceiling; on the right hand of the anteroom
you go into a very fine saloon, with a large bow
window opposite the chimney. The room is 64 ft. by
24 in the bow; 33 wide, 20 high. Out of the saloon you
go thro' two small rooms with cases of manuscripts, over
which are modells of the remarkable ruins about Rome;
represented in cork. You then go into the library, the
dimensions of which I have been so stupid as not to
remember. It is, in effect, three or five rooms, one very
large one well-proportioned in the middle each end divided off by pillars, in which recesses are chimneys; and a
large square room at each end, which, when the doors are
thrown open, make it appear like one large room or gallery.
I never saw so *magnificent* and *so pleasant* a library,
extreamly well lighted, and nobly furnished with everything that can inform and entertain men of learning and

virtü. The only objection to ye house is 42 stone steps, which you must ascend whenever you go up to ye lodging appartments. When you are there there is no fault to find, as they are fine rooms, and very commodious ; five compleat appartments—a bedchamber, 2 dressing rooms, and rooms overhead for a man and a maid-servant *to each*. One of these appartments is Lord and Lady Bute's, and 4 for strangers. Up another flight of stairs leads to the attick, where there are as many appartments as compleat, but not as lofty. The furniture well suited to all. The beds damask, and rich sattin, green, blue, and crimson; mine was white sattin. The rooms hung with plain paper, suited to ye colour of ye beds, except mine, which was pea green, and so is the whole appartment below stairs. The curtains, chairs, and sophas are all plain sattin. Every room filled with pictures; many capital ones : and a handsome screen hangs by each fireside, with ye plan of ye room, and with the *names* of the hands by whom the pictures were painted, in the order as they stand. The chimney pieces in *good taste* ; no extravagance of fancy; indeed, throughout the house that is avoided. Fine frames to the pictures, but very little guilding besides, and the cielings elegant, and not loaded with ornament. A great variety of fine vases, foreign and English, and marble tables. I think I have led you a dance eno' to tire you, and wish I may have given a description plain enough to understand. I must not omit one part of our entertainment, which was a clock organ, which is an extraordinary piece of mechanism, and plays an hour and a $\frac{1}{2}$ with once winding up. There are 30 barrells, of which the principal are Handel, Geminiani, and Corelli; the tone is mellow and plea-

sant, and has an effect I could not have expected. It is
a vast size, and has a great many stops, and I had rather
hear it than any of their modern operas or consorts :
many parts are judiciously brought in, and some parts
of Handel's chorus's tolerably executed. But after all I
heard and saw at Luton I cannot say that on my return
hither Bulstrod had lost any of its charms, but its own
merit is great, but its owner stamps a double value upon
it. The Dss of Portland's best compliments salute Calwich. I am so glad all is so well at Ilam. The Dss of
Portland was brought to bed last Wednesday of a fine
boy,[1] which I hope will live; they have *only* Ld Titchfield beside, and have lost 2 sons. The Dss of Leinster
is certainly married to her son's tutor !

The Hon. Mrs. Boscawen to Mrs. Delany.

Colney Hatch, ye 29 Sept., 1774 ![2]

I feel myself just now much oblig'd to my ser^t, who
has brought me a scrap of paper, and says, " Pray, mad^m,
cou'd you be pleas'd to send this to Mrs. Delany ? " for
it gives me a very good pretence to write to you, my
dear madam. Has the Duchess of Portland been
well this extraordinary wet season ? and how does it
agree with you, my dear madam ? Is Mrs. Port as well
as your heart can wish, and her little ones after the de-

---

[1] William Henry Cavendish Bentinck, second son of the 3rd Duke of
Portland, was born 14th Sept., 1774. He was a General Officer, and Governor-
General of India.

[2] When Mrs. Boscawen dated her letters in full she often added a note of
admiration, which probably was intended to attract Mrs. Delany's attention
to what she did *not* always remember to do.

sire of her own? I know your kindness to me and mine will require that on my side I should give you some intelligence of us. I did not leave Bill Hill till Thursday, and then I repented it sorely, finding my spirits quite sunk when I got out of that friendly society, and came to my own dreary mansion, &c., &c., &c. Lady Gower, too, had most kindly desir'd me to stay with her as long as my daughter did, but besides that her departure was uncertain, depending upon the stay Mr. Leveson made at Bath, I was really asham'd to trespass so long on her compassion, and had indeed business that ought to be dispatch'd, so I took a resolution, and kept it to my cost. I left my charitable noble hostess (but shall *always* remember her goodness to me), I parted with my dear daughter—and I have been exceedingly oppressed ever since; not that it affects my health at all, for that is perfect. Mrs L. was to set out yesterday for Badminton, where Mr. L., who is recover'd, thank God, will meet her, and then proceed to their mansion near Plymouth for—a long long time. The Duke of Beaufort went to Dover, and staid there 3 days for the arrival of the Dss Dow^r, and the young Duchess waited for her Grace in London, and tells me she never saw anything so pleasing as the two young ladies, not only the beauty of Lady Mary, but the manners and agrémens of both.

And now, my dear madam, I must add one more egotism, wch is, that having had the honour of an invitation from Lady Leicester to come to Holkham with Lady Gower, whose kind project it was, I purpose to avail myself of their goodness, if I continue well.

I have seen but one gossip, and she told me that

Lady Falm.[1] protested to everybody that wou'd hear her
that she "*wou'd part with my lord*," but I shou'd fancy her
ladyship wou'd revise that resolution, tho' 'tis very im-
material whether she does or not. Adieu, my dear
madam. Present my best respects to the Dss, and believe me ever your very affec[t] serv[t],

F. BOSCAWEN.

Mrs. Delany, Bulstrode, to Bernard Granville, Esq., at Calwich.

Bulstrode, Oct. 10th, 1774.

I have not waited for an answer to my last long letter,
knowing my dear brother always writes when he is able;
I conclude therefore you are not even as well as when
you last wrote, and then you seemed to have to make a
great effort. I often say to myself: "*Why art thou so
disquieted, O my soul?*" &c., when I reflect on *your* suffering state and *my* inabillity of being of any *real consolation*
to you. But I humbly hope it is not want of confidence
in that gracious Providence who only knows what tryals
are necessary, and who chastises out of love and kindness, to crown us in the end with glory and immortality!
These *rays of light* for a time dispel the gloom which the
veil of mortality interposes; but the most comfortable
future hope cannot, and I believe ought not, to extinguish the affectionate feelings of human nature. They
are meant as cordial supports under pain and affliction,
and as incitements to make us practice those virtues and
that faith which are to be our guides to eternal peace.

------

[1] Wife of Viscount Falmouth, the elder brother of Admiral Boscawen.

I flatter myself you may, at this time, feel the good influence of the fine weather we have at present. The long course of damp weather was certainly very trying to invalids. The Duchess of Portland, I think has been much affected by it, and has had an attack of her rheumatick complaints; I thank God, the violence of the pain is abated, but it robs her of the enjoyment of her garden and park, except out of the window, but the hares feed as usual, and have a circle of food prepared for them every evening : there are never less than between 20 and 30 at supper !

The disolving of the parliament has put all parties into a bustle, but as I am no politician, and only judge from what I think will be the natural consequence of it, I can't help rejoycing that much expense of fortune, and morals will be saved by it, and the only loosers, I think, will be the *alehouses* !

Lady Dartmouth's having a daughter[1] after 8 sons in succession, is great joy to all the family. Lady Willoughby has had a fine boy.[2] I had a letter this morning from Lord Willoughby, with a good account of all the family. I believe I wrote you word that Mr. Lightfoot was returned from Cornwall, from whence he has brought *several* curious *wild plants*; but much disappointed with not having been able to get any of the curious minerals ; and so was I, for he told me if he succeeded I should come in for a little share : no amusement gives me so much pleasure as my shells and fossils, and every acquisition, tho' ever so small, if good of its kind, adds to my

---

[1] Charlotte, only daughter of William, 2nd Earl of Dartmouth, who married, in 1795, Lord Feversham.

[2] "13th Sept., 1774, the Lady Willoughby de Broke, of a son."

pleasure. I hope it is not only the beauty and variety that delights me ; as it is impossible to consider their wonderfull construction of form and colour, from the largest to the most minute, without admiration and adoration of the great Author of nature. Every thing of that kind now bears an *enormous* price, so that were it not for the Duchess of Portland's bounty, I have small chance of *additions* to my collection. I have been happy with a good account from Ilam. I hope our dear Mary will be supported under the arduous task of motherly cares, but she acts upon the best principles. I am sorry Mr. Marsh has left Ilam. He is a substantial loss. The Dutchess of Portland desires me to add her best wishes and compliments.

It is evident, from the letters of Mrs. Delany to Mr. Granville at this period, that he had renewed his correspondence with her, (which seems to have been much interrupted from the time of Miss Dewes's marriage), but that he *did not wish* to see her ; and it is probable that she did not like to go to Ilam during his illness on account of its contiguity to Calwich, as she often alludes to her regret that she could be of no real comfort to him.

Mrs. Delany to Mrs. Port, of Ilam.

Bulstrode, 14th Oct. 1774.

I had the pleasure of your letter yesterday, and dear as your words are to me, I cannot wish you to write a line more than is quite easy and convenient. You are so well employed in your attention to your domestick duties that it is almost pity to interrupt them ; and yet I have two strong reasons for desiring to do it : one is to offer you a little amusement and relaxation, as I fear your too great solitude, having no good female assistant; and the other my own tender anxiety that cannot be satisfied by any other hand so well as your own, when you are able to write. We wait with eager impatience for the brilliant heat of the Derbyshire coal, and much obliged to you both for sending it so expeditiously.

I am glad your neighbours are inoffensive. I wish they were agreable and entertaining, that you might the less feel the loss of their worthy landlord. I heartily wish Lady Wrottesley's housekeeper may answer her character, that there may be an end of your turmoils in that important article, and that Mrs. *Cotchet* will have no *Crotchets*. Mrs. Boscawen does not come here. She has a relation come to stay with her till she goes into Norfolk with Dow^r Lady Gower, which will be next month. She has had the comfort of a good account from her son abroad, and Mr. Leveson is quite recovered. Our dear Duchess is very well again, only a little weak, and to-day she ventured into the chapel. Whilst we are enjoying sweet peace in this delightful place, the world is in a *hurry-durry*; but according to my little politicks the King and his Ministers never did a wiser thing than in dissolving the Parliament; and indeed it is universally approved of, as it must certainly be a means of saving much expence and *intemperance*. Some heroick ladies, I hear, have entered the electioneering list, and have *harangued* upon the occasion. Her Grace of North-umberland[1] has *signalised* herself with intrepidity. I

---

[1] "The Duchess of Northumberland," Anne, daughter of John, Earl of Bute, who married, 2nd July, 1764, Hugh, 2nd Duke of Northumberland.

hear, Lord Cowper [1] is certainly to be married to a Miss Gore that went abroad for her health, where they met, *and little Cupid bent his bow.* But I hear the match is not to be concluded till a year hence : so much the better for the lady, for *if* his lordship continues constant, he will be *more* worth her acceptance! I hear also he has notified it to Lady Cowper, and she has *at last* hopes of being ranged among the dowagers! Lord Mahon,[2] Earl Stanhope's son, is to be married to Lady Hester Pitt. Lady Blessington [3] is dead, and has left Admiral Forbes twelve hundred pound a year, a fine pair of *diamond earings*, and a fine set of child bed-linnen! To the eldest *Puss* a small pair of diamond earings, a pearl necklace, and a quantity of table-linnen to Puss *the second*. All her plate plain and gilt also to the admiral. To Miss Molesworth, that lived with her, five thousand pounds and a very fine diamond necklace.

I had a kind letter last post from Cal. My brother seems rather worse. I pray God support him. I hope the clavicord is not quite neglected. What resolution are you come to about Miss Sparrow?

---

[1] George Nassau, 3rd Earl Cowper, married, in 1775, Anne, daughter of Francis Gore, Esq., of Southampton.

[2] Charles, Lord Mahon, afterwards 3rd Earl of Stanhope, married, 19th Dec., 1774, Lady Hester Pitt, eldest daughter of William, 1st Earl of Chatham.

[3] In Berkeley Square, the Hon. Lady Dowager Blessington died, Oct. 4th, 1774.

The Hon. Mrs. Boscawen to Mrs. Delany.

Glan Villa, 20th Oct., 1774.

I hope you have miss'd me, my dearest madam. You see I appear again! When I get to Holkham, I shall have something better worth your hearing, from hence I can only tell you that I am busy making a new walk, wch I find of great use in employing me continually and out of doors, so that I am quite weary by the time it is dark; after tea is my hour of writing. Nothing can obliterate from my memory and my heart the Duchess of Portland's kindness to me; I am sure you must have admir'd it, and possibly have promoted it by imparting as much of my last letter as excited her Grace's compassion; so valuable an effect of it, and so flattering a mark of her friendship! My beloved ladies have had a delightfull three weeks together at Badminton, and parted only yesterday; when Mrs. Leveson proceeded West with *y^r cousins* great and small, and the Duchess of Beaufort and her little tribe remov'd to Oxfordshire for the hunting season. I have had letters every day, the sisters taking by turns which shou'd try to amuse me by very agreeable pictures of their occupations, their children, and their own perfect satisfaction in being again under the same roof, wch had not happen'd for a twelvemonth. Elections too take up much room in every body's letters, tho' the Duke of Beaufort was *so lucky* that Glostersh. was quiet and *Monmouth quiet too!* Not so poor Cornwall, wch is, on the contrary, *quite distracted.* Perhaps you think I am for Sr Wm Lemon.[1] No indeed, I have

---

[1] William Lemon, of Carclew, M.P. for the county of Cornwall, was created a Baronet, May 24, 1774. He married Jane, daughter of James Buller, of Mowal, Esq., in the county of Cornwall.

given my interest for the old members, who were nominated and approv'd at the meeting. I cannot but think
it great presumption in *boys* to set a great county *in a
flame* (as the phrase is, and indeed but too *apt*), and
therefore I cannot admire Sr George Cornwall.[1] Indeed
he went farther and broke his word at the first setting
out—ce qui n'est pas bien debiter. Did you see a ballad
on that subject in the newspaper? If not, I can send it
you, for I saw it to-day—an *envelope* to some *lupin seeds*!

I have never told you perhaps how much it pleas'd
me to know that Mr. Lightfoot was in any shape benefitted by my letters, mais cela va sans dire, for surely I
shou'd have wish'd to have had the satisfaction of his
Cornish tour more compleat, and his researches more
successfull than they seem to have been.

I have been indulg'd in examining a letter wch my
young companion, Miss Sayer, has had from her mother,
who, living at Richmond, hears many things and sees
many persons, and sometimes meets his Majesty walking
upon the green (with his bro^r-in-law) like any other
inhabitant of Richmond. I shall transcribe one article:
"I hear Sr W. Duncan[2] is dead at Naples; it seems L^y
Mary and he did not live well together; au contraire,
he us'd to say: 'a wife did very well to snuff the candles,'
wch you'll think is like 'Henriette de Bourbon, ôtez mes
bottes.'" I will also send you some lines of Voltaire,

---

[1] Sir George Amyand, Bart., who on his marriage, in 1771, with Caroline,
only child and heiress of Velters Cornewall, of Moccas, Esq., Herefordshire,
assumed the surname of Cornewall. He succeeded his father-in-law as M.P.
for the county of Hereford.

[2] William Duncan, M.D., Physician Extraordinary to King George III.,
was created a Baronet, Aug. 14, 1764. He was of the same family as the
Earls of Camperdown. Sir William married the Lady Mary Tufton, eldest
daughter of Sackville, Earl of Thanet. He died Sept. 1774.

wch my good cousin sends her dau^r, and says they are addressed to the Princess of Prussia, and that they may probably be very old, tho' new to her. I have a charming letter from Lady Gower to-day, who seems very busy, spreading a new carpet on *Bel Ombre* and in great spirits. She is so good to let me name or alter the day for our journey ; at present it stands for ye 3rd.

Y^r ever faithfull

F. B.

Mrs. Delany to Mrs. Port, of Ilam.

Bulstrode, 21st Oct., 1774.

Alas, my dearest child, you call upon me for advice that I am little capable of giving ; but your good sense and observation, the rectitude of your mind and principles, and the fervent desire you have to make your dear children happy, will give you assistance in a task of *all others* the *most arduous,* as your management must suit their *different* tempers. Your gentle, good-humoured dove must *not* be *roughly* opposed, but led with a soft rein, but a *rein* there *must* be, tho' a silken one ; the human mind is so apt to encroach on too much liberty that it must not be trusted. Whenever *our* little darling seems negligent or inattentive it should not pass by unheeded, and I am sure your tenderness will find means of gaining your point without severity, and avoid commands that may be difficult. The most essential ground is to teach them such a love of truth that upon *no account* they will tell a lye ; and that might easily be obtained with a good disposition could you keep the fair sheet of paper without being blotted by nonsensical people, who think you cruel if you insist on your child's being obedient.   However, we must take the world as it is, and guard against its *foibles* as well as we can.   You can *easier* guard against its vices because they are glaring, and a good heart startles at their hideous form ; but we must guard well the *avenues* to them, and court truth and humility to take us under their wing, and be our guardian angels.   As to your son John I have less to say : a good school if he grows unruly will *tame him ;* but even *a preparation* for *that* will be necessary, or the *discord* will never be resolved into a *concord.*   I am glad you ride, and that the weather favours you.   I long to know how you found my brother, and how the *meeting* agreed with you, it is so long since you have met !   You may be sure any one belong⁵ to you will be welcome to my house.   Mary Butcher knows the day. I have already ordered rooms, and bed well aired.   I suppose Miss Sparrow returns no more to school ; and you will have an additional task to exercise your judgment upon : the subject a delicate one—for tho' she does not want for sense or good nature, they have hitherto met with many things to warp them.   And I look upon schools as necessary *evils,* which under *some circumstances* are unavoidable ; as the cabals, the party-spirit, the fear of the governess, the secret and foolish indulgences of the maids, sometimes teach dissimulation, jealousy, resentment, and revenge,—a sad train, and as mischievous as the ichneumon fly that gets into the chrysalis of the poor innocent caterpillar, and devours its vitals : but do not be frightened, my dear Mary.

Mrs. Delany to Mrs. Port, of Ilam.

Bulstrode, 28th Oct., 1774.

Well, the box is come, and all its pretty and curious contents safe and welcome. The sparr (or rather chrystalization) and mundic in the coal is very curious and much admired. You know how pleasant it is to offer a mite to our dear, kind Duchess, and you may be sure I gave her the *best bits*, and also bestow'd a specimen on Mr. Lightfoot, who thinks it worthy the acceptance of a philosopher, and desires me to tell you he values it more as coming from Ilam. The fossils are good in their kind; the Dss having all those kinds, I keep them for my own little cabinet, but shall delight in them more for the sake of the giver than the gift. But tho' I have (or meant to have) made our acknowledgements, I have not done with the subject; for you must inform us of their birth and parentage, particularly of some brown mosslike substance that was pack'd into the largest cockle, and a little brassish, coperish, goldish thread-like stuff adhering to a bit of slate or coal, and which has puzzled even Mr. Lightfoot to find out without you inform us where they were found, whether on rock or tree, or bog? you must be very minute in your account; nothing less can satisfye such accurate enquirers.

I am heartily glad the visit was so well over. I own I was anxious about it, and fear'd your being too much agitated by it; but I suppose you *know* my bro^r wrote to me by the hand of his secretary (John) *an account of it himself!* Were his " Nancy " 16 instead of 3 years old, I should suppose he was desperately in love, and he seems no less satisfied with you. What pleasure it gives me when I think he acts a kind part by those I love so tenderly! not only on their account, but his. I was diverted with the history of *cropping* the hair and the reason for it, but I *agree* with *him* about the growing of the hair down the forehead. Besides it being a very dowdy fashion, it is a *pernicious* one to the growing of the hair if suffer'd too long in that state, and prevents the hair from growing handsomely to the face. To hang in a careless way about *half an inch* may do very well.

What a confidence I have in your goodness to me, my dearest Mary, to tell you so frankly my opinion; but tho' I tell it, I by no means insist on its being complied with, but shall be pleased with what you think best.

Well, but to proceed. *I am order'd* to *send* a *cloak*, a *muff*, a *fan*, a *pair of gloves* (send me a pattern glove). The cloak is to be of the richest damask (blue or green) and edged with furr. I suppose he means the flower'd *sattins* that are made for cloaks, but the D — says she is sure *he means* the richest Genoa damask. I wish you would tell me which of the colours you like best. I should think *blue*, and trimm'd with ermin. If she is not as *averse* to touching it as she was to *the lamb*, it may be a good way to reconcile her to it. I was delighted with the good acc^t of y^r self and all your doings. You are saved this time from one of my enormities, by my being in haste to finish a flower for my hortus siccus;[1] and to-morrow there will be an end

---

[1] "My *hortus siccus*." Unless Mrs. Delany also made a collection of dried plants she must have here again alluded to her great and wonderful work of *the Flora*.

of all industry for some time,—Duke and Dss of Portland, Miss Walpole, Coll. Bentinck, Mr. L'Anglois, come
for some days.

Mrs. Delany to Bernard Granville, Esq.

Bulstrode, 31st Oct., 1774.

I was much obliged to my dear brother for his letter,
dated 22nd, and for employing an amanuensis, as it
procured me a longer letter without your having the
trouble of writing. I saw too plainly by your kind
termination that you were not well enough to do it yourself. I will wave this painfull reflection, earnestly
praying for your support and relief. I am much pleased
with your approbation of *our little goddaughter :* she is a
fine child, and, I thank God, in good hands. I think
her mama will have a very proper attention to her, and
will not trust her from *under her own eye.* I was impatient to have you see her, but feared it might be too
much for your spirits. When she was with me, I found
her very tractable, with gentle usage; but a harsh word
quite overwhelm'd her; so that I think a silken twine
will guide her best; and as she has *great observation* and
quickness, she will give but little trouble to her teachers.
I am quite of your mind about her hair *not* being suffered
to grow too low on her forehead, (tho' the fashion is
universal,) and it makes *all* the children look *like
dowdys.* I will execute your kind commission for her as
soon as I go to town. We have had a whole month of
the finest autumn weather, and gone out every day. The
Duke and Duchess of Portland, Miss Walpole, and Col.
Bentinck came yesterday, and stay till Tuesday. The Dss

just recover'd of lying-in of a second son likely to live,
indeed I may say a fourth son, for she has buried two;
Lord Titchfield is a fine boy, and at school.

You don't remember I have some money of yours in
my hands. You sent me a bill of thirty pounds, and I
believe your upholsterer's bill was but £26. I shall attend
to your kind caution about reading, and not read longer
than is perfectly easy; I never read more (and seldom so
much) as *two hours together*, but rest between, and chuse
good prints for candle light; and that only three days in
the week, for Mr. Lightfoot, who comes to read prayers
on Wednesdays, always stays till Saturday morning; and
the evenings he is here are spent in philosophical specu-
lations. He is now arranging all the Dss of Portland's
insects and fossils, which afford great entertainment, and
I think it is impossible to consider the formation of the
meanest worm without its having *the effect of praise and
admiration for the great Creator*; and if we are so affected
by such a minute part of the works of God, what must
we be if we follow the chain to the highest being? We
may well say with Milton, " These are thy wondrous
works, &c.!" I had a letter this morning from Mrs.
Sandford. She is pretty well, and trying to amuse herself with a pretty garden she has now got to the house
she has removed to in Bladud's Buildings. Having a
good deal of furniture by her, she took the house un-
furnished, not with any intention of settling down there,
but as it was convenient, and more comfortable than
lodgings. She thought when she left it it might turn to
good account, as such a sort of house is much sought
after. She is very busy preparing her ground for plants,
and she is to have some from Bulstrode, for they are

extravagantly dear at Bath, and she will be glad of the superabundance of any of her friends' gardens that can conveniently be conveyed to her. Mrs. A. Viney hopes Bristol will be of service. I wish it may; but *there* is another deplorable instance of the havock unruly passions make in the human mind when under no restraint; a wise person said they were " excellent *servants*, but terrible *masters*." They were undoubtedly designed to be subservient to good purposes, but they destroy our own peace of mind as well as torment all about us if we suffer them to tiranise. I recommended " *Self-Knowledge*," by Mason, but fear it came *too late* to do *her* any good! We hear no news. The last extraordinary appearance has been the Dutchess of Northumberland *every day* on the hustings, haranguing the populace.[1] Her Grace had an appartment in one of the houses there, where she received company every morning.

The Hon. Mrs. Boscawen to Mrs. Delany.

Glan Villa, 2nd Nov., 1774.

At length I send the ballad, my dear madam, which will cost more than the just price of ballads, viz.: one halfpenny, and what is worse it will put out your eyes with the *fillagree* print. I have found it but this morning, the news papers being mislaid.

I finish'd my walk just in good time, and now am about to remove from this *very* retired cottage to Holkham, where we shall arrive, please God, next Wensday. I

---

[1] Election for Westminster, Oct., 1774. Candidates—Lord Percy, Lord J. Clinton, Lord Mountmorres, Lord Mahon, and Mr. Humphrey Cotes. The two former were elected. Horace Walpole said, the Duchess of Northumberland sat at a window in Covent Garden addressing the mob.

was thinking of you last night, my dear madam, while I read a little book, entitled " An Extract from the Observations, made in a tour to Italy, by the Chev. de la Condamine." These observations are chiefly sur l'histoire naturelle, fossils, metals, &c. &c. While I perused this little book that came in my way, I said to it, " Mrs. Delany wou'd like you." I hope you have some agreeable study, for the evenings are long, tho' they can never appear so where you are ; you understand I mean *with whom* you are, for *place* alone will not do, it is the *presence* of the friend that brightens the eye and dilates the heart. May you long enjoy this greatest of blessings, of which no one is so worthy. Tho' such a sincere benediction is a good ending to a letter, yet I would enliven mine with something, if I knew where to have it. Shall I copy a Cornish letter, wch says, " What I most condemn is Mr. Pitt's descending to personal abuse ; on opening the business at the meeting, he told the publick that Sr J. M. was a man of no capacity, that neither he nor his ancestors ever did any good for the county ; in short, all he said was (I fear) only intended to raise a mob, and mislead the ignorant ; and so far the purpose was answer'd, for the mob was altogether on his, and his friend's side." Have you *a notion*, my dear madam, of *Mr. Pitt* with *a mob* at his heels ?

Lady Fra^s Conway[1] is certainly to marry Lord *Lincoln*, I am told by Miss Burgoyne,[2] who had just seen

---

[1] Lady Frances Conway, daughter of Francis Seymour Conway, 1st Marquis of Hertford, married, May 22nd, 1775, Henry Pelham, Earl of Lincoln, son of Henry, Duke of Newcastle. The Earl died Oct. 22nd, 1778, during the lifetime of his father.

[2] Probably one of the daughters of Sir Robert Burgoyne, Bart., and of the Lady Frances Montagu, his wife.

Lady Grandison[1] in her way from Bristol. Lady Villiers[2] quite recover'd. Lady Eliz. Stanley[3] is just now with her mother[4] at Richmond. You know, dear madam, that your friend there is now Countess *Dowager* Cowper,[5] and that the earl *is marry'd* to Miss Gore, of Southampton![6] I am much pleased to hear you have good accounts of Ilam ; and that Mrs. Sandford is of my trade, and *become gardener.* Alas ! the cause to similar.

Adieu, my dear madam, I will not tell the postman on this *outside*, how truly I am yours. I believe I will borrow Mr. Condamine for you, and send it to Whitehall ; 'tis not worth buying. I hear nothing but good from Antony House, (*now* Chateau Leveson.)

Mrs. Delany to The Right Hon. Viscountess Andover.

Bulstrode, 3rd Nov., 1774.

It is an age since I heard from, or wrote to, dear Lady Andover ; the latter to be sure is my own fault, and a grievous fault it is, as perhaps it has delay'd my hear-

---

[1] Elizabeth Villiers, who was created Countess Grandison in her own right in 1766.

[2] Gertrude, daughter of Francis Seymour Conway, Earl of Hertford, and wife of Lady Grandison's only son, who succeeded his mother in the earldom.

[3] Elizabeth, only daughter of James, 6th Duke of Hamilton, married, June 23, 1774, Edward, Lord Stanley, afterwards 12th Earl of Derby. Their son Edward, 13th Earl, was born April 21st, 1775.

[4] Elizabeth Gunning, then Duchess of Argyll.

[5] Georgina Carolina, daughter of John Carteret, Earl of Granville, widow of Mr. Spencer, and of William, 2nd Earl Cowper.

[6] George Nassau, 3rd Earl Cowper, married Anne, daughter of Francis Gore, Esq., of Southampton.

ing from her ladyship, and lost a pleasure that I well know the value of. And what can I say for myself? The want of materials to make my letter acceptable,—that I know will not be allow'd, for, am I not at Bulstrode, rich with materials to occupy a pen, were it worthy of such a subject? Am I not at the elbow of the dearest friend in the world, and the most entertaining? Then, where is the cause of this non-writing? Alas! it is not to be said without mortification, *age* and *stupidity*, which at times so " clouds, *my poor abilities*," (as a celebrated patriotick orator says in his speech at Bristol,) that I am good for nothing! but nothing can rouze me more powerfully than a letter from dear Lady Andover to assure me she is well and happy, and that a certain paragraph of the resignation of a friend, (who can ill be spared from the station he has honour'd) is false.

I can now with truth, I thank God, tell your ladyship that the Dss is very well, and the rheumatism gone which paid her some time ago a very unpleasant visit. The Duke and Dss of Portland, Miss Walpole,[1] and Col. Bentinck came here last Saturday, and staid till Tuesday. It never ceased raining all the time, which made it *very sad*. We are now consoling ourselves, with books, work, butterflies, fungus's, and lichens: they entertain us and tell us pretty moral tales; they *banish* scandal and politicks, but not *one moment's remembrance* of the friends we admire, respect, and love; so your ladyship sees no employment can exclude you from the

---

[1] Miss Walpole. Probably one of the two daughters of Mr. Horatio Walpole, afterwards 2nd Lord Walpole and Earl of Orford. He married, 12th May, 1748, Rachael, third daughter of William, 3rd Duke of Devonshire.

party ? Happy were it real, instead of ideal, would it make dear Lady Andover's

Most affectionate and most obed^t humble ser^t,

M. DELANY.

The Dss desires her love ; mine I beg to Miss Howard. When does y^r ladyship think of London ?

The following Rules were written by Mrs. Delany, probably by Mrs. Port's request, for the benefit of Miss Sparrow.

Bulstrode, 13th Nov., 1774.

Rise at 7, sacrifice to cleanliness in the first place ; neatness of person and purity of mind are suitable companions : then, with awfull attention, say your prayers, return thanks for the blessings you have received, and pray for their continuance and for grace to make the best use of them, &c. &c. If you have time, before breakfast read the Psalms for the morning in French, and some French lesson ; most likely you may be called upon to read them afterwards in English. Write 3 or 4 lines, as well as you can, to offer to your friends at breakfast. Suppose you take in hand Mrs. Chapone's letters to her neice ; begin at page 3, " *Hitherto you have,*" and *don't* exceed 6 *lines of her book at a time,* it will imprint it on your mind, and it would be an excellent exercise for your memory to get the historical and geographical parts of it by heart. I know no book for a young person (next to the Bible) more entertaining and edifying if read with due attention : I must again repeat, *not* to write more than *six* lines at a time, and that in perfection ; for if you grow tired you will grow *careless*, and *that* is the bane of all improvement. I hope I need not recommend to you neatness and regularity in taking care of cloaths, &c., keeping them in nice order, and proper repair *not depending* on its being *done for you*. Employ *two hours every day in plain work*, and *making up your own things* ; it is an accomplishment necessary for every gentlewoman, and when you are in circumstances to make it less necessary or convenient you will be better able to know when it is well done for you. But this is not to exclude, at their proper seasons, works of ingenuity ; if you have learned to draw, give *one hour* to that *every day*, but *not* to interfere, with what is more necessary. As the cleanly part of your dressing will mostly be done when you first get up, bestow as little time on *dress* as possible, but let it always be neat and suitable to your circumstances (or position,) and never *extravagantly in the fashion*, which is very vulgar, and shows levity of mind. Be always punctually ready for your meals ; it is very impertinent to make anybody wait for inattention or idleness, and the attention of young people should always be awake to do everything with propriety ; after dinner retire to your room, and amuse yourself with anything that is *not study* for an hour, or walk if it is allow'd you, and the season proper for it, till you receive a summons to books or work for the evenings ; the occupations of the day must of course vary with the season, and rules give way occasionaly as engagements at home and abroad may sometimes interrupt them. Walking or playing with your little cousins may enliven part of your time ; and your good sense and observance of the rules laid down in regard to them, will guard you against any wrong and mistaken kindness, and make you carefull and particular in all *your own* words and actions; as your good nature would be extremely hurt to *bring them under correction* by *your example.* You are now of an age to know how very improper it would be for you to interfere in their management, and that of the family; and be assured the only way to be beloved and happy, (even in a parent's house,) is to be humble, modest, attentive, and complying towards those who have taken you under their wing, adhering strictly to truth, and never *see* or *say* what is no busyness of yours, but be always civil and affable in your behaviour to the servants; you will then raise no jealousy or envy among them, and by not herding with them, you will gain and maintain their respect, and the confidence and friendship of the friends you are with, who have your happiness at heart, and are the only persons you should open your mind to without reserve. Avoid *intruding* on them when they may *like to be alone,*—reserve on those occasions shows *observation and respect;* and the evening will close as the day began.

These are rude hints to be improved upon and filled up by *a better capacity!*

————————

Mrs. Delany to Bernard Granville, Esq., at Calwich.

Bulstrode, 14th Nov., 1774.

I am so apprehensive of my insignificancy that nothing can gratifye me so much as to find I can *add a few minutes of satisfaction* to my dear brother, and never wish'd so much as I do now to have talents equal to the desire I have of doing *it.* Don't think of answering any parts of my letters but what are necessary, and I shall then write on without remorse, well assured your indulgence will excuse what is wrong, accepting the will for the deed.

I am sorry your kind favours to *your little Nancy*[1] and *my little Mary* must be postponed so long, but I will not lose a day as soon as I go to town. I don't know whether I ever mentioned to you Mr. Granger's[2] biographical account of all the persons (from the King to the artificer) whose prints have been published in England, till the Revolution; it is usefull and entertaining, as it is very authentick and pleasant to have recourse to when you meet with any character that you are uncertain about the time or place he lived in, and the general character he bore. His first intention was to direct collectors how to class their portraits of remarkable persons, and he has thrown into the bargain little anecdotes that enliven it. It is four thin quartos, the price two guineas. An appendix is lately come out, much of the same size, and I suppose may be another half-guinea. The author is a clergyman of a very good character. I don't recollect what I said of Miss Viney (*Mrs. Viney*, as she *will* be called, and *not Mrs. Mary V——*), but I meant that her passions had got such a dominion over her that I fear'd they were incorrigible. I hope the ice of age will abate the fire of youth, and by making her more gentle and humble will open a happiness to her view which hitherto has been clouded by the turbulence of her disposition. I wish it for her own sake; I wish it still more for her

---

[1] "*Your little Nancy*," and "*my little Mary*."—Georgina Mary Ann Port, whom Mr. Granville chose to call "Nancy."

[2] The Rev. James Granger published a valuable work, entitled "The Biographical History of England," in four vols., 8vo. He died in 1776.

good sister's sake, who has been almost a martyr to her humours. But this tryal perhaps was graciously sent her to exercise that patience and resignation which, in the end, will obtain for her an eternal weight of glory. If we could fix our minds steadily on the *great reward* in store who could swerve from virtue? It is only when we lose sight of *that* that we go astray, and then, in order to restore us to the right path, our great and mercyfull Benefactor reminds us of our mortality and our dependance on him by sickness and sorrow; and if we make a right use of those friendly monitors we must bless the hand that gave the blow. I *am happy* with the account you give of the present state of your mind, and pray most earnestly for your support under so severe a tryal. I fear I have omitted what I ought to have told you, the pleasure you gave *our* dear Mrs. Port in your approbation of her little girl, and she charged me to tell you so. I hope she will prove a blessing to her mama. I will transmit to Mrs. Sandford your kind wishes! she always gratefully remembers the friendly regard you have always shown her. A *twig* from Calwich or a few seeds would be valuable to her for the sake of the place and its owner; but the Dutchess of Portland has been so good as to amply supply her garden. Carriage from hence to Bath is easy. I would give you a sprinkling of news if I could. Tho' of no consequence to you your young people should know how the world goes. My Lord Mayor's[1] stroke of palsy in the midst of his exultations, and Mr. Bradshaw's[2] miserable end when

---

[1] John Wilkes, Lord Mayor, Nov. 9, 1774. Frederic Bull, Lord Mayor for the previous year.

[2] Mr. Bradshaw, Secretary of the Treasury, committed suicide, by shooting himself in Nov. 1774.

arrived at a fortune far beyond his deserts or pretensions, are lessons to humble mortal vanity and ambition.
Lord Townsend is another instance of the insufficiency
of fortune and talents if not properly made use of. He
is *undone* in his fortune, and from possessing above 18
thousand a year, retired into the country to live on one
thousand a year! with the sting of having involved his
family in distress, when, had he acted on right principles,
he might have been an honour to them and his country.

Lord Berkeley,[1] one day last week, coming from London in his post chaise between 5 and 6 o'clock, ten miles
this side London was attacked by a highwayman. As
soon as he came to the chaise door Lord Berkeley shot
at him with a blunderbuss. He rode off, and the
footman behind the chaise fired another pistol at the
man, which made him reel and drop off his horse and
he expired in a few minutes. Some say the highwayman
fired a pistol into the chaise and wounded Lord Berkeley
in the head. These are dismal anecdotes, I wish I had
better to send you.

My love to y[r] chaplain. Adieu.

The Hon. Mrs. Boscawen to Mrs. Delany.

Holkham,[2] 15th Nov., 1774.

I have promised you, dear madam, large letters from
hence, but I shall fail in the performance I doubt, not

---

[1] Lord Berkeley was stopped by a highwayman, when passing in a post-
chaise over Hounslow Heath, in the dusk of the evening of Nov. 11th. The
highwayman was shot by Lord Berkeley's servant, and his accomplices discovered.

[2] Holkham, Norfolk, the seat of the Cokes, Earls of Leicester.

for want of matter most assuredly; volumes might be fill'd with what I see daily in this magnificent palace, but I am unequal to the description, and more likely to tell you how I wander about it, *losing my way.* Lady Leicester is often so good to be my guide, and to-day shew'd me a shorter way to my apart^mt, but it has to me been a *new* egarement, *another way to wander!* When I am bound to the library I find a bedchamber; in short, I walk many a furlong (I had almost said mile) that I do not intend, but everywhere such objects present themselves,—such pictures, such statues,—that I willingly halt on the road, whether the right or the wrong. We arrived here last Wensday to dinner, had a prosperous and pleasant journey, save that the poor beasts that drew us were quite worn out with 2 Newmarket meetings, and the preceding election, so that when we found a dead horse upon the road, we observ'd that ours had not life enough to take offence at it! We cou'd get no farther than Newmarket the first night, tho' we *never* went with but one pair of horses. At Houghton [1] (which we did not stop to see) the immense plantations gave me a greater respect for *Sir Robert* [2] than I had ever entertained for him when he rul'd these realms. The country all around is *entirely bare,* as if there was some *strict law* that *not a tree, not a shrub,* should shade *the turnips!* Houghton appears, and all is forest, woods, groves for many miles. Here also are great plantations, but no very old trees, you may believe, like the beeches at Bulstrode, but a great extent of *plantations,* more than

---

[1] The seat of the Earls of Orford.

[2] Sir Robert Walpole, afterwards Earl of Orford, Prime Minister to King George II.

enough to inform the country that trees *will grow* in Norfolk: but no one here seems convinc'd of this truth, and *no tree is propos'd to the earth*! but in these two principalitys. Here is a lake that charms me very much, and seems to me to be *much* the most beautifull feature of the dehors; I am not, however, able to judge, not having as yet been in a carriage since I arriv'd, except to church on Sunday. My Lady Duchess will tell you how advantageously the church is mounted on a round hill w[ch] commands a prospect of the sea; but perhaps her Grace did not see in what manner her noble cousin [1] has repair'd and beautify'd this church. I was quite surpris'd when I came into it. The inside is striking, all new work of L[y] Leicester's, y[e] cost £1100, so that you may believe it is compleat. But, my dear madam, I do not commend you by any means for not having seen this palace, of which you are so worthy. I learnt this after-

---

[1] Thomas Tufton, 6th Earl of Thanet, and his wife Catherine, fifth daughter of Henry Cavendish, 2nd Duke of Newcastle, were the parents of Lady Leicester, Lady Gower and their sisters. The following table explains the relationship between Lady Leicester and the Duchess of Portland.

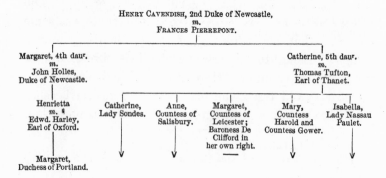

HENRY CAVENDISH, 2nd Duke of Newcastle,
m.
FRANCES PIERREPONT.

Margaret, 4th dau[r].
m.
John Holles,
Duke of Newcastle.

Catherine, 5th dau[r].
m.
Thomas Tufton,
Earl of Thanet.

Henrietta
m.
Edwd. Harley,
Earl of Oxford.

Catherine,
Lady Sondes.

Anne,
Countess of
Salisbury.

Margaret,
Countess of
Leicester;
Baroness De
Clifford in
her own right.

Mary,
Countess
Harold and
Countess Gower.

Isabella,
Lady Nassau
Paulet.

Margaret,
Duchess of Portland.

noon of L^y Leicester that you had never been here. I think you *must* come, I don't say in winter, for her lady^p tells me there " is *nothing* between her and *Norway* ;" but in summer, my dear madam, surely you would be well entertain'd. There is one room, called the landscape-room, full of Claudes and Vernets, that wou'd please you well. Other pictures, especially the Duke d'Aremberg by Vandyke and two Pietro Cortono's, I leave to my Lady Duchess to describe to you. I know both her Grace and you will be glad to hear these noble ladies enjoy perfect health. I think it is curious to see my L^y Leicester work at a tent-stitch frame every night by *one candle* that she sets upon it, and *no spectacles*. It is a carpet she works in shades—tent-stitch. Lady Gower and I walk out every day at noon, often L^y L. is of the party, and seems to be a very good walker. They are both vastly kind to me, and I am exceedingly obliged to them.

My dear madam, you will believe I have no news to tell you. While I was in London my *wretched* neighbour at the next door but one (tho' I thought him most *prosperous*) shot himself. You will understand I mean Mr. Bradshaw, tho' I believe you do not always read newspapers. I saw Ld Mahon [1] when I was in town ; I thought him *remarkably silent,* and should never have guess'd it was he that harangu'd the people so as to be heard *quite across Covent Garden!* Adieu, my dear madam. My paper does not suffice for all the salutations and respects that Holkham sends to Bulstrode.

Hastily but very affectionately yours,

F. B.

---

[1] Charles, afterwards 3rd Earl Stanhope.

Mrs. Delany to Mrs. Port, of Ilam.

B., 18th Nov., 1774.

Your letter, my dearest Mary, which I yesterday received, was doubly welcome from beginning with such interesting anecdotes.   What can be more natural than to *delight* in the dawnings of understanding as they break out in your children? and what can be more *delightfull* to your A.D.? not all the wise sayings of philosophers or witticisms of the beaux-esprits! I was quite *delighted* with the little *moon*skins so like their dear mama.   You see how it has led me into " *delight,*" " *delightfull,*" and " *delighted.*"   Sir Phillip Sidney in his Arcadia cannot be more guilty of reiteration! You have made me impatient for the acquaintance of Owen Feltham.[1]   I have sent to Mrs. Dunoyer to get it for me; I like your quotation extreamly; but as I hope to get the book, I would rather receive four pages of your own sentiments when you can do it without hurting yourself with too much writing.   I am in no hast to go to London; for I have here such a happy enjoyment of my dear friend's company as cannot be expected in London; she is a gem of inestimable price, and worthy of being preserved with the utmost care! Your little offering of fosils have the honour of being deposited in *the* cabinet, and what is still more honourable are more esteem'd as coming from " *our dear Mary.*"   Mrs. Leveson is at Leveson house ("Anthony" that was) near Plymouth; you may see *its picture* in Borlace's Natural History of Cornwall if

---

[1] Owen Feltham, author of " Resolves, Divine, Political and Moral," died about 1678.

you have it ; it formerly belonged to a Sr Willm Carew.
Mrs. Boscawen is gone with Lady Dr Gower to Holcomb ; returns the beginning of Decr. I hope the new
scene, and change of air and exercise will be of service to
her spirits. She has indeed borne this late loss beyond
expectation, for he was dear to her as a child, but his
conduct had been unamiable aud careless, and often gave
her much uneasiness, which must have loosen'd in some
measure the tender strings of affection ; but she has two
worthy daughters, who make it their study to give her
consolation ; and what can do it so effectually as the
attentive tenderness of a real friend ? Well may I say it
under this roof ! and when addressing my dearest Mary,
whose filial love is such a cordial to me, I am glad Miss
Sparrow had a good journey, and that you think her
improved. Her good sense I hope will make her behave
herself in such a manner to her good friends at Ilam as
to make them and herself happy. We search abroad for
that thing call'd happiness, and it as constantly eludes
our search, and all the time like a thing long lost we find
it in *our pocket* ! *Home* is the *first place* to search for it
in, and having *found it there*, we shall want it nowhere
else. Last Monday I went to Windsor to breakfast
with Mrs. Walsingham, and also made a visit to Mrs.
Egerton, both in Windsor Castle. The Duchess was
afraid of venturing ; but I always find exercise do me
good when I don't hazard catching cold by it. Perhaps
you think we go on here in an uninterrupted course of
philosophy and rational amusements, and talk of nothing
but the wonders of the four elements ; but we have our
episodes, our little anecdotes, that if penn'd by the
sublime and beautifull paragraph writers, might make

a figure in story; but you must take it in vulgar phrase.

A young gentleman, Lord Creiton, son to Lord Dumfries of Scotland, arrived at Beconsfield about ten days ago; lodged at the King's Head; went to make a visit to Mr. Waller, who, not being at home, his butler thought it incumbent on him to do the honours of the place to this travelling young nobleman, and for the time he staid at Beconsfield attended him everywhere; an unlucky shower of rain wetted his lordship to the skin, and he condescended to borrow a suit of clothes of the butler, and a watch from a watchmaker's at Wickham, and walked off with both, leaving a reckoning of *seven* pound unpaid for at the inn. About the same time as Lord Godolphin was drinking his tea with Dr. Bentham of Oxford, a young man, came into the room with his coat almost torn off his back, apologizing for his abrupt appearance; that his name was Lockwood, son to an acquaintance of his lordship's; that he was returning to Oxford, but a highwayman had robbed him of his watch and money, and left him in that deplorable way. Lord Godolphin's[1] compassion opened his heart and purse, and he gave the man six guineas, and Dr. Bentham, who was going in his chaise to Oxford, offer'd to carry him, and he did. When they came there the young adventurer said he must go on to Woodstock to see his relations; marched off, and has never been heard of since! it is supposed that the pretended lord and the squire were the same identical person. In his tours round Beconsfield his master of the ceremonys brought

---

[1] Francis, 2nd and last Earl of Godolphin. He died 17th Jan., 1766. His sister Mary married William Owen, of Porkington, Esq., Salop.

him to Bulstrode; but when he came into the court his heart failed him : he was taken with a sudden stitch, said he "was subject to fits, and must go immediately to an apothecary." I suppose, seeing such a number of servants, he was apprehensive of discovery. Lord Godolphin has given his two nieces, Miss Owens, five thous^d pound a piece, and five hundred pound towards the building of a college at Cambridge (I believe); these benefactions, I hope, will rub off the rust of avarice it was thought he was a little addicted to, and the pleasure he must feel in making others happy, encourage him to go on. I know nothing of the Foleys, tho' Miss Foley owes me two letters. Lord Clanbrazil not in parliament; depending on *Lord Godolphin's* interest made no other, and *he* was under an obligation to give his to Lord Caermarthen. It seems strange that his father, Mr. F., did not bring him in; but there is no accounting for narrow minds. Encourage your young pupil to read history, particularly of England, and to give you an account every day of what she reads. No novels, but don't seem to *forbid* them, only in speaking of them disapprove generally of their falsehood and insignificancy; for if you *make them* of too much consequence, it will excite curiosity, and at best they too often take up the time from things of more utility. So ends my dictatorship.

You have a new cousin, Lady Bridget Tolmache,[1] brought to bed of a son : he would have come in better time when she had a good estate for him. Lady M.

---

[1] Lady Bridget Tollemache, wife of the Hon. John Tollemache, and daughter of Robert, 1st Earl of Northington.

Somerset[1] and Lady Betty Compton,[2] who will undoubtedly lead the fashion this year, wear their hair as
Ben says in Love for Love "*Top and topgallant.*"[3]

Mrs. Delany to Mrs. Port, of Ilam.

Bulstrode, 25th Nov., 1774.

I am glad, my dearest Mary, you approve my plan.
Your partiality embellishes my little works, and the goodness of your heart deceives your head in that one article.
Praise from those we *love* doubles the satisfaction of receiving it, and stamps a value on it, whether owing to
their affection or judgment. We can never think it
flattery from *them*, and a just sense of our own demerits
should guard us from the rock of vanity, and be a spurr
to make us do our best to deserve what partiality bestows.

I will make the best enquiry I can after *Wright
Mandrest, Wright Healing that was.*

I thought of Mrs. Jackson for you (if to be had), and
spoke about her to Mrs. Sandford when she was in
town. She had had an intention of taking her herself,
but Mrs. Viney had *set her up* on so high a footing that
she took upon herself in such a manner as nobody could
reasonably submit to. She expected to be one of the

---

[1] Lady Mary Isabella Somerset, youngest daughter of Charles, 4th Duke of
Beaufort.

[2] Lady Elizabeth Compton, only daughter of Charles, 7th Earl of
Northampton. Lady Elizabeth married, in 1782, Lord George Augustus
Henry Cavendish, afterwards Earl of Burlington.

[3] "*Love for Love,*" by William Congreve, published in 1695.

company at all times, and was very troublesome. There
is no end of such indulgences, and all the inconveniences
that attend them. These notions are as mean as their
origin, which makes them *proud* of *appearing* what they
have no pretensions to be, and it cannot be too much
guarded against. The articles agreed to when you engage with such a sort of servant should be strictly ad-
hered to, and then any little indulgence will be an
obligation, and the moment they advance too far put a
check immediately. There is *no medium:* when they
cease to be servants, they attempt to be mistresses.
Mrs. Sandford will not part with the person she now
has, but if she ever should, and you should then want
one, she will certainly think of you. She says she has
an elder sister, who she thinks would be more desireable
for you, if her friends will let her go to service, and has
every accomplishment that fits her for such a station
except experience, as she has never been in service.
Mrs. Johnstone has applied for Lady Jersey, but her
father and mother are unwilling to let her go into a
large family without *an assurance* of their *great regularity*.
They have kept for some time with great reputation a
French school at Bristol. Mrs. Sand[d] thinks if she could
be obtained for you she would be a treasure. Her name
is Vranken. I don't know what to say about her youth,
but that's a fault mends every day.

I am glad you have got one of my dear councellors in
your neighbourhood. It is long since I heard from
Calwich.

The newspapers killed Lord Cadogan,[1] but he has

---

[1] Charles, 2nd Baron Cadogan, who died 24th Sept. 1776.

been at the opera in good health laughing at the paragraph. I am sure you will be glad to hear that Miss Goldsworthy is made sub-governess to the young Royals at St. James's; most likely Lady Cowper has already informed you, and that Lord Cowper is not to be married till next year. Mrs. Dashwood was saddly shocked with the manner of Dow[r] Lady Effingham's [1] death, who was her aunt. *Beware* of standing too near the fire in a combustible dress !

Mr. Mason is in town, but he may be gone before I get there. He is like a meteor, and blazes but for a moment. His visits as bright and as short.

The long story of the adventurer, which I told you in my last letter, has a sequel. He went to Welbeck, borrow'd one of the Duke of Portland's horses (the Duke that day not at home), went a hunting, calling himself Captain Crofts (alias Crafts), the second day met his Grace, and " thank'd him for the use of his horse." The Duke replied *he was " very sorry his servant had been such a fool as to lend him a horse "* (having been let into the gentleman's character), upon which Captain C. made off, but left the horse behind.

Mrs. Delany to the Viscountess Andover.

Bulstrode, 27th Nov., 1774.

The Duchess-dowager of Portland was so good to you my dear Lady Andover, as to take the pen out of my hand and postpone my acknowledgements to another

---

[1] The Dowager-Countess of Effingham was Anne, widow of Francis, 1st Earl of Effingham, and sister of Robert Bristow, Esq.

opportunity; but alas! all is spoyl'd by her Grace telling me this moment that I *must write* and send y^r lady^p the history and adventures of my young Lord Creighton, son and heir apparent of the noble Earl of Dumfries, of the kingdom of Scotland—how he first of all personated the young nobleman at Beconsfield, where he intended a visit to Mr. Waller; he not being at home, the butler to do honour to his master, offer'd his service to show him about, upon w^{ch} *my lord* determin'd to stay some days at the inn, where he was so courteous and affable that (they thought) to be sure he "must be a *lord*." Bulstrode was a principal object but unluckily my lord as he was coming into the house was seized with *a stitch*, said he was subject to fits but always had warning, and must immediately go to an apothecary. They trotted on to Uxbridge, where at a watchmaker's he saw a watch that took his fancy—unfortunately had left his purse at home—" S^r, will you trust me, my friend—here will answer for me?" "Surely, my lord." A shower of rain wetted his lordship, but his guide supplied him with a sute of cloths; when he return'd to the inn he bespoke a dinner for himself and friends, and said he must make a visit to his "cousin, my Lord Godolphin," but should be back to dinner—he was as good as his word in *one* particular, and went to Lord Godolphin, whom he found at breakfast; but made not his appearance in the shape of *my lord*, but as a young gentleman on his road to Oxford who had met with robbers, who had taken his money and watch, and had torn the cloaths almost off of his back, but as he was son to a particular acquaintance of his lordship, his name Lockwood, he hoped he would lend him six guineas. His deplorable figure, his dolefull ditty, and

the son of an acquaintance, so moved my Lord Godol[n]'s
compassion, that *his heart and purse-strings both were open*
and he not only gave him the money, but Doc[r] Bentham[1]
of Oxford, who was there, offer'd to carry him in his
chaise, as he was going thither; the offer was accepted,
and when they arrived at Oxford the youth said he must
go on to see some friends at Woodstock before he settled;
here they parted; which way his genius led him is not
known; but his next exploit was a visit to Welbeck, the
Duke of Portland not at home; he called himself "Captain
Croft," and borrow'd one of the duke's horses to go a
hunting; the second day he met his Grace, and with
infinite modesty thank'd him for the use of his horse.
The duke, aware of his extraordinary character, said he
was very sorry any servant of his should be such a fool
as to lend him one of his horses; upon w[ch] the intrepid
Cap[n] march'd off. Lord Lincoln met him on the course
and invited him to dinner, but having afterwards some
hint given him of his deserts, order'd him to be pursued,
but he was *too nimble* for his pursuers! But this is *not
all*; he tried his skill on Lord Essex at Cashioberry, but
his lordship who has the wisdome of the serpent, said he
"never gave money on such occasions, but he was welcome to a bit of bread and a glass of wine," and took
care to have him watch'd safe out of sight. It is a misfortune that attends many historical facts, that there
is a dificulty in settling the exact chronology of them —
and so it is with our hero; for authors differ about the
last mentioned transaction, and not quite sure of the
name he assumed, but all agree that he is a *very great*

---

[1] The Rev. Edward Bentham, D.D., Senior Canon of Christchurch, Oxford,
and Regius Professor of Divinity. He died Aug. 12, 1776.

rogue—witness 6 guineas from Lord Godolphin, a suit of cloaths formerly belonging to Mr. Waller's butler, the watch, and above seven pound he left unpaid at the inn. Now if your lady^p is tired to death, you cannot say I did it, but the Duchess of Portland, who could have told you all this in a dozen lines, concise and clear. I have a great mind to revenge the injury done you, by exposing your friend and sending you a libel she has receiv'd from Albemarle Street that exposes her Grace and the odd company she keeps; and I can tell you, madam, she has defrauded your lady^p of something that belongs to you—now if you love riddles this may amuse you by your chimney-corner, I had much rather it were to be by mine; but you mortify me to the last degree in speaking of coming in such doubtfull terms—my great relyance is on Miss F. Howard and your sweet little Lady Maria; their amusement and improvement will gain the point so much wish'd for by,

Dear madam,

Your lady^ps most obed^t hum^bl ser^t,

M. DELANY.

The affectionate compliments of Bulstrode salute Elford; hope Ld Suffolk is now free from the gout.

My lord's sudden *stitch* at Bulstrode was occasion'd by his seeing *my man* in the hall, as he *apprehended* he knew him.

Mrs. Delany to Bernard Granville, Esq.

Monday.   Bulstrode, 28th Nov., 1774.

My first busyness shall be to execute your kind commission for your little " *Nancy*."   I feel loth to leave the
perfect tranquillity of this place and enjoyment of the
Dss' company; we read and like the *same* books, we
talk them over without interruption, we are fond of the
same works; and the pleasures of these occupations are
increased by participation; in London I have the
pleasure of seeing *her* most days by *my own fire-side*,
but the bustle of the world does not afford the same
edifying subjects of conversation, except when we moralize on its folly and vanity; *not* that there are not *many*
virtues to admire and imitate, but they are almost lost
in the *crowd*.   I am a little sorry, too, to bid adieu to the
sociable hares; I counted thirty last night as they were
regaling themselves at their round table under the
windows.   But the enemy has been abroad, and killed ten
brace very near the park pale, which was very ungentle-
manlike!   My friend deserves better treatment.   So ends
my lamentation for leaving Bulstrode, but I thank God
I have a home that suits me very well, and I endeavor
to enjoy the blessings preserved to me, as it is my duty.
The painfull recollection of my dear brother's sufferings
would render all my endeavors to that purpose ineffectual,
did I not consider it is the will of that gracious Being
who alone knows what is best for us.   My greatest mortification in London is not being able to go constantly
to church, tho' so near me, as catching cold in the beginning of winter makes me a prisoner by necessity, and
unable to go out at all.   I am fond of an old fashioned

book, Dr. Patrick's Pilgrim,[1] and have just met with a
very comfortable paragraph, that "sometimes God bestows more favours upon sick men in their beds, who
can pray in no other manner than by humiliations and
prostrate submissions of their *wills* to him, than he doth
upon some others who spend many hours on their bended
knees in that holy exercise." You see I lay hold of
the indulgence you give me, and send you my thoughts
without reserve; a long absence naturally leads us to
make our letters like conversation; when one has hopes
of frequent meeting, we suppress many things to communicate them personally; but at best, writing is an imperfect communication. I should be glad to enliven my
serious reflections with some amusing paragraph. We
have heard nothing by the newspapers, but they are
false talebearers. It is certain that Lord Holland[2] is so
ill that it is thought he can't recover. His distemper the
dropsey. Lord Clive's[3] sudden death has raised strong
suspicions of the manner of it, tho' I have heard nothing
certain; what a deplorable end to all his ambitious
views! A large field for moralising! and I shall relapse
if I don't hasten to some other subject. I hope I shall
catch our nephew Bernard before he leaves London, and
if you recollect any thing you wish to have sent in the
box with the little girl's things, let me know in time.
I have just begun a book the Dss of P. recommends as
well written in French: *l'Histoire de François Premier,
Roy de France, par Mon. Gaillard.*

---

[1] The Parable of the Pilgrim, by Dr. Symon Patrick, Bishop of Ely; born
1626, died 1707.

[2] Stephen, 2nd Baron Holland. He died 16th Dec., 1774.

[3] Robert, 1st Lord Clive, died 22nd Nov., 1774.

In Mr. Granville's handwriting on the back of this letter—

Half a hundred of non parielle apples.

Ditto golden pippins.

A dozen of Civill oranges.

A silver scoop to eat the apples, or I shall not know how to manage.

The apples must be fair and not bruised.

The apples to be of the large sort which are best for scooping.

The Countess Cowper to Mrs. Port, of Ilam.

Richmond, Dec. 3rd, 1774.

My dearest Mrs. Port,

Many thanks for your last agreable letter, and for conveying mine to Mrs. Henzey. I hope your little boy is quite well again, and that you have not suffer'd by y[e] good nursing. I had the chicken-pox in labour of Lord Spencer, w[ch] lasted so many days, that y[e] distemper was over with me before he was born. There was no appearance of it upon him, but when he was ten days old it appear'd, and he was very full. Lady Bridget Tollemach was brought to bed of a son on y[e] 30th ult., and Lady Jane Halliday[1] the next morning of her 4th son, to whome I am to stand god-mother. I am much pleased with Miss Goldsworthy's preferment. Lady Charlotte Finch[2] has not only show'd her friendship, but

---

[1] Lady Jane Tollemache, daughter of Lionel, 3rd Earl of Dysart, married, 23rd Oct., 1771, John Delap Halliday, of the Leasowes, county Salop.

[2] Lady Charlotte Finch, daughter of Thomas, Earl Pomfret, and wife of William Finch, Esq. Lady Charlotte was Governess to the Princesses, daughters of George III., and Miss Goldsworthy, Sub-governess.

also her judgement in recommending her to her Majesty for sub-governess to y[e] young Princess, as she is in every respect qualified for such a trust by her *morals, manners,* and *accomplishments.* The salary is £300 per annum, and a table and an apartment in the house. As y[e] Prince of Mecklenburgh [1] made me a morning visit last Monday, I had an opportunity of saying *many agreable* things concerning her. Her own fortune is £2,000, w[ch] was left her by her grandfather. Her mother had £10,000, but her father spent it all. Mrs. Le Grand comes here on y[e] 5th instant to spend y[e] winter, and Lady Mary Mordaunt leaves me on the 12th, and goes into Bedfordshire to her friend Mrs. Gordon. She desires her love to y[o]. I was at my *neighbour's* last night. They both look ill. I was as usual *roasted.* Every one in my house sit close to y[e] fire (except myself), and have (of course) caught colds. I have as yet not had any, notwithstanding y[e] *furnaces* I enter. When from home, my nightly *cold bath* (meaning my bed) I really believe prevents my catching cold. Mr. Port will *shiver* at this account! My best complim[ts] to him. Lady Mary sends hers to you. God bless you and y[rs]. My dearest Mrs. Port, think sometimes of

Y[r] affec[t],

S. G. COWPER.

---

[1] His Serene Highness Prince Ernest of Mecklenburgh-Strelitz, second brother to Queen Charlotte, arrived in England 18th June, 1774.

Mrs. Delany to Mrs. Port, of Ilam.

St. James's Place, 20th Dec., 1774.

Now I will ramble away after my usual manner, and like Swift's gossip *tell all I can think of.* The important box at last is gone to Calwich, and I suppose as soon as you can safely venture you will go there, with *his* little "Nancy" and have a summons to receive its contents, as he has set his heart upon seeing the effect they will have on the little darling. It contains the two hats with rufled hat-bands (which I hope are not crushed), a cuckow for little George, the cryes of London, and a set of flappers for Johnny, a memorandum book for *Mary the Little,* and an almanack for *Mary the Great.* The hollows stuffed up with bisquet.

I am truly sorry for good Miss A. Landers loss.

Yesterday, and not before, Lord Mahone was married to Lord Chatham's daughter. Lord Chat. sent to *Lord Temple*[1] to name the day before Xtmass. Miss Nugent,[2] Lord Clare's daughter, a very pretty well-behaved girl, just 16, to be married to Mr. Pit, just of age. Lord Cathcart's[3] two eldest daughters destin'd to the Duke of Athol and a Scotch Mr. Graham, men of good characters and great fortunes. The youngest Miss Cathcart some

---

[1] Richard Grenville, 1st Earl Temple, who died 11th Sept., 1779.

[2] Mary Elizabeth, only daughter and heiress of Robert, Earl Nugent, married, 16th April, 1775, George Grenville, who succeeded to the Earldom of Temple on the death of his uncle in 1779, and was created Marquis of Buckingham, 4th Dec., 1784.

[3] Jane, eldest daughter of George, 9th Lord Cathcart, married, 26th Dec., 1774, John, 4th Duke of Atholl. Mary, the second daughter of George, Lord Cathcart, married, in 1774, Sir Thomas Graham, afterwards Lord Lynedoch. Louisa, youngest daughter, married first, in 1776, David, Earl of Mansfield; and secondly, in 1797, the Hon. Robert Fulke Greville.

time hence to a son of Lord Abercorn's; but she is too young.

The world, after all, is not so much depraved as we often think it, for all these young women have been chosen, not altogether for beauty, but they are remarkable for their *proper behaviour*, and I hope it will encourage reserve and modesty. You could hardly have expected it from an elève of Lord Clare's. She is the only one of the set that has any considerable fortune.

The American affairs are now the only topick of conversation.

I am reading l'Histoire de François Prem^r, and last night was struck as apropos to *my Cinthia* with the following paragraph :—

"La première femme de Franc^{s1} premier, Roy de France, la simple et vertueuse Claude, avoit pour devise une pleine lune, avec ses mots :

Candide et bienfaisante aux ames candides.

Cet astre (ajoute l'historien) réjouit ceux qui n'ont point de mauvais desseins, et qui ne cherchent point les ténèbres, pour cacher leurs mauvais actions."

Last Tuesday I had a party to dinner: Dss Dow^r of Portland, Mrs. Montagu, her son Mr. Frederick Montagu, the Bishop of Litchfield, and Mr. Mason. It was an agreable day. The Bishop's sensible cheerfull conversation, with great politeness, was an excellent contrast to Mr. Mason's shyness, and Mrs. Montagu's sprightly and inoffensive humour unfolded the poet's reserve, and they play'd an excellent trio till nine, when a rap at the door dispers'd my com-

---

1 "Histoire de François I^r." by Gabriel Henry Gaillard, author of other historical works. He was born in 1728, and died in 1806.

pany. Had they known who was coming they would not have hasten'd away. It was poor Mrs. Boscawen, who call'd to take her leave before she went to the Duke of Beaufort's to spend her Xtmass. He has taken "*Blandford Lodge*," formerly Cornbury!

I had the satisfaction of going to church last Sunday. I could not venture in the very cold weather, but I miss'd the good Lord Dartmouth, who called with 2 of his youngest sons before I return'd home. A visit from F. M. made me some amends. Nothing was ever more amiable than Mr. Mon. attention to his mother. Amongst all my friends in London, she next to my dearest friend at Whitehall would be my greatest loss. Her affection and integrity, her excellent principles and knowledge of the world, makes her very valuable, and preferable to many whose manner may be more engaging.

I saw Lord Willoughby in sad spirits, tho' he hopes Doct[r] James has been of some service to Lady Willoughby.

Mrs. Delany to Bernard Granville, Esq.

St. James's Place, 22nd Dec., 1774.

Tho' I am almost afraid a long letter may be troublesome to you to read, I cannot help indulging myself, depending on my dear brother's not reading it but when he can do it most at his ease; I therefore begin with my commission, as probably it may prove the only part of my letter of any consequence. I have just sent to the Ashbourne carrier a box with a dozen Ceville oranges, half a hundred nonpareils, half a hundred golden pippins, and have taken the liberty of putting in a little bundle for Mrs. Port, as too small to send by itself. I have not been able to get your silver scoop yet, tho' I bespoke it immediately, for I could find none ready made. I would not wait for it, as I thought you might want the fruit; but I have tucked into Mrs. P's parcel an ivory one, en attendant. There goes also, tied on that box, a small one with superfine jarr raisins, as the confectioner, Koffin in the Haymarket, assures me; they have them now made up in those little boxes; if they are not what you like let me know sincerely, that I may mend my hand. Smith grumbles extremely that the fruiterers will not now allow *more* than 50 to the half hundred! Apples in general this year are small. There are no good French plums to be yet had.

Lady Stamford and her new-born son in a good way. I wish I could say as much of Lady Willoughby, who has such an obstinate jaundice that nothing has been yet able to conquer. She is now in *Doctor James's* hands, who cured Lord Stamford and Lady Rockinghame of the same complaint. I pity her family, as she is a worthy woman and greatly esteemed, and we cannot well spare such. I never saw two men so dejected as Lord Willoughby and Lord Guilford: they have both call'd on me. This world is a sad wilderness when we lose those that have made us happy in it; and whilst we remain in it self-love will make us lament when (for the sake of those we love) we should rather *rejoyce;* we are ready to do so for all advantageous earthly acquisitions that fall to the share of our friends; but we must be more angellick than humanity can attain to resign them without regret and sorrow, tho' for their eternal happiness.

People are going out of town to spend their Xmas.

The marriages that are, and are to be, as follows : Lord Mahone, Lady Hester Pitt; Mr. Greenvil (*your cousin's son*) to Miss Nugent, Lord Clare's daughter, a great fortune, pretty, and well-behaved; Lord Cathcart's 2 eldest daughters to the Duke of Athol and Mr. Graham. Great estates and good fortunes, and everybody speaks well of the young ladies. The American affairs are perplexing and require great adroitness in the Minister. Incendiaries are busy to raise discontent; but these are matters too high for me. I wish for peace and grace to enjoy and employ well the *plenty we possess.* The approaching season naturally fills the heart with thanksgiving for the blessing of so wonderful an event, and expands it with kind and fervent wishes to all our fellow-creatures. I don't know how to express mine to my dear brother, but they are constant for his happiness here and hereafter.

―――――

The Hon. Mrs. Boscawen to Mrs. Delany.

Blandford Park, 27th Dec., 1774.

I remember well, my dear madam, you bid me take notice that I ow'd you a letter; but I doubt it is the hopes of being *paid* one (rather than the love of justice) that induces me to write. The state of this family, I thank God, is very pleasant to relate and behold. All well—hormis la pauvre Duchesse qui est très malade tous les jours pour l'être davantage dans quelques mois d'ici. I had rather it had not been so, but I never

reckon such events in the number of misfortunes. Alas!
I am but too well acquainted with real ones ever to
make imaginary ones. Methinks I will go back to my
journey and tell you that I had the finest winter day
that ever was seen, and at Salt-Hill à point nommé Mrs.
Walsingham arriv'd (for I requested her so to do), and
I had a conference with her of 3 hours, which was very
agreeable to me; all that while my horses refresh'd themselves so well that they trotted on to Henley over a
beautifull country, gilded by the setting sun. Next day
I proceeded to Oxford, which is always venerable and
pleasing, and at Woodstock they told me the Dss of
Beaufort was come to meet me, and I sh^d find her at Blenheim, which I did accordingly; but first I pass'd thro'
as much of Blenheim Park as shew'd me the *vast* superiority of taste in the days of George 3^d from those of Anne
the first. Blenheim is now as beautiful as it is magnificent, and the water which *only* "an emblem of *her*
bounty flow'd," now is worthy to represent that of
another Duchess better known to you and *very unlike*
her Grace of Marlboro'. It spreads, it adorns a country,
and looks like the beautous Thames.

> Tho' deep yet clear, tho' gentle yet not dull ;
> Strong without rage, without o'erflowing full.

One improvement might be recommended to the
princely Marlboro', and that is to make roads like those
which our friend, Lady Gower, wou'd make if she had
half his purse. The road from Woodstock hither is odious,
but having got into my daughter's chaize, I was so
pleas'd to see her, and found so much to say to her, that

it cheated the weary (and very rugged) way. I found
my dear boys at the porch in great joy to see *gran.*, and
I found indeed a sweet scene here. It must be charming
in the summer, such uneven ground, such venerable
beeches and old riven oaks, such a valley full of clear
springs, and the hills beyond, the view of Charlbury—
"all full of amenity" (as somebody says) and delightfull
landscapes, but I cannot find *the* rocky cliff *you told me
of.* I prowl about the park very much, for it is not
dirty, except in gateways or places of much resort; nor
do I hear any thing of Cowley's House ;[1] did it over-look
the water ? If so, it is now the farmer's house. The
mansion is in itself noble, and must have been very agreeable when it was fill'd with Vandykes and their successors,
living and worthy to *keep them company.* At present
the house and tatter'd furniture is so delabrés that I
understood perfectly the meaning of the (foreign) maître
d'hôtel here, who said : "His Grace shou'd be here, to
live here, and *not pay* his Grace of Marlboro'." However
he *does* pay the D. of Marlboro' £400 a year, half of
wch he receives again from a farmer who hires the park
and covers it with sheep and cattle of all sorts. The
more *remote* parts he ploughs, but the whole is a very
agreeable view from the terass and from my window. I
have a very comfortable bedcham^r and 2 closets upon the
ground floor, south aspect. But the beds above stairs
are *old velvet rags,* except the Duchess's own apartment,

---

[1] Abraham Cowley, the poet, was born in London in the year 1618, and
died at Chertsey in 1667. A picture of his house is engraved with—"Here
the last accents flowed from Cowley's tongue."

w^{ch} *is whole.* In general the hangings above stairs are
tapestry. I have been at Ld Lichfield's [1] and at General
Boscawen's,[2] and Capt. Pigot's:[3] the two latter are lodges
in the adjacent forest, both pretty indeed for a solitary
wild forest scene. You will not expect a piece of news
from hence, and yet I will tell you one: Lady Yates is
going to be marry'd to the *Bishop of Rochester!* You
will say perhaps: " I know it already from our common
friend, Lady E. Clive [4] and I approve it very much." So
do I indeed, and I have a great esteem and affection for
Lady Yates, so that I shou'd be very sorry if her choice
were not wise, but indeed I think it is. There is to be
cour plenière at Blenheim these holidays, I think near
30 guests, in general la belle jeunesse. One of them
has halted here in her way, Lady Sefton,[5] who remains
till to-morrow or next day. I have just had a very comfortable letter from Mrs. Leveson. Adieu, dear madam.

P.S. Quick lime and white of egg is the best ciment
for China.

---

[1] George Henry Lee, 3rd Earl of Lichfield, died in 1775, when his title
reverted to his uncle, Robert Lee, 4th and last Earl of Lichfield, who died in
1776, when the title became extinct in that family.

[2] The Hon. George Boscawen, fourth son of Hugh, 2nd Viscount Falmouth,
and brother-in-law to Mrs. Boscawen.

[3] Thomas Pigott, of Knapton, Esq., Queen's County, afterwards a Major-
general in the Army.

[4] Elizabeth, daughter of Robert Clive, 1st Earl of Powis.

[5] Isabella, second daughter of William, 2nd Earl of Harrington, and wife of
Charles William Molyneux, 1st Earl of Sefton.

Mrs. Delany to Mrs. Port, of Ilam.

St. James's Place, 27th Dec., 1774.

Surprised at your date? (" Wolsley Bridge.") Yes,
surely ! I fear the dear children's coughs are very bad
that you quit at this shivering season your own comfortable house for an inn, and I fear a very indifferent one.
My sweet little bird ! How earnestly I wish it were in
my power to come to her, and she should not " *want me
sadly.*" You say your plan was *to go Wolesley B. first,*
which implies your going further. I am sorry Mr. P.
has not been well. Great is my consolation that Miss
A. Lander is with you a sympathising friend, and the
service, the comfort, and pleasure she must know you
receive from her I hope will do her spirits good, and
cheer her good heart. What *says Calwich* about your
journey. How are they there? It is very long since I
heard. I suppose Miss Sparrow is with you. She is of
an age now to be usefull, and her good nature, I dare
say, will make her exert herself. Lady Stamford goes
on well. Her rheumaticks charm'd away by bathing her
face and neck with a water Dr. Ford prescribed, and if
it will keep I design to send you a pint of it, for fear
your pain should return. Lady Will^r still in the same
way in Dr. James's hands. My good little friend in
Han^r Square confined with one of her terrible coughs,
but I thank God I was stout eno' to spend yesterday
with her. Did you receive my letter with a nonsensical
advertisement enclosed in it?

Mrs. Delany to Bernard Granville, Esq.

St. James's Place, 31st Dec., 1774.

I don't know how it came to pass, but my dear brother's last letter, dated the 20th instant, did not come to me till last night, and I began to think it long since I heard from Calwich. I do not wonder you should be affected by the extream cold, which I suppose must still be more severe in the northern countys than under the influence of the London smoak, and yet we are obliged to have recourse to cloaks and *double hoods* by the fireside. I had the comfort of going to chapel on Xmass day well wrapped up, and caught no cold. I endeavour to use exercise at home by making errands for myself from one room to another, which, tho' they lye in a small compass, is better than no exercise. When I can go out, the Dss of P. is so good as to let me have her coach, for since my fall *I can't* go in a *chair*, as it cramps my knees, and the motion gives them pain—the only inconvenience, I thank God, that now remains.

Your distinction between the two French ladies is very just, but from the very beginning there seems to have been reserve and art in Mad^{me} de Main^{n}, and the reverse in Mad^{me} de Sevigné. Indeed, they acted in very different scenes of life. Your observation regarding the *effects* on *temper* in the early part of life is certainly true, and the *impressions* taken in *extream youth go very deep* more or less, according to the natural disposition. You have so true a *sense* of charity and *justice* that I have no doubt of your making such a disposition of what you have in your power as will most essentially give you that comfort and consolation I most earnestly pray you may be blessed with to your last moments.

I hope the boxes are arrived by this time. They talk now of a match between Lord Egremont[1] and Lady Mary Somerset. I believe I mentioned it before. He is a pretty man, has a vast fortune, and is very generous, and not addicted to the vices of the times, which, if he were, would soon entangle even his great fortune. His kind and generous behaviour to his mother, his brother, and sisters, show a goodness of heart that I hope will have *some influence* on his contemporarys. My pen freezes in my fingers. I shall long to know how your *little Nancy* will receive your kind gifts. She will be all astonishment. I will communicate your thoughts about the *milk* charity. It is an excellent and sure mode of relief.

Mrs. Stainforth has an additional employment, and I suppose an additional salary. She was housekeeper to the King, and she now has the care of the Queen's appartment. She is a *charitable* and *good woman, as well* as her Royal mistress.

Lady Willoughby, they hope, is something better.

George O'Brien, 3rd Earl of Egremont, who died *unmarried*, 11th Nov., 1837.

Bulstrode ? 1775.

[The commencement of this letter has not been found.]

MR. WALPOLE, the patron of the arts, seeing something uncommon in her perseverance, lent *her* [1] some fine miniatures and enamels, which she has copied admirably, and goes on rapidly; so you may believe she is delighted *here*, where there is such gratification for genius of every kind. Wednesday evening Mr. Pennant [2] came, and is here still, and yesterday Mrs. Walsingham spent the day here, and made it very agreable. I mentioned the Duchess of Leinster's [3] marriage to her son's tutor, but I called him by a wrong name—his name is Ogleby. People wonder at her marriage, as she is reckoned one of the proudest and most expensive women in the world; but perhaps she thought it incumbent (as Lady Brown [4] said of her Grace) to "marry and make an honest man of him." I pity her poor children, and it is supposed that this wretched proceeding has made Lady Bellamont [5] more ready to accept of that miserable match. The Dowager

---

[1] " *Her*," probably Lady Bingham, afterwards Lady Lucan.

[2] Thomas Pennant, Esq., the eminent Welsh antiquary, whose valuable works are well known. He was born at his family place, Downing, Flintshire, 1726, d. 1798.

[3] The Lady Emilia Lennox, d. of Charles, 2nd Duke of Richmond, and widow of James, 1st Duke of Leinster. She had seventeen children by that marriage. She became a widow, Nov. 19, 1773, and married, secondly, William Ogilvie, Esq., by whom she had other children.

[4] "Lady Brown."—Margaret, daughter of the Hon. Robert Cecil, second son of James, 3rd Earl of Salisbury, married Sir Robert Brown, a banker at Venice. (?)

[5] On the 22nd July, 1774, the Earl of Bellamont married the Lady Emily Fitzgerald, sister to the Duke of Leinster.

Duchess of Beaufort is come to England. The Duchess of Kingston, who has been some time at Calais, has a ship of her own, which she sends on her errands to England, &c. She expected its return, and on hearing it was coming into harbour, she went to the strand and immediately on board, and asked the captain " if he had brought her birds ?" " *No, madam, I have not brought your birds, but I have brought Captain Hervey.*" Upon which her grace-*less* Grace hurried out of the ship with all possible speed. I want to hear the sequel, when I do you shall. I can write no longer ; my ink is puddle, my pen a skewer, my head stupid, but my heart ever yours.

M. D.

Mrs. Delany to Mrs. Anne Viney.

St. J. P., 11th Jan., 1775.

My last accounts from Ilam were rather better, but not from Calwich. I have nothing to hope from thence but that the goodness of God will support my dear brother under his sufferings, and that in the end they will prove *blessings ;* but glorious as *that expectation is,* it is impossible not to feel the present affliction as a subject too grievous to dwell upon ! I heard a sweet new instrument called the *celestinet,* the improvement, *if not* the invention of Mr. Mason the poet. His gentlest muse is not more harmonious and pathetick. I know your sister will long, as well as yourself, to have it described, but that is past my skill. I can give you a sketch, but not a finished piece. The shape is that of a short harpsi-

cord, with the same sort of keys, and played on only
with the right hand in the same manner ; and at the
same time you draw with your left hand a bow like the
bow of a fiddle, that runs in a groove under the keys,
and by proper management presses on the wires and
brings out a delicate, exquisite sound, something between the finest notes of a fiddle and the glasses. It is
not above 2 feet long and 1 foot and a half in the
broadest part, where the keys are, which are placed on
the top of the instrument in this
manner. It is set on a table, and
is best accompanied with a piano-
forte or harpsicord. Mr. Mason plays
charmingly, with *great expression*. I
must own tho' that Handel's majestic
musick is too deeply implanted on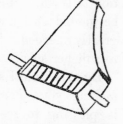
my soul to suffer me to delight (in general) in modern
flimsy Italian music. This being a curious invention I
could not help giving you a detail of it, and perhaps
have tired you.

I don't know how to condole with Mr. Newton for
his loss, if such it may be called, for in so deplorable a
state as the poor woman was in it is a happy release.

You may enclose your letters to Col. Egerton, Grosve-
nor Street. The seal you take notice of is after a true
antique, and reckon'd very fine. What I shall seal this
with, is Garrick's head.

Mrs. Delany to Bernard Granville, Esq.

St. James's Place, 14th Jan., 1775.

I hope my letters are not troublesome to my dear brother, but I cannot satisfy myself without writing, tho' I beg at the same time you will not attempt writing to me but when it is easy. I had an opportunity of giving your receipt for the jaundice the very evening I received it. Lord Willoughby was with me, and desired me to make his acknowledgments for your kind attention to them. He copied it out, but I hope it will not be wanted, as I have the satisfaction to hear that she is greatly mended. They talk of her going to Bath to recruit her spirits, which have been much depressed.

By this time I suppose you have had the pleasure of making your *little Nancy* happy with your favours. It is pleasing to see the different workings of a young mind, and every discovery of sensibility and attention is delightful. Her mother devotes herself to her children, and, added to her natural good sense and religious principles, adheres closely to the maxims and rules of her *own* most excellent mother,[1] whose memory is so dear to us all!

The Dss of Portland is well. My good little friend Mrs. Montagu has been very ill. Her son has been in Nottinghamshire, assisting at Lord Ed^d Bentinck's election, and the success has paid his trouble. Lady Stamford is just out of her lying in of her 7th child;[2] 6 are living, 3 sons and 3 daughters. Lady Weymouth has had 12; eight alive, 3 sons and 5 daughters. I had,

---

[1] Ann Granville.

[2] The Rev. Anchitel Grey, third surviving son of George Harry, 5th Earl of Stamford, was born 16th Dec., 1774, and died unmarried, 20th Dec., 1833.

last post, a letter from Lady Clanbrassil, dated Dundalk. The Dowager Lady Clan[11] is very fond of her, and she seems happy, but hankering after her English friends, and much chagrined at her lord's not being brought into the English Parliament. They come some time in March. Foleys not yet come to town. Mrs. Chapone[2] will soon publish a volume containing her poems and some essays. I believe I first put it into her head to try and make herself some reparation for the poor advantage she made of her last excellent work, receiving *but fifty pound* (for which she sold the copy to Walters), and he has made *above £500 of it!* She laughed when I press'd her to this publication, and said she should most likely lose the little reputation she had gained; but *if* it raised her a sum of money that it *would be convenient*. But I think *now* her name to it will make it sell very well.

The newspapers have given you a string of matches that *have* been; those that *are* to be are, Lord Lincoln and Lady Frances Conway;[3] Duke of Dorset[4] and Miss Damar,[5] Lord Milton's daughter; Mr. Grenvil, Lord Temple's heir, and Miss Nugent, Lord Clare's daughter. The last pair were invited to dine at Lord Temple's one

---

[1] The Dowager Countess of Clanbrassill was Lady Henrietta Bentinck, third daughter of William, 1st Earl of Portland, and widow of James Hamilton, 1st Earl of Clanbrassill.

[2] Mrs. Chapone published, in 1775, Miscellanies in Prose and Verse.

[3] Henry, Earl of Lincoln, eldest son of Henry Clinton, Duke of Newcastle. He married Frances, fourth daughter of Francis Seymour Conway, Earl of Hertford.

[4] John Frederick, 3rd Duke of Dorset. He married, in 1790, Arabella Diana, daughter of Sir Charles Cope, Bart.

[5] The Hon. Caroline Damer, daughter of Joseph Damer, Baron Milton (created, in 1792, Earl of Dorchester), born 1752, and died unmarried in 1829.

day last week; Lady Temple not well eno' to dine below, but met them in the drawing-room at their coffee, dress'd in all her diamonds, which she had all new set, and are prodigious fine, most of her own purchasing. She told Miss Nugent that "after that day they were no longer hers, but desired to see them upon her, who would become them better." A good *substantial* compliment.

I suppose you are not ignorant of the strange behaviour of Mrs. Vernon, who has *discarded* her husband. The immediate offence, I think, has been his going to see Lord Vernon when he was ill without her permission. She is in Wales, and has written him a letter to say she could bear his temper no longer, and would not live with him, and that she would be contented with two thousand pound a year, rent-charge, and to live on her estate in Wales. To which (*as well he may*) he readily agreed, but desired he might keep his daughter with him, their only child. She answer'd, "with all her heart, she did not care about her." There's the fruit of marrying *solely* for fortune, for there could be no other motive. Her want of beauty was no evil, but her want of temper, to a notorious degree, has made him a miserable man ever since he married, and he bears a good character among his acquaintance. My tattling has run away with me, but it may amuse your companion. I have not been unmindful of his stall at *Litchfield*, and think he is now in a better train for it than before; and when the present prelate goes to take possession, I believe you will think it proper he should go and pay his respects. He is a very worthy, good man, besides his *great* talents, and his manner and conversation so agreeable and so well beloved, that I don't know his equal in his station. If you approve I will send him a letter to deliver to the Bishop.[1]

Mrs. Delany to Mrs. Port, of Ilam.

St. J. P., 19th Jan., 1775.

Mr. Boyd[2] has been sadly used by his son-in-law, Mr. Trevanion, and not much better by his daughter. How few fathers are blessed like Mr. Dewes in children! To-day I spend at Whitehall, but all things must give way to a little hint I received last night from no less a person than the Lady *Premier*,[3] that the *next* vacancy that falls among the commissioners of the Lottery Office would be conferred on B. D., so I suppose now it may be depended upon, but be silent even to Calwich till the bird is actually in hand, of which you shall have immediate notice. As to Welsbourn, I acquiesce in all your reasoning, and if there are *no mountains* more difficult to surmount than those of Derbys[he], I shall, please God I am well and able, do my best to climb them, but *cannot* break thro' my rule of more than *a month's stay*, and am sure you will not press me; but this is a sort of a castle, the prospect is pleasant tho' distant, and if it can be brought to pass, what part of summer will suit you best?

---

[1] Dr. Richard Hurd, Master of the Temple and Preceptor to the Prince of Wales, appointed Bishop of Lichfield in 1774, afterwards Bishop of Worcester.

[2] John Boyd, Esq., married, first, Mary, daughter of William Bumsted, Esq., of Upton, co. Warwick. Their daughter Elizabeth married John Trevanion, Esq.

[3] Frederick, Lord North, was First Lord of the Treasury from Feb. 6th, 1770, to March 27th, 1782.

I don't know when my friend will make her excursion, but that is the time that would suit me best. It must be in the longest days, and not later than August. I am afraid by your not having yet had a day fix'd for Cal. that my poor bro^r is worse. In his last few lines he said *he was "worse than common."* Pray God support him. I am much obliged to you and Mr. P. for your kind venison present. I am glad it is *not* to be in town on Friday, as I should then have bestowed it on those who (tho' worthy of good things) can command them whenever they please—viz., *Duchess D^r of Portland, Bishop of Litchfield,* Mrs. Montagu and her son, and Mr. Mason, who dine with me on Saturday, but on Sunday your brothers come, and I will treat them with your venison. *Miss Vrankin* (but if she comes to you *pray* let her be called *Mrs.*) is a sort of servant so much sought after, that they raise their demands *very high.* I am convinced sixteen pound a year is as much as you *ought* prudently to give, but if she only boggles at that, and twenty will content her, I will make it up to her if on tryal you approve of her. Lady Tweeddale has paid me the ten guineas for the Xtning; shall I remit it to you? On Sunday I accepted Lady Wallingford's invitation to dinner to meet the Dss of Portland, and in the afternoon went to see Lady Jersey,[1] after dinner, found only her lord and Lady Ancram.[2] From thence to the Duchess

---

[1] George Bussey, 4th Earl of Jersey, married, in March, 1770, Frances, only daughter and heiress of Dr. Philip Twysden, Bishop of Raphoe.

[2] William John, Lord Ancrum, eldest son of the Marquis of Lothian, married, in 1763, Elizabeth, only daughter of Chichester Fortescue, Esq., and grand-daughter of Richard Wellesley, 1st Lord Mornington.

of Montrose's,[1] where I was to meet our *Duchess*, and *she* insisted on my going with her to Mrs. Montagu (Hill Street). Was dazzled with the brilliancy of her assembly. It was a moderate one, they said, but infinitly *too numerous* for *my senses*. My eyesight grew dimmer, my ears more dunny, my tongue faultered, my heart palpitated, and a few moments convinced me that the fine world was *no longer* a place for me, tho' I met with encouragement eno' from beaus and belles, who gathered about me like so many gay birds about an *owl*, but my wisdom prevailed for once over my vanity! I kept very near the door, (not advancing so far as the carpet,) and whisper'd the Dss that I was going home, which I did as soon as the door opened for more company. Her Grace soon followed me, and by a comfortable quiet hour of her all-healing conversation, and a dish of good tea, was refresh'd, and had full amends for my past toyls. The next day proving fine, and finding I was not realy the worse for y⁰ preceding day, I couragiously resolved to make a circle of visits, and went to Dowʳ Lady Gower (at home), to Lady Dartmouth (at home), to Mrs. Keene,[2] now in a charming house in Stable Yard, next door to Lord Harrington's;[3] found her at home also, and her little girl, a fine child. I shall send your message to Lady Willoughby. She is now in Dr. Warren's hands, who gives hopes of her recovery.

Tuesday morning I had a visit from Mrs. Chapone,

---

[1] The Duchess of Montrose was Lucy, daughter of John, 2nd Duke of Rutland, who m., 1742, William, 2nd Duke of Montrose.

[2] Elizabeth, d. of George, Viscount Lewisham.

[3] William, 2nd Earl of Harrington. He m., 11th Aug., 1746, Caroline, eldest d. of Charles, 2nd Duke of Grafton.

and whilst she was with me in came the Duchess of Devonshire, so handsome, so agreable, so obliging in her manner, that I *am quite* in love with her. She ask'd most kindly after you, made apologies for not having been to see you at Ilam, but hopes when you have thoughts of favouring her with a visit at Chatsworth, that you will *not* come in a formal way on her day, and that she came to me in a morning to break thro' all ceremony between us, and to desire I would give her leave to call on me sometimes. I can't tell you all the civil things she said, and realy they deserve a better name, which is *kindness* embellish'd by politeness. I hope she will *illumine* and *reform* her cotemporaries!

Mrs. Delany to Mrs. Port, of Ilam.

St. James's Place, 24th Jan., 1775.

Your brothers dined with me on Sunday, both very well, and staid with me till past 8; they were hurried on first coming to town, or I would have enticed them into my circle, which seldom begins *to fill* till that hour (as you know). *Their* Lord Chancellor's[1] lady came in soon after, *Lady Stamford* came just before they went, and the evening closed with Mrs. Boscawen, Mr. Montagu, and the Dss Dow^r of Portland.

Yesterday Lord Willoughby came in the evening, something cheer'd by Lady Willoughby's amendment, wch I hope is such as may now be depended on; their children

---

[1] The Hon. Henry Bathurst, created Lord Apsley, was appointed Lord Chancellor, Jan. 23, 1771. He succeeded his father as Earl Bathurst, 1775, resigned, 1778. His second wife, whom he married 14th June, 1759, was Tryphena, daughter of Thomas Scawen, Esq.

are well, the youngest a fine promising boy. I saw the
eldest at Lady Dartmouth's one morning, but he was
not set out to advantage in such a brilliant groupe; he
is grown tall, but a poor-looking creature, which is
grievous, though perhaps he may have such qualities of
the heart as will recompense for other defects, and the
want of an engaging appearance may save him from the
slippery paths and precipices that endanger those of
more shining and lively parts.

The comfortable accounts of you and yours, my dear
child, are truly a cordial to my spirits, and enable me to
support the conflict between *nature* and *reason* in regard
to my poor brother, whose present situation is deplorable
as to all that regards this world, unable to give or receive pleasure, and struggling with pain and sickness; I
endeavour to cast a veil over that sad scene, and to hope he
has, *in the main*, made a good use of his tryals, and that
when it pleases God to finish his sufferings he will receive him into his holy habitations—this I earnestly pray
for, and submit to his blessed will. My poor brother's
errors have been owing to a temper never properly subdued: it has clouded many good and agreeable qualities,
it has corroded his spirit with suspicions, and it has made
him and his friends unhappy; but I must own, though I
have suffered at times *inexpressibly* by its cruel effects,
and tho' they have in some degree abated, they have by
no means extinguished my affection. I am afraid I have
said too much on the subject! my heart *was full*—and is
now reliev'd. I think by his last letters there is a great
alteration. I find he was not well eno' to see " *his little
Nancy* " (as he calls her), but he has sent her things: pray
tell me if they came safe, and how she received them ?

I am now in expectation of Mrs. Boscawen, who is to convey me to see some Chinese rarities.

Mrs. Delany to Bernard Granville, Esq.

St. James's Place, 25th Jan., 1775.

This is trying weather for us, my dear brother; you, I fear, feel it more sensibly than I do, for, I thank God, I support it tolerably well, or rather am supported by that gracious hand whose mercies are infinite; for even when sorrow and sickness bear hard upon us, if we attend to the call, it opens our eyes and hearts, it makes us recollect past errors, brings to our aid *contrition* and *repentance*, and joyfull hope; and tho' our mortal part shrinks at sufferings, our immortal part soars to *everlasting happiness. This*, my dearest brother, is *true comfort*, and compensates (even in expectation) for the sorrows of this miserable world. We have also innumerable blessings to recollect and be thankful for; our joys and sorrows conduce to the same happy end, fill us with gratitude and humble resignation to the blessed will of Providence.

The Bishop of Litchfield,[1] I find, approves very much of old Jeremy Taylor's works; he says there are in his works more *good sense, just argument, learning, knowledge, and true piety* than in most authors who have written on the same subjects; but his stile not being modern, and his works numerous, they are now little known or read. He has just published a little treatise

---

[1] The Hon. Brownlow North, Bishop of Lichfield and Coventry, was translated to the bishopric of Worcester in 1774.

of Dr. Taylor's—a shilling book, which he hopes will be read—to prove the undeniable truth of the revelation of the Gospel; he sent me one and desired me to recommend it. I will get one and send it to my nephew John, which I can do by dividing it under two covers. I think the Bishop has been mistaken in *not* putting his own name to it, as he *is* the editor, which would certainly gain many readers. I should suppose that when the living of Bromshal falls, that John will have a good chance for it, as the last time but one that I saw Ld. Willoughby he expressed much concern that when his application came it was too late. They hope Lady Willoughby gains ground. The Duke of Glocester is in much danger, tho' something better than he has been. They are going abroad, they say, as much on account of circumstances as health. Want of œconomy, and her foolish extravagance, has much distressed their affairs. Our nephews dined with me yesterday, and seemed pretty well. Bernard looks thin. It is a great comfort to me their being in town, as they bestow all their idle hours on me.

Mrs. Delany to the Rev. J. Dewes.

St. James's Place, 7th Feb., 1775.

MY DEAR NEPHEW,

My affectionate wishes to my dear brother, and best thanks for the Oriental agate, the finest I ever saw; but that is the least part of its value to me. Tho' late accounts have been far from satisfactory, absence and distance magnify our apprehensions. Whether our pains and sufferings in this world are sent as punishments for

past offences or tryals of our obedience to the will of
Providence, we are sure they are sent *in mercy*, and not
only to refine and prepare the sufferer for a state of eternal joy and happiness, but as lessons and examples to all
around them.　The situation of seeing a dear friend in
such a state would be insupportable without reflections
of this sort, and the opportunity of showing them a
grateful and tender attachment, and of endeavouring, to
the utmost of one's power, to give them some relief and
support our greatest consolation.　It *is grievous not* to
be able to do it!　I will get Mrs. Chapone's Miscellany
as directed.　Tho' an ingenious work, moral and useful,
it is *not* so interesting as her *last* work.　I am well in
health.　I have not yet been able to get the little essay
of Dr. Jeremy Taylor's, published by your present Bishop;
they are not published yet in general, that I have he
gave me.　Your brothers are well, and dined with me
on Sunday last and the Saturday before; and just as
we were going to sit down, a note came from the D. Dss
of Portland to beg I would be so charitable as to give
her a dinner, for y^e *tide* was so high it *drove her out of
her house!*　She is most kind in her enquiries and wishes
about my dear brother, and as I never go out in the
evening, she comes every day.

Mrs. Delany to Bernard Granville, Esq.

St. J. Place, 11th Feb., 1775.

I have some time debated with myself whether I should
write to my dear brother or not till I had the comfort of hearing he was better; but his *own* kind words

that told me *my letters gave him consolation*, has determined me; and I should feel happy indeed if I thought
that could be the case; but you have a better comforter,
who will accept and reward your pious resignation under
such great sufferings—the only thought that supports
my own spirits.

The world is in a bustle about the American affairs,
but I am no politician, and don't enter into those matters.
Women lose all their dignity when they meddle with
subjects that don't belong to them: their own sphere
affords them *opportunities eno'* to show their *real consequence*. A *pretending* woman, and a *trifling, ignorant*
man, are *equally* despicable; and after all the endeavours
to make what is generally called " a figure in life," what
does it all avail, when we come to our bed of sickness,
and consider mortality? There, the humble, penitent,
believing Xtian, may look down with pity and compassion upon the false glories of the world—and, in the
midst of anguish, blessed with the hope of eternal happiness, be able to rejoice. This, commonly, is the situation at that trying hour, of all who have acted on
honest principles; tho' error and passion may, at times,
have warped them out of the right line.

I had a visit the day before yesterday from Lady
Spencer, who told me she expected Lady Cowper for a
few days, till *the tide* had subsided. Last year, to the
great distress of her domesticks, she braved its waves,
tho' her lower floor was a *foot under water*. Lord Cowper's match with Miss Gower is *not* to be concluded till
the end of the summer; they are both still in Italy.
A match is talked of between Lord Stormont[1] and

---

[1] David, 7th Viscount Stormont. He married, secondly, in 1776, Louisa,
third daughter of Charles, 9th Lord Cathcart.

Lady Harriet Stanhope,[1] Lord Harrington's daughter, and a match between Lord Trevor [2] and Mrs. Johnston (the late Bishop of Worcester's sister.) The latter, I believe, *without grounds*, and only reported on account of Lord Trevor's love of money, and the Bishop's having left his sister *all his fortune* for her life. Here interrupted by a visit from the Marchioness of Tweeddale, who is well in health, and better in spirits. She asked me who my letter was to, and desired her best compliments.

My fervent prayers constantly attend you.

Adieu.

Mrs. Delany to the Rev. John Dewes.

St. J. P., 14th Feb., 1775.

I thank you my dear nephew for your letter, which I received last night; it was a great relief to me to hear my dear brother was better. The *resign'd* state of his mind is my *greatest consolation*, as *such reflections* must be so to him. The hope of what we call (falsely indeed) happiness in this world, is very delightful to us, tho' we know, at best, how transient it is. What must the hopes of sublime and everlasting happiness be to those who truly put their trust in God, with faith and humble confidence in our Redeemer! *Sensations* that must give

---

[1] Lady Harriet Stanhope, daughter of William, 2nd Earl of Harrington. She married, 15th March, 1776, the Hon. Thomas Foley, who succeeded his father, in 1777, as Baron Foley.

[2] Robert Trevor, 4th Baron Trevor. He married, in 1743, Constantia, daughter of Peter Anthony de Huybert, of Holland. In 1776 he was created Viscount Hampden, and died in 1783.

us a foretast of the blessings hereafter, where peace and
joy will take the place of pain and sorrow! I forgot in
my last letter to my brother to mention one thing, before I have the enamelled picture of Lady Stanley taken
out of the box; which is, that I design to leave Calwich
the *original* portrait by Houseman;[1] and, if it would be
any satisfaction to my brother, I will send it down to
Calwich immediately; I also intend to leave my *father*
and *mother*, Lady Johanna Thornhill,[2] and Lady Dysart,[3]
as I think all the family pictures should be collected together. But if my brother continues in the same mind
about the enamel-picture, I will have it done immediately
with as much care as possible, tho' there is some hazard
in unsetting enamel for fear of chipping the edges. If
you think saying all this to my brother may be troublesome to him, don't mention it, and I will do what he
desired as soon as I receive y[e] answer.

The Dowager-Countess Gower to Mrs. Delany.

Pall Mall, 15th Ffeb., 1775.

D[r] M[rs] Delany has strangely *mis*-aplied her *apologys*
w[n] she bestow'd 'em on me; I must find fault, and say
w[t] I think, and I hope hereafter she'll think y[e] same:
y[t] from *her to me, they are absurd.* I have found y[e]

---

[1] This picture is now (1861) at Welsbourn, in the possession of Bernard
Granville, Esq., great-grandson of Ann Granville (Mrs. Dewes), and has been,
by his permission, engraved for this work.

[2] Lady Johanna Thornhill was daughter of Sir Bevil Granville. This picture
is also in the possession of Bernard Granville, Esq.

[3] Lady Dysart, daughter of John, 1st Earl Granville; also in the possession
of Bernard Granville, Esq.

Philosopher's stone, just enough to turn Mrs Swan's subscription of 5^s into *guineys*, wch I send inclos'd, not being certain wⁿ I shall see you, and reading that her necessities call for iṁediate relief.

I conclude Mrs Montagu (or Ann Payton,) have heard ye false report of my having gain'd a cause in Chancery by wch I've recover'd a large sum of money, y^t is to be distributed amongst poor housekeepers; 'tis *void of all foundation*; there's nothing particular to be given at this time, but coals (*from my ffather's charity*.) I believe there are some yet undisposed of; if Mrs M. would have three sacks for this Ann Payton, I will send her an order for 'em, y^t is ye quantity allotted to individuals. Wishing next post may bring ye best news from Calwich,

Remain y^r faithfull,
M. Gower.

Mrs. Delany to Bernard Granville, Esq., at Calwich.

21st Feb., 1775.

Tho' I have reason to apprehend that my dear brother has been rather worse lately, not having had any account of him from his own hand, I have not yet executed your commission about Lady Stanley's picture, as there is no way of having the ring fastened to it in any shape without unsetting the picture; it is not at present fast in its setting, and I should think it would be better to have it set in a shagreen case, and the stones of *the ring* placed as a crown on the top, and then they will both be strong and secure from accidents, which it is not at present, and on the back her name

may be engraved. I *have had* Doct^r Delany's picture
done in that manner. It is my intention to leave to *Calwich*, the original of that picture of Lady Stanley, and if
it will be any satisfaction to you I will send it you
directly. I also intend for the *same place* my father and
mother's portraits, Lady Johanna Thornhill's, your own,
and Lady Dysart, that all the family pictures may be
together, and your great room (gallery) I should think,
would hold them all very well. If you have any objection to altering the setting of the enamel picture, who-
ever you bestow the box and ring upon with an in-
junction it *should never be used as a snuff-box*, I should
suppose you might depend on their observation of your
request. I am afraid all I have said about the enameled
picture will be troublesome, but I wish to have it done
to your satisfaction. I am sensible at this time your
thoughts are better employ'd, and lead you to the contemplations of those rewards promised to a pious and
patient resignation. We begin life encompass'd by our
passions, which were designed (did they not take a wrong
bias) to be incitements to generous and virtuous actions,
but by little indulgences, prejudices, and evil example, the
hurry and false glare of life, and persuading ourselves it
is time eno' to scrutinize our own actions, we are deluded
till graciously called to order by *disappointment, sorrow*,
and *sickness*; our eyes then are opened to our natural
and acquired infirmitys, and what our *pride* formerly
charged upon others our humbled state brings home to
ourselves! We are thankfull, tho' in a painfull situation, for the opportunity allowed us of settling our
worldly affairs with justice, kindness, and prudence; we
resign ourselves to his blessed will who *chastiseth in*

mercy, and will crown us with loving kindness, who promiseth comfort and salvation thro' Jesus Christ to all penitent offenders. What consolation is this! May my dearest brother feel the full effects of such contemplations by a constant and exalted hope. Most earnestly wishing to hear a better account of your health than I can flatter myself with the hopes of, Adieu.

Mrs. Delany to Bernard Granville, Esq.

St. James's Place, 29th, 1775 ?

I have been longer than usual without writing to my dear brother, and waited in hopes of saying when I should send the communion cup, &c., but have been put off from day to day, and will wait no longer. I am uneasy when I don't write. I hope the plate will be finish'd the beginning of next week, and it will be what you wish to have. My over-caution about the enamel picture prevented my doing just what you wanted, for had I taken it out of ye box and set it in a chagrine case, I believe you would have liked it better, and that may still be done and ye box none the worse for it, or you may unhinge it and keep it in the top as a case to it.

I have not been very well lately but I thank God I am much better, and a little air and exercise will strengthen me. The Dss of Portland talks of our going next Friday to Bulstrode, and it is at present such exceeding hot weather that I shall be glad to remove to a purer air than London, but I would have all my letters directed to me S^t. J. Place, and have sent you some franks for your secretary.

I have amused myself lately with Mr. Mason's publication of Mr. Gray's Memoirs,[1] and liked them extreamly. Mr. Mason's zeal for his friend is very amiable. I have sent the book to Mrs. Port, and if you like to hear any of the letters you can send to her for it. There are some serious ones that I think you will approve of; one to his unhappy friend on his leaving his chambers at the Temple (or Lincoln's Inn, I don't know w^{ch}), and his consolatory letters to his mother and Mr. Mason.

I can only add my affec^{te} wishes.

I hope to send the plate next week.

Mrs. Delany to Mrs. Port, of Ilam.

[Part of a letter.] 1775?

Don't let what I say on this subject distress you, my dear child, for to give vent to oppressions of this kind is an inexpressible relief, and *my sufferings* will end *with his!* His pres^t state is such as to make a *happy release* to be wish'd, and *such*, I trust, his will be. Providence has corrected him in mercy, and I trust will accept of his humiliation and resignation. His errors have *not* proceeded from vices. Few men can boast of so much innocence in those respects. An unhappy temper meeting in early youth with many disappointments, was *aggravated*, having had too little contradiction and government in childhood. The subject (tho' a sore one)

---

[1] Published in 1775.

runs away wth me. I'll say no more. Mr. E., Mr. M., and y^r bro^{rs} dine with me to-morrow. I am afraid the latter stay but a little while longer, therefore ans^r this directly.

What added yesterday to my flutter was *Mr. Weston's nephew* bringing me a box from Calwich, containing an agate snuff-box *he* has given me, and Lady Stanley's picture in enamel, which is to be set in a case, and on asking how my poor brother did, *he* answer'd " very bad indeed !"

Mrs. Delany to Mrs. Port, of Ilam.

St. James's Pl., 21st Feb., 1775.

Alas! what can I say about my poor brother. He seems at present to have a *reprieve,* but it is attended with so much weakness as to make his present situation very alarming. Why should I say alarming : it is indeed being too selfish to wish the continuance of a friend's life on *such* painful terms, and under *such* a *hopeless disorder*, were I *not* shut out from all personal communication with him ; and, *as it is*, all I ought to do is to pray for his support under the great tryal, and that his sufferings may atone for all past faults. I have written to him to-day. It is a painfull and serious task, but he takes it kindly, and that enables me to do it.

Your brothers dined with me yesterday. They have, as usual, been kind and attentive to me. I shall have them only this week. To-morrow I have ask'd them to meet the Dss D^r of Portland, and celebrate *your birthdays.* Dr. Ross and Lady Wallingford to be of the party. *How* warm, *how* affectionate, my wishes will be on the occasion, let ye justice and kindness of your heart tell you! for *I cannot.* The most refined sensations of a heart are not to be expressed.

Mrs. Boscawen has just been with me; always full of kind enquiries after you. Lady Cowper came to town last Wednesday in order to be at the Dss of Devonshire's concert on Friday last. She made me a visit on Thursday morning as *good-humoured, fair, and comely* as usual, and much we talk'd about *our* god-daughter the matron of Ilam! She came to me again on Saturday evening, and met the (our) Dss. She was full of her grand-daughter's magnificence; her own jewells and her commissions from Lord Cowper for jewells for his lady elect, whose picture in water-colours he has sent her (like a Savoyarde,) pretty eno' tho' not ans^g her character for beauty, but I suppose it does not do her justice. Lady C. is gone again to Richmond this morning.

A match is talked of between Lord Stormont and Lady Har^t Stanhope.

Poor Lady Primrose˜has had a happy release. I have not heard how she has left her affairs. Mrs. Vesey has been afflicted. My little solitary dinner waits for me. Mr. and Mrs. Boyd are very obliging, and supply me every week with nosegays. Everybody is good to me, and I wish I was more worthy. I hope Miss Sparrow is very well, loves work, practices her French, and holds up her head: tho' I do not think *les Graces* are to be all in all, they ought not to be neglected.

Mrs. Delany to Mrs. Port, of Ilam.

St. J. P., 28th Feb., 1775.

The accounts from Calwich are beyond my expectation, and I feel my spirits relieved when I think my poor brother's pain abated, for his sufferings are infinitly more grievous than the apprehension of his being happily released from them. This morning your brothers have turned their backs on London : great is my loss of their company. Bern^d has had a letter from John *to encourage* his coming to Calwich after the assizes. Last Friday Dow^r Lady Gower was with me till eleven at night; went to bed as soon as she went home; at twelve was called up by an express that came from Holcomb to say that Lady Leicester[1] was very ill, and to desire her to come to her directly. She set out as soon as it was day. We have heard no particulars, and can expect none till to-morrow at soonest. My poor Mrs. Montagu is in *great distress;* she loves those sisters mightily! it has been a friendship of above fifty years standing! There is something *melancholy* in *keeping one's ground,* and seeing our cotemporarys drop off, till one stands quite alone! Melancholly, indeed, it would be, but for the hope of meeting them again in a glorious state, with all their imperfections done away. This idea is innocent and rational, and I am indulged in it by a dissertation,[2] I have lately read on the reasons for expecting that virtuous men will

---

[1] The Right Hon. the Countess of Leicester, at her seat at Holkham, in Norfolk, died 26th Feb., 1775.

[2] Four Dissertations.—1, On Providence; 2, on Prayer; 3, on the Reasons for expecting that virtuous men shall meet, after death, in a state of happiness; 4, on the Importance of Christianity. By Dr. Richard Price, born 1723, died 1791.

know each other and meet in a state of happiness. The author a Mr. Price, published in 1768; perhaps you have it: there are other dissertations with it—on Providence, on Prayer, &c.

I have heard nothing more from the Premier, and fear the *gracious message* was only a sop to silence me for some time. Lady Willoughby still mends, but has now and then a little return. The Duchess of Beaufort continues very indifferent. Mrs. T. Pit[1] is brought to bed of a son, and very well at Boconnoc.

Mrs. Delany to Mrs. Port, of Ilam.

St. James's Place, 10th March, 1775.

I am glad my packet came safe, and thank my dearest Mary for her account of herself, &c., most heartily wishing increase of health and happiness and a *continuance* of that divine elixer *contentment;* for let our situation be ever so great or so affluent, a mind not disposed to enjoy rationally the blessings of fortune is much more unhappy than the labourer who gains his livelyhood by the sweat of his brow, who is *honestly industrious* and *thankfull* for his small gains ! The longer I live in the world the more I am convinced that the happiest people are those who make the *best* of *their lot* and keep their minds *untainted* with ambitious views. Ambition's ladder is very treacherous ; when you have taken one step you are deluded to another, not considering your airy situation, and that if a step fails your fall is so much the more dan-

---

[1] March 1st, 1775. The lady of Thomas Pitt, Esq., Member for Old Sarum, of a son and heir, at Mr. Pitt's seat in Cornwall.

gerous for having left the ground you stood on before.
I do not mean that this lesson is wanting at Ilam, where
innocence and peace, with every virtuous inclination,
possess one of the most beautiful spots in England. O,
my Mary! I really can say with Cato, *I am sick of this bad
world*, when I suffer my imagination to wander among
the multitude; it would be more supportable could one
select a number of any considerable magnitude *not*
affected by the great whirlpool of dissipation, and (indeed I *fear* I may add) *vice*. This bitter reflection arises
from what I hear *every* body say of a *great* and *handsome*
relation of ours[1] just *beginning* her part; but I do hope
she will be like the young actors and actress, who begin
with *over* acting when they first come upon the stage,
and abate of her superabundant spirits (that now mislead her) and settle into a character worthy of applause
and of the station she possesses; but I *tremble* for her!
which has led me into this tedious animadversion.

I will look out all my blue muslin; I believe I have
eno' for another chair and a bottom to that you have.
I wish, my dear child, I could *as easily give you* a
month's work as provide you with materials, but, as I
have said before, there are *greater* difficulties to surmount
than climbing your stupendous hills; you *know more*
than I can explain, *some of them*; but should there be
such an amendment in your neighbourhood as to make
a meeting desirable it would abate one difficulty; but
to be *so near* and *not to see him*, or to see him in such
a state of suffering and to be unable to give him any
consolation, requires more fortitude than I am possessed
of! Your tender feelings will see this in a true light.

---

[1] Georgina Spencer, Duchess of Devonshire.

I thank God I enjoy more health than most people of my great age, but I am unable to *struggle* with fatigue of body or mind, and have *a dread* of giving *pain* to those I wish most to give pleasure to, *which* I know must be the case should I have any complaint at a distance from those who are used to attend me when I am not well; but I don't say this as absolutely determin'd *not* to venture *if circumstances encourage me!* The *time* must depend on our dear respectable Dss. I am so bound to her by the most tender affection that I can't determine till I know her determinations for the summer. I should rather think, if possible, that May would be the most desirable month.

Lady Gower is come to town, but sees nobody nor receives any messages; nor is Lady Leicester's will yet known, but it is supposed she has left everything that was in her power to her *sister*, and then of course it will go to *her* son, Mr. Leveson. The title of Clifford, which Lady Leicester[1] had, is now in abeyance.

Lord and Lady Clan[1] are on the road to England. Nothing is talked of now so much as the ladies *enormous* dresses, more suited to the *stage* or a *masquerade* than for either *civil* or sober societies. The 3 *most* elevated plumes of feathers are the Dss of Devonshire, Lady Mary Somerset, and Lady Harriet Stanhope, but some say Mrs. *Hubert's*[2] exceeds them all. It would be some

---

[1] On the death of Sir Thomas Coke, Earl of Leicester, 20th April, 1759, the Earldom and minor honours became extinct, and the extensive estates devolved upon (the son of his sister Anne) Wenham Roberts, Esq., who assumed, in consequence, the surname and arms of Coke.

[2] Query Mrs. Hobart? Albina, daughter and coheiress of Lord Vere Bertie, married, in 1757, the Hon. George Hobart, son of John, 2nd Earl of Buckinghamshire.

consolation if their manners did *not* too much correspond wth the lightness of their dress! but the Lady H. Stanhope[1] is *much commended* for the propriety of her behaviour.

Mrs. Delany to Bernard Granville, Esq.

St. J. Place, 12th March, 1775.

I think it very long since I wrote to my dear brother; I have wished to do it oftener, but I had an apprehension you were worse, and I was not in spirits for an employment that always gives me much satisfaction when I think it does not *disturb you*, for I have nothing to offer you that can make amends for *that*.

I have got the ring, that is the turquoise and little brilliants, set in the box over the picture, in the strongest and safest way I cou'd. I would not venture to have the enamell moved out of its present setting, as there is always danger of chipping the edges and cracking the portrait. If you like to have the original I will send it you immediately, and let me know what you want beside. Don't spare employing me. I have money eno' *of yours* in my hands, as you remitted me thirty pounds, and I have not laid out half of it (for you) yet!

Mr. and Mrs. Leveson are at Anthony in Cornwall, the house that was Sir William Carey's, which *they* have hired. Lady Leicester's will not yet declared by Lady Gower, but as she and her sister always lived in strict friendship, and there is no other sister, it is generally supposed that Lady Leicester has left everything that

---

[1] Lady Harriet Stanhope married, March, 1776, the Hon. Thomas Foley, son of the 1st Lord Foley (2nd creation).

was in her power to Dow^r Lady Gower, and to Mr. Leveson after her; some say 20, others 40 thousand pounds. I hear Mr. Cook *complains* that he must *buy* cattle to stock his grounds, and *even cart-horses*—very hard indeed for a man who comes into the finest and best furnished house in England, with seventeen thousand pounds a year! Lady Leicester has laid out *many* thousand pounds she was *not* obliged to do in furnishing the house, and more than she was requested to do by Lord Leicester when he died, for he left it unfinished. Beside she allow'd young Mr. Coke for travelling expenses five hundred a year, so that the present possessor of Holkham is very ungrateful indeed to complain.

Political matters seem now to run smooth, excepting a few newspaper squibs, and they dye in the firing. The bustle of the world goes on as usual, and we who sit by our fireside, wonder at "*the madness of the people,*" and with declining years feel an inward contentment that we are retiring even from the sound of it, and have time allowed us to prepare for a happy change.

I will not venture to trespass longer, and hope it is unnecessary to add how

Affectionately I am yours,

M. D.

The Duchess of Portland says I must never omit her best wishes. Thank God she is well.

Mrs. Delany to Bernard Granville, Esq.

St. James's Place, 28th March, 1775.

One of my spring colds has prevented my writing to my dear brother for some posts. I thank God I am well now, and as a proof I ventured to St. James's Chapel last Sunday to hear *your* excellent Bishop preach; his text was, " *Never man spake like that man.*" I wish my memory could have retained eno' of it to set down on paper, that I might communicate to you the satisfaction I received from it. It explained the wonderful efficacy of our Saviour's words, their dignity, their simplicity, and the blessings we derive from his mission—a subject that must necessarily lead us far above mortality, and heal *all our wounds* and *infirmities,* which (comparatively speaking) will *last but a day,* and *joy cometh in the morning*—a joy everlasting. These are great comforts, my dearest brother, and I most earnestly beseech God that you may feel their full force.

I hope my last letter, with an account of the small appointment I had obtained for Bernard, was not disagreeable to you. I thought it would rather please you when gained, but that it was better not to teize you with an expectation of what might not have succeeded. The commission begins as soon as the lottery is appointed, which, they say, will be about the beginning of next term. I have sent your box with Lady Stanley's enamel'd picture in a parcel I have sent Mrs. Port.

The death of Lord Bristol [1] has made way for Lord

---

[1] George William, 2nd Earl of Bristol, died unmarried, 18th March, 1775. His second sister, Mary, married George Fitzgerald, Esq.

Weymouth,[1] who is to succeed him; he has left vast estate, some say above £17,000 a year. Five hundred pounds a year to his sister Lady Mary Fitzgerald, and many other legacy's. The present Earl in so bad a state of health, it is thought he will not long enjoy it. Lady Leicester has left Mrs. Montague, Han[r] Square, two hundred guineas. Adieu.

Mrs. Delany to Bernard Granville, Esq.

St. James's Place, 6th April, 1775.

I was much obliged to my dear brother for his letter by the hand of Mr. Ber[d] Dewes; it is some consolation to receive a letter of his dictating. I wish my memory was able to comply with your request of setting down on paper parts of the Bishop of Litchfield's sermon. He dwelt much on the dignity and great simplicity of our Saviour's words; how wisely he evaded, by the most pertinent questions, satisfying the vain curiosity and wily snares of those who sought to kill him, that it might be fulfilled what was said by the prophet, that he was to be a *Lamb without blemish*; and therefore carefully avoided saying anything the Jews could possibly lay hold of as (wrong or) criminal. How noble in every respect his conduct was! My head is bewildered when I try to recollect, tho' at the same time I hope I feel the good effects of so excellent a discourse, and if I can will try if I can obtain a sight of the manuscript. When I read those parts of the Bible where our Saviour speaks, I am

---

[1] April 7th, 1775, the Right Hon. Lord Viscount Weymouth, to be Groom of the Stole, in the room of the late Earl of Bristol.

each time more attentive and delighted than before, with the gracious and wonderful language, so clear in every *material* point to every capacity ; though the beauty of it must appear in a stronger light to those of the liveliest and best informed judgments. I have just been reading some of Mr. Mason's sermons that Mrs. Sandford recommended to us. They are very comfortable indeed ; I am *particularly* pleased with the discourse on the *use of afflictions,* and his two last sermons in the second vol., where he makes a comparison between the Israelites passing through the wilderness and over Jordan to the promised land, and our passage thro' this world.

Nobody has yet seen Lady D^{wr} Gower, or know from her the particulars of Lady Leicester's will ; but from the Cooks, they say she has left 6000 among nephews and nieces, and the residue to Lady D^{wr} Gower, amounting to 40 thous. pound. Mr. Winnington, son to Sir Edward Winnington,[1] a good man, and an estate of above £3000 a year, has made proposals for Mr. Foley's youngest daughter, but she is so young Mr. Foley will not give his consent that they should be married now, nor engaged absolutely ; but if they like one another, 2 or 3 years hence, he shall give his consent. But this must not to be mentioned.

---

[1] Anne, youngest daughter of Thomas, Lord Foley, and Grace Granville, his wife, married, 12th Sept., 1776, Edward, eldest son of Sir Edward Winnington, Bart.

Mrs. Delany to Mrs. Port, of Ilam.

St. J. P., 27 April, 1775.

I hope my dearest Mary will have reason every day more and more to approve of her engagement with Mrs. Vranken, and that she will be such a deputy under your inspection, and with your advice, as to relieve your spirits from the too great anxiety they have undergone. I was truly touched by your last dear letter, but surely those sensations that arise from true friendship pay one for many bitter pangs, which a long absence must at times occasion. In this fluctuating world we cannot *always* settle down just in the spot and in the neighbourhood we wish—*that* is out of our power, but to endeavour to be contented with our lot, to delude absence by the intercourse of letters that *speed the sweet intercourse between soul and soul*, to scheme for meeting, and, if not convenient and practicable, to acquiesce, resigning our will to the great Disposer of all things—*these are* in our power, tho' it will cost us some pains and trouble.

Now, my dear M., don't take it into your pretty noddle that I mean all this by way of preamble to *not* making you a visit. It is only writing as I should speak; just what rises at the moment the pen blots the paper! but I can't indulge you or myself with saying *I will come.* Should it please God to give me courage to undertake (at my years) so long a journey, to be *so near* Calwich, and *not go*, it *would* appear strange, and mortify me saddly! and *should* I be admitted, I cannot answer for my own weakness. To see him in so suffering and hopeless a state would *affect me greatly*. This, indeed, is the truth, wch can be told only to you; for as to the journey, tho' I am certainly feebler than two years ago, I *should* have *courage eno'* to venture.

I think I shall remove to odoriferous Bulstrode on Friday next, which will enliven my spirits and give me strength, as it always does.

I am in hopes your bro^rs will be in town to-night, that I may have 2 or 3 days of them. Did I tell you Lady Cowper had appointed last Tuesday for dining with me and Lady Frances Bulk.[1] I invited Mr. Bulk. and Lady M. M.[2] to meet them, but Monday night a letter came to say the Countess had a " sniveling cold," and could not come, so I put off the rest of the company, and the Countess comes on Tuesday next, but desires a tête-à-tête dinner with me. I hear she is *greatly chagrined* at her g. d^rs conduct, and I fancy she wants to unburthen herself. And now I must talk of your agreable friend Mrs. Jodrell,[3] who, before this reaches Ilam, will have made you a visit, and will tell you I was very well when she called upon me. I like her very much, and was sorry to see so little of her. Her sister[4] did not come with her the last time. Did you sound Bern^d? I *did*, and he gave me no more encouragem^t than his elder bro^r! Indeed, at present *he* has no *pretensions*, unless *little Cupid*

---

[1] Lady Frances Bulkeley, eldest daughter of Charles Mordaunt, 4th Earl of Peterborough, married the Rev. Samuel Bulkeley, of Hatfield, in Hertfordshire.

[2] Lady Mary Mordaunt, sister of Lady Frances Bulkeley.

[3] Mrs. Jodrell.—Frances, eldest daughter of Francis Jodrell, Esq., succeeded, on the death of her grandfather, to the Yeardsley estates in the co. of Chester. She married, in 1775, John Bower, Esq., who took the name of Jodrell.

[4] Elizabeth, sister of Mrs. Jodrell, inherited the Twemlow estates, and married, 21st Sept., 1778, Egerton Leigh, of West Hall, Esq., in High Leigh, Cheshire.

takes his part, and there has been no opportunity for that.

I am impatient to hear again how you approve of Mrs. V. on further acquaintance, but *don't* let your liking of her and natural indulgence lead you to make her *too familiar*, and to forget the station she is in, as that will give her *less* consequence with the young people. I know P.'s good humour and comicality will lead him to *joke* wth her sometimes, but *his judgem^t* will correct that, as *he knows* there is a great difference between *civility* and *familiarity*; the *one* will teach her what is *due to him*, the *other* would be toute au contraire; and tho' she seems very steady, knowing, and prudent for her age, you must consider she *is* very young, and may learn a great deal from your advice. I think when you have any company it would be best for her to dine above stairs with G. M. A., and use her to it *at first*, or she may think it hard afterwards. Sr Ed^d Winnington's son, of Worcestershire, is fallen desperately in love with Miss Anne Foley, just 14 year old, and has proposed and is accepted, but not to be married these two years; but this must not be told to anybody. For Godsake, my dear Mary, don't let *my little Porty* think of anything but her lessons and her doll at 14 years of age! What behaviour and conduct can be expected from children's being so soon introduced into a state of life that requires the utmost prudence? but Mr. F. gives him a good character, and his estate joins Witley.

Consider before you determine about Fanny's[1] going to any water-drinking place with only so young a person as V.!

---

[1] Miss Sparrow.

Mrs. Delany to the Rev. John Dewes.

Bulstrode, 8th May, 1775.

I fear the Indian sweetmeets are not as tender as they should be, and the quince too sweet; but I could not meet with any better. I took the liberty of adding a pot of Smith's orange marmalade, which is tender and sharp, and to fill the box I added a few maccaroons. I hope the essence of lavender was right, and that my brother approves of the silver cup. The foot screws off and fits into the cup, and the plate for the bread serves for a cover. I contrived to have it as compact as I could, that you might, on occasion, easily carry it in your pocket. The silver is hammered thin, in a particular manner, to make it light, and at the same time so hard that it will not easily bruise. It was made by Hemmings in Bond Street. He told me he thought it would come to about £6 or 7, but when he brought it home with his bill it was only 5*l.* 18*s.* 0*d.* I had the Glory, &c., engraved on it, and hope my brother will like it. The box was sent last Monday by Bass's waggon. We came here on Friday; it rain'd violently all day; but yesterday and to-day have been fine. I am just returned with the Dss of P. from the kitchen garden, and have seen Mr. Granville's scarlet geranium in high beauty. Adieu.

Mrs. Chapone to Mrs. Delany, St. James's Place.

Wardour Street, May 12, 1775.

Dear Madam,

I was truly sorry not to see you before you left town. You are very kind in the solicitude you express

about my health. I have indeed been a poor suffering
mortal since I saw you, and cannot say I am even yet
restored to ease, tho' nearer it than I have been for a
long time, and Mr. Broomfield insists upon it that I am
in the way to be well; and I believe him or *not* according as my spirits are high or low!

I owe you a thousand thanks for the great pleasure I
have enjoy'd in reading the precious remains of that
noble poet and amiable man Mr. Gray, whom I now love
as well as admire. What charming fragments has he left,
scatter'd with the negligence of a rich prodigal! and what
pity that they were not finish'd! I am pleased to see
that so sublime a genius could trifle agreeably, and cannot
but wonder when I am told that he was not a pleasing
companion; for he is so pleasant, so easy, so humorous a
correspondent, that I should have expected much delight
from his conversation. The lively good-humour with
which he bears the ill-judged censures cast on his noblest
works seems to show a good temper and a dignity of
character which secured him from the *mortifications of
vanity.* The picture he draws of his friend Mr. Mason,[1]
and the manner in which that friend has managed and
preserved the treasures he left him, makes one wish for
Mr. Mason's acquaintance. Upon the whole I do *not*
know that I have received more pleasure from *any publication* than from this.

Poor Mrs. Montagu is at present in a most distressful
situation. Mr. Montagu is in the last stage, but instead of sinking easily, as might have been expected
from so long and gradual a decline, he suffers a great

---

[1] Mason's Life of Gray was published in 1775.

struggle, and has a fever attended with deliriums, which are most dreadfully affecting to Mrs. Montagu. If this sad scene should continue I tremble for the effects of it on her tender frame; but I think it must very soon have an end, and she will then reconcile herself to a loss so long expected, tho' I doubt not she will feel it very sincerely. He is entitled to her highest esteem and gratitude, and I believe possesses them both.

I send the book with this to your house in St. James's Place. I am, dear madam, with every good wish,

Your most obliged and aff^{te} serv^{t},

H. CHAPONE.

The Hon. Mrs. Boscawen to Mrs. Delany.

Glan Villa, Saturday night, 13th May, 1775.

I have meditated and thought upon obeying your commands ever since I came here, but the quiet of the place and the dullness of your poor friend have concur'd to make her sensible she had nothing to say worth your *hearing*. You make no complaints of weather, my dear madam, and I do not wonder at it, for Bulstrode is delightfull in all weathers. For my part I have starv'd with cold, and have burnt my billets without mercy. To-day, however, I went to London for a few hours, and there I found it warm enough. Mrs. Walsingham carry'd me to the Exhibition and entertain'd me very well, only I spent more time there than I cou'd afford.

Afterwards I visited poor Mrs. G. Boscawen,[1] and

---

[1] General the Hon. George Boscawen, next brother to Admiral Boscawen, died May 3, 1775. His widow was Anne, daughter of John Morley Trevor, of Trefallyn, Esq., North Wales.

then Lady Edgcumbe. I am very glad to hear so good an account of your friend Mrs. R., and of the satisfaction she has (and feels) to find you well and tending toward that perfection which (some authors say) *you* have got nearer to than comes to the lot of most people. We won't enquire how far they are mistaken! but proceed to say, that as Mrs. Vranken thinks her daughter has *need* of a director, she is not the person we want, for it is that *very director* or governess we would have to superintend not only the children, but *those* who *look after them*. I ask pardon, therefore, for giving you any trouble upon the matter.

I reckon Mrs. Montagu will be gone to Bill Hill by the time you receive this, for our (penny) post goes to sleep on Sunday, and moves neither hand nor foot. I hope L^y Gower will find how much pleasanter it is to hear a friendly voice than to live as if one were ship-wreck'd (one alone!) upon a desert island. I do not despair, my dear madam, of meeting you yet at Bill Hill this summer, tho' both of us will require much invita-tion, in the apprehension of being troublesome. I do hope my dear Mrs. Leveson will move east e'er it be long; mais silence là, s'il vous plait, for I would have her announce it herself. The Dss of Beaufort is much better, I thank God. I hope Mrs. Port is well. Adieu, my dear madam, I beg you will present my best respects to the Duchess, and kind complim^ts to Mrs. Montagu. I expect every moment to hear that her namesake in Hill Street is become a widow.

I am ever my dear Mrs. Delany's very
    Affectionate, faithful, and obliged servant.
                    F. BOSCAWEN.

Mrs. Delany to the Rev. John Dewes, at Calwich.

Bulstrode, 26th May, 1775.

My poor brother's uneasy state is a severe tryal of his pious resignation ; and tho' we must feel pain and sorrow as human creatures, our heavenly Father at the same time sends us consolation by the blessed hope of *everlasting happiness.* One should imagine *that* thought wou'd raise us above mortal anguish, and certainly in a great measure it does, it at least mitigates it greatly. When we suffer pain, it shows us what insufficient creatures we are to help ourselves ; it makes us recollect our infirmities of body and mind. It calls us to repentance of our offences, and supplication to the Almighty power, who alone can relieve us, and whose mercies are infinite. *For what is required of us, but to show mercy, to do justice, and to walk humbly with our God?* It is a distress to me, that I have not been able this year to go into Staffordshire ; I should not think of spending any time at Calwich, as, at this time, it might not be convenient to my dear brother ; but if I were in his neighbourhood *I could come to him* if it would be *any manner* of comfort or use to him, and am sure if he thinks it will, I *will certainly,* please God to give me strength, *do it* ; and trust you will let me know *sincerely what he wishes to have me do?* I hope he liked the silver chalice and plate. Lord and Lady Clanbrassil are expected here for 2 or 3 days. We go out every day, and the Dss of P. is very well ; her best wishes. Mr. Ed[d] Montagu [1] is dead.

---

[1] The Hon. Mr. Montague, uncle to the Earl of Sandwich, died May 20th, 1775, in Hill Street, Berkeley Square.

He has left his widdow everything, real and personal estate, for ever. Only charging it with a legacy of £3000. If her *heart* proves as good as her *head*, she may do *abundance of good*; her possessions are *very great*. *Mr.* Boyd of Danson [1] is made a baronet, by y[e] interest of his friend Lord Dartmouth; *he*, his lady and daughters are going abroad for their healths. Adieu.

The Hon. Mrs. Boscawen to Mrs. Delany.

Glan Villa, y[e] 29th May, 75.

I know, my dear madam, you will be pleas'd to hear that I have got some very agreeable company in my cottage: neither more nor less than my dear Mrs. Leveson and her little son, a very fine hearty chubby boy. I cou'd not help taking some steps on my side to meet them, and on Thursday last I went to London with my Lord Chief Baron and Lady Smythe, who had spent the day here; next morning I rose soon after the sun, and set forwards for Salisbury, as I intended, but at Stockbridge had the satisfaction to discern a chaize standing, on w[ch] were certain hieroglyphicks that belong'd to *Leveson* and *Boscawen*; beside that I cou'd also discern within the inn-gate my serv[t] conferring with a lady, instead of getting me fresh horses: but not to make a very long story of a very pleasant one, I din'd with my dau[r] at Stockbridge last Friday, and bro[t] her

---

[1] John Boyd, Esq., of Danson Hill, co. Kent, was created a Baronet 2nd June, 1775.

and Co. hither to dinner on Saturday. She cou'd not pay
her duty to Lady Gower in passing without lengthening
her journey very much, wch her young travelling companion found full long enough, beside that I cou'd *not* have
waited on Lady Gower, *without* her permission, nor cou'd
Mrs. Leveson have cast me off upon the road after I
had gone so far to meet her ; but she hopes to receive
Lady Gower's summons, (whenever it is agreeable to her
lady^p to see her and the child,) and will always be ready
to obey them. Mr. Leveson remains at Plymouth till
after Ld Sandwich has made his annual visitation to that
port.

My dear madam, I beg the favour of you to send me
the name and title of that efficacious liquor which you gave
me for the Duchess of Beaufort: the phial was wrote
upon " Godfrey." The next day the Duchess of Portland was so good as to send me a fresh bottle, (also
mark'd " Godfrey.") This I have bro^t hither, and have
had occasion to apply it to the deplorable face of my
dairy maid, who has been in agonies of rheumatick pain
all the winter, has had blisters, teeth drawn, course of
bark, everything that cou'd be thought of, and all to no
purpose ; till at length the Duchess of Portland's bounty,
(w^h has cur'd many an *aching heart*,) has also cur'd this
poor creature's *aching head*, and now she can milk her
cows, and make her butter with a great degree of ease
and comfort ; but as she has sometimes little returns and
mementos of her late misery I sh^d be glad of another
phial (I have one not quite finish'd), exactly the same as
that the Duchess and you gave me ; by what *title* then
and description am I to ask for it *at* Mr. Godfrey's
chemist in Southampton Street, Covent Garden ? Be

pleas'd to direct to Colny Hatch,[1] Midd^x; to pardon my sending you a double letter, qui ne vaut pas le sou of a single one ; to present and accept my dau^{rs} respects and mine to the Duchess and yourself; and to believe me Most truly and affectionately yours.

The Hon. Mrs. Boscawen to Mrs. Delany.

Glan Villa, 5th June, 75.

My good Madam,

I feel so frequently a disposition of mind very unlikely to amuse any body, and especially those who so kindly wish me easy and happy, that I am (very properly) deterr'd from sitting down and giving a picture of it. Indeed, during the past week having had the favour of two letters from you, I shou'd certainly have wrote—if my thoughts had not been at Boston, and alas! my cares also ; I do not mean that I give credit to all these stories of the insurgents (and as yet we have no other), but— the sword is unsheath'd! and it cannot be but its *glare* must be painfull in eyes so *sore* as mine.

How beautiful must your charming Bulstrode be this bright, clear day ! I heard of its charms by Mr. and Mrs. Southwell (who spent a day with me), and who visited it last week, but I chid Mr. Southwell for not going into the house, as he is fond of pictures—he wou'd have receiv'd much pleasure ; as to the dehors he was

---

[1] *Colney Hatch* was the name of the place where Mrs. Boscawen's country house was situated, and in allusion to her own maiden name, Frances Evelyn Glanville, she called it " *Glanvilla.*" Sometimes she prefixes the name of the hamlet and sometimes that of her house.

charm'd, and in many excursions they have lately made
within 20 miles of London, but nothing has delighted
them like Bulstrode, or seem'd *worthy* to be *nam'd* with
it. Lady Gower in a very kind letter to Mrs. L. tells her
the small-pox is so near Bill Hill that she wou'd by no
means have her come yet.   This suits our plans particularly—and the present situation of the Dss of Beaufort.
We expect her now in a short time; that wch she has
pass'd in perfect quiet at Badminton had greatly improv'd
her health and strength, I thank God.

Your friends, L^{d}[1] and L^{y} Mansfield, are enjoying Ken
Wood in perfect health. Mr. and Mrs. Ramsay, who din'd
with me to-day, paid their respects there and saw them
as they came along.   My dear madam, I delight in your
Sallet and the *Oil* thereof, for, tho' I can do *nothing* that
you do, I have a great mind to fancy that I love every
thing that you love, and always I desire much oil in my
sallet.

The news of states and potentates concern not me, but
I have been hurt to see the papers fill'd with dreadfull
calamities ; the fire in Cov. Garden, the still *more horrible*
one at Chester, the wrecks ! the hurricanes ! I am much
better pleas'd when our newsmongers are occupied solely
by their favourite subject—the *liberty of the citizens*,
happily exerted of late in attacking *their custards*, and
giving sheriff Lewes a black eye !

Adieu, my dear madam.   My young ladies desire to
present their best compliments to you, and join me in

The Lord Chief Justice of the King's Bench, who married, in 1738, Lady
Elizabeth Finch, daughter of Daniel, Earl of Winchelsea and Nottingham.

respects to the Duchess of Portland and very sincere wishes for her health and yours.

Believe me, my dear madam,

Your most faithfull and affectionate servant,

F. Boscawen.

Mrs. Delany to Mrs. Port, of Ilam, at Welsbourn.

Bulstrode, 11th June, 1775.

My dearest Mary,

I hope this will find you safely arived at Welsbourne; that you had a good journey; and the pleasure of finding your father well,—happy, I am sure, they will all be in having you with them, and happy should I be, could I take myself there for a few days; but that depends on concurring circumstances. The most convenient time to me would be when the Dss of Portland goes to Weymouth. *If* the *regatta* goes on, the Dss proposes going to town for two or three days; and I have a little busyness will call me there at the same time, from the two and twentieth to the five and twentieth. On our return to Bulstrode, Lord and Lady Weymouth and their family come here for a week, and I tnihk it would not be right to leave Bulstrode at that time. I must get you to make an apology for an impertinent thing I shall do by your father, which is, sending down a matrass for the bed that may be allotted me, as I am not a very good sleeper, and must have the sort I am used to. It is long since I heard from Calwich; as you have never mentioned seeing my poor brother, I suppose you have not been there. Don't speak of my thoughts of coming to Welsbourne, as it is uncertain, and as I wish my brother may *not know it.*

Last Friday we had an extraordinary visitor here ; Mr. *Whang at Tong* ; thus he writes his name :—

You know the Chinese write perpendicularly. He came with a Capt. Blake, who has taken him under his protection, and has had him instructed in necessary knowledge. He is a young man ; I believe I gave you an account of him and his dress some time ago. Lady Andover is at Lord Suffolk's at Sunbury, about 16 miles off, near Hampton Court ; in a melancholy way, with her poor little g. daughter, who is past all hopes of recovery. We go to-morrow, please God, to see her ; I shall have no time to add to this letter, and think it long eno'. My best compliments to all ; so says her Grace.

Mrs. Delany to Mrs. Port, of Ilam.

1775.

Lord and Lady Clan[1] came on Friday, and go this evening. I like him mightily ; he is good humour'd, easy, well-bred, and *deep* in search of *botany*, which has afforded an ample field for *conversation*, to which our cousin, you know (of old), does not contribute much, and is still as dolorous (entre nous) as if she was not so

---

[1] Lady Clanbrassill.—Grace Foley, daughter of the Hon. Mrs. Foley (Grace Granville), whose husband was created Lord Foley.

happily settled. Yet she seems sensible, too, of that; but her langour of spirits and want of exertion seems insurmountable; she sees without speculation, and hears without reflection, and all the rare beauties of Bulstrode can hardly extort an assent to other people's admiration; but not so her lord, for he takes notice of everything, tho' we shall not regret enjoying by ourselves our books, our work, and our rambles; but I am really spoyled for *common conversation.* The knowledge, the *spirit,* the frank communication of my dear friend here is an *un*common blessing! and how thankfull am I to *be able* to enjoy it. I have no news to impart; the Duchess of Northumberland greatly recovered.

Miss Johnston's death (the maid of honour) must have been a great shock to her friends, who had just placed her in a situation so desirable to her; but she *is* removed *from a precipice!*

The Hon. Mrs. Boscawen to Mrs. Delany.

(5th page of a letter.)

You will hardly expect any news from Glan Villa, now that L^y Mayne is remov'd from this neighbourhood. We have nobody in it qui appartient au grand monde; nor indeed do we want anybody, having frequently friends from Lon^n. The heat and dust begin now to forbid those favours also. Did I tell you that I had seen Mrs. Montagu since her widowhood?[1] She

---

1 The Hon. Edward Montagu, uncle to the Earl of Sandwich, died in Hill Street, 20th May, 1775.

sent to ask me when I was in town. She intends to go
abroad before winter; at present her health obliges her
to go to Tunbridge. The young ladies will be carry'd
abroad to get husbands, as two Miss Gores, Miss Burrell,
and Miss Seymour have done. I hear the regata [1] goes
on. Mrs. Walsingham and I agreed to ask of the Duchess
of Portland a window in her garret to behold the same.
What say you, my dear madam. *Will you* prefer our
petition, and be of our party ?

Please to direct to Audley Street.

The Hon. Mrs. Boscawen to Mrs. Delany.

Glan Villa, June 23rd, 75.

I return you many thanks, my dear madam, for de-
lineating your steps to me. Surely I should have trac'd
them carefully till they had brought me into your
presence, if I were worthy of it, or capable of enjoying
such a satisfaction; but a weight of care and anxiety
oppresses my mind, and renders me very unfit for the
pleasure of meeting you at Whitehall this evening; but
I hope Mrs. Leveson will be there and enjoy your company. I hope, too, she will present my thanks to the
Duchess of Portland for her goodness in allotting me a
place. Whether the regatta had tempted me or not, the
good company was such an attraction as I should cer-

---

[1] A regatta (the first entertainment of the kind held in England) took
place on Friday, the 23rd of June, 1775, on the Thames. The Dukes of
Gloucester and Cumberland were present in their barges, and many of the
foreign ministers, &c. The entertainment concluded with supper, concert,
and ball at Ranelagh.

tainy not have resisted had I been at all able to enjoy it. I hope you won't get cold, which, methinks, will be no difficult matter, considering that with the extreme heat we have a violent wind : at least so it is in this cottage, wch makes very unpleasant sort of weather, for when the burning sun departs it leaves you to the stormy wind, and there is none of that still and tranquil evening air wch so amply rewards the uneasiness of a hot day. You will return to Bulstrode to-morrow, but this will kiss your hands first, and wish you all manner of good. Do not imagine I read any news papers. I soon found it necessary to leave that off. O cruel *patriots* to rejoyce in the blood of y^r countrymen, provided you can wade thro' it to the Treasury-bench. It is from *hence* those deluded wretches are encourag'd to ruin themselves and distress others. Heaven vouchsafe to help us !

Mrs. Walsingham must have enjoy'd the party you describe, and was worthy of it.

Adieu, my dear madam.

> Y^r ever affectionate,
> Faithfull servant,
> F. Boscawen.

The Hon. Mrs. Boscawen to Mrs. Delany.

> Glan Villa, Wensday.
> (After June 23rd, 1775).

My dear Madam,

Excuse this penny worth : it is only to beg Mrs. Smith will put up 3 shifts instead of one, for the weather is so hot (yesterday it was quite sultry) that I am sure this airy cottage on a hill will be better for you than the vale of St. James's.

Au reste—I have had to-day by the post a letter from my poor dear boy at Boston ; he assures me that he is in perfect health, and I thank God I shall be in perfect spirits to-morrow when I have such friends to visit me. A remains of Barnet Fair will so *guard* her Grace to London, and a moon towards the full will so light her and prevent any dusky evening, that I trust she will have no fright, and be in no hurry to leave us to our meditations, tho' they shou'd be (as most likely they will be) on her kindness and goodness. I am vastly glad to hear Lady Weymouth is well.

F. BOSCAWEN.

Poor Mrs. Chapone has been very ill, but is recovering.

Mrs. Delany to Bernard Granville, Esq., at Calwich.

Bulstrode, 26th June, 1775.

I have been longer than usual without writing to my dear brother. Could I offer him anything in his present uneasy state that could lessen his sufferings I should write more frequently, but I know his own reflections are of more real use to him than anything I can say, tho' suggested by the *truest affection!* The long continuance of heat we have had did not agree with me, and I fear encreased your complaints. I have been better since I was let blood and the weather is grown cooler. I was in town three days, and saw our nephews, very well; they are very kind and affectionate to me, and the *difference* I see in *their* behaviour to what I *hear* of *other* young men, makes them truly valuable. We returned to Bulstrode on Saturday; the rain made it comfortable, but it was much otherwise in London. The Duke of Portland was robbed of his purse with twenty guineas, and his watch, just as he left Putney on Friday night, tho' he had two servants that rode close to his coach. The Dss Dow^r of Portland, thank God, is very well; she desires me to make her best compliments and wishes to you. Her botanical garden prospers, and her health is much strengthened by her attention to it. How happy would it be for the world if they delighted more in *natural pleasures*, which lye open to everybody, instead of racking their brains and time to invent *irrational* entertainments, that besides the expense of fortune and constitution, put a stop to every serious consideration, and which lay in no store for the hour of pain and tryal, when nothing can support them but a conscience void of offence towards God and man, a *relyance* on the mercy of God, and *submission* to his will, with the joyful hope of eternal happiness! I am afraid I have made my letter too long. I will only add my warmest wishes. Adieu.

This was probably the last letter of Mrs. Delany's to her brother. He died on 2nd July, six days after it was written. The painful and lingering illness of Mr. Granville, which had been a source of sorrow to Mrs. Delany for a considerable period, had been aggravated by the impossibility of personally administering to his comfort. At one time he appeared anxious for frequent letters from his sister, especially on religious subjects; at others all intercourse on his side ceased, and it appears that her offer of going to Calwich was not accepted. Hopeless of his recovery, Mrs. Delany admitted to her niece that his release from a state of continued suffering would be a blessing and relief, but yet the trial, when it came, was very painful. She had ever retained her attachment to the remembrance of what he *once* was to her, and as long as life lasted hope lingered, and she evidently caught at every little trait of kindness in the expectation that the "*Bunny*" of *the past* would reappear! There is nothing in the style of the above letter which indicates immediate alarm, and it is probable that *at last* his death was unexpected, but no letter has been found giving an account of his last moments or announcing his death. At the expiration of seven years from the date of Mrs. Dewes's death, the Dean of Down died, and *seven years* after his death Mrs. Delany lost her brother! but her piety, her energy and good sense had not deserted her, and she *again revived* to be a *still greater* object of interest, reverence, and admiration to all her surviving relations and friends, as well as to the world around her. Mr. Granville left his own epitaph, and over it the following words were written—

" *The inscription for the monument that is to be at Elaston.*"

Under the epitaph was a pen and ink sketch, of which a *fac simile* is here given, which was intended to show in what part of Ellaston church his vault was to be made and his monument erected.

Under this sketch were these words :—
"I would have the vault where my coffin is to be put full nine foot deep, and lined with a good brick or stone wall."

Mr. Granville was buried in Ellaston church, and the inscription on his monument is as follows—

Here lies interred the body of
BERNARD GRANVILLE,
who trusted in the mercy of Almighty God
for the forgiveness of his sins
through the merits and mediation
of
Jesus Christ, the Saviour and Redeemer
of mankind.
He was the son of Bernard Granville,
and great grandson of Sir Bevil Granville,
who was killed in the civil wars,
fighting for King Charles the First,
on Lansdown, near Bath, in Somersetshire.
He died at Calwich, July the 2nd, 1775.
Aged 76.

The above epitaph is nearly the same as the one found among his papers, but in the original MS., instead of the " *civil wars*," the words were—" *The wars between King Charles I. and the Rebbells.*"

The Hon. Mrs. Boscawen to Mrs. Delany.

Glan Villa, July 5th, 75.

Indeed, my dear madam, I shall not defer my visit till you begin to wander, nor think of catching you upon the road, but pay my respects to you before you set out, and wait on you with my best wishes for your pleasant journey, attended with all manner of agremens, and prosperity of every kind. At the present writing you are on your march *to Eton*, and y^r pleasant assignation at the Provost's, the thoughts of which quite refreshes my imagination; to know of so many whom I love and honour so charmingly associated and assembled really does one good, unless one were subject to the fell disease of *envy*, which I am not: *few people* taste the charms of society so much as Mrs. Walsingham, as indeed *fewer* contribute *so largely* to them! *She* has *celebrated* these charming parties (especially one at Bulstrode), and I was quite glad that she enjoy'd a pleasure she is so peculiarly worthy of. The Duchess's approaching excursion and y^{rs} must be a great loss to her. I wish, dear madam, you may execute y^r purpose of calling on Lady Gower, sans prejudice, however, of the longer stay, wch I hope you will find occasion to make at Bill Hill when y^r humble servant shall be there, wch will hardly be till towards autumn I imagine. At present I am in hourly expectation to hear of a new grandchild ; however, the Duke and Duchess of Beaufort were here yesterday both in perfect health. Mrs. Leveson has had a very kind letter from Lady Gower, warning her of the spreading of the small-pox in her neighbourhood, so that it would be improper to carry the child there as yet ; it is vastly well here, and thrives and walks alone : and it suits Mrs. Leveson too not to remove to Bill Hill before her sister is in a fair way of recovery, or indeed abroad again, since her convalescence will be *very triste* if she does not attend it. As for me, I own to you, dear madam, my mind is in a very uneasy state ; I *cannot help* thinking of my poor dear only remaining boy, and I cannot think of him without *great agitation and anxiety!* Thank God we have heard from him again ; I have had a letter from him, dated the 9th of May, and Mrs Leveson one since, dated ye 13th, in which he gives her a very circumstantial account of the unfortunate skirmish, in which he lost an invaluable friend, Lieu^t Knight, an officer of his regi^t, who had taken a great kindness for him, and was (by all accounts) a person of extraordinary merit. My poor George laments him most pathetically; indeed his whole letter, wch freely expatiates (to his sister) upon many subjects, is a most masterly performance, and nobody that read it would guess the age of the writer; yet to me the only very pleasant part is that in wch he tells her that the "climate seems to him better than that of England, one reason of which may be that he has never had an hour's illness since he has been in it." Indeed I should add that the expressions of duty and affection towards me, the care that he is under lest I should be uneasy at his situation, and the desire he expresses that his sister (whom he supposes at Plymouth) should spare me all the time she possibly can—all these are earnests of my future comfort in him, if it pleases God to spare him! But I ought not to have named this subject to you, my dear madam, who are so kind and compassionate towards me. Mrs. Leveson and I have made 2 expeditions together, beside that wch she made sole to the birthday and regatta. We have been at Hatfield (perhaps I told you), and since at Wimbledon to spend a day with our good friend my Lord Chief Baron and Lady, who lent us guards on our return, for the Duke of Portland had been rob'd two days before, and Lady Rockingham[1] was so afraid of the same fate, that she, being on the road when she heard it, *stopt* at Putney, and *there lodg'd* at her apothecary's. We, tho' not quite so cautious, got safe to London, and next day visited my poor sister Frederick[2] at her villa, and the following we spent at

---

[1] Mary, daughter and heiress of Thomas Bright, of Badsworth, Esq., Yorkshire; and wife of Charles Watson Wentworth, 2nd and last Marquis of Rockingham.

[2] Lucy, daughter of Hugh Boscawen, 1st Viscount Falmouth, and sister of Admiral Boscawen, married Sir Charles Frederick, K.B. She died in 1784.

Greenwich with some particular friends, who told us Sir Gregory Page [1] was about to depart this life very gently and in a good old age. My dear madam, I am proud to resemble you in anything, and therefore was vastly pleas'd to find you are *re*-reading Mess[rs] Mason and Gray l'un portant l'autre, for that is every night our occupation, and has been for some time past—a very agreeable one. I read aloud while Mrs. L. works, and, as you observe, we quite chew it and dwell upon its taste; having discover'd, I think, many bits that were not selected at the first hasty reading. But I have a good mind to tell you what my ingenious friend Miss More [2] says of them, or rather of their editor. I sent the book to her when first it came out, doubting if she cou'd presently find it at Bristol; she was vastly pleased with it, and says of Mr. Mason, "Never was a more generous editor or a more faithfull friend. What an exquisite pleasure does he take in doing honor to the departed! May his *own* fame meet with *such a guardian,* and his *own life such a biographer!* His *candour and modesty* in this work are *as* admirable as his *taste and talents* in all his preceding ones." Mr. Gray too has his share of his sister poet's panegyrick, and she is delighted, she says, "to be admitted into his closet." She adds, that lately she met at the Dean of Gloster's a sister of that young Mr. West who was Mr. Gray's friend, that she too has been a child of sorrow, and but for a lucky acquaintance with the Dean of Gloster, who had taken

---

[1] Sir Gregory Page, Bart., of Wricklemarsh, in Kent, died August 4th, 1775, at the age of 90.

[2] The well-known Hannah More.

her home, was falling into want and indigence. She is a widow, I believe her name was Williams, and advanc'd in years. I think you did Mr. C. F.[1] too much honour to want to see him; for *my part* I shou'd *like* to *send him to America* and Orator Burke[2] with him. Great proof it would be of *their eloquence* if they could persuade that *turbulent people* to *be quiet* and enjoy their own happiness and plenty! It seems Lord Chatham has fail'd in that attempt, and that the Plan of Pacification and Bill he bro^t into ye H. of Lords is held in the *utmost contempt* by the Congress! I forget who told me this— not the newspapers, for I have been oblig'd to leave off reading them. Adieu, my dearest madam; much health and pleasure attend y^r steps.

Countess Cowper to the Rev. John Dewes, at Calwich, near Ashbourn, Derbyshire.

Richmond, July 12th, 1775.

SIR,

I have received ye favour of y^{rs}, and I congratulate y^n upon y^r increase of fortune, w^{ch} *I do not doubt* y^r making a good use of; but I fear Mr. Granville has *not* acted kindly by y^r brother Bernard. Y^r close attendance merited a recompense.

It was always a *pleasure* to me to call y^n "*my chaplain*," as I thought it made the son of my amiable friend,

---

[1] Charles James Fox.
[2] Edmund Burke.

in some measure, *belong to me.*   But I am very glad you
are so well provided for; and I shall always remain
Y^r sincere,
Humble servant,
G. C. COWPER.

Mrs. Delany to Rev. John Dewes.

Welsbourn, 17th July, 1775.

I have not been well, which has prevented my writing
sooner. I received your letter this morning, and am
obliged to you, my dear nephew, for y^r kind invitation.
I expect the pleasure of seeing you in London, as I hear
you are going thither, and I propose, please God, being
at my own house on Saturday next, and *you know too
well,* I hope, how much I am interested for a family so
dear to me to doubt of my satisfaction in everything
that contributes to their real happiness.

I wave saying much about the late event at Calwich,
it has *already cost me too much sorrow.* I am sure your
honest heart would *not* believe me if I said I "was satisfied" with the disposition of my brother's fortune, and
I am much deceived in my dear John if a *less partial* disposition would not have been more agreeable to you.   I
am *far* from thinking you did *not* deserve an ample
recompense for the uneasy life you have led for near 4
years past, but it was your lot to be chosen to that task.
The events of this world are guided by an unerring
Providence, and prosperity is sent as a tryal of our
virtue, as well as adversity.

I have *no doubt* of your generosity, as far as it lies in

ˣ Bernard and your sister Port,
elly used; and I pray to God to
I have been so much weaken'd
tho' I am, I thank God, better
ted, I am too weak for a hurry;
ing my journey into 3 days: the
ck, 2nd at Henley, 3d to dinner
pe you and your broˣ can drink
fternoon, and dine with me on
quite satisfied with Mrs. Port's
spirits, tho she   them.

Bernard Dewes, Esq., to Mrs. Viney.

25th July, 1775.

DEAR MADAM,

As you know the reason, I have no doubt you
will excuse my not answering your obliging letter sooner.
The disposition Mr. Granville has made of his estate
I must own has disappointed me much.   He has left me
but a very small part of it, not that I in the least regret
what he has done for my brother John, for *he is indeed*
worthy of any good fortune that can happen to him, but
taught, as I have been *from my infancy*, to expect from
Mr. Granville a considerable estate, I had of course
formed schemes for my future life accordingly, which
must now be greatly contracted.

My best wishes attend your sister.

Believe me, dear madam,
Your very sincere friend
And humble servant,
BERNARD DEWES.

L 2

Mrs. Delany to Mrs. Port, of Ilam.

St. James's Place, 29th July, 1775.

I will not wait for a letter from my dearest Mary from Ilam, tho' most likely this evening will bring me one, with the happy information of her having a good journey home; that change of place has agreed with her, given her better nights; that her dear babes are well, and her dear P. ever kind and attentive; to close all, that the dear spinsters are enjoying the delights of the superb beauties of Ilam, and that I know will compleat your satisfaction.

I have had the company of your dear bro'' 3 times to dinner, and to-morrow they are engaged to me. The *more* I converse with them the *greater* is my esteem of them. John stays *purely* out of kindness to Bern'', whose little employm' has obliged him to stay in town; they are impatient to return into Staffordshire, as you may believe, and to see their friends at Ilam. I hope, tho' the disappointment *has been very great* to my dear Bernard, that time will reconcile him to an event so unexpected by him. He has *no corroding passions* to deal with; he is *neither avaricious nor envious*; his resentment arises from *sentiment,* to be dealt with *unkindly,* when he *must* be conscious he *did not deserve it,* and this must hurt a generous nature; but he does not say a murmuring word; and his bro' John seems in the midst of his own great acquisitions to feel *so sensibly* what *must pass* in Bernard's mind that I am sure he will do all he can to soften the disappointment; but there must be time to consider what can be done, or what he may have in his power; but they seem *quite satisfied* with *one another.* I believe they go out of town on Monday next, as I shall (please God) if Lady Gower is at liberty to go then; but she is waiting in town to put in her claim to the peerage of Clifton[1], now in abeyance; I hope she will get it; tho' Mr. Southwell has been very vigilant in his pursuit of it before L^y G. took a step towards it. She has been so obliging as to invite my two nephews to spend two or three days at Bill Hill whilst I am there, but they will hardly allow themselves that time now, and I have not seen them since; it was last night she spoke to me.

Lady Weymouth has spent an hour or two every evening but one since I came home. Mrs. Dashwood, Lady Wall^d, Mrs. Boscawen, Mrs. Leveson, Lady M. Mordaunt take their turns, and the day before yesterday Mrs. Tomlinson spent the whole evening. The mornings are filled up with my usual employments, wch I shift often, as I think it better than a long application to any one. I want my amiable *little bird* to tempt me with a pretty flower, and so *that work* at present is idle, and will hardly be renewed till I go to Bulstrode.

The disposition of Mr. Granville's property to the third instead of the second son of his sister, Ann Granville (Mrs. Dewes), was a matter of surprise and regret to Mrs. Delany, who considered that, as Bernard, the second, had been brought up with the expectation of being his heir, and had not offended him, that it was unjust to prefer his younger brother;—but the result was eventually the same, as Court, the elder son of Ann Granville, dying unmarried, Bernard succeeded to his father's estates, and John of Calwich fully justified the opinion entertained of him by Mrs. Delany, and was one of the most benevolent, liberal, and kind-hearted men that ever lived.

---

[1] Query, Clifford.

The Dowager-Countess Gower to Mrs. Delany, St. James's Place.

Bill Hill, 6th Aug., 75.

M^rs. Leveson was so good as to tell me by Tuesday's post you had not had a return of ye disorder, had also an opportunity of hearing on ye 3rd ye same, and w^n ye post came had this good news confirm'd under d^r M^rs. Delany's own hand, wch gave me great satisfaction; not-w^thstanding, (had you ye doc^rs leave to come here,) you cou'd *not* have my consent, being prepossess'd this late disorder properly attended too will be a means of establishing an un-interrupted health, (wch I so much desire long to continue); and I shou'd be misserable wth ye apprehension I broke into; and even Bulstrode sh^d not be gone too in a hurry, tho' there are many things to be said in favour of y^t journey, y^t can't be said for this. I'll sum up all in these few words : *pray* in ye first place *take care of yor health*; something I hope will hapen to put off her Grace's journey, she is always better for being at Weymouth, so 'tis wishing her well. I am not worth a ffrank, but rich, in thinking I've felt yor regard to yor most faithfull

M. G.

P.S. About *once a week* let me know how you do.

The Hon. Mrs. Boscawen to Mrs. Delany.

Glan Villa, 14th Aug., 1775.

Not a word did hear of you yesterday my dear madam, nor shall to-day; such are the *charms* of the penny post wch refuses to *stir out of town*, or come into this country on a Sunday. I must make myself amends for this fast, and to-morrow I do hope for the great feast of beholding you with my eyes, and hearing you (tho' in y^r gentlest voice) with my ears, both which I might have had on Saturday last 'tis true, and I refused, for which Mrs. Smith will love me the better as long as she lives, and you, my dear madam, will not think me a savage or insensible to y^r kindness : no—but a carefull considerate affectionate friend, that fears to stir or deviate a hair's breadth from the line trac'd out by the skilfull physician ; for you must know my dear friend that 'tis *not* in this case that "love casteth out fear:" no ! fear establisheth itself with all its torments at first, which are afterwards soften'd into *cautions*, by wch milder name mine were discernable last Saturday and did not escape your just penetration I persuade myself. Shall I have the honour (and great pleasure) to see the Duchess of Portland to-morrow ? I had that of writing to her to Weymouth, from whence her Grace was departed or ever my letter arriv'd ; for to say the truth it was a little tardy on your account, my dear madam, as I did not presume to tell her Grace fibs, and the truth was much too unwelcome to be told at ye time of my g. daug^{rs} christening wch was the subject of my letter.

Mrs. Leveson and her spouse are at Bill Hill, both missing their child very much. I doubt L^y G. wou'd not suffer him to come because of the small pox in her neighbourhood.

The post waits. Adieu, my dear madam, I intend to appear slily to Mrs. Smith[1] to-morrow between 1 and 2, but shall not proceed any farther unless she encourages

---

[1] Mrs. Delany's waiting woman.

me, and Dr. Turton licenses. Ever with earnest wishes
for your entire and perfect recovery,

Your most affectionate,

F. BOSCAWEN.

Mrs. Delany to Mrs. Port, of Ilam.

St. James's Place, 29th Aug., 1775.

I every moment expect the *spinsters,* as they came to
town last night and are at Mrs. Berk^{ys}.

I was afraid your late visiters gave you more *pain*
than *pleasure.* *Time* and *sickness* make *great revolutions*
in the disposition of *some people,* and tho' they do not
obliterate tender sentiments, often embarass them with
troublesome companions—such as *unreasonable expectations, quick resentments,* &c.—and had we not humanity
eno' to make allowances for these deficiencies there would
often be a total alienation of affection. When we feel
in ourselves *the havock* that a depression of spirits makes
not only on *our temper,* but *our understanding,* it raises
that compassion towards our fellow-creatures which we
at times feel so much the want of; but then when that
is the case, why fly from home, or go anywhere but for
means of cure. I hope the travelling will have had a
good effect; before I seal my letter I will let you know.

I hope your visit to Calwich was not too much for
you, and that all its present inhabitants are well and
happy. I have not had a line of enquiry from your
father since I left Welsbourne, but I assure you I do not
take the omission ill, for it is his way. I should have
written to dear Mrs. Mead but have been forbidden so

strictly not to write much, that I reserve it for those to whom it is of most consequence; tho' now I begin to creep out of my trammels, and have been out three times, and dined last Friday at Whitehall for the first time; had the comfort of going to early chapel last Sunday, and spent two hours in the afternoon yester. with Lady Weymouth, her tenth day;[1] she seems low in spirits, and weak, but they say is full as well as can be expected. Our dear Dss is so well satisfied that she leaves me her deputy to take care of the little Viscountess during her absence, from to-morrow till next Saturday; and at Lady Wey—s earnest entreaty she has consented to go for that time to see Lady Bute at Luton, which I am glad of, as so long a confinem^t in London, and so much in a close room, is very bad for her nerves. I suppose if Lady W. goes on well she will go to Bulstrode the latter end of next week.

Lady M. Mordaunt[2] sat with me an hour last Sunday; she is well and has had good success with her nursing, and goes back to-day with Lady Cowper, who comes to town to dine with Mrs. Cowper—and *here in came* the countess full of *health, spirits,* and *good humour*, but I had rather she had come another morning to have spared my spirits, as I was in expectation of our other friends, who came soon after. Indeed I think Mrs. R. is grown very thin, and seems weak, but otherwise as well as I expected to see her. She was full of lamentation of the

---

[1] Elizabeth, the thirteenth child of Thomas, 3rd Viscount Weymouth, was born Aug. 19th, and died Aug. 22nd, 1775.

[2] Lady Mary Anastasia Grace Mordaunt, second daughter of Charles, 4th Earl of Peterborough. On the death of her half-brother, Charles Henry, 5th Earl of Peterborough, Lady Mary succeeded to the Barony of Mordaunt, of Turvey, and died in 1819.

trouble she had given at Ilam, but seemed much pleased with the place, &c., and is in love with *my sweet little bird.*

Mrs. Delany to Mrs. Port, of Ilam.

St. James's Place, 5th Sept., 1775.

It is very true, my dearest Mary, that under all the events of this life, even those that most nearly touch our sensibillity, there is consolation and reason for us to be thankfull; when we can lay aside just our own immediate sufferings, and consider the wisdom, and goodness, and loving-kindness of the Almighty Disposer of all things. I make no doubt but that you will go on well, and prosperously; *enjoy* the roses of life, and *not provoke* its thorns! The accounts y^r late guests have given me, even of your health, (circumstances consider'd) have been satisfactory, your domestic happiness in so tender and attentive a husband, your lovely children, your care of them, which tho' checquer'd with some anxiety on the whole, is a blessed employment, to cultivate their minds to sow good seed, and root out (or rather prevent) the tares, and to lay, by their *submission to your will,* the *chief* foundation for *their* happiness, as well as *your own,* present and future; cherishing a rising hope of their being a real blessing to their family, and all they are connected with. This subject raises a melancholly recollection of an *unbridled* will, that overthrew *many virtues* that *might* have made an *illustrious charact^r*! Everything I hear from everybody of y^r bro^{rs}, raises them in my esteem. I need not say, my dearest Mary, how much you share it, and what a happiness it would be to see you

all happy together, but I must (at present at least) enjoy
the report of it; but my dear faithfull Mary, do you
mean to deprive me of my hoped for visit? and when
may I flatter myself about it? Not at all I promise
you, if attended with the least fatigue or inconvenience
of any kind; you must be honest. How long we shall
stay at Bulstrode, if we go, is at present uncertain, but I
should suppose not longer than the end of Novr. Now it
will not be proper or prudent for you to come so late as
after Xtmas; beside, then weather and roads grow worse,
and you may fear rains, and snows; this you see con-
tracts your time and may make difficulties. You know
how welcome you will be to *my very heart*, but I would
rather give up that hope than draw you into trouble.
*" Intent on her my love forgets its own, nor forms one wish
but for her sake alone."*
I thank God I am pure well, and grow stronger, as
you shall judge. Thursday, breakfasted at Kenwood.
Friday morning, made a visit to the spinsters. Saturday, rested at home for prudent reasons. Sunday, went
to church, our *errant* friends dined wth me, full of com-
mendations of the beauties of Ilam and its inhabitants
acknowledging great kindness and civility, and lamenting
their own troublesome state while there. I think, indeed,
poor Ravaud much emaciated and in a precarious state,
but she says she is better and Mrs. Shelley thinks her so;
they seem both in good humour, and in admiration of
y^r charity and attention to your poor neighbours. They
dine here tomorrow and meet the Dss of Portland, who
sends her love to our Mary and thanks for the intelligence about the picture. I am glad you like your new
neighbours, but a *distant cautious* civility 'till you know

more of them, will be best. Yesterday morning I spent
near four hours in seeing the pictures at ye Queen's
House. They are a *charming faultless* collection. In the
evening I was with Lady Weymouth, she is well but has
not got up her spirits. Mrs. Dashwood is at Tunbridge.
Lady Wallingford blister'd, and confined with a bad
cold.

Lady Mary Somerset has had a fever, and continues
very languid, she is ordered to the sea. Everybody is
in fears for her, and think of her poor sisters, but I hope
she will recover and be as happy with the Marquis of
Granby as there is reason to think she will; he is commended, and she very much so; *quiet* in her manner
and *unpresuming*, which is greatly preferable to more
lively parts *when* in the *contrary extream*. Lady Cowper
is to have a magnificent lighting up of her fine room on
ye 9th or 11th. She has *beat the drum*, and volunteers will
flock in, tho' she seemed distress'd for want of *maccaronis* but to obviate that she told me she had invited
Lady Harrington and desired her to bring as many men
as she can pick up; but I believe I may apply to *her*
lady^p what Mr. Foote did to the Dss of Kingston, that
"the Cupids had forsaken her long ago."

On Thursday next I have promised Mrs. Bos^n to
make her a visit at Glanvilla and stay till Friday
morning.

Without any previous notice the King, Queen, and
the two young princes were yesterday at Bulstrode and
drank tea there, which is all I have heard at present from
a *carter!* that brought me fruit from thence by the Dss.
orders. Don't you remember Ned Salmon's letter about
a royal visit some years ago? it was admirable! I

am afraid there is no such good scribe there now. And
poor Mrs. Evans, ye present housekeeper, is not so adroit
as her predecessor. I dare say she curtsey'd every
minute—" *Yes*," or "*no*," *my lady, an "please your
majesty,*"—and she will be terribly puzzled to arrange
her account of their observations and graciousness.

The Dowager-Countess Gower to Mrs. Delany.

Bill Hill, 6th Sep^t., 75.

How c^d my d^r good Mrs Delany venture to write to
me after I had absolutely forbid her so to do, have not
dar'd to write to her till now, least she sh^d think of
answering it. I have often heard of her great amendm^{ts}
from divers hands; my last acc^{ts} assur'd me of her perfect recovery, wch I must say rais'd my spirits and gave
me infinite satisfaction.

I rec̃ed a very obliging letter from ye D of P.; pray
wth my best respects, tell her Mr. Ffoot's [1] letter is carefully preserv'd among all my favorite peices.

Have you heard anything relating to y^t affairs of importance to me and mine, wch took up much of my
thought and care, w^n last in town? We are told my
antagonist says, he's sure of succeeding; if it is determin'd,
why not declar'd? ... Leveson is gone to London to
see some sea acquaintance just arriv'd; I expect some
news to night by him. Mrs. Leveson desires her best
complim^{ts} to you; among ye many disap̃ointm^{ts} y^s world
is full of, wee c^d not have her son here, ye leting y^e

---

[1] Probably Samuel Foote, the comedian, who died in 1777.

inoculated people walk abroad has spread ye small pox all over this country.

W^n ever 'tis not hurtfull to you to write, 'twill be a cordial to yor faithfull (friend) to hear you are well. The hectick is quite gone, and I seldom cough ; ffruite has been ye cure, in wch I have indulg'd, tho' not very good.

The Hon. Mrs. Boscawen to Mrs. Delany.

Glan Villa, 20th Sept., 1775.

My dear Madam,

You had omitted to date your letter, but it seem'd to have been wrote on Thursday. On your arrival at Bulstrode you had just such weather as I wish'd you. I beg to hear from you. I bribe you with some verses ; perhaps you have already seen them, for it is from Lady Gower that I got them. She sent them to Mrs. Leveson. One paragraph of her letter is " The Barony,[1] I think is in *imminent danger*." I hope therefore her ladyship is easy on the subject! By the ship wch is just arriv'd with Mrs. Gage[2] I have the satisfaction

---

[1] The Barony of De Clifford having fallen into abeyance on the death of Thomas Tufton, 6th Earl of Thanet, between his five daughters, the King terminated that abeyance by conferring it upon the Earl's third daughter, Margaret, wife and widow of Thomas Coke, Earl of Leicester. Her death in 1775 placed the Barony again in abeyance, and in 1776 it was conferred upon Edward Southwell, grandson of Lady Catherine Tufton, eldest daughter of Thomas, 6th Earl of Thanet, and of her husband, Viscount Sondes. Had the abeyance on Lady Leicester's death been terminated in favour of her sister, Lady Gower, the Barony would have descended to her son, the Hon. John Leveson Gower, the husband of Mrs. Boscawen's eldest daughter.

[2] Margaret, daughter and heiress of Peter Kemble, Esq., of New Jersey, married the Hon. Thomas Gage, Commander-in-chief of His Majesty's forces in North America. General Gage was the second son of Thomas, 1st Viscount Gage, and the father of Henry, the 3rd Viscount, who succeeded his uncle, William Henry, the 2nd Viscount, in the title.

to hear that my soldier and his captain (Evelyn) were well on the 20th of last month.

Mrs. L. presents her respects. I beg mine to the Duchess. I have just received a charming account of the Gloster meeting, delightful music and *successfull canvass*. They are very sensible of Mrs. Delany's goodness in writing, and very desirous to hear of her health.

The verses enclosed by Mrs. Boscawen were entitled "The Pleiades," the first line is—

> "With Devon's girl so blythe and gay,"

The two last lines—

> "To this vain world I'd bid adieu,
> And *pass my* life, and *think* with Crewe!"

It would be needless to insert the whole, as it has been so recently published in the Literary Remains of Mrs. Piozzi, where it is entitled "The Planets," and said to be written by Charles Fox. Another copy of verses in the above work is called "The Pleiades," said to be written by Mr. Chamberlayne, ending—

> "But if I dare to talk with Crewe,
> My ease, my peace, my heart adieu!
> Sweet Greville! whose *too* feeling heart
> By love was *once* betrayed,
> With Sappho's ardour, Sappho's art,
> For cool *indifference* prayed:
> Who can endure a prayer from you
> So selfish and confined?
> You should—when you produced a Crewe,
> Have prayed for *all mankind*."

Mrs. Delany to Mrs. Port, of Ilam.

Bulstrode, 1st Oct., 1775.

I hope Miss Sparrow will not fall into the absurd fashion of y^e *wasp-waisted* ladies. Dr. Pringle declares he has had four of his patients *martyrs* to that folly (indeed *wickedness*), and when they were open'd it was evident that their *deaths* were occasioned by *strait laceing*, and it is said Lady Mary Somerset's *complaints* have been brought on by it, tho' I fear beside that *hers* are constitutional, and the poor Duchess of Beaufort (for she *can feel* for herself) is in a melancholly situation as she apprehends this pretty blossom is fading away like her sisters. It is truly a melancholly story; just on the brink of being as happy as high state and honour could make her, and united to a young man who really bears a good character in these times. I think I should pity him the most if his heart has not been cast in the fashionable mold, and tainted by the vanity and dissipation that reigns; but such whirls of pleasure keep off those tender sensations that a more thinking and rational being would feel most exquisitely; yet Lord Granby is said to be very good-natured and much attached to Lady Mary. The Duchess of Beau^t wants to take her abroad immediately, but Lady Mary won't bear the thoughts of it, tho' I suppose the Marquis would attend her. Dowager Lady Lothian[1] and her daughter Lady Emily

---

[1] "Dowager Lady Lothian." Lady Caroline D'Arcy, only daughter of the Earl of Holdernesse, and widow of William Henry, 4th Marquis of Lothian. She had one son, William John, 5th Marquis of Lothian, and two daughters —Louisa, married to Lord George Lennox, and Amelia Wilhelmina Frances, (called "Lady Emily Kerr,") married, in 1783, to Major-general John Macleod, Director of Artillery at Woolwich.

Ker went away this morning; they have been here ten days; both sensible, lively, and well-bred; Lady Emily not handsome, but altogether a good figure and well fashioned, is very good humoured, and seemed as easy and cheerfull as if engaged with people of her own age. She loves reading, writing, and musick; no turn to any other amusements; has a pretty voice, but it has been *squawlified* by the bad taste of the present performers: how *remote* from *melody!* Pleasant as they were, we are well pleased to be alone and go on with our own routine of employments, which are not all such as amuse everybody. A new acquaintance has been introduced here deeply skilled in the science of moths and butterflies.

[The end of this letter is missing.]

The Dowager-Countess Gower to Mrs. Delany.

Bill Hill, 10th Octr., 75.

I expect and hope to hear Bulstrode has done its part, and quite restor'd d^r Mrs Delany to her health and strength; I have a notion it has great capabillities: and y^t ye D^s of Port^d has also found its good effects, to w^m I desire my best respects, and y^t y^e *increase* of her ffamily may be an *increase* of joy to her; I won't repeat this by writing to her Grace, knowing 'twill be mended by yor report. I was much entertain'd wth ye description of Ffoote's antagonist's[1] coach, yatcht, &c., one knows

---

[1] " Foote's antagonist."—The notorious Duchess of Kingston. Foote wrote a drama, in which he introduced a part called " Lady Kitty Crocodile," intended to ridicule the Duchess. He informed her of it, in the hope of extorting a large bribe for its suppression, but the Duchess took the more effectual and less expensive measure of obtaining the Lord Chamberlain's prohibition of the performance.

not w^t *to name her—alias, alias, alias*; she has ye assurance now to be at Thorsbey. W^ts come of her law-suite and trial? The ladies in general are *all* politicians, 'tis ridiculous to hear 'em talk of America, and *how well* they judge, and *govern it* in *their own* imaginations; 'tis pity they are not taken into ye Privy Council!

I sopose you've seen L—d Chomondeley's[1] epigram, Mr. Garrick's petition to Mr. Stanley, and y^e *Pheiades*. L—y Hyde gave me some of 'em, who has, wth her whole nurssery, been at Durham, to see L—y So. Egerton[2] (who is in her usual way still); they saw every body's house, and vissited both going and returning; among the rest Trentham. L—y H. seem'd to be pleas'd wth ye l—y of ye house[3], but for y l—d, they only said he *"was there."* They brought here only their two eldest sons, were returning from ye West, from vissiting Mr. Hyde's[4] borough (who bestow'd on me some ffranks); 'tis charming to be so lively so long, for they are realy birds of passage.

Poor little Phipps is dead, comonly call'd L—d Mulgrave;[5] I've been told he wrote prittily in *verse*, but I never saw any of his performances.

Mrs Mountagu stays longer in ye countrey y^n her son, to see Mrs Ffountayne; I wish she may not stay too

---

[1] George James, 4th Earl of Cholmondeley, was born in 1749, and in 1815 created Marquis of Cholmondeley.

[2] Lady Anna Sophia Egerton, daughter and coheiress of Henry Grey, Duke of Kent, and wife of the Hon. John Egerton, Bishop of Durham.

[3] Lady Susannah Stewart, daughter of Alexander, 6th Earl of Galloway, and the third wife of Granville, 2nd Earl Gower, who was created Marquis of Stafford in 1786.

[4] The Hon. Thomas Hyde, afterwards 2nd Earl of Clarendon, called "Tommy" by Lady Gower in former letters.

[5] Constantine Phipps, 1st Baron Mulgrave, died Sept. 13th, 1775.

long, for she has many waters to pass, and we seem under ye influence of some very watery planet. She complains much of her eyes, I fear wth reason; her writing shows it.

The cough has been so kind as to leave me long since, as long ago as ye juicy ffruites came in season; my grapes are sweet, and w^th *in* my reach, those *out* of it *shan't sower me*; ye magnolias still bloom, and I'm hôle enough to be pleas'd wth these *rural* ffriends y^t *won't deceive me*. I wish for you to partake of ye sweets, tho' perhaps I wish you ill, having all where you are in higher perfection. Long may health and haṕiness bless ye inhabitants of Bulstrode.

Mrs. Delany to Mrs. Port, of Ilam.

Bulstrode, 15th Oct., 1775.

The folio dated from Matlock was truly welcome, and I feel my obligation the more, as it convinced me that my dearest Mary, " *true as the needle to the pole*," thinks of her A. D. in all places! I am glad you have taken a snatch of Matlock, and think it was well judged after your flutters; for tho' it is a bustle, it is *not* of the wearing nature of anxiety! And *why not dance?* I should have delighted to have seen you *trip it on the light fantastick toe.*

I thank you, my dear *little bird*, for wishing to see me and your little table;[1] they are both ready to receive you

---

[1] This little table matched a little cabinet, in the Editor's possession, made from a design of Mrs. Delany's, and by her orders, for her great-niece (here called her "little bird"). They were of dark wood, inlaid with her favourite pattern of husks and berries in a lighter wood.

M 2

when time and convenient opportunity will permit. I
shall then be reconciled to organs and drums in the
street, under my window; at present they are very
harsh. You say nothing of Miss Sparrow; I suppose
she is pursuing her studies with Mrs. Vrankin, and I
hope will make a good use of her time. Where is Mr.
Edge?

We came here on Wednesday morning, and found
Mr. Lightfoot, and a Mr. Yeates, a brother in philosophy,
who staid till yesterday, and, on Friday morning, came
Lady Weymouth and her 3 eldest daughters, which
enlivens our scene, brilliant as it was before. I don't
know how long they stay, but not long, as Lord Weymouth, who comes to parliament from Longleat, and the
Queen's Majesty will have demands on the little Viscountess.

The Hon. Mrs. Boscawen to Mrs. Delany.

Glan Villa, 18th Oct., 1775.

My dear friend, what is it you tell me? that the
Duchess thought of *me* when she sent her commands *to
Paris?* You will make me proud and vain to have any
place in such a head and heart! yet I don't believe you
will quite disallow my first, natural little wish, that this
precious gift, being so valuable for the giver's sake,
shou'd have been *less so* in gold and exquisite work than
this very fine *jewel* is, for I can hardly call it less; and
such I am sure it is, to be accompany'd with the
assurance of the Duchess's friendship. Tell me, my
dear madam, if you *have seen* her Grace's picture printed

in the St. James's Chronicle ; I have carefully taken a copy of it, for time has not at all alter'd the principal features.

The sketch you gave me of Madame *de* Montagu n'est que trop ressemblante, and much I *fear* that she will *never* be Mrs. Montagu[1] an English woman again ! I wish she would learn by heart her friend, Mrs. Chapone's Chapter of Simplicity, wch surely is a better thing than egotism or boasting, or affectation of any kind ; but how *little temptation* has she to *affect* any thing, when she has *such* natural endowments ! but so it is, and I own I apprehend qu'elle reviendra de ces courses *tout à fait gatée*.

Subscriptions to Dr. Beattie[2] had been better in the omission than in the observance I shall always think, and *if* he does *not* publish (wch his ill health may possibly cause) every body else will think so. One wou'd not "give occasion to the enemies of the Lord to blaspheme ;" and Dr. Beattie, whose character is delicate (if I may so speak), has many enemies, I have heard, among those whom we sh^d think *not* averse to blasphemy, tho' they call it " *Philosophy*."

I send you un quartrain of Ld Lyttelton's to L^y Brown, sent to her but a little before his death. Mr. Leveson sent them to his wife, having heard them repeated at Mount Edgcumbe, where he seems to have taken up his very pleasant residence for several days, during the entertainment and reception (wch was magnificent and

---

[1] Mrs. Montagu (Elizabeth Robinson).

[2] Mrs. Montagu was the warm friend and patroness of Dr. Beattie, and to her he dedicated the first collected edition of his poems.

elegant) of the Duke and Duchess of Northumberland,[1]
(also Mr. Bowlby and Lady Mary,[2] who came with their
Graces to Mount Edgcumbe,) going to their newly pur-
chas'd seat in Cornwall (Werrington). L[d] and Lady
Algernon Percy[3] (to whom *it is said* they have *given it*)
did *not* come with them, but went to Lon[n] from Cornwall,
in order to proceed with all haste to the South of France,
for his lord[p] spits blood. I return you many thanks for
telling me Mrs. Port is well, for it is always most welcome news to me. I was vastly glad to hear of Lady
Weymouth and the 3 graces *in her train* (and whom she
is training) were at Bulstrode. They must have given
and receiv'd much pleasure. My excellent friend, Mrs.
Walsingham, will certainly breakfast with you the very
first opportunity she has, having too much taste and
good sense to lose any opportunity of enjoying such
society and conversation. I have heard nothing from
America since the 18th of Aug[st]; the rigours of winter,
added to all the misery that was there before, is bitter to
think of, and I will not speak of this sad subject to you
who have so much compassion. Indeed it is high time I
should take my leave. Lady Gower may indeed despair of the barony (long since surely) but I do *not* think
she cares much about it. I have thought her spirits
much sunk since her loss of Lady Leicester, and to you

---

[1] Sir Hugh Smithson, Bart., married Lady Elizabeth Seymour, only child
of Algernon, Duke of Somerset, and in 1766 was created Earl Percy and
Duke of Northumberland. The Duchess died, Dec. 5, 1776.

[2] Lady Mary Brudenell, second daughter of George, 3rd Earl of Cardigan,
married, first, Richard Powys, Esq., second, Thomas Boulby, Esq.

[3] Lord Algernon Percy, second son of Hugh Smithson, Duke of Northumber-
land, married, June 8, 1775, Isabella, daughter of Peter Burrell, Esq., of
Beckenham. On his father's death, in 1786, he succeeded to the Barony of
Lovaine, and in 1790 was created Earl of Beverley.

and me all these long evenings alone, listening to the
wind and the rain, wou'd not be the way to raise them.
It is now many weeks since she has resided *quite alone*
in her lonely mansion in the forest, and will be many
months, I believe, before she comes out of her solitude ;
for I understood she did not mean to come to Lon^n till
towards the spring, if at all ; but if this was a resolution,
I hope it will be *rescinded.* I cannot think her present
life is good for her in any respect (but that I shou'd
decide upon it *she* wou'd think a little impertinent I
believe). I am sure my best wishes attend her.

Your little cousin, John Leveson Gower, gains upon
me every day, tho' I *don't intend* to admit him into my
heart, I can tell him. Alas! that is too dearly paid for
very often! His mother and I talk of you, my dear
madam, and indeed are much y^r humble servants. Present my gratefull respects to the Duchess, and let me
know, if you please, if you go to London next week.
Once more adieu! God keep you in health.

Mrs. Delany to Mrs. Port, of Ilam.

Bulstrode, 23rd Oct., 1775.

I am sorry I had not given orders sooner for the
spermaceti candles. I will write to Mr. Mark Fair, at
Hull; for *work and read^g* I love *short candles,* for meals
long ones. I am afraid the late rains and short'ning days
will prevent your going to your agreable friend, Mrs.
Joddrel, which I am sorry for ; the conversation of those
we know to be worthy as well as ingenious is very delightful and rare.

I have of late been inform'd of some transactions of

your new neighbour, that obliges me to repeat my caution: an artful unprincipled man is a very dangerous animal; but when one *knows that* to be the case it is easy to keep a *due distance* and yet be civil. I know you will forgive me, and take it in yᵉ right light. *He* has been the ruin of many that he has laid snares for: but I will say no more on this chapter, for a word to the wise is sufficient.

Lady Weymouth and her three eldest daughters left us on Wednesday, all parties sorry to part; but her lord and her royal mistress expected her that day: to her succeeded Lady Bute and her two daughters, Lady Caroline[1] and Lady Louisa Stuart;[2] *nobody* is more agreable in conversation than Lady Bute, her natural and improved good sense and knowledge of the world is a never failing fund when she has spirits to exert her talents, which is not always the case. Lady Caroline is a *genius* in painting and musick, and has made a great progress in both; she has a clear sweet voice, under good managemᵗ, and *less* of the *fashionable yell* than most of her contemporary's; she is extremely good-humoured and sensible, but is one in whom many pleasing accomplishments are a little hurt by an awkward habit: she has *no affectation*, but a *trick* of a laugh at whatever is said or that she says herself. I should not mention this, but as it has proceeded from want of attention in her training up, which makes it *so necessary* to be watchfull from infancy, and check in time any propensity to tricks.

---

[1] Lady Caroline Stuart, 5th daughter of John, Earl of Bute, married, 1st Jan., 1778, the Earl of Portarlington.

[2] Lady Louisa Stuart, the youngest daughter of John, Earl of Bute, died unmarried, 4th Aug., 1851.

I think *my sweet bird* very free at present, if she has left off her little bashful way of lifting up her shoulders and elbows; but she has no odd tricks which she *can* learn *from you*, wch is a matter of much consequence.

The Hon. Mrs. Boscawen to Mrs. Delany.

Glan Villa, 1st Nov., 1775.

Certainly, my dear madam, I should, as you suspect, have sent you not only a civil dun, but indeed a very anxious one (for I have heard that you have not been well) if I had not been totally engross'd by a distress which now, I praise God, begins to subside. Last week Mrs. Leveson and I went to Lon^{n} to see the Duke of Beaufort, and others of our friends whom the Parlia^{t} call'd together : there it was that enquiring after Bulstrode I learnt that you had been indisposed. I went to y^{r} house and spoke to y^{r} maid, but she only told me that you were well at Bulstrode. I found she had not heard lately; so I promis'd myself I wou'd write to you by Saturday's post to enquire; but alas! on that day we were sent for hither to the child,[1] who had been sud-denly seiz'd with a convulsion fit. Luckily an eminent physician, Dr. Garrow of Barnet, was at dinner in this village at the opposite house, so that the child was instantaneously assisted, and four of his poor teeth were lanc'd before he was out of his fit; the doctor remained with us, and when we arriv'd the child was reliev'd and

---

[1] John Leveson, afterwards Gen. Leveson, father of John Leveson Gower, of Bill Hill, Berkshire, Esq. (1860.)

asleep. Next day he had another fit, w[ch] I was able to conceal from his mother, who, tho' she has suffered much, will not I hope be hurt by this distress. On Monday the child began to amend and his high fever to abate (Sunday he was let blood by a leech) ; since that time he seems gradually advancing towards a recovery, I thank God, but it is interrupted by grievous pains of his teeth, so that it will be a work of time ; but as he is a brave strong fellow, I trust he will struggle thro' all these sufferings. Tell me how you do, my dear madam, and whether you are quite recover'd of the indisposition w[ch] you had when the Lady Stewarts[1] went to Windsor, and w[ch] they spoke of to Mrs. Wals. Did you flatter yourself that writing me so delightful a letter as that I receiv'd to-day, and extending it to 5 sides, as if you wou'd imitate *my character* (while y[r] own is inimitable)— did you flatter yourself, my good friend, that I sh[d] never once miss the chapter of " Health " w[ch] is totally pass'd over in silence tho' so important to me. This is a question that I must have answer'd, my dear madam, there- fore I will depend upon the favour of another letter, not of 5 sides, but of 5 lines, just to speak of y[r] health as it is. What satisfaction will it give me if it be as I wish it ! Have you not pity'd poor Lady Sussex,[2] my dear madam ? She has been often at this village with her sister (Mrs. Durell) of whom I have enquired after her health, and have had a very bad account, her agonies

---

[1] " *The Lady Stuarts*," the daughters of the Earl and Countess of Bute.

[2] Henry Yelverton, 3rd Earl of Sussex, was twice married ; first to Hester, daughter of John Hall, of Mansfield Wood-house, Notts, and secondly to Mary, daughter of John Vaughan, of Bristol, Esq. No dates of these marriages are given by Burke, but as there were no children by the second, the Lady Sussex here alluded to must have been the first wife.

having been great. My lord has made a will wch cuts off this ungratefull child with a shilling, but it is to be hop'd he will live to cancel it and forgive her; but it must be a very bad child I sh^d fear that can plant a dagger in her parents' breasts in return for all their care and tenderness: *such* a *child too!* The boldness amazes me. She was 16 last June! Lieut. Gould,[1] her husband, is the same young man who was wounded and taken prisoner in ye first action with the Americans; he came over after ye 2^d (being exchang'd) and came to me at my son's desire to bring his letters and assure me of his safety, he and my boy being in the same regi^t. Gould is not a soldier of fortune, but has a small estate in Nottinghamshire in possession, his father being lately dead. One of his sisters is marry'd to Lady Sussex's bro^r, *from whence* I suppose this unhappy connection arose; but all this is *better* known to the Duchess Dow^r of Portland, the Lady of Welbeck, &c., &c.

Mrs. Montagu you know never got further than Canterbury, and return'd ill to her own home, where she will remain this winter. I did not see her when I was in town, but was going to her in consequence of her desire, when I was sent for to our dear child.

Mrs. Leveson is a little uneasy about Lady Gower, not having had any answer to her two last letters; she has therefore not yet told her of the child's illness, but intends to do it now that all apprehensions of danger are over, thank God! Little guessing that any were so

---

[1] Barbara, the only surviving child of Henry Yelverton, 3rd and last Earl of Sussex, married, Oct. 27, 1775, Lieut. Edward Thornton Gould. Their son succeeded his grandfather, the Earl of Sussex, in the Barony of Grey de Ruthyn. Lady Barbara died before her father.

near, we spent one very pleasant evening in London
with Lady Edgcumbe and Mrs. Walsingham, *both* in
high song! The Duchess of Beaufort is now at Stoke,
waiting upon the Duchess Dow[r], to whom she carries
her two eldest dau[rs], having last week carry'd her two
eldest sons: for her Grace *will not* come to Badminton.
The marriage[1] will bring my daughter to London I hope.
I doubt if I shall return with her as has been proposed;
y[r] *cousins* I think want me most, at least such is the
present appearance. I know not when we shall remove
to London, but whenever you do, my dear madam, I
shall be very desirous to come and see you; be pleas'd
to tell me therefore, and mean time believe me most
truly most affectionately yours,

F. B.

Mrs. Delany to Mrs. Port, of Ilam.

Bulstrode, 5th ending 6th Nov., 1775.

My thanks for yours of the 28th Oct[r]; it was most
welcome, as it brought me such good intelligence of the
health of Ilam. Has John quite recovered his voice?
and has Mrs. Vrankin still such an ascendant over him
as to *bring him to order?* and saving papa and mama the
trouble of reproof, or the greater trouble of seeing him
refractory. I hope Mrs. V. continues to deserve your
good opinion—always remember me kindly to her; and
has she been able to make Fanny as *tidy* and *observant* as
you wish her to be? *Early wrong* indulgences are

Mary Isabella, youngest daughter of Charles, 4th Duke of Beaufort,
married, Dec. 26, 1775, Charles, Marquis of Granby, who, in 1779, succeeded
his grandfather as 4th Duke of Rutland.

hardly ever rooted out,—a striking lesson to those who have infants to train up, not to neglect or indulge them in humours that are *never* afterwards to be conquered. Nothing is easier (if soon eno' begun) than making a child obedient and humble; nothing so *unsurmountable* as obstinacy and pride when suffered to grow with them; it so *totally* corrupts the heart and *perverts* the understanding so that they grow insensible to the impressions of tenderness or gratitude. They think they have a right to decide and cannot submit to the least controll. If their disposition is violent and passionate they are quarellsome and provoking; if *sulky* they *grow false* and *cunning,* and baffle every intention that means to save them from the evils of the world.

The Hon. Mrs. Boscawen to Mrs. Delany.

Glan Villa, 13th Nov., 1775.

MY DEAR MADAM,

I flatter myself you have no right to any more *influenza,* for I think you was the first in that fashion; if so, how many have follow'd you? better to copy you in anything else—in some of your imitable perfections, and not in the infirmities of a cold and a cough.

The letter which my Lady Duchess was pleased to entrust me with I trusted to nobody, but carried it myself to Mrs. Durell's gate, and I doubt not she has acknowledg'd it, as she call'd upon me next morning to beg I would inform her if Bulstrode was in Bucks, and I advis'd her to direct to her Grace rather at Whitehall.

I saw Lady Sussex's coach in this village to-day; I hope she is better, but her sister told me the shock and affliction had made her extremely ill: every one must pity her. Strange that her daughter alone had *no compassion*; "no bowels" for her parents, nor thought what they must endure. Dame Nature as well as Mrs. Modesty were chas'd away upon this occasion.

My dear madam, you say not a word of removing to London, and I must not say a syllable of wishing for it till a bill of health can be given, and the influenza be spent. I do not much like Mrs. Leveson's going to her pretty south room the day after to-morrow. She expects Mr. Leveson in town this week, he and his *other* wife (the *fair Albion*) being parted. Mrs. Leveson had a letter from Lady Gower to-day.

Mrs. Walsingham has had the influenza at Windsor, and her little girl[1] was also drooping when she wrote to me. I have sent her y^r message.

I purpose to remain here 5 or 6 days after my *company* leaves me (I shall miss them, great and *small*, very much), just to pay my debts and wind up my bottoms, and then settle in winter quarters in Audley Street, wch I know I shall not like so well as this cottage; for tho' the weather has been very bad I seldom fail of a walk or airing, or both, and find business in my garden to plant or remove. I have been *enlarging my borders*, wch sounds well, as in a figurative sense it may mean purchase of lands and increase of demesne; but to tell you the truth it must be understood in the *literal* sense, for my borders are enlarged just 14 inches d'un bout

---

[1] "*Her little girl*."—Charlotte, who succeeded to the Barony of De Ros, and married Lord Henry Fitzgerald. She was mother of the present Lord de Ros, and of Admiral de Ros, now living (1861), of the Countess Cowley, the Hon. Mrs. T. Boyle, Mrs. Broadhurst, and Mrs. Frederick Pare, now living (1861).

jusqu'à l'autre, and being well enrich'd with good mould, have such a profusion of jonquils, ranunculus's, and tulips and hyacinths sett in them that when I have the honour to see you in the month of May, you shall fancy yourself in Flora's own cottage.

T'other day I carry'd Mrs. Leveson to see a (China) tea-tree in blossom at Mr. Lee's at Totteridge,[1] where also the hot-house and green-house pleas'd us extremely. This morning we have been at Hadley to visit Mrs. Smith, but she was in bed with the *influenza*. Mrs. Chapone has had it in London, but is better, so I hear is Mrs. Montague.

Lord Granby has taken Lord Cholmondeley's[2] house in Picadilly, his lordship (with that *unreasonable* long name) being remov'd into his uncle's part of his late legacy.

And now, my dear friend, I know you will be so good to present my congratulations to my Lady Duchess on Lord Weymouth's appointment. Affairs do indeed go on very prosperously in Glostershire. In one of the Duchess of Beaufort's letters I remember these words. " *How much* are *we* obliged to Mrs. Delany and to Mr. Dewes !" I hope her Grace will have an opportunity to express so much by the pleasant side of your fire, when Lady M. Somerset is marry'd ;[3] by that time I conclude (viz., early in the next month) you will be in London. Meantime all health attend you, my dearest madam, and

---

[1] A celebrated nurseryman, who cultivated rare exotic plants.

[2] George James, 4th Earl and 1st Marquis of Cholmondeley.

[3] The Lady Mary Isabella Somerset, youngest daughter of Charles, 4th Duke of Beaufort, married, Dec. 26, 1775, Charles, 4th Duke of Rutland, then Marquis of Granby.

that possest I need not add, " happiness," but I will *allow* your word " *administratress*," and I understand it.

Ever your affectionate faithfull, F. B.

Lord Pitt[1] returned home; why may not my poor boy do so too?

Treat me with a kind little letter after my daughter is gone, that is if you have leisure and inclination: at all events I will write to you when I get to London. Mrs. L. presents her respects to the Duchess and to you.

John Dewes, Esq., to Rev. Mr. Dewes (afterwards Granville), at Calwich, near Ashbourn, Derbyshire.

Welsbourn, 22nd Nov., 1775.

DEAR JOHN,

I had yo[r] lr̃e of the 6th inst., and was very glad to hear that you and yo[r] bro[r] and the rest of our Staffordshire ffrends were well, which is the chief I have now to say to you. We go on here much in the old way, and I think are as well as usuall. Mr. Venour is just returned from London, says he saw Court there very well; he called on young Hewit at Oxford, both as he went and as he return'd, and found him very ill of a violent ffever both times, and seems to doubt much of his recovery.

I am sorry to hear of the death of poor Gregson. I gave him a shilling when I was last at Ilam, upon condition of his keeping it to entertain himself with at

---

[1] John, afterwards 2nd Earl of Chatham.

Xmas, which he promised to do, so if he kept his word he lost his money!

I am sorry cock shooting is so bad with you; as I never go myself, nor converse with those who do so, I know little how it goes on here.

Pray tell Ffrank I recẽd his letter of the 13ᵗʰ inst., and am very sorry to hear my young horse is so·ill, but hope he is got well again before now, as he seemed to think him a little better than he had been ; and as to his comeing home, as he waits for the recovery of the horse, I shall not expect him till I see him. Mr. Lucy's company left him a few days agoe. Mr. Aylworth is come and is very well. I sent compliments to him, but have not yet seen him, which is all I have to say at present, but that I am (with love to Bernard)

Yʳ mᵗ affectionate ffaʳ,

J. D.

You may tell Ffrank that his wife is very well.

The Hon. Mrs. Boscawen to Mrs. Delany.

Audley Street, yᵉ 25ᵗʰ Nov., 1775.

Yes, indeed, my dear madam, I have thought it a very long time since I had the satisfaction to hear from you, and therefore I went yesterday a pilgrimage to yʳ house. The sight of the *dear round window*[1] made me break my word ; for whereas I had promised I would *not* wish you in town for fear of the influenza, I have certainly been guilty of that wish every afternoon since I came, over and above the morning in which I visited your

---

[1] A painted glass window in Mrs. Delany's house in St. James's Place, which there is reason to believe was brought from Delville.

maid and I had a conference with her. I ventured to tell y^r friend in Hanover Square that you are well. I sat with her above an hour this evening, a very pleasant hour of conversation with her amiable son (who nurses her most tenderly I believe), and with Mr. Geo. Montagu, who was in high song. To tell you that Mrs. Montagu *is well* I certainly *cannot!* she has a cough, and has had this fashionable cold very severely, as it affected her breath, but she is much better. She beg'd me to call upon her frequently, wch is a sign of good spirits. I hope to give you a still better acc^t the next visit I make, and it shall not be long first. I hope L^y Andover is well. We call'd at her door this evening to inquire, but of course did not go in so soon after her arrival. I have also been to visit Mrs. Montagu, Hill Street, only L^y Townshend [1] was there, and in her best manner very chatty. Y^r cousin, Mr. Leveson, is come to town, and looks mighty well: his lady wife was of my visiting party to-night, and thought Mrs. Montagu better than when she was in Han. Square ten days ago to wait on her. I want to tell you some news, but know none. Ld Granby's [2] marriage rather delay'd by L^y Mary's having the influenza ; doubtfull if it will happen before Christmas ! Mr. Foley's [3] marriage determined ; that you know better than I can tell you. L^d and L^y Edgcumbe went from hence t'other night to a very par-

---

[1] Anne, daughter and coheiress of Sir William Montgomery, Bart., second wife of George, 4th Viscount Townshend, created Marquis Townshend in 1787.

[2] Charles, Marquis of Granby, afterwards 4th Duke of Rutland, married, Dec. 26, 1775, Mary Isabella, daughter of Charles, 4th Duke of Beaufort.

[3] Thomas, afterwards 2nd Lord Foley, married, March 15, 1776, Henrietta, daughter of William, 2nd Earl of Harrington.

ticular entertain[mt] at the French ambass[r]. A gentleman (for *so* he is it seems) spoke and acted a French tragedy so perfectly that all his audience wept, and he himself, se blessa de son propre epée, and wept also when he came to the lady's distress, wch he represented most pathetically, and in a *female* voice, for he chang'd his tones so that a blind person would have concluded there had been the whole dramatis personæ. Adieu, my dear madam. I will write ag[n] soon, and not send such a shabby scrap with the seal in a corner; my next shall go down to Whitehall. I get no influenza, being (as you know) tough and hardy. My best respects wait on the Duchess. Adieu, my dear friend.

Most faithfully yours,
F. B.

Mr. Fit*zpatriot* (as L[d] Edg. calls him) spoke well.

The Hon. Mrs. Boscawen to Mrs. Delany.

Audley Street, y[e] 2nd Dec., 1775.

Two such summer days as yesterday and this fair morning I cannot see without thinking of my dear and honour'd friends at Bulstrode, where I reckon they are enjoy'd in perfection.

My dear madam, I saw many of your friends last night, but before I give an account of my *gaieties,* w[ch] are not common, I will speak of my business lest I shou'd forget it, for indeed I have been already once reminded of it. Mr. Southwell asked me last week if I wou'd apply for a Glostershire vote. I take it to be Mr. Levers who is a freeholder; if not, it is some other of

her Grace's upper servants; but I am pretty sure it is
Mr. Lever, and to-day Mr. Southwell came to know if
I had comply'd with his request, and with what success?
for I understand they are going to form their lists,
Berkeley and Chester being *more vehement than ever!*
Wou'd you believe, my dear madam, that it is reckon'd
£30,000 will be spent upon this contest. Mr. Southwell
added that there must be subscript^{ns}, for if Mr. Chester
spent £10,000 of his own it must be reckon'd very
handsome. For my part I reckon it *very foolish*—mais
chacun à leur gré—we see wise and respectable personages too often engage in such costly struggles. I
know, my dear madam, you will be so good (with his
gracious sovereign's license and protection) to ask Mr.
Levers if he will give his vote to Mr. Chester, and enable
me to make answer to my employers.

I dare say Mrs. Montagu little suspects that I told
her a fib and did not write on Thursday; but you must
know, my dear friend, that I went out of town to my
cottage in the morning, and there I found so much to
do, so many wallflowers to plant, with one nonsense and
another (being alone), that I did not get home till ½ past
4. By that time my dau^r was come to dine with me;
and as soon as we had had a little chat (pour la digestion)
Mr. and Mrs. Soame Jenyns[1] came on an early visit
previous to their evening party of quadrille. I did not
chuse to be deny'd *to them,* and these excellent *evergreens*

---

[1] Soame Jenyns, of Bottesham Hall, M.P. for Cambridgeshire, was the
only son of Sir Roger Jenyns. He was born in 1704, and twice married,
but died without children, Dec. 18, 1787: he was distinguished as a scholar
and a wit. Sarah Jenyns, the celebrated Duchess of Marlborough, was of this
family.

look perfectly well, rather younger than older, I think, nor has any influenza presum'd to visit them. By the time they departed *my drum* began to arrive, for I had a whist-party consisting of Edgcumbes, Southwells, and two or three more friends, who staid longer than the last bell tingled, so that you see why I did not write on Thursday. I sh^d not wonder if you were to add, "O, time enough in all conscience," for this dull epistle may be waited for with *great patience.* I wish I cou'd enliven it with giving you any idea of Monsr Tessier,[1] but that is impossible. I had the favour to be invited as his audience last night at my neighbour's Mad^e l'Envoyée de Portugal. There was Lady Holderness, Lady Bute (who looks very well), Lady Jerningham (also well), les dames du corps diplomatique, L^y D. Thompson, Mrs. Howard and I ; le Comte Orloff,[2] his height *Patagonian*, his diamonds *Mogulian*, their quantity *immense indeed!* A Prince de Holstein (between whom and C. Orloff there

---

[1] Horace Walpole, writing to the Countess of Ossory, Nov. 23rd, 1775, says—"On Sunday night I was singularly entertained at Monsr de Guinés', who gave a vast supper to the Prince of Hesse, and the goddesses most in fashion, as the Duchess of Devonshire, Lady Sefton, &c. We were twenty-eight at supper ; but before it, *a Monsieur Tessier*, of whom I have heard much in France, acted an entire play of ten characters, and varied his voice, and countenance, and manner, for each so perfectly, that he did not name the persons that spoke, nor was it necessary. I cannot decide to which part he did most justice, but I would go to the play every night if I could see it so acted." Monsr Le Tessier was a native of Lyons. Walpole also says—"Madame Pinto came to see my house t'other day, and told me in Portughée-French that '*pou*tetre she detourned me from making des petits vers.' I hate to have a scrap of reputation, and had rather anybody thought I could not write my name, unless all Dame Pintos had the simplicity of Balzac's neighbour, who assured him he had a profound respect for him and *messieurs ses livres.*"

[2] From the description given by Mrs. Boscawen of the Count's gigantic stature, this would appear to have been Alexis Orloff, who strangled the Emperor Peter III. Alexis was the brother of Gregory Orloff, Prime Minister and favourite of the Empress Catherine II. There were three other brothers.

is not, I have heard, much love lost or found), but he is a very agreeable sensible young man I fancy, at least he appear'd to me so, as he talk'd to Madame de Pinto (our hostess), the Prince of Hesse,[1] and most of the foreigners. Not Mons[r] de Guines, for he has had twice at his house this extraordinary entertainment, once tragedy and once comedy. Mad[e] Pinto told me it w[d] be tragedy last night, she believed, but on y[e] contrary it was le Mariage de Julie, a very agreeable comedy, full of satire, full of wit and pleasantry, and above all most entertaining and surprising, from the gestures and tones of the performer (I cannot call him reader, as he seldom look'd at a book of the play that lay before him) ; and of these I shall say nothing but that it greatly exceeded my expectation, w[ch] was, however, greatly rais'd by L[d] and Lady Edgcumbe's description, who had seen the same piece at Mons[r] de Guisnes.

I shall not pretend to tell you any publick news if I heard any, as you wou'd probably be much better inform'd. L[y] Blandford within these two days is said to be much better, and her bone not so unlikely to unite as at first it appeared to be. I send you a copy of Mrs. Walsingham's charming *vision*. I sh[d] give you an argument, wch is that speaking of an indiscreet marriage of a père de famille, she said, "I wonder how long the years of discretion last. I figure to myself they are like a hill, wch when you atchieve y[u] may soon go down on the other side, and if you do the descent will be steeper the lower you descend." This (à peu prés) was her metaphor,

---

[1] Frederick, Landgrave of Hesse Cassel, then the widower of the Princess Mary of England, fourth daughter of King George II.

wch having commended she sent it me drawn out in this agreeable form. I shall have it again at y^r leisure. Mrs. Montagu, Hill Str. I have not seen lately, when I did she seem'd pretty well. You see I have got a grande envelope that the post-office clerks may not again read mes sornaises.

Your sincere friend,
And obliged serv,^t
F. BOSCAWEN.

P. S.—I have not seen " *the Sprinkler*," nor did I know my bro^r Admiral[1] was a *poet*. That ever the correspondents, was hinted to be L^d L^t. is a wicked bookseller's trick to make it sell, and deserves to be punish'd. I once began the Female Quixote, but did not finish, with my cousin Miss Glanville or Miss Evelyn, I forget which (both equally my name wch I *never lent*). Y^r cousins are well, only little John still at times tormented with teeth, but his father is grown so fat and looks so well that I was surprised to hear t'other day that he intended to go to Bath. I know not when Mr. Southwell[2] will be declared *Clifford*, or Mr. G. Pitt *Morley*; but I have heard that 6 other patents are fill'd up (not sign'd), Hawke, Amherst, Rider, Polwarth, Cust, ye 6th perhaps is *Mr. Foley*, but he was not named by my informant.

---

[1] The Hon. John Forbes, Admiral of the Fleet and a General of Marines, brother to George, 4th Earl of Granard.

[2] In 1776 the abeyance consequent on Lady Leicester's death was terminated by the Royal assignment of the Barony of De Clifford to Edward Southwell, Esq., whose mother was the eldest daughter of Catherine, Lady Sondes, the eldest sister of Lady Leicester and the Countess Gower.

The Hon. Mrs. Boscawen to Mrs. Delany.

Audley Street, Dec. 6, 1775.

I return you thanks, my dear madam, for your early announcing to me the grant of our petition, which I as speedily made known to Mr. Southwell, who was going to the Duke of Beaufort at Blandford Park to hunt. But as both these gentlemen are at this present writing still more keen for *votes* than for *foxes*, I know they will think themselves much oblig'd to the Duchess of Portland for her powerfull assistance, and to Mr. Levers for the promise of his vote. There has been an acharnement in this canvass rather illiberal (but perhaps you will say it is always so). Mr. Berkeley's friends began, by casting reflections *upon the memory* of Lord Botetourt,[1] wch surely is *very unworthy*. The Duchess of Beaufort took a copy of it and sent it me. I have just found it (putting a drawer to rights) with ye printed answer; I shall enclose them both as to a Glostershire lady, our good friend and ally; you will burn them, but my dear madam, what you will not burn is some stanzas of Mr. Jenyns's, wch I have the merit to have *caus'd*. He and I were talking of Dr. Tucker's[2] last pamphlet,

---

[1] Henry, 5th Duke of Beaufort, Mrs. Boscawen's son-in-law, was the maternal nephew of Norborne Berkeley, Baron de Bottetourt; which Barony his mother, the Dowager Duchess, inherited from her brother, who, according to Burke's "Extinct Peerage," died in 1776.

[2] There was, in the last century, more than one writer named Tucker. The one here alluded to was doubtless Josiah Tucker, D.D., a Welshman, born at Laugharn, in Caermarthenshire, in the year 1712. He proceeded from the grammar school at Ruthin to Jesus College, Oxford, where he graduated. He took orders and became Chaplain to the celebrated Bishop Butler and a

and of his plan to cast off ye Americans. Mr. Jenyns said he was a proselite to it, and I answer'd that it seem'd to resemble a piece of mechanism I had heard of, introduc'd in the make of a carriage, that if y^r horses are unruly and kick, you may by means of a spring pull up a peg or plug, and off goes the fore-carriage, horses, and all. Mr. Jenyns said my metaphor was admirable, he lik'd it mightily. I answer'd that he cou'd with great ease make an epigram of it. Yesterday he sent me the enclos'd verses in an envelope, which said that he "return'd the child to its true mother, that it was a pretty child, and ought to have had a more elegant mantle." But I believe you will think the mantle is pretty too.

My dear madam, I do not know a word of news that can amuse you. I am afraid Sir Charles Saunders is dying, and that is ill news. You know perhaps that Mr. Foley[1] had the galantry to cross the sea to meet Lady Hariet Stanhope at Calais; Lady Sefton went no farther than Dover; all are returned safe, and your cousins are well, except y^e *small* man and his *great teeth.* Good morning to you, my dear madam; Mrs. Dunbar[2]

Prebendary of Bristol Cathedral. In 1758 he was appointed to the Deanery of Gloucester. Through a long course of years he published various political pamphlets and theological works. Between the years 1773 and 1777, he published several tracts on the American war. He was beloved, respected, and admired, and died in 1799.

[1] Mr. T. Foley married, March 15, 1776, Henrietta, fourth daughter of William, 2nd Earl of Harrington. On the 18th Nov., 1777, he succeeded his father as 2nd Baron Foley.

[2] Maria, daughter of the Rev. Mr. Hamilton, of Monaghan, Ireland, and wife of George Dunbar, Esq., who, in the year 1781, succeeded to his father's baronetcy.

arrives, so does Lady Edgcumbe. I shall have time only
to say

Ever yours
F. Boscawen.

The Dowager-Countess Gower to Mrs. Delany.

Bill Hill, 8th Dec^r., 75.

I sopose ye cold you complain'd of was ye fashionable
one, was glad to hear it lasted not long. Here I'm so
out of ye world and beyond all reach of ffashion, y^t I
and all belonging to me have hithertoo escap'd; poor
Mrs. Mountagu has not, she has been extreamly ill, for
this reigning disorder has affected her in ye highest
degree; I'm now inform'd she is much better.

I'm always hapy to see ye D^s of Port^d here, or anywhere; wish I c^d do such things as once rais'd yor
apprehensions, but y^t tyrant *Time*, &c., has dwindled
me into being fit for nothing but home.

I'm surpriz'd at ye Admiral's [1] poetick genious coming
to him *so late*,—his great ffortune, and y^e " Sprinkler "
must have had violent effects; tho' I know *not* w^t y^e
" *Sprinkler* " is? ye poem seems to have humour. By
ye news papers all London seems to be in a flame; w^n I
was last there for a few days, *all* ye ladies *I saw* knew
how to govern America better y^n ye K—g, Council, or
Parliam^t; 'tis wonderfull, w^t pains some take to make
y^{m}selves ridiculous. I'm inform'd you pass yor Xmas at
Bullstrode. I believe I shall eat my pye in London, tho'
against my inclination and apetite, for I wish not to
change place.

---

[1] The Hon. John Forbes, Admiral of the Fleet, and a General of Marines,
second son of George, 3rd Earl of Granard.

Where're I am shall always be d^r Mrs. Delany's most faithfull

M. GOWER.

My best respects and good wishes always attend ye D^{ss} of Portland.

The Hon. Mrs. Boscawen to Mrs. Delany.

Dec. 14, 1775.

My business, as you will learn, my dear madam, is with her Grace, but I cannot make use of your envelope without addressing a little word to you, and telling you that last night I saw your friend, Mrs. Montagu, who really seems quite hearty. She longs for y^r arrival. Her son was with her, and he told me that Mr. H. Walpole having ask'd Mr. Mason where the Duchess of Portland and Mrs. Delany were, the latter answer'd, *"in the country, fox-hunting."* Whether this is a poetical license or no in our great poet, you best can tell. I have related exactly what I was told. Afterwards I went to Mrs. Vesey, where there *were fine ladies indeed!* Dss of Devonshire, L^y Jersey, L^y Claremont, Mrs. Crew, &c. I got near Mrs. Walsingham and Lord Edgcumbe, Mrs. Dashwood was there and look'd very well.

I am interrupted, my dear madam, and expect company at dinner, so that I will only add my best wishes, and assure you that I am ever

Y^{rs} most affectionately

F. B.

Mrs. Delany to Mrs. Port, of Ilam.

St. James's Place, 21st Dec., 1775.

MY DEAREST MARY,

No Mr. Port—no Bernard!—By my letter from
Mr. P. last received, I did not much expect him, as he
seemed not quite fixed, and when he is, I suppose I shall
know the day. I came to town on Monday, a day or
two sooner than I intended. I *must* be *in the fashion* in
my old age, 'tis the vice of the times ; and have a little
of the "*influenza*," and I thought it best to advise with
those I was used to, which made the dear Duchess easy,
tho' she could not come with me, as her house was not
ready. I thank God, I am now only a little weak, all
feverishness is gone, and have no other prescription
given to me but quiet and diet, and *no physic.* Yesterday I was surprised with our dear Duchess's calling here
between 5 and 6, in her way to Whitehall, as I did not
expect her till to morrow. But alas, she must submit to
the general enemy. She was *blooded yesterday,* and they
send me word she had some sleep, and is better to-day ;
I shall hear again before I seal my letter, and will let
you know. I have seen Lady Bute, Lady Andover, and
Miss Fanny, Mrs. Dashwood, Mrs. Boscawen, Mrs.
Leveson, Lord Guilford; by seeing so much company,
you may be assured I am pretty well. My good little
friend in Hanover Square is confined with the gout, and
no likelyhood of our meeting soon, for I will not venture out till the fogs are dispersed. I am a little impatient to hear how you have managed about F. I
suppose you continue in the same scheme, it will not be
till after Xtmass. Much is said about the Dss of King-

ston s tryal, which she will not stand if she can help it.
But everybody wishes she may have her due. They say
Lord Lytelton [1] is so charmed with the cleverness of Mrs.
Rudd [2] (*adores a mind so like his own*) that they say he
has adopted her as his mistress—and what mischief may
not *two* such *heads* and *two* such *hearts* do? It is frightful to think of. That human creatures should be so
depraved! Mr. T. Foley and Lady H. Stanhope are as
fond as doves (happy if as innocent); did I tell you Mr.
Foley pays his debts, settles £3,000 per annum in
present, and makes a settlement after his death of
£10,000 a year. I hear of nothing but balls and high
heads—*so enormous* that nobody can sit upright in their
coaches, but *stoop forward* as if they had got the children's *chollick*. Surely there is an influenza of the *brain*,
which must account for the present vagaries, and be
some excuse. Lady Weymouth has just been here from
Whitehall, and says the Dss is much better.

---

[1] Thomas, 2nd Lord Lyttelton. He succeeded his father in 1773, and died
27th Nov., 1779.

[2] Mrs. Margaret Caroline Rudd. Horace Walpole, writing in April, 1775,
says—" The town is very busy about a history of two Perreau's and a Mrs.
Rudd, who are likely to be hanged for *mi*sapplying their ingenuity. They
drew bills, instead of rising from the pillory to pensions, by coining anecdotes
against the author and friends of the Revolution. As Mrs. Rudd has turned
evidence, I suppose as soon as her husband is executed, she will have eight
hundred a year to educate her children." Dec. 17, 1775, he says again—
" Mrs. Margaret Caroline Rudd's history would make as large a volume as
Madame de Kingston's. She sent her lawyer a brief of which he could not
make head or tail. He went to her for one more clear: ' And do you imagine,'
said she, ' that I will trust you, or any attorney in England, with the truth of
my story? Take your brief, meet me in the Old Bailey, and I will ask you
the necessary questions.' At her trial she *did* write sixty notes to him, with
such artful interrogatories that she was acquitted, and the whole court shouted
with applause." Dec. 20, 1775, Walpole again writes—" They say Mrs. Rudd
has been at the play in Lord Lyttelton's chariot. If the Duchess is acquitted
I suppose he will take her, to show he is convinced of *her* virtue *also*, and
wronged her innocence."

Mrs. Ravaud to Mrs. Delany.

Bath, Dec. ye 22nd.

My dear A. D, some people's friendship, like *Bath fires*, are extinguish'd if not continually watch'd and stirr'd; not so with ours, it keeps quietly burning without raging in flame and noise; and when sickness or other necessary interruptions of this foolish world will allow us time we set done and enjoy its comfortable warmth with double pleasure. What need then to tire you or myself with impertinent excuses, nor will I importune with lamentations at our not meeting in London, were we frequently went in a morning while we were at Lady Westmoreland's; but shall only inform you, in the good John Trot style, that we are (thank God) very well at this present writing, hoping that you are so too, with all your appurtenances; for you really have so many strings to your bow, *alias your heart*, that 'tis most wonderful if they all keep in order. From Lyme I can give a good account, not from Mrs. Sandford (she has renounced *all* correspondence with *this place*,) but from Master Daniel, who says his mama is pretty well, he and his brother quite so.

How does this weather agree with you, and with that Duchesse, si aimable et si bien aimée? This severity is not usual before Xtmass, but we must not complain after the very fine season we had last autumn. Mrs. Lambard has just left us, much improved by the Bath waters; she is not esteemed a very wise *head*, but I that *esteem hearts* as the *first* object in the human composition, respect her for her *grateful* manner of speaking of the Dut. of Portland; 'tis certainly due to her Grace, but

who, my dear madam, pays *their debts?* especially such
as those which are more properly debts of honour
than such as are usually call'd so. Ma Kitty court *les
Champs*, je n'ose par bienseance dire *les rues*, mais ce que
j'ose hasarder c'est de vous assurer, qu'elle unit ces vœux
aux miennes, non seulement pour tous les biens de cette
vie passagere, mais pour celles d'un monde, et d'un bon-
heur qui ne finira jamais ; nous tacherons d'etre digne
de telle bonne compagnie, et puisque le tems ne nous
veut pas fournir l'occasion de nous revoir, nous espére-
rons en l'eternité ; en attendant, ma chère tante peut-
être que le chapitre des accidens, me donnera le grand
plaisir de vous confirmer en propre personne, que je
suis votre, &c. &c.

. M. M. R.

Mrs. Delany to Mrs. Port, of Ilam.

Dec. 26th, 1775.

Our dear amiable Dss has been very ill with the influenza, wch brought on her rheumatism and cramps. The
account was better last night, and they hoped she would
mend fast. It is sad not to be able to see her, but if I
attempted it, it would only hurry her spirits, and at
pres^{t}, indeed, she is not allowed to see anybody but
Lady Weymouth, who is so good as to send or call on
me twice a day to tell me how she is. And now I must
touch again upon the F——ds : *his* art and falshood is
most dangerous when he meets with those that are free
from those bad qualities. His conduct has been so bad
that he is shunn'd even by sharpers ; and he is so quarrel-
some and easily affronted that nobody knows when he

may break out, even in civilized company. I would ask no questions about him of B., but it would mortify me saddly if John has encouraged any acquaintance, for as a clergyman he would be a very improper companion indeed. My hope is, that as he (F.) is quite blown upon, and only subsists by artifice, that he will soon quit ye neighbourhood. It is difficult to withdraw an acquaintance that by appearing so agreable has advanced so fast, and if I did not go upon sure grounds I shou'd certainly have avoided the subject.

I am glad Mrs. Savage has been with you. How valuable is an honest heart! and such only are worthy of my dearest Mary.

The pheasants, I am sure are well bestow'd, and I hope will enjoy their charming situation, and increase and multiply. Tho' I hope to gain by it, I shall be sorry when you lose Mr. Marsh; but you have such a delightful charge at home to employ y^r time that I hope, with the company of Miss Mead, reading, and musick of y^r own sweet fingers, it will not lye heavy on your hands nor be filled up disagreably. Make my kind wishes and complim^ts acceptable to all that contribute to your happiness. Adieu.

I had a letter lately from Mrs. Ravaud.

Mrs. Viney is coming to London with Lady Hope, who is *returning* to the Indians.

Lord Granby and Lady Mary Somerset are married this day, and go immediately out of town till ye birthday.

I hear a charming account of Lady Willoughby.

CHAPTER XXV.

1776—DECEMBER 1777.

Mrs. Delany to Mrs. Port, of Ilam.

St. James's Place, 15th Feb., 1776.

I have huddled over business to come to the letter so strongly tinctured with old maidism. Don't mind it, my dear Mary: it was *cross* and *impertinent;* but suspicion and spleen, and insatiable curiosity, turn everything topsy-turvy, and they hurt themselves in the main more than others. Yet I do not wonder you were *vext* for a moment; but I hope it has vanished with the smoak of the letter. Indeed, our dear Mrs. San^d is a strong contrast to the aforesaid. Her gentle and sensible mind always is ready to *heal* and *not* fester a wound. No one discerns or apprehends more the consequences that may attend particular circumstances, but when unavoidable she makes it her busyness to lessen and not aggravate the cares of a friend, and *that* is friendship. I hope you and Mr. Port will have no reason to repent of the step you have taken; at least you gain a year for farther consideration. Your quotation and observation of Mr. Gray's sentiment very just; in short, compose your thoughts about ye matter, for you had nothing else to do at this juncture than what you have done, and I am sure in everything that can be in her power to do to make you easy you may depend on our friend in Bladud Buildings. Lord Granville[1] *died on Tuesday,* and *with him* the title, *so* the *honours and name of Granville are no more* (except Mrs. B. Gran.[2]), and " so the fashion of the world passeth away !"

> " We read each monument, we sigh ! and while
> We sigh, we sink ; and are what we deplor'd,
> Lamenting or lamented, all our lot."—Dr. Young.

This would be a melancholy reflection *did all end here ;* but to a well-informed and pious mind there *is* a consolation that *blunts all the arrows of adversity,* beside the enjoyment of many blessings to soothe and sustain us in our progress, for which we cannot be too thankfull !

Lord Granville has left his estate to Mr. Thynne for *his life,* and has entail'd it on Lord Weymouth's second son, and a thousand pound to Lady Cath. Hay, which I am glad of.

Last Sunday your bro[rs] dined with me, and in the afternoon the Bishop of Litchfield came. They all dine here to-day (meaning my neph[s] 3) with Doct[r] Ross, and the dearest of duchesses, and *our* dear Mary will not be forgot. The thaw has let loose everybody, and everybody is running everywhere ; eno' to turn one's sober brains ! They are so good as to *take me en passant,* and from eight to ten my little circle is pretty well filled ; et pour faire

---

[1] " The Right Hon. Robert Carteret, 2nd Earl Granville, Viscount Carteret and Bailiff of the Isle of Jersey, died 20th Feb., 1776." As this letter is dated 15th Feb., Lord Granville could not have died 20th, as here announced.

[2] " *Mrs. B. Granville.*"—The Hon. Elizabeth Granville, Lady of the Bedchamber to the Princess of Wales, daughter of George, Lord Lansdowne.

la bonne bouche, my dear Dss stays till they are *all gone!* I am sometimes tired, but on the whole it is good for me, as I cannot read by candle light as much as I used to do. Last night I had Lady Wey., Lady Stam^d, and a short visit from Lady Frances Bulkeley, who came on purpose to enquire after you, which she did most kindly. I had also her Grace of Queens^y, *very droll* about the fashionable heads. She says "they are too bad to look at," and so she "*only* looks at the ladies buckles ;" and " to mortify them for their folly she advises everybody to do the same." What do you think? I am just come from my neighbour Christie's, and have seen the famous Madona and Child painted by Vandyke. It cost 2500 louis d'ors, and they talk now of asking £4000. It is truly a most perfect, beautifull, and agreable picture. The expression of devotion in the Virgin, and dignity with beauty in the Child, are exquisite, but it *is* a large sum.[1]

My spirits have been a good deal affected for my good little friend Mrs. Mon^u, who I think still in a precarious way. She expects the Dean and Mrs. Fountain. Apropos, the ingenious Genealogical Tree was the *invention* and *execution* of Mrs. Fountayne, on purpose for you. All her children got it by heart, and on my saying I thought it would be very usefull she sent it me.

---

[1] Walpole says, 27th Dec., 1775—"If Lord Ossory has a farthing in the world to spare, he may buy a Madonna and Child, by Vandyke, at Christie's, for four thousand guineas, for which I would not give four hundred if I were as rich as General Scott. *It is a fine picture*, but yet I believe Vandyke was the father no more than Joseph."

Mrs. Delany to Mrs. Port, of Ilam.

St. James's Place, 22d Feb., 1776.

May every *joy* and *felicity* that can bless my dearest Mary in this world, and conduct her to *those* that will know no end, attend her in every circumstance of life. Truly my heart is so full of acknowledgements on the return of this day, dear to me on a *double account,* that it is more than I can express; but thro' your hands I convey my sincere congratulations to your dear husband on the happy occasion, with my very affectionate compliments.

Our dear Duchess dines with me to-day, Dr. Ross and Lady Wallingfᵈ. I had asked your brothers to meet them, but by a mistake of the day, and my not mentioning it time enough, they were engaged, but to-morrow they all come to me to celebrate. I have put on *all* my *birthday geer, new white sattin,* best covers on my chairs, and the knotting furniture of my bedchamber, with window-curtain of the same. Tender recollections and warm wishes will supply the place of bonfires and illuminations, an offering more worthy of the occasion than what is prostituted to every (factious) *patriot* unworthily *so-called.* Can any thing in the world more strongly prove the strong political tincture that infects every human mind at present, that even on the most foreign occasions a dash will appear; or why *should I* bring in a *patriot* by head and shoulders? Indeed, my dearest Mary, *I am sick* of the mischiefs of politicks. They tear asunder the very vitals of friendship; set familys and friends at variance; and, to compleat our ruin, *vice and extravagance knows no bounds.* Happy, truly happy! are they that are out of the way of this contagious influenza, whose lot is fallen into such a situation as to preserve their rational faculties by a peaceable and innocent enjoyment of that " *state of life to which it hath pleased God to call them.*" And now I have given vent to my dull moralization, let us talk like people of this world, but first I must tell you I have had a visit from old Cuz Fo., excessively chagrined and out of humour notwithstanding the peerage [1] in view, and which I suppose will soon take place; but the dispute between him and his cousin H. has risen to such a height that all is *fire and confusion* between them, and he is very cross about his son's match. I think he has been ill-used in regard to his election, and most ungratefully so by his son Tom hitherto; for he (the father) has done *everything* he could *in hopes* of a reformation. I said all I could to quiet him in regard to the alliance he so much dislikes. The young lady, certainly, has behaved herself *remarkably well*, considering the disadvantages she has been under. I have never heard anything materially wrong laid to her charge, and she is insinuating and agreable, which may gain her such an influence as to bring about a reformation that would make him (Mr. F.) amends for other disagreable circumstances. He has made a bargain with his son, that neither his daughters nor himself shall go to Lady H.'s assembly, and the story is mended by saying " *he* would not be left in a room alone with Lady H. for the world." Miss Nanny Foley's match will now be soon concluded. The ladies headdresses *grow daily*, and seem like the Tower of Babel to

---

[1] Thomas Foley, Esq. (the husband of Grace Granville) was created Baron Foley, of Kidderminster, 20th May, 1776. His cousin Thomas, 2nd Baron Foley, died unmarried, 8th Jan., 1776.

mean to reach the skies! I hope Miss Madge in the
Election Ball[1] has made you laugh. I gave it to Bernard to send with your other things. I gave your lottery ticket to Bernard, who, I believe, is this morning
gone to pay his respects to Lady Cowper, from whom I
suppose you receiv'd an account of Lord Granville's
death. I don't hear he has left her a legacy, which I
think she *had* a good title to. She denies their being
any truth in the report of Lord C—r and his lady being
parted; but report, ever ready to maintain her malice,
won't give it up. Some say she is coming over with
her father to lye-in. It is strange such an occasion
would not bring him over to his own country.

Mr. Wortley Montagu's wife *is dead*. *If* he marries
again, and has a son, they say Lady Bute's great estate
will go to that son, *from* her own family, which will be
very hard. But I have no good authority for this. She
was here yesterday evening to meet the Duchess of P.,
and Dash very miserable on parting with Lady Jane
M'Cartney, perhaps for ever, as she and Sir George[2]
set out this morning for his Government in Canada,—
one of the cruel effects of play and indiscretion; a large
debt contracted with the late Lord Holland, that has
now fallen upon him, and obliges him to go out of
England to retrieve his affairs. They are happy in one
another, and I have in every other respect heard Sir

---

[1] "An Election Ball," in Poetical Letters from Mr. Luke, at Bath, to his
wife at Gloucester; with a poetical address to John Miller, Esq., at Batheaston
Villa. By the author of the New Bath Guide, published by Dodsley in 1776.

[2] Sir George Macartney married, 1st Feb., 1768, Jane, second daughter of
John, Earl of Bute. Sir George was employed upon several diplomatic
missions, particularly in an embassy to China, and was created Baron
Macartney, 8th June, 1796.

G. M. commended. He is a sensible, agreable man. This debt was on his setting out in life. I long impatiently to hear of your good friend Miss Sanders' arrival at Ilam; her attention to you will relieve me from some cares. And so with all your wits about you, you could not find out the riddle *A E I O U.* I am much pleased with your account of Miss H. Mead. You made her very happy, and her good mother also, of consequence. I can give but a poor account of my little friend in Hanʳ Square. She is sometimes better, and sometimes worse. On the whole, I see little amendment. She always enquires most kindly after you and yours. Next week I fear will hurry her too much. The Dss of Queens. is in town, and *I am in high favour* at present, and her G. in very good humour. I very seldome see Lʸ Dʳ Gowʳ; her afternoons are devoted to a particular set, and she is constant in her kind attention to Mrs. Montagu, and that is of more consequence than my seeing her. She retires much from her acquaintances, and takes little pleasure in anything. What a blessing it is to be able and inclined to enjoy those advantages that are within our reach? to be *resigned* when Providence seems fit to withdraw those gifts that were lent us, but *gratefully* to *accept* and *enjoy those that remain.*

Mrs. Delany to Mrs. Port, of Ilam.

St. James's Place, 6th March, 1776.
Wednesday night.

Your letter to-day, my dearest Mary, was my best desert, and whilst your two brothers, Mr. Marsh and

Mr. Edge, were drinking your health I read your letter.
They went to the oratorio, and I have had my visiters,
Mrs. Dashwood, Mrs. North, Dss. D. Portland, and
Lady Stamford, and whilst my supper is preparing I
snatch up my pen to tell you of *my exploits* of the week.
Imprimis : Sunday had the comfort of going to early
chapel, and caught no cold ; on Monday dined at Lord
Guilford's with Bern^d (poor John so bad a cold he could
not go). Yesterday at eight o'clock I went to Lord
North's with the Duchess D^r of Portland to hear Mon^r
Tessier read a play. I think his fame must have reached
even the Alps of Derbyshire. He is by birth a Frenchman,—some say of low degree, and some say that he is
come of a respectable family, but that some faux pas (still
a secret) obliged him to leave France, and he chooses
London for his stage, and puts himself under the protection of the French Ambassador, by which means he
was introduced into good company, and his extraordinary
talent for reading a play has made him much in vogue ;
with such variety of tones and actions (tho' sitting all
the time with a table before him), that if your eyes were
shut you would think there were different act^rs for all the
parts. He has the play on the table before him, which
he looks at very seldom. It was a comick piece called *La
Mariage de Julie.* I lost a great deal of what he said,
not having for some years heard any conversation in
French, it was too rapid for me to follow as close as I
wished, but enough remain'd to make it both surprising
and entertaining, and I bore all the bustle of it tolerably
well. The company assembled for the entertainm^t consisting of a good many of the *bon ton ;* waving plumes,
preposterous *Babelo*nian heads towering to the sky,

exciting both my wonder and indignation at their immense folly, worked up my spirits more than my attention afterwards to the performer, and during that time all was *hush*. I had the pleasure of meeting all my acquaintance among Dartmouths and Norths, and had a thousand enquiries after you. Pretty modest Lady Bagot[1] was there, and we talked about you, and she wished you were nearer neighbours. I did not get home till past eleven, and was more sensible of being tired yesterday than the night before, being *much amused*, which kept up my spirits. To-day I am very well, and every moment expect the two Lady Clives,[2] Archdecon Clive and his Lady, Miss Ducarrol (*my harpsicord in tune*), and your brothers.

I wish I could give you a better account of Mrs. Montagu (my friend), but I am far from satisfied. Our dear Mrs. Sandford is happy in her little William's having had the small-pox by innoculation, and quite recovered under Dr. Wall's care, who is still at Bath.

I believe after all I must dunn you for your *sprig'd chintz* (not the pettycoat), for I have been obliged to add two more chairs in my drawing-room, and want it to complete my set of covers, and I *can't match* it with *anything* the least like it. My company has just left me, Miss Ducarrol played some of my Mary's musick really very well; but they were so attendrissante that they

---

[1] "*Pretty, modest Lady Bagot.*"—Louisa, daughter of John, 2nd Viscount Bolingbroke, married, 20th Aug., 1760, Sir William Bagot, who was afterwards created Baron Bagot, 17th Oct., 1780.

[2] Robert, Lord Clive, the famous General, married, 15th March, 1752, Margaret, daughter of Edmund Maskelyne, of Purton, Wilts, Esq. Lord Clive died 22nd Nov., 1774.

have left me as *melancholly* as an *old cat.* Lady Cowper
came in the midst of the musick, and was much pleas'd
with it : she came to town yesterday to hear Mon[r] Tessier
at Devonshire House, and stays till Saturday. *She* is
saddly afraid you will *be rusticated* by living so long in
a distant country. I answered, "*Well grounded principles
were permanent, and I would answer for yours;* but had
you been bred up only to *fiddle faddle,* you would have
fiddle faddled all your life." But she was very *kind* in
enquiries and good wishes, and so I forgave her.

When the Mills's come to town, as they generally do
about Easter, they could bring the chintz with them, as
it may be folded up to take little room. Lady Cowper
asked me "why Miss Sparrow was away ?" I told her that
she might have the advantage of masters, w[ch] could not
be had in the country ; and the thoughts of her wanting
those advantages, and being neglected during your confine[t], made Mr. Port and you determine on this plan for
a year or two, and she seemed to approve of it very
much. Lady M. Mord[t] is come to town, and Mrs. Le
Grand returns with her ladyship to Richmond.

I am delighted with my dear little Mary's abilities
and her diligence. I was one morning at Wedgewoods
and found Mrs. Bentley at home, who enquired after you
and Mr. Port, and very particularly after your fine girl,
and was in raptures about her. As to Johnny's not
speaking plain yet, it is of *no consequence*, he will prattle
fast eno' in a year or two hence ; and if he takes so well
to French it should be encouraged. Mrs. A. Vrankin
I hope always speaks French to them.

Mrs. Delany to Mrs. Port, of Ilam.

St. James's Place, 2d April, 1776.

I have some dependance on Mr. Marsh and Mr. Edge recollecting and amusing you with what may have passed during that time ; and they can also tell you I am, I thank God, well in health, and put on *as good a face* upon yᵉ matter as *age and wrinkles will allow,* tho' *not* so *beautifull, young,* and *blooming* as my contemporary the Duchess of Queensbury ! Apropos, what sort of an answer from Mrs. Granville ? she did not say in her note that enclosed her letter whether it was " yea " or " nay ;" however I am glad you ask'd her, as she might have thought it an oversight had you not. Mrs. Ann Foley called on me yesterday with my little god-daughter, who is a sweet babe. Yesterday Mr. Foley and Lady Harriet[1] came to town to settle in their new house in Park Lane, next door to Lord Holderness. They were in town one day to be presented to the King, but the Queen was not well enough to be in the drawing-r., so that ceremony is but half over. Miss Betty Foley[2] was presented the same day. Miss Nanny waits till she is a bride, which I suppose will be in a month or six weeks. Sir Edward Winnington (the lover's father) is in town on that account ; the peerages will not be declared (they say) till the breaking up of the sessions. Our dear Duchess con-

---

[1] Thomas 'Foley, Esq., afterwards 2nd Baron Foley, married, 15th March, 1776, Henrietta, 4th daughter of William, 2nd Earl of Harrington.

[2] Miss Elizabeth Foley, third daughter of Thomas Foley, 1st Baron Foley, died unmarried 13th Oct., 1776.

tinues charming well, and has ventured to some assem-
blys; to-morrow she eats her dinner tête-à-tête with me,
and we propose going together in the evening to Mrs.
Walsingham, by invitation, to some musick—I hope
catches and glees. My good friend in Hanover Square
is much in the same uncertain state of health. Mr.
Halifax does not think her case desperate, but at her age
what hope of such a recovery as will make her life comfortable to her? She has been a good deal hurried with
the Dean of York and his family having been a month
in the house with her; the Dean almost as great an
invalid as Mrs. Montagu. They set out yesterday for the
Bath. They are all worthy good people, and very constant and kind in their enquiries after you. I have seen
Lady Jersey[1] two evenings this week to meet her mother,
who is gone out of town to-day with her general, in
order to go to Ireland for two years. Lady Jersey
lamented very much not seeing you at Ilam, which she
admires *prodigiously*. She *is* very fine, *superbly à la
mode*, and has lost much of her prettiness, and will soon,
I fear, lose her life if she continues her present absurd
and ruinous course of life. It is a pity, for she wants
neither parts nor sensibility; but every good quality is
lost in vanity and the love of what is *falsely* called
"*pleasure.*"

Lady Stamford speaks in raptures of your charming
Mrs. Jodderel. I find the mother's marriage has proved
a sad affair, and the young lady's match is off.

---

[1] "*Lady Jersey.*"—Frances, only child of the Right Rev. Philip Twysden,
Bishop of Raphoe, married, in March, 1770, George Bussey, 4th Earl of
Jersey.

Mrs. Delany to Mrs. Port, of Ilam.

St. James's Place, 9th April, 1776.

Cousin Betty [1] is so much taken up with her family
and new allies that I see little of her. My pursuits are
chiefly by my chimney corner, and those who love and
like me, find me there without ceremony; but I must
brag of an *extraordinary* honour on *an extraordinary day*!
(a propos, I enclose a discourse, which I believe you will
approve of.) After the duty of Good Friday morning was
over I had anonced *Mr. Thoˢ Foley*, who has not vouchsafed to take the least notice of me *since* his *mother's
death*! I own I give the credit of this civility to his
fair *bride*, who *is very well bred*; and sincerely wish her
influence may prevail in points of higher consequence, for
I look upon exact civility as a Christian virtue, it is a
part of benevolence, and has the grace of humility; it
checks self-sufficiency, by a gentle acknowledgment that
the person you wish to oblige is worthy of your attention,
and at the same time lays them under an obligation of
such a return as must be pleasing and engaging in
society; a *wilfull* omission of civility is *un*pardonable,
an *ignorant* one pitiable—so ends my chapʳ on civility,
and now I return to my visitor. I received him
graciously, all things considered, and told him I was glad
he gave me an opportunity of wishing him joy in person.
He brought compliments from Lady Harriet Foley, who
" desired leave to come and see me whenever it would be
most agreeable to me." He behaved easyly, and *look'd*

---

[1] " *Cousin Betty*."—Hon. Elizabeth Granville.

very happy, which gave me pleasure.   You may be sure
I left L^y H. F. at liberty to come when most conven^t to
herself; and she came next day between two and three,
very polite, a very fine figure, and *I think* very pretty;
her address is remarkably pleasing, but there is a
particular affectation in speaking now practised by the
present *" bon ton,"* in twisting their mouth, and *spreading
it* out to shew their white teeth, that appears to me *a great
blemish,* but it is in vain when people can perswade
themselves that a *fault* is a *perfection* to hope to see it
amended; this leads me to your darlings, and early
watchfulness may prevent bad tricks (*the MS. torn.*)   I
don't think severity will do if *too often repeated,* and as he
is a sensible child, perhaps treating him with some contempt when he is in his *tantrums,* or not seeing him at all
that day, nor suffering him to keep company with sisters
and brothers, but put to bed without seeing you or his
papa, and not being worthy to ask your blessing till the
next day, when you suppose he will be a good boy.

[End of letter missing.]

Mrs. Delany to Mrs. Port, of Ilam.

St. James's Place, 15th April, 1776.

I begin to-day for fear of interrupters to-morrow; at
present I am in as quiet a solitude (excepting London
cries) as if on the top of Bunster or pinacle of Thorp
Cloud, for all the world, great and *small,* are gone to
Westminster *Hall!*[1] This accidental rhyme is enough

---

[1] The trial of Elizabeth, calling herself Duchess of Kingston, for bigamy,
before the House of Lords, took place in Westminster Hall, on Monday,

to draw me into a poetical rhapsody, and had I as fluent a tallent as the author of " the Election Ball," I have subjects enough to have added a second part. *The solicitude for tickets, the distress of rising early to be time enough for a place, the anxiety about hairdressers,* (poor souls hurried out of their lives,) *mortifications that feathers and flying lappets should be laid aside for that day,* as they would obstruct the view from those who sit behind;— all these important matters were discuss'd in my little circle last night. Bernard dined here, Mrs. Boscawen came by appointm^t in the evening to settle their going together this morning to the tryal; here they met at seven, and went together in Mrs. Boscawen's coach. Bern^d had his ticket from the Duke of Beaufort. How long it will last, nobody knows. I *bravely refused* a ticket for the Queen's box, and going with our dear Duchess, for I feared the bustle my spirits would be in now unused to such splendid appearances, and doubted whether my eyesight and hearing would have been at all gratified, as both those senses *are* a *little* clouded by old Father Time. So I content myself with my own chimney corner, and have resigned my place to one more worthy of it. My young men return hither to a mutton chop as soon as the busyness of the day is over.

Tuesday, 16th.

To go on. Nothing now is thought of but the *Duchess of Kingston's* tryal, for *such* she is till publicly declared otherwise. I waited no longer for my guests than half

---

15th of April and several following days. She was pronounced Guilty, but claimed her privilege of peerage to be exempt from corporal punishment, which was allowed, and she was discharged on paying the fees.

an hour after four, and at 7 they came starved, having
been twelve hours fasting; and eat their little dinner
voraciously (mutton chops and lamb pye, lobster and
apple puffs), drank their coffee between eight and nine,
and then came to my little drawing-room, where they
found Lady Mary Mordaunt and Mrs. Gordon. The shew
of the tryal was *awfull*, and *splendid* beyond imagination;
but very little more done than a preparation for what's
to come, and nobody can guess yet what time it will
take. The prisoner walk'd in very decently, dress'd in
black silk, two damsels in mourning attending her, and
led in by a person also in mourning. I have enclosed
you what passed to save writing some lines, tho' very
likely you have it in your own paper. After Lady M.
M. and Mrs. Gordon went away, Mrs. Boscawen and
Mrs. Leveson came in, and Bernard held forth, and gave
them an account of the proceedings of the day very
clearly and concisely, and they were much entertained.
He brought a cold to town with him, but I hope has
bustled it away. He desires his love to you and blessing to his godson Bunny,[1] and was sorry he could not
attend him to church in person. Mrs. Granville (who
by the by *sets up her cap as high as anybody*) brought me
a paper with five new guineas, wch I am answerable for
on demand. Lady M. M. has been very ill with a fever
first, and since a cough and hoarseness, wch tho' much
lessen'd is far from well. I suspect Miss —— will soon
enter into an engagement not easily shaken off; but she
has not made me her confidante, and I avoid as much as
I can giving her an opportunity. She is in great spirits,

---

[1] "*Bunny*."—The Rev, Bernard Port, Vicar of Ilam.

and looks very *blooming*; she talks of going out of town in a week, but I think she does not know her own mind.

The Duchess of Portland went in the Queen's box to the tryal, liked it very much, dined at home at four o'clock, and Lady Andover, who went with the ticket I was to have had; they don't go to-day, but come to me in the evening. I find Miss Sparrow is now with Mrs. Sandford, and she is attentive to all studies going forward, and seems desirous of information, and speaks and understands French much better than she expected to find she did; as to manner she is *gauche*, and will, I fear, always be so; but as she does not want for sense and good nature, I hope those faults that have gain'd ground for want of *early* good habits will be conquer'd for her own sake as well as for her friends, and I most heartily wish they may. I am sure your good heart and good will to her, will make you happy to accomplish so good a work. I am sure you will shew her every mark of kindness in your power by engageing her affection, wch may be more effectually done at a distance than near. *Virtuosos* and *visiters*, all morning have fortunately for you stopt my career, and saved you the fatigue of another page. Every tender wish to Ilam.

Mrs. Delany to Mrs. Port, of Ilam.

St. James's Place, 27th April, 1776.

What a pleasure did my dearest Mary bestow upon me in giving me so lively a picture of her domestick

happiness! Long may you be blest with every circumstance that can contribute towards it. I am confident
that if every individual *wou'd* try to enjoy *rationally* the
lot which *falls to their share* they would not find that
desireable and amiable dame (*call'd Happyness*) so coy as
she is generally thought. Her benevolent disposition is
universal, but her favours must be attended to, and they
must be accepted *in the manner* she seems most inclin'd
to confer them. On *those terms* the king on his throne
may well support the weight of his crown, and the poor
man eat his morsel with thankfulness, each acting in their
proper character altho' the *favorite* seat of happyness
seems to be in scenes of life removed from the tumult
and temptations of the world, unmolested by ambition
and its attendant perplexities, but without the corroding
cares of poverty, and the mortification of a dependant
state upon the assistance of others : what gratification
amongst the rich, the gay, the admired and admiring
throng can ever equal the serene but delightfull reflection
that you *are doing your duty* to all the objects of your
affection! that you enjoy all the beauties of nature, and
have leisure to reflect on the greatness and goodness of
the Giver of all good gifts! the sensation of gratitude these
reflections must raise in the heart cannot be exprest ; and
we must look down with pity on those mistaken beings
who while they think they are grasping at *happiness* are
in the contrary road to it. Happiness may seemingly
retire sometimes under the disguise of losses, trials, or
worldly disappointments, which in the train of life may
happen, and indeed in some degree must, but you are
sure of *finding her* again with *added lustre;* and under
resignation there is always future hope.

Much cause of speculation—much hurry—has the late grand tryal occasion'd. Greatly to the general satisfaction, the shameless Dss is degraded into as shameless a countess. Surely there never was so thorough an actress. Garrick says "*she has so much outacted him it is time for him to leave the stage;*" but that does her too much honour; one should search the jails amongst the perjured notorious offenders for a paralell to such an infamous character. She has, however, escaped the *searing* of her *hand*, and is turned over for condign punishment to her *conscience!* It was astonishing how she was able to speak for three-quarters of an hour, which she did yesterday, but it was *labour in vain!* Bern[d] was there *four days*, and so much fatigued with sitting 10 or 12 hours in one place that he gave up the last day, but he was at the most entertaining part of it. I have desired him to send you at the same time "Variety," a poem to married people (if you have it not already), written by Mr. Whitehead,[1] the best of his performances. I am very sorry for poor Mr. Sneyd and his poor children. I fear by your account there is small hope of Mrs. Sneyd's recovery. Your observation and quotation are very well applied, but the hand that sends the tryal can always sustain the sufferer.

---

[1] "Variety, a Tale for Married People," by William Whitehead, Poet Laureate.

Mrs. Delany to Mrs. Port, of Ilam.

St. James's Place, 29th April, 1776.

I can't stay till to-morrow to thank my dearest Mary for her kind and entertaining letter, with so good an account of you and yours, and your agreable visit to Calwich. I don't wonder you *feel your freedom*, which indeed as you say is "worth gold;" but your *mind* is rich whatever your *purse* may be; the *first* is a never failing fund, the *latter* is subject to thieves, &c., so I wish you joy of the substantial part, and may you long bless and be blessed. I enclose you a receipt which Lady Stamford gave me on my telling her how ill poor Mrs. Sneyd[1] was; and she wishes she may be prevailed on to take it, as it has done great cures, to her certain knowledge. She also sends some *tips* for your *toes*, which you may *tack on* in what colour you like best. Lady Wey. I hope has got a little respite, they are both very valuable, and *an example* to their sister peeresses. Miss Thynne[2] is much *im*proved and *ap*proved wherever she makes her appearance, which is but seldome, for her prudent mama brings her forward *very cautiously*. The present romping age is not very inviting, tho' I don't think I have heard of *as many* pranks this winter as the last, indeed everybody has been so much taken up with the modern *Moll Flanders*[3]

---

[1] "Mrs. Sneyd."—Penelope, daughter of Thomas Kynnersley, of Loxley, Esq., and wife of John Sneyd, Esq.

[2] Louisa, eldest daughter of Thomas, 3rd Viscount Weymouth. She married, Nov. 19, 1781, Heneage, Earl of Aylesford.

[3] Miss Chudleigh, the Duchess of Kingston, whose trial for bigamy had just taken place.

that nothing else has been talked of. She is now gone to the Pope for absolution, but the Meadows's have not done with her yet.

Our cousin T. F. and his belle moitie[1] are gone to make a visit to Newmarket, tho' they say she endeavoured to diswade him from it. I fear no reformation is to be expected, he has *so often broken his word.* I dine to-morrow at Foley House, and Wednesday at Whitehall to meet Weymouths and Clanbrazils. Since I wrote last I had a visit from the Dss. of Gordon,[2] she *is beautiful indeed.* Lady Bute brought her here under a pretence of showing her my herbal on purpose to treat me with her beauty. She is very natural and good humour'd, but her *very* broad Scotch accent does not seem to belong to the very great delicacy of her appearance. I must finish to-morrow, for I have written thus far by *owl light.* The grand assembly at the Queen's caudle drinking[3] fills my little circle every evening, as that ceremony is over at nine. I have sent your letter to Lady M. M. I tenderly felt my *dearest bird's* sensibility, may it never be engaged by an ungratefull or unworthy object. Sweet child, *how I love her !* I am dressing a doll for her ; but oh, sad chance, the friseur who had her in hand let her fall and broke her nose, and as some of her clothes are made and her *tête* also fitted, it will be some time before I get another doll that will do. You must copy out

---

[1] The Hon. Thomas Foley and his wife, Lady Henrietta, daughter of the Earl of Harrington.

[2] Duchess of Gordon.—Jane, daughter of Sir William Maxwell, Bart., married, in 1767, Alexander, 4th Duke of Gordon.

[3] The Princess Mary was born April 25th, 1776. She married her cousin, William Frederick, Duke of Gloucester, July 22nd, 1816, and died 30th April, 1857.

" *Moll Flanders*," for I have not time ; the *spring flowers* now *supply me with work*, for I have already done since the beginning of March *twenty plants*. I'll make your speeches to Madam Bess. Your brothers and Mr. and Mrs. Mills dined with me last Sunday—all very well. Pray tell your bro^r John *I miss him very much*, but he is in so much a happier scene I won't repine. Providence has given him a *good* and a *benevolent disposition*, and has bless'd him with ample means to gratify it,—long may he enjoy it. The Duchess of Queensberry has not been well and, confined a good while, but is better. My poor little friend comes on very slowly. I had a "*how d'ye*" to-day from Lady Cowper. I suppose she came to town to enquire after the Queen. Lady Tweeddale still in town. Lady Cath. Hay[1] much in the same weak declining state, and making herself and all about her unhappy with her unaccountable humours. Lady Frances Tolmach called on me one morning : all the family seem to think Lady C. H. in danger now, and that she has brought it on herself by mismanagement. I went one morning last week to see Mrs. Pit's little girl at Craven Hill, a mile from Knightsbridge turnpike, and to gather a nosegay. She is a fine upright, good humoured girl, a year younger than Mary. When I told her I had a little darling girl afar off she said—" O, and why won't you bring her to see me ?" I was touched,—and for fear of the like I will close my 2^d sheet. No words can say how
Affectionately I am y^r own,
M. DELANY.

---

[1] Lady Catherine Hay, wife of Captain William Hay, of the 2nd regiment of Foot Guards, daughter of the Marquis of Tweeddale, died 25th Aug., 1776.

In this letter Mrs. Delany states that she had finished "*twenty plants*" since the beginning of March. These plants were all the most perfect representations of Nature as to form, colour, light and shade, and perfection of perspective. This is the second time she alludes to this marvellous work, at first called her "Herbal" but afterwards her "Flora." The manner in which the idea first struck her was as follows: Having a piece of Chinese paper on the table of bright scarlet, a geranium caught her eye of a similar colour, and taking her scissors she amused herself with cutting out each flower, by her eye, in the paper which resembled its hue; she laid the paper petals on a black ground, and was so pleased with the effect that she proceeded to cut out the calyx, stalks and leaves in shades of green, and pasted them down; and after she had completed a sprig of geranium in this way, the Duchess of Portland came in and exclaimed, "What are you doing with the geranium?" having taken the paper imitation for the real flower. Mrs. Delany answered, that "if the Duchess really thought it so like the original, that a new work was begun from that moment;" and a work was *begun* at the age of 72, and *ended* at the age of 85, which no other person before or since has ever been able to rival or even approach.

Mrs. Delany to Mrs. Port, of Ilam.

St. James's Place, 14*th May*,[1] 1776.

A day that always leads me into a wilderness of recollections on the many turns and changes—the many pains and pleasures—that I have experienced in the course of seventy-six years ; *various* have been the events ! and tho' I have enjoyed many blessings (above all that of tender and valuable friends), *the sorrows of my heart have been enlarged* ; and taught me that this world is not made for happiness, unless we could be as perfect as we ought to be. This being the case I have no reason to regret that my glass is so far run ; but to submit with thankfulness and humility to what is to come. Great reason, indeed, I have for thankfulness, who still enjoy more friends, more health, and more cheerfulness of spirit than most at my age ; and these reflections do not arise, my dearest Mary, from my being at this time ill, for I thank God I am much better than for some days past. How thankfull ought I to be for the many kind friends who spare me everything in their power that they think will ruffle me. I am sure I may place my dearest Mary at the head of them. At the same time I don't love to be deceived ; for when I suspect I don't know the exact truth my imagination is apt to form chimeras. Your account of your pleasant days at Calwich made me *very happy*, and particularly your renewal of your musick. Whenever you can come in the way of a good master you will do well to take some lessons. I know nothing of Kelaway but there is a Richardson[2] much commended.

---

[1] The birthday of Mary Granville.

[2] Query, *Richards*.

Miss Ducarol play'd here last Thursday three hours. I treated your brothers and Mr. Williams with her. She is a very ready and clever player and enters into the designs of the different masters; is ma*jestic*, *pathetic*, *harmonious*, when she plays Corelli, Geminiani, Handel, but *scours away the keys* with the *modern musick!*

I don't wonder you liked The Correspondents;[1] the sentim[ts] are new and pretty, *some* letters better than others. The Letters of a Lady from Italy to her friend, are Mrs. Miller's[2] of Bath Easton; very conceited, they say, and not worth buying. Did I send you the Russian Letters?[3] they are natural and informing.

Mrs. Delany to Mrs. Port, of Ilam.

St. James's Place, 28th May, 1776.

Miss Dolly Mode's box[4] just pack'd up to go to the carrier next Friday, containing—imprimis: a lady *à la mode* in accoutrements—but in every other respect *toute au contraire*, for she can neither rouge, nor giggle, nor run away; she is nail'd down to her good behaviour, and when you set her at liberty, the nails must be carefully drawn out, (after the books, boxes, &c., that are at the top of the box, are taken out,) the nails that fasten the

---

[1] The Correspondents; an Original Novel, in a series of Letters. Published in London, 1775.

[2] Letters from Italy, describing the manners, customs, &c., in the year 1770-1, to a friend residing in France; 1776. By Mrs. Miller, of Bath.

[3] Letters from a lady who resided some years in Russia, to her friend in England; with historical notes. London, Dodsley, 1775.

[4] "*Miss Dolly Mode*" was the name given by Mrs. Delany to a doll which she dressed in the fashion of the time, and which was preserved for years as a specimen, not only of the fashions, but of Mrs. Delany's wonderful skill and ingenuity.

two boards on the outside of the box must then be taken out, and the boards carefully taken up before Miss Dolly can gain her liberty; then the thin paper that wraps her up to be unpinn'd, which will discover a broad blue ribbon that fastens her down (round the waist) to the box, and ditto across her legs. I leave the rest of her unpacking to your delicate fingers. I hope to hear she arrives unrumpled—*feathers and all*. A box with miss Dolly's things, a parcel with pamphlets, and the copy of a .countenance sent to you by Bernard, and also from him a book of musick you desir'd him to get, and if I could have packed in *everything* I wish to send to Ilam it would have been a *rich box*, but I, alas! have nought but love.

The Duchess of Portland is much better, and drank tea with me the two last evenings, and comes to-night. Talks of going to Bulstrode on Wednesday, and I hope to follow her on Friday. As to your A. D. she is a flaunting frollicksome old gentlewoman; and was on Friday last at Mrs. Walsingham's catches and glees, and staid out till past eleven o'clock. She was much entertained with the musick, which was as well perform'd as possible; she was also a little amused, and abundantly astonished at the piramidal, touring *Babel*onian head-dresses, and the busy hum; *not only* of female voices (tho' I must acknowledge they predominated). Well did the witty man say, at a late assembly to Miss Seymour, that "now he *had seen* the Tower of Babel and had *heard* the *confusion of tongues*" (for you must understand *she* speaks several languages and all imperfectly). But all was hush as soon as the musick began, but the moment it was over the vociferation was wonderfull, as if they had gather'd new force from the pause. To-morrow your brothers and I dine at Foley house. I fancy I shall find them a little out of humour with the loss of the Herefordshire election. Lady M. Mordaunt has been very ill, and looks sadly. She and Mrs. Gordon called on me one morning last week and were going out of town soon. I was surprised with the performance of Lady M. M. in a copy of two dead partridges in water-colours; not finish'd, but as far as she had done them they were charming, and she tells me (which is surprising) that she *cannot* draw *an outline* of anything, but Mrs. Gordon does that part for her!

Mrs. Delany to the Viscountess Andover.

St. J. P., 27 May, 1776.

I am infinitely obliged to dear Miss F. H. for her kind information of your having had a good journey to Elford; which time, and summer, and the succession of beautiful and rural objects, I hope will render pleasant, and salutary, to my very dear Lady Andover. According to decorum this ought to be address'd to Miss F. Howard, but as she flatters me with saying a letter to your ladyship will be acceptable, I lay it at y^r feet, and should not have staid for that encouragement, could I have said that our precious friend at Whitehall was quite well; which now I trust I can with a good conscience add; as her doc^{tr} has left her, as well as her fever, and she has appointed Lady Bute to meet her here this evening. I cou'd now very naturally fall into a lamentation for the loss I have felt, since a certain most amiable Viscountess and her amiable daughter have forsaken my little nitch. I have spent as much time as I could at Whitehall, and

Ilan^r Square (*where* I find very little amendment,) but the cold winds have made me "*wrap my old cloak about me,*" and stay at home several days.

I sometimes am conceited eno' to think myself a sober decent ancient dame; till temptation comes in my way —and then alas! *I am frail.* Last night I was invited by Mrs. Walsingham to hear catches and glees; *impossible* to resist, and *without* our dear friend (who was too prudent to venture), I went early to get a snug corner; for an hour it was dumb show, and I was amused with the variety of waving heads, dangling lappets, and all the flutter and tinsel of the present mode. My good stars brought Lady Bute to take her place next me, and drive away little Mrs. V——n. Was not that lucky? tho' for *a crab* she was very sweet, notwithstanding my having avoided any communication for 2 years past. When the songsters begun, wch was about 8, I was indeed vastly delighted, for they performed admirably; and such were their powers, that the instant they begun the universal babble ceased, and all was silence and attention; but when the song was over, the prattlers, as if they had received fresh forces from that silence, made such a tumult of strange sounds that the confusion of Babel was never so well express'd; it was a jayl delivery of tongues! it not only *astonish'd* me, but actually gave me the *head-ach*; however the next sweet song made me amends, and I slept well, and am well after all. The Dss of Q. has crept out, but I have not seen her, she says she is but little better.

Mr. W. Montagu's death,[1] and Lady Bl—ke's elope-

---

[1] Mr. Wortley Montagu, son of Lady Mary Wortley Montagu, died at Padua, 30th April, 1776.

ment with Mr. G. Bosc—n, (not our friend's son) can be no news to your ladyship, nor Miss Mundi's marriage, which is soon to take place with Sr Roger Newdigate.[1] I hope very soon to have the pleasure of hearing from dear Lady Andover. You have ever been so indulgent to me, present or absent, that I feel forlorn without those kind testimonies of favour to

Your ladyship's most affec^te and
Obedient hum^le ser^t,

M. DELANY.

I beg my love to Miss F. H. I am sure I need not say the Dss of P. always attends you both.

Mrs. Delany to Mrs. Port, of Ilam.

Bulstrode, 9th June, 1776.

I am very sorry, my dearest child, for your disappointment and vexation; not surprized at it, knowing the disposition of *the person*; who with many good qualities, wants those tender feelings, and that politeness, so necessary to correct *selfishness*; *which* when indulged will not bear the officious kindness of friends, if *not* offer'd at the *particular moment* they think most convenient! The want of that delicacy makes them insensible of the pain they give, and cou'd their hearts be open'd at once to the tenderest sensations of affection,

---

[1] Hester Mundy, 2nd daughter of Edmund Mundy, of Shipley, Esq., in Derbyshire, married, 3rd June, 1776, Sir Roger Newdigate, Bart.

they would have many regrets, and be miserable for ye distress they had given, for they *certainly* persuade themselves that *they* are *always in the right!* This being the case, we can no more change their nature than our own; it is our best and wisest way not to lay it in their way (when we can avoid it) to treat us with coldness, and Providence perhaps has so designed it, that our nearest and *dearest* connections shou'd be our most particular care (not omitting other social duties), and that where *they* are concerned no sacrifice is to be made. You are happy in an attentive and affectionate husband, lovely children, and a pleasant habitation; your fortune, tho' not large, with œconomy and content, is such as will afford you many comforts. These are all *substantial* blessings; and tho' attended with some anxiety, doing your duty by them is (and will be) *a support;* and the many delights of their company will prove a recompence. So, my dear M., enjoy them: go abroad when health and kind invitations encourage you, and take the different dispositions of people, not as marks of any intended unkindness, but as *constitutional.*

I hope my last letter to Welsbourn, and *Miss Dolly Mode*, have afforded you some amusement. As to my own part I have everything I can wish for in the constant tenderness and delight of such a friend as our inestimable Dss; unless I could remove Ilam within a day's journey. Tho' so long an absence has been painfull to me, it has been unavoidable on both sides, and that is a consolation; for had it been possible, we should have met, as our inclination is mutual, and I never quit *resting on hope*, which often opens a pleasant view. *Rigid* **Wisdom** says, *"Don't hope*, and then you will not be disappointed;" but your philosophers are *rare talkers*, and *sad comforters*.

To-morrow the Duchess of Portland expects Lord and Lady Dartmouth and Mr. Montague, I hope for some days, but I fear not above 2. Lord Dartmouth's good taste and good breeding will make him delighted with everything, and delight everybody at Bulstrode; he never was here before.

I began my letter to-day, as I have made an appointment for to-morrow with a very fair lady called "Lychnidea."[1] If I neglect her, she will shut herself up, and I shall see her no more.

Monday.

The fair lady was true to her appointment, and we parted friends.

Mrs. Delany to the Viscountess Andover.

Bulstrode, 9 June, 1776.

I have been impatient to write to my dear Lady Andover ever since I had the favour and pleasure of her most kind letter, to return her my best acknowledgem[ts] for it; but I have been for some days past good for nothing; but being now as well as in reason I can expect to be, I take up the most perverse pen in the universe. Her Grace has made two notable discoveries (for *idleness* has *not* been the consequence of confinement); one is that exercise is *not* necessary to health, and the other (contrary to the received opinion of all gardeners and farmers) that rain does *not* improve verdure; these ob-

---

[1] Mrs. Delany made a beautiful representation of a white and lilac lychnidea from nature.

servations, with many others, may some time or other appear in the Philosophical Transactions!

We have seen nobody since we came, but Mr. Lightfoot and a philosophic friend of his. I have been busy at my usual presumption of copying beautifull nature; I have bungled out a horse chesnut blossom [1] that wou'd make a fine figure in a lady's cap, or as a sign! To-morrow the Duchess expects Lord and Lady Dartmouth and Mr. Montague: my last account of his mother was rather better. The beauty of Bulstrode in spite of the weather is not to be described, no more than her Grace's transport at seeing one of the hares suckle its 3 young ones in the court before the drawing-room window! Another piece of extraordinary good fortune also attended the Dss this morning: 4 old nightingales with 4 young ones, were brought to-day in a cage, which she set at liberty with her own fair hands.

I hope Miss F. Howard is not idle; I know but of one fault she has, which is not doing justice to her own genius, and a little inclin'd to hide her tallents in a napkin; now I desire her to *display* it on fair *paper* or *vellum*, and let the world judge if I am not in the right in giving her this advice. By the bye supper has been on the table 3 quarters of an hour. Hark! I hear her Grace's footsteps, and luckily your ladyship is released from any more nonsense at this present writing from

Dearest Lady Andover's

Most affect^e and obed^t,

M. Delany.

---

[1] "I have bungled out a horse-chesnut blossom."—It would be impossible to imagine, without seeing it, the wonderful imitation of nature in the spike of horse-chesnut blossom, with its leaves, here alluded to.

Mrs. Delany to Mrs. Port, of Ilam.

Bulstrode, 16th June, 1776.

I must tell you that the portrait so kindly received, acknowledged, and cherished, was *no gift of mine;* but I was to be silent till I heard whether you knew it. Most traiterously was I drawn in by my good friend Mrs. Boscawen, unsuspecting that she wou'd be accessory to such a superannuated exhibition. I consented to her bringing with her one morning Mr. Gosset to see my pictures; and whilst she was discoursing with me, and consequently fix'd my attention to her, thinking the artist was looking about him and criticizing, I turn'd my head about and discovered him at my elbow, modelling my antiquated profil:[1]—had he been working in colours he might have *added roses* to my palid withered cheeks! I exclaimed—I expostulated—but my betrayer was inexorable, tho' at the same so soothing with her kindness that I submitted. Bernard came in and caught us in the fact, bespoke a copy instantly unknown to me, brought it to me finished as I was packing up y^r box, and desired me to send it to you without saying anything of it—which I perform'd; and if any thanks are due, they are *his right.* No part in the whole transaction gave me so much pleasure as his immediatly communicating, what *he* seemed to set *so great a value* upon to my dearest Mary. Indeed he has a kind heart, and how blest am I in the attention and regard I receive from those whom my heart with a maternal fondness delights

---

[1] This profile, beautifully modelled in wax, is in the Editor's possession.

in, and who on all occasions are so ready to listen and advise with me, and to communicate their own thoughts. How happy would it be for youth and age did they oftener mutually pay and receive; for the experience of age when accepted with deference and kindness, and the cheering and sprightliness of youth when they meet, are like sunshine and shade, set off one another, and are delightfull and salutary.

I had a letter from your brother Bern^d the morning you left Welsbourne, with ye same account as y^u give of Mr. Dewes, a quick recovery of strength is not to be expected at his age.

The weather was cruelly bad whilst Lord and Lady Dartmouth and Mr. Montague were here, last Monday, Tuesday, and Wednesday. Lady Weymouth came on Thursday evening with her 4 eldest children; Friday was favourable for the kids to bound over the lawn, &c., and they enjoyed every fair moment; unwillingly they were parted with yesterday.

It now rains desperately, but I hope it will forbear next week, when Mr. Mason and Mr. Montague are expected here—apropos, I must tell you another pretty-ness of your bro^r Bern^d; he took an opportunity when *Mrs. Montague* was airing, to hang up in her drawing-room *another effigy* of the same phiz! Great was her astonishment.

The Hon. Mrs. Boscawen to Mrs. Delany.

Glan Villa, 19th June, 1776.

Very luckily for me, my dear madam, your last favour has no other date than "Tuesday," so I will by no means examine or try to find out how many Tuesdays ago it is since you gave me so kind a proof of your remembrance. I have just caus'd the white dog's house to be mov'd from the sunny to the shady side, it is a convenient mansion, and he seems to grow and thrive. You never told me his name, so I call him "poor fellow," and he jumps upon my apron a little indiscreetly. I have had some visitors, two short ones from my dear Mrs. Leveson and her boys; they repair en famille to Lady Gower's most hospitable retreat to-morrow. Her lady^p has also sent me a most kind invitation to come when I please. I shall be apt to ask you, my dear madam, a little *advice* upon that subject, as whether you wou'd not counsel me to go *when Mrs. Delany goes.*

Lord and Lady Edgcumbe have spent a day with me, and it was a very fine one. Mr. and Mrs. Cole enliven'd a rainy one. Yesterday I saw a guest arrive at my gate just as I was sallying forth to my early walk, but little thought it was one that wou'd make my breakfast quite a feast—my own young soldier, who having rece^d at Monmouth orders to repair to Edinburgh, obey'd them so alertly that he was his own messenger. I think Scotland will be a pretty summer tour, but he that has *the good of the service at heart* assures me he shall "never get so many recruits anywhere as at Monmouth," where all the Duke of Beaufort's militia assist him, and where, I suppose, *if* the *truth was known,* he is more fêted and considered than he has any chance of being among strangers. Just now he is gone up to the War Office to give an account of the recruits he has enlisted. He is not a man likely to bring me news or I wou'd defer closing this till his return. My best respects wait on the Duchess; I hope her health is perfect.

Mrs. Delany to the Rev. John Dewes, at Calwich.

Bulstrode, 28th June, 1776.

I am sure your dear sister is always glad to visit Calwich, for you make a place that was *once very awful to her,* very pleasant ! I wish I cou'd share it with you both, but my race is too far run to undertake long journeys, and I must look forward to that time when happiness will be in perfection, and endeavour to make myself worthy of it. Your prosperity, my dear John, as well as your bro[rs] and sister's, must ever be the chief objects of my best wishes. I once mention'd that if you found any of my letters to your late uncle[1] that you wou'd let me have them, and also a letter of Lady Granville's to me; when they come easily in your way. Send them me the first opportunity.

I am pretty well and so is Smith.[2]

----

[1] This desire for the return of her letters accounts for so few having been found to Mr. Granville in early years.

[2] " Smith."—Mrs. Delany's waiting-woman.

The Hon. Mrs. Boscawen to Mrs. Delany.

Audley Street,   Monday, June 30th, 1776.

I fully intended to have acknowledg'd by this post (at large as I am apt to do) the pleasure of your kind letter of the 22ᵈ, but the event of Mr. Chase Price's death,[1] which has brought me hither, leaves me hardly leisure to say in two words that I was vastly thankfull for the most welcome intelligence of yʳ recovery, which I hope is perfect, or something very like it, and that I shall have the satisfaction to hear so very soon. I have seen Mrs. Price (my half-sister), whose shock and surprise is very great; she was gone to Brighthelmstone to fetch away her girl. She receiv'd a letter *from* Mr. Price on Saturday evening (*he had been dead then many hours*) wrote on Friday in exceeding good spirits, and giving reasons why he did not himself come to fetch her as he intended. He din'd abroad, it seems, on Friday, and appear'd to be particularly well, for he has had a mortal disease, I am persuaded, a long time, and at length it ended him instantaneously, for he appeared to be in a profound sleep when his servᵗ found him dead on Saturday morning. Mr. Evelyn has got Mrs. Price, his sister, at his house (having left her girl with Lady Bathurst), where I have been all this morning and am now returning. He and his wife are very kind and friendly to her, so that I shall go back to Glan Villa to-

---

[1] Chase Price, of Norton, Esq., M.P., married Sarah, daughter of Mrs. Boscawen's father by his second marriage, and consequently her "half-sister." The genealogy of the Price family is given in Burke's "Dictionary of the Landed Gentry," but without dates.

night, having left Mrs. Leveson and her boys there. I am glad you have seen Mrs. Sandford and hers. God bless you, my dear madam! take great care of yourself. Present my best respects to the Duchess, and believe me

Y^r very affectionate friend,

And faithfull servant,

F. BOSCAWEN.

The Dowager-Countess Gower to Mrs. Delany.

Bill Hill, 30th June, 76.

I have taken pen and ink out of Mrs. Mountagu's hand to thank d^r Mrs Delany for her kind intentions to us; c^d she inform me of her certain time of coming here my chaize sh^d attend her hour. We are all hapy in ye hope of seeing her, and not one lion in ye way on this side ye Thames. The *alloy* is great, from ye shortness of ye time allotted.

Mrs. Mountagu assents to all above, bids me says she's much better a-days and her nights rather better,—I think her much stronger. I have something curious y^t I'm sure must amuse. *Mother Magnolia* has more buds y^n I can count, her daughters are all fruitefull, and ye 2 standards in ye parterre show for bloom y^t ne'er bloom'd before! This rural news is all wee rusticks have. 'Tis surely none y^t wee are, d^r mad^m,

Ever y^rs,

M. G.

A. M.

All respect and good wait on ye Dss of Portland.

The Hon. Mrs. Boscawen to Mrs. Delany.

Audley Street,
Monday night, near 12, (*query*) June, 1776.

I was going to tell you how y^r dog breakfasts with me and is kindly treated, and that "love me love my dog," &c., but not at all, for I must talk upon very different subjects. Good news from America, I thank God. Lee *taken prisoner*,[1] Carleton[2] too *victorious*, and being attack'd, has repulsed the enemy and given them a *total defeat!* This I hope you will hear particularly to-morrow; but what you may not hear so soon is Lord Bruce's resignation! (rather Lord Aylesbury, I believe, for I think he had kiss'd hands both as Govr and as Earl;)[3] was vastly well rec$\tilde{\text{e}}$d by his little master as well as his great one, and yet he has resign'd and is gone into the country, the Duke of Montagu, his brother, being Govr in his stead—Dr. Hurd *continues.* If nobody tells you this by to-night's post, I might have begun my letter like Mad^e de Sevigné, and said, Voici la chose la plus merveilleuse, la plus miraculeuse, la plus, &c., &c., &c. Lady Bruce has done all this mischief, tho' parading about Bath in good health. I am sure you will be sorry as I am for all that will be

---

[1] Charles Lee, a distinguished military officer, accepted, in the year 1775, a commission from the American Congress, and served as a Major-General under Washington. He was made prisoner by the English forces, taken to New York, and treated with much indignity by General Howe. After the surrender of General Burgoyne, Charles Lee was exchanged as a prisoner.

[2] General Sir Guy Carleton was, in 1786, created Baron Dorchester for his eminent services during the American war. In 1776 he defended Canada successfully against the American Generals Arnold and Montgomery.

[3] Thomas Brudenell, Baron Bruce, born in 1730, married, in 1761, Susanna, daughter of Henry Hoare, of Stourhead, Esq., Wilts. On the 8th of June, 1776, he was created Earl of Ailesbury. After holding the office of Governor to the Prince of Wales for a few days, Lord Ailesbury suddenly resigned it, and was succeeded by the Duke of Montagu.

said to the discredit of this well-intentioned nobleman, tho' weak, doubtless, on this occasion, at least so it appears. I carry'd *two* Mrs. Delanys to wait on L^y Gower to-night: her Ladyship chose one with a *handkerchief* and *breast knot!*[1] Y^r dog has run away once, but being sent for to St. James's Place, was there found and brought back. Take care of y^r health. Cannot say a word more—last bell tingling.

I have been at Osterley Park all day wth Lord and Lady Edg. and Mr. Leveson.

The Hon. Mrs. Boscawen to Mrs. Delany.

Glan Villa, Thursday, July, 1776.

" O'er the small mansion as I lonely range,
Condemned at every step to feel the change,"

I seek the garden,—there I am not better satisfy'd unless it is with the sympathy it expresses, for it is become quite cold and comfortless. The bower which you distinguish'd with peculiar honour is cover'd with seer leaves, which the hollow winds blow " frae the tree." I look'd at the moon last night, but 'twas in a burr; and then it rain'd, but not a fine generous shower to restore our *green* grass—no—only some tears of vexation at your departure.

Thus it is with us, but you, my dear madam, are, I hope, quite happy in being restor'd to your inestimable friend, and enjoying the delight of seeing her in most perfect health. I trust she was satisfy'd with yours and the good looks you carry'd from hence, not diminish'd, I

---

[1] The wax cameo which the Editor has is in a hood without any " *breast knot.*"

hope, by the heat of your noon-tide march. I could have excus'd the General's arrival just at the moment of decampment, for I did not tell you how gratefull I felt for all your kindness to me, nor how sorry I was to loose the hourly experience of it. I return you a thousand thanks, and attend you with as many good wishes; for fear you should not read them right my pen delivers them in ropes as thick as those which war against the cows. Adieu, dear and much honour'd friend! no pen can tell you with what truth, affection, and gratitude

I am yours

F. B.

The Hon. Mrs. Boscawen to Mrs. Delany.

Glan Villa, July 6th, 1776.

Tho' you are not apt to be mistaken, my dear madam, yet you certainly was in the name of the Judge who try'd my cause before you, and acquitted me so handsomely: his name was not *Vanity*, believe me, but *Sagacity*, and a most just and upright judge he shew'd himself, for I was not guilty of any of the crimes laid to my charge; nor treachery nor indifference were mine, and I am surpriz'd that I could ever be accus'd of such odious delinquency.

Since I had the pleasure of y^r letter I have been in London, saw Lady Edgcumbe, who had been at Park Place, and heard news of Lord Winchelsea's [1] surprizing voyage, wch I was sorry for, as Lady Charlotte [2] will probably be very anxious and miserable on his account.

---

[1] George, 8th Earl of Winchelsea and 4th Earl of Nottingham, succeeded his uncle, Aug. 2, 1769. Horace Walpole says—"I shall not send to America after Lord Winchelsea for his spirit."

[2] Lady Charlotte Finch, eldest sister of George, 8th Earl of Winchelsea.

Miss Vernon's marriage [1]—what a number of countesses, besides 2 duchesses among those cousin-germains. Marlbro, Grafton, Carlisle, Thanet, Holland, Brook, and Warwick—pretty well! Poor Lady Harriett Foley [2] was the subject of compassion : driven from her home (if indeed she has ever had any since her marriage), jewels seiz'd, cloaths seiz'd : (these last I think she got again ;) but it seems she has no pin-money or settled maintenance at present, so she may be reduc'd to a dernière chemise !

I have been in care lest our charming friend Mrs Walsingham should be dispossest of her castle and driven out of your neighbourhood, of which she is so worthy and so fond ; but she tells me that tho' she has trembled she begins to be secure again. What delightfull reports you tell me of! Yes, indeed, my dear madam, I shou'd like to be of such parties, nobody more : but in my northern corner I have nothing, so it will not be amiss to treat my eyes at least (whatever becomes of my understanding). This I mean to do by a progress as far as Burleigh,[3] so far I intend to go with my Lieu[t] in his way to Scotland ; and after we have admired all the beauties, ancient and modern, of that superb place, we shall part at Stamford, my son to proceed (with my blessing) to his station, and myself to return, pian piano,

---

[1] Henrietta, daughter of Richard Vernon, Esq., and grand-daughter, maternally, of John, 1st Earl Gower, married, July 9th, 1776, George, 2nd Earl of Warwick.

[2] Lady Harriet Foley, 4th daughter of William, 2nd Earl of Harrington. She married, March 15, 1776, Thomas Foley, who succeeded his father as 2nd Baron Foley, Nov. 18, 1777.

[3] Burghley, the seat of the Marquis of Exeter.

to this cottage, stopping perhaps to see any thing fine or curious on yᵉ way, *especially* Lord Melbourne's.[1] After this petite equipée I shall think of visiting my daughters, both of whom kindly beckon me. I have very pleasant accounts from Bill Hill, and (lately) a most kind letter from Lady Gower to invite my son to come and visit his sister before he goes (but as he saw her in London he does not allow himself this indulgence, being on the point of setting out). I am very glad to hear Mrs. Montagu is so much better since her residence in Berkshire. I hope she is now easy enough to enjoy the place and the company. That of her son and Mr. Mason must have been very pleasing to her, as it was also to my daughter, who regretted their departure. And now, my dear madam, I will bid you adieu.

Mrs. Delany to Mrs. Port, of Ilam.

Bulstrode, 8th July, 1776.

My dearest Mary will for a wonder receive a short letter by this post ; not want of inclination, but actually time, for the Dss of Portland and I have had some curious MSS. lent us that we have been obliged to read and return to-morrow, wᶜʰ with company here, and visiting our neighbours, have exercised body and mind. A short journal, and then adieu.

On last Wednesday came Lady Cork,[2] full of her cruel circumstances, her Lord's unkindness, her sister-in-law's

---

[1] Melbourne Hall, now (1861) in the possession of Viscountess Palmerston and the gardens still preserved as laid out in 1612.

[2] Lady Cork.—Anne, daughter of Kelland Courtenay, Esq., married, in 1764, Edmund, 7th Earl of Cork and Orrery.

wiles, and her girl being kept from her, all deplorable
for there is no unkindness towards her that they do not
exercise, even endeavouring to blast her reputation, very
unjustly ; her spirits are in continual agitation, and she
can talk of nothing else, I wonder she keeps her senses.
The frowns of fortune are bad to bear, but the unkindness of friends unsupportable without such a degree of
resignation as is difficult to attain tho' well worth our
while to cherish it as a never failing friend.

On Wednesday evening (near 9) walks in Mrs. Berkeley, (unexpected,) with an intention to return for a
lodging to the White Hart, Gerrards Cross ; but her hospitable hostess wou'd not suffer her ; so the even^g past ${}^{\cdot}$y^e
better for it, and the tide of lamentation was turn'd into
chitchat, and questions and answ^{rs} ab^t London, and its
environs, whither the 2 ladies resorted on Thursday
morning : in the evening we went and paid a visit to
Lady Jane Halyday and L^y Fan. Tol. now with her,
but did not find them, and on Friday they returned
the visit. Yesterday we made a visit to Mr. Drake
and his family at Shardelois,[1] a charming place. To-
day we expect Mr. Bryant, and on Tuesday the Dss
goes a little journey in search of plants ; and I to Bill
Hill ; and we propose, please God, meeting on this spot
on Friday next to dinner.

I had a kind visit from Bernard before he proceeded
to Staffordshire, hope he had a good journey, and that
you are all happy together.

How did Miss Joddrel like Calwich ? Your account
of her is very pleasant.

---

[1] William Drake, LL.D., of Shardelois, near Amersham, Bucks.   He
died in 1796.   Now in the possession of Mr. Tyrwhitt Drake (1860).

Lady Cork was robb'd just by Kew Bridge the day she left us. She dined at Windsor, which made her too late.

The Hon. Mrs. Boscawen to Mrs. Delany.

1776.

MY DEAR MADAM,

I have been twice to wait upon Mrs. Montague, Hanover Square, and was, indeed, surprised at the great amendment of her health, her spirits seem perfect. She wears her hat, and *speaks* of blindness, but 'tis not to be perceived or even suspected by her guests,—I wish it were as unknown to herself. She talks of visiting you when you come, and seems so desirous of it, that I hope she will accomplish it.

Yesterday I was told by a lady that she had met Lady Strathmore[1] with serv[ts] still in mourning, but *wearing white favors in their hats* (as at a wedding), also that in the chaise with her, sat an ill-looking man, from whence inference was made that she was marry'd to some Italian.

Lord Maynard[2] has announced to his sister, in form his marriage with. . . Miss Nancy Parsons (for I think the *title* of Mrs. Horton is doubtful); it is not at all so

---

[1] John, 9th Earl of Strathmore, m., in 1776, Mary Eleanor, daughter and heiress of George Bowes, of Gibside, Esq., in the county of Durham. He died in 1776, and his widow, the Countess of Strathmore, m. Andrew Robinson Stoney, Esq., who took the surname of Bowes, as the Earl, her first husband, had done. Her son, the 10th Earl of Strathmore, left the Durham estates by will to his cousin, John Bowes, Esq.

[2] Charles, 2nd Viscount Maynard, married, in 1776, Mrs. Anne Horton. He died without children in 1824.

that this Circe was well known at the time Lord Maynard was born—is this a *charrade*, or only a phenomenon ? I don't at all know what the former word means. Pray send me some charrades (or may not I say pray bring them), but I shall not guess them as you do. I have not heard from Mrs. Walsingham this age, nor, indeed, wrote to her, or anybody else except to my son in Scotland, where you hear the famous Princess D'Aschkoff has carry'd her's for education. T'other night I play'd whist (at Mrs. Vesey's) with General Potemkin![1] who was the person that took yᵉ rebel Pugatchef with his own hand. I have seen Monsʳ de Noailles[2] "*chere Madᵉ de Montaigu !*" his appearance is very agreeable. Mr. and Mrs. Jenyns are as flourishing and as pleasing as any evergreens in her Grace's shrubberies, they do me the favour to come here to-morrow to meet Mr. and Mrs. Cole. I have ask'd *Madᵉ de Montagu* to come and tell them a little about Paris, but she makes no answer. It is very well for you, my dear madam, that my coach is come, and my daugʳ is waiting.

Ever your faithfull and affectᵉ servᵗ,

F. Boscawen.

A letter from Cornwall, tells me that a ship arrived at Falmouth from Lisbon, says the K. of Portugal is certainly dead.[3] But his death is concealed from the people.

---

[1] Prince Gregory Alexandrovitch Potemkin, the favourite minister of Catherine II. He died in Oct., 1792.

[2] Louis, Viscount de Noailles, who in 1803 was killed in a sea-fight against the English.

[3] Joseph, King of Portugal, died Feb. 4, 1777.

The Hon. Mrs. Boscawen to Mrs. Delany.

Glan Villa, this hot Thursday,
July 16th, 1776.

I write, my dear madam, to enquire how this African
weather agrees with you, and with my Lady Duchess ;
and also to tell you that I did not omit to deliver your
message to Mr. Cole,—you have probably been inform'd
long since. Mr. Cole express'd great indignation at the
bill in general, and the enormity of many of its articles
quite beyond example. I doubt if you have got Mrs.
Walsingham in *your neighbourhood* yet, and I have pro-
fitted by her excursion. She made a charming one to
Cambridge and to *Burleigh,* and then repos'd herself (after
les delices de Capua) with me. I cannot say the thin
walls of my cottage are calculated for hot weather, or
that we know very well how to convey ourselves to yon
spreading oaks, whose dark shade seems to invite us.
At present I am sitting in my closet, doors and windows
all open, and tho' ye window is full north, and the horizon
not within miles, yet the air that comes in seems to be
sent from some *camp-oven,* where many rations of ammu-
nition bread are actually baking ! I want a pretty pigeon
to fly to Bulstrode ; but I must be content to give a
penny, and wait three days. But here is the post, and if
I do not sign, seal, and deliver, he will be gone. Best
respects wait on the Duchess, and earnest wishes for
perfect health to Bulstrode.

From Bill Hill advices bring that Mrs. Montagu is
surprisingly well, and Mrs. Montagu *la grande* is gone to
the North.

The Hon. Mrs. Boscawen to Mrs. Delany.

Glan Villa, 22nd July, 1776.

I congratulate you, my dear madam, on the more moderate weather, and myself on the hopes of enjoying your company next week. Monday, by all means, in *my* returning chaise if anything makes you prefer it, else I shou'd think it was beyond comparison pleasanter to come in *your own* much better equipage, for, if my horses stay long in London, to rest there, you will come just in the heat of the day; and if they do not bait, then, they will be lazy, having gone their ten miles;—in short, they will be tedious compar'd with your brisk equipage: beside that, having nothing to do but to repose yourself when you arrive; but *I will give you leave* to halt at y[r] friends at Ken Wood if you choose it! Sufficient that I receive you, next Monday, in good health, which God grant! We *shall* be quite alone, which will be pleasant to us both, I think; and when the Duchess knows that you are with a friend that (next to her Grace) loves and honours you, she won't hurry away so soon from a station which I flatter myself will be very beneficial to her health. Now you must know, ladies, that I shall be in town soon after you receive this, and shall wish to wait on you *both*. But how? why 'twill be impossible, as I shall stay only from twelve till two!—unless Mrs. Sandford comes to fetch me, or both my dear ladies receive my gratefull visit to them in my own back parlour. My house is a chaos of painters and whitewashers!

If nothing of this can be done, then by these presents I express my sincere wishes for Mrs. Sandford's health, and that of her fine family—for her good journey, and perfect success in all her undertakings and prospects for them.

For you, my dear friend, *I trim my bower and make my garden fine*; to see you enjoy it will be a most heartfelt pleasure to

Y^r very affectionate faithfull servant,

F. BOSCAWEN.

Miss Sayer begs her respects. I carry her away to-morrow, her father so requiring.

The Dowager-Countess Gower to Mrs. Delany.

Bill Hill, 24th July, 76.

Being call'd to London, I desir'd Mrs Leveson, (who likes to be so employ'd,) if she saw yor writing among my letters, to inform you I was not at home, wch she tells me she did; I c^d not bear to think of apearing one moment insensible of ye kind vissit you made me, and flatter myself the shortness of it was not choice, y^t it will be made up to me w^n circumstances permit; much delighted to read, you call'd it an airing, and y^t it was crown'd wth ye hapiness of ye D^s of P—d's returning better for her expedition.

The sincere little woman,[1] set out on ye travelling plan she fix'd on w^n you was here; I saw her twice in London, in good spirits, and rather better for her journey so farr; have heard of her from Mr. G. Mountague's y^t she was as

---

[1] Mrs. Montagu, of Papplewick.

well there as usual; some wise people wonder at her
undertaking; she is best judge w^t is most easy and co-
venient; it is *very material* how and where one lives, but
quite *im*aterial in my opinion where one dies!

An old acquaintance, tho' no intimate, ye D^s of Newcastle, is no more.[1] Various are ye reports of her illness,
and ye disposition of her ffortune.

As to myself, ye cough is very little. I've began
ye bark, wch I'm told will take off y^t lassitude wch has
so long hung upon me: I like ye medicine, because it
causes no confinement, nor no sort of mark to discover
ye taking it, and of course can't furnish conversation on
so disagreeable a topick as a calamity.

The charming ugly boy[2] improves daily in cleverness,
but not one word does he speak. I conjecture 'tis from
contradiction y^t is implanted in human nature; for y^e
profound talkers were trying to make him speak a year
ago.

All respects wait on Bullstrode.

The Hon. Mrs. Boscawen to Mrs. Delany.

Glan Villa, this hot Tuesday, 31st July, 1776.

What shall I say for my elegant handkerchief? Why
that I shall never wear it without thinking of my dear
and much honour'd friend; but for that I want no

------

[1] Lady Harriet Godolphin, widow of Thomas Pelham Holles, Duke of
Newcastle, died 28th July, 1776. She was daughter of Lord Godolphin, by
Henrietta, eldest daughter of the great Duke of Marlborough, and possessed a
large share of her mother's wealth.

[2] Lady Gower's eldest grandson, John Leveson Gower.

memorial but the remembrance of her kind visit, and
the agrémen it spread over this little place, now dull,
brown, solitary, and unpleasing! Every day I visit the
morning bower because you liked it, but the flowers are
all drooping, and the very leaves sere and yellow; indeed,
my dear madam, we are *scorch'd and burnt up;* but I
refresh my imagination with thinking of the stately
grove at Bulstrode; such deep shade, such lofty canopies,
can at any hour tempt you abroad, or if you postpone
your excursions in the garish eye of day, you are now
suffer'd to take them by *moonlight,* and may very safely
do so, for their is neither damp, nor dew, nor (to all
appearance) any moisture left upon the face of the earth.
This day se'nnight I purpose, please God, to set out
on my travels (tho' at present my coachman is sick,
wch is very inconvenient). I have just received a letter
from the Dss of Beaufort, who condoles with me on
losing you, and begs that I will "return you her *sincere
thanks* for the honour you did her sons in taking such
kind notice of them," wch I find they have made the subject
of their letters to her. In their last visit I carry'd them
to Judge Willis's, where we sat (very pleasantly) in a
green-house, or rather conservatory, where I counted 16
roses (my own the largest, I might safely add). Among
us was Mrs. Williams,[1] who got near me to talk of you,
and I was not averse. Among us, too, was the widow
of Genl Wentworth, of other times: this lady signed
the Test in the year 1711, so we *know* she is 91, but
how much more she does not choose to tell, tho' *more is
suspected:* she seem'd neither *deaf,* nor *blind,* nor *lame,*

---

[1] The sister of West, Gray the poet's fellow-student and friend.

but she had march'd (in a great, heavy, close coach) at least 6, if not 7 miles in that extreme heat to see Madam Willis, so that we need *not* reckon her *understanding* perfect!

I have purchased 2 lots of poor Mrs. Aislabie's plants, of wch there has been an auction. One was all orange-trees, the other have long names, of which I send you a specimen, but the pots themselves (so entitl'd) were as familiar to my ignorance as geraniums, orange-leav'd mirtle, azorian jessamine, &c.

Adieu, my dearest madam. The sun gains upon my blue room, and I must quit it as y^u us'd to be *driven* from *your cabbin over head*; I wonder now at the hours I *suffer'd* you *to* spend there by yourself, and could almost regret that I was not as impertinently as I ever shall be affectionately yours,

F. BOSCAWEN.

The Hon. Mrs. Boscawen to Mrs. Delany.

Bill Hill, Augst ye 2^d, 1776.

MY DEAR MADAM,

I arriv'd here on Monday evening, and found the noble lady of the mansion in perfect health and *alertness* as usual; her's and my younger friends thriving exceedingly under her auspices and kindness; besides the little boys' round faces I find my daughter is grown fat as butter; mais c'est le pais de cocayne, or, in other words, we all live in clover. I find a prodigious change of climate, so much hotter here than in my northern cottage that I want a garment of the fashionable gauze!

Next Monday you will be pleased to direct to Badminton. Lady Gower, however, most kindly requiring me to halt again here on my return, and *then* it is that I must hope to see you, my dearest madam, for the cottage (you perceive) is abandoned which you purposed to have honour'd with your presence. It shall be a dormant patent which I shall claim whenever I can find a probable opportunity : meanwhile we will exchange our different coins, but not inquire wch is *gold* and wch is *poor Cornish tin!* the merit of discerning is something, and to that I shall lay claim, and pretend to be assay-master. Hot! very hot! and I am *very stupid.* Lady Gower says " *Delany calls me the Salamander:*" and I am sure I understand why, for her lady^p looks perfectly cool, while Mrs. Leveson and I appear to have *dress'd her dinner!* Mr. Leveson is at Portsmouth. He is only gone on a visit to some of his comrades.

I do indeed enjoy the good news from Quebec. Heaven grant us more from the southern provinces, and perfect success to Genl Howe ; that is what I long for in trembling expectation, for there, methinks, the miscreants will make their chief stand : we shall not hear while the east wind lasts. How many hearts ache that have their dearest concerns engag'd in this unhappy conflict! Lady Bute has a very fine son there (as I have heard mine say). Pray, my dear madam, does Dr. Beattie belong to the University of Aberdeen, or that of Glasgow ? if to the latter I shall beg a few lines of you, to introduce my son, now quarter'd at Paisley, near Glasgow, under the command of Captain *Charles Stuart,* (memorable name!) But let me not forget to tell you that Lady Gower begs in case you shou'd happen to see Mr. Drake, of Amersham, that you will ask him if his ice-house succeeds well : she is going to build one after the same plan, and gave me this message to you, over and above her best respects and compliments to the Duchess and yourself.

We study'd and admir'd the eclipse. La belle lune vont se planter sur le sommet du grand ormeau, when the eclipse began. At length, when the whole was cover'd, it seem'd to be only with tortoiseshell, and one still discern'd the circle of the moon; this surpriz'd us. We expected a covering of ebony, opaque and black. I watch'd till she emerg'd again. L^y Gower was overtaken by sleep, and left the moon in distress, but her lady^p *sits out* by moonlight, and *walks* by moonlight, so that we seldom come in till half-past 9. Magnolias innumerable perfume the air and delight the eye at the green-house; 23 have blown, as many more (at least) are coming. Adieu, my dear madam. Excuse this dull letter; heat makes one more stupid than ordinary.

Ever your faithfull

F. B.

Mrs. Delany to Mrs. Port, of Ilam.

Bulstrode, 5th Aug., 1776.

Tho' the King and Queen drink tea this evening at Bulstrode, and the Dss of Portland threatens to produce me among the *antiques*, I am composed eno' to thank my dearest Mary for her letter of the 22nd, and hope y^r agreable party succeeded to your wishes. It is very pleasant to see the improvements of our manufactures, and to consider how many poor people are supported by it that otherwise would be starving, or following desperate courses for their maintenance; but I fear it is a

great sign of ye sad depravity of our nation that tho'
there is *all manner* of encouragement and employments
to engage them beside defending their country from re-
bellious oppression, &c., that there should at this time be
so much robbing, but I am very apt to think those .dis-
honourable collectors are *more* among the *middling* than
poorer sort; everybody in all ranks and degrees live *above
their fortune,*—avarice, vanity, and pride make spendthrifts. Surely an hour's reflection on their conduct, had
they any principles, would show them how much more
disgraceful it is to run in debt than to *retrench* in order
to *do justice*, or to live within bounds in order to prevent
what in time must bring ruin and disgrace to their
families. I am led to these reflections on having heard
so much lately of our *cousins*, but it seems I have thrown
away some compassion, for it is now (among *a certain set*
of the *bon ton*) thought a good joke that Lady H. F.
was handed out of her own house into her coach by two
bailyfs. Ah! poor bashfulness! Ah! gentle modesty
where are ye flown? Effronterie and extravagance have
taken your places.

What a shocking account of L^y Tyr.! Every day produces some circumstance to her disadvantage. Indeed,
the present state of the publick world would make one
wish to turn hermit, to avoid the mortification of hearing so much of the impropriety of those who are brought
into the world; but I am thankful that those who are
most dear to me, are placed in such a position that they
may avoid all these evils, and enjoy the true blessings of
Providence, by a rational life, and do their duty towards
God, and man.

I suppose *the travellers* will be impatient to return, and

that philosophy, and searching after curiosities; will yield to more interesting pursuits, and prospects of domestick happiness will be *more* aluring than those of distant countrys, and I hope on their nearer approach will not disappoint them; they have (as far as I can judge) great reason to expect a reasonable share of felicity, as they act upon rational and good principles.

I am sorry Bern⁽ᵈ⁾ had not my letter, as there was something that required an answer. He was so good as to communicate to me his *first* thought of Miss De la Bere, and to ask my opinion before he proceeded. What I had heard of Miss D. for some years had made an impression with me in her favour, and her appearance and manners confirm'd it. He also gave me an account of what his father had done, and that he intended to lay it before her father: w⁽ᶜʰ⁾ I suppose was well received, but his hurry and engagem⁽ᵗ⁾ for *the tour* prevented his telling me any more, and tho' I designed (as I thought it would be proper) to write to Miss De la Bere, to say how much I was satisfied with my nephew Bernard's choice, I did not care to do it till I heard from him again.

Friday Mrs. Middleton and Miss Drakes dined here; Saturday Mrs. Anne Egerton, a neice of hers, and a Miss Carter of Lincolnshire, who they say is very clever; in the evening came the renowned Mr. Burke—take him *out* of politicks, and he is very entertaining—he brought a Mon⁽ʳ⁾ Nicolaide, a Grecian, who was full of *silent* admiration; and yesterday came Col⁽ˡ⁾ Egerton his lady and 2 daughters. Don't you think her Grace is glad these civilities are over? On Wednesday we shall return to a feast of reason: Mr. Briant and Mr. Lightfoot spend the day here. On Thursday Lord and L^y Beaulieu [1] dine here, and then, till Tuesday the 13th, I hope we shall have a tranquille enjoyment of Bulstrode. On *that* day the Duchess seems determined to go to Weymouth. I shall go to London for a day or two, and then to Luton or Bill Hill.

Did Bernard remember to speak to you about the curious fosil (like threads of brass or gold) you sent the Dss of Portland 2 years ago? she wants to know where it was found, and if a bit more can be had.

Love to my dearest bird!

Monday night.

The King and Queen came a little after six. The King drove the Queen in a low chaise with a pair of little white horses. Lady Weymouth attending them in another chaise and 6 grooms on horseback, but no other attendants. The Dss of Portland met them on the steps before the hall-door. I was in the dressing-room belonging to the blue damask apartment. They were so gracious, as to desire me to bring my book of flowers, and I have neither time nor assurance to tell you all the things they said. They staid till 8 o'clock.

---

[1] "Lord and Lady Beaulieu."—Isabella, daughter of John, Duke of Montagu, married (after the death of her first husband, William, 2nd Duke of Manchester), Edward Hussey, Esq., who assumed the name of Montagu, and was created Earl of Beaulieu.

Mrs. Delany to the Viscountess Andover.

Bulstrode, 12th Aug., 1776.

Have I, or have I not, been remiss, in writing to my dear Lady Andover ? For to own the truth my diminished brains, are bad at recollection : and I have of late been so embarrass'd with the beau monde, and royal favours, that it is no wonder I shou'd be forgetful of my own doings. However, I am not so bad as to forget the constant goodness of my dear Lady Andover, and have a certain affectionate and faithfull corner in my heart, from whence gratitude flows in abundance ; nor am I grown so insensible to what is elegant and entertaining, as not to be happy in receiving her letters, were that all their merit.

Now your ladyship says, " *Well, I know all this, but tell me what my dear amiable Duchess has been doing all this while, and how she does?*" As to her Grace's health, I think she only wants her favourite physician the sea air, to strengthen her ; which she proposes going towards on Tuesday next the 13th. Infallibly I shou'd go to Elford, were it not for unsurmountable obstacles ; as it is, I shall, (please God,) after spending 3 dull days in London, proceed to Luton, and from thence to Bill Hill ; where I shall stay till ye day of the Duchess of Portland's return from Weymouth. Great have been our visiting exploits, 15 struck off the list ; numerous have been the visitors of all sorts and sizes, male and female, from the K. and Lord Mans^d down to Ed. B—ke ;[1] from the Q. and Lady Wey. down to Miss Wheat !

On Monday evening between six and seven came their Serene Majesties, in a chaise with a pair of horses and

---

" *Edmund Burke.*"—It was probably at Bulstrode that Mr. Burke observed in Mrs. Delany the combination of mind and manners which caused him to speak of her in such terms as made a deep impression on Dr. Johnson.

grooms attending. Lady Weymouth came with them,
(and no small additional pleasure.) All things were
prepared for their reception, and the drawing-room
divested of every comfortable circumstance. I pleaded
hard with her Grace for permission to go that day to
London; she was inexorable; but I still had hopes that
so insignificant a person would be overlooked, and that
I shou'd be fully gratified with seeing their royalties
thro' ye window, or thro' the keyhole! but I was mistaken, and Lady Weymouth was sent by the Queen to desire I would bring the *hortus-siccus*. I obey'd, and what
does your ladyship think?—that I was miserable, or
wish'd myself at York?—no truly—I was charm'd and I
was pleased, and I even wish'd they had staid half an
hour longer. They did great justice to dear Lady Weymouth's merit, and spoke not only with approbation, but
with kindness, of everybody they knew our most dear
friend had a regard for; nor was *Lord Suffolk* and *Lady
Andover* forgot! In short, had I been told that the
King and Q. had made the Dss. of P. a visit of two hours,
and that she was neither weary nor hurt by it, I cou'd
hardly have believed it—but, indeed, they seem'd to
receive great pleasure from it themselves, took notice,
and admired everything; and above all I am sure the
possessor of what gave them *so much* entertainment. I
had my panicks that she wou'd stand till she grew faint,
but the K. and Q. insisted on her sitting down the
greatest part of y^e time.

The Dss of Portland's affection^{te} complim^{ts} salute
Elford, as well as those, (with the best respects,) of dear
madam, your lady$^{p's}$

Most faithful and obed^t,

M. DELANY.

The Dss of Portland went to Windsor the next evening to make her proper compliments in person to the K.
and Q. without meaning to see them ; but they knew
better than to lose the pleasure of her company, kept
her to drink tea, and kept her so late, that I grew not
only impatient, but anxious, forming a thous^d *bug a boos*,
but she came home safe, and pleased. Lady Wey. and
her family set out for Long Leat on Friday last.

Lord Cathcart [1] died this morn^g. This was begun at
Bulstrode, ended in St James P. not a soul in town.

The Hon. Mrs. Boscawen to Mrs. Delany.

Badminton, 18th Aug. (Evening,) 1776.

Can one think of a dear friend every day, and never
speak to her, pens and ink always offering their assistance.
But there is one thing, as necessary as all these which
does not present itself, and that is *the writing-hour*. " Le
voyez vous. Je dis que non, ni moi je vous le jure."
Such was Monsr Coulanges's song upon another occasion,
and it is very applicable to this. The weather is so fine
that we live much out of doors, and when we are within,
as we sit in the library, 'tis in vain to leave me to my
occupations *the shelves* find me in *so much*, that instead
of writing three letters, (wch perhaps I had prescrib'd to
myself,) I have not wrote three words ! But I need not

---

[1] Charles, 9th Lord Cathcart, died 21st July, 1776. Lord Cathcart served
as Aide-de-camp to the Duke of Cumberland at Fontenoy, and was for some
time Ambassador to the Court of Russia. He married, in 1753, Jane, daughter
of Lord Archibald Hamilton ; and was succeeded by his eldest son, William
Schaw, afterwards Earl Cathcart.

give you, my dear madam, the history of my busy idleness, for tho' never idle yourself, you have great indulgence for those that are so, (provided always they are not in *mischief*,) and you can make allowances too for little people that love dearly to come into granmama's room, if she will invite them.

Next week I return home, and shall halt at Bill Hill. When I was there in my way hither I found Lady Gower pure well and in very good spirits. She walks as usual in the *hottest hour* of the *hottest day*, but had disus'd riding on horseback; 'twas *only* on account of *the flies*, however.[1]

Adieu, my dearest madam. All hands here are walk'd forth. Else I shou'd be charg'd with many complim^ts to you from my dau^r and her two sons, that you were so kind to. I beg my best respects to the Duchess, and that you will be assur'd whether I write it or not that I am always most gratefully and most affectionately yours,

F. BOSCAWEN.

The Duchess of Portland to Mrs. Delany.

Weymouth, Aug. 23rd, 1776.

My dearest dear friend, I have worried you with two immoderate long letters, and I believe in both stopp'd short in the middle of a sentence (lest I should be too late for the post) ; your dear delightfull letters are the joy of my heart. The other day I was on the beach, the

---

[1] Lady Gower was seventy-five when she disused riding "*on account of the flies.*"

wind blew a brisk gale; I got into a little sand grotto, and read your charming letter over and over while Mrs. Le Cocq was travelling about in search of shells, butter-flys, and plants. Mr. Lightfoot desires his best comp^{ts}; he goes away on Monday, and I hope to set out next Thursday. He has traversed all the island of Portland in search of plants, but has met with nothing new, neither animals nor vegetables—and has been very sea-sick, but he will give you a better history of his adven-tures than I can do, for I have no time as I expect visitors, and they will stay till it is too late for the post. Heaven send us a happy meeting on Thursday next, and let me beg of you to dine at 3 o'clock, as I shall not come till the evening. Best comp^{ts} to Lady Gower.

I am, my dearest friend,

Most affectionately yours,

M. C. PORTLAND.

Saturday.

The Duke of Portland's cause is finally decided, which is *very comfortable*.

The Dowager-Countess Gower to Mrs. Delany.

Bill Hill, 4th Sept., 76.

My serv^{ts} brought me tranquility wth yor letter, and pleasure to think anything belonging to me c^d be usefull to you: yet it had its alloy, as I had flatter'd myself I sh^d hear ye thumb was restor'd to its natural *ton*. An-other pleasant incident; ye postillion met ye D^s of P. in perfect health, he reported; this proves obedience brings a blessing. If you had not obeyed my com͠ands, I c^d

not have had this good news. I am deeply in yo[r] debt for y[e] days you bestow'd upon me ; tho' *few* in number, they were *all* you had. I ever desire to be thus involv'd.

I send this in a ffrank of Mrs. Bos : Mrs. Leveson says her mother has forgot to tell you how much she is yo[r] h[ble] serv[t], desires I w[d] make up y[e] deficiency. Leveson joins his respects, and his son tells us daily by signs, " *Mrs. D. is gone !*" I, and all, desire our best complim[ts] to y[e] D[s] of .P., and my congratulations she is returned quite well. Mrs. Walsingham is come. Adieu, d[r] M[rs]. Delany.

The Dowager-Countess Gower to Mrs. Delany.

Bill Hill, 13th Sept, 76.

D[r] M[rs] Delany's letter of the 2nd inst. made me very haṗy in confirming y[e] good acc[t] my serv[t] brought of her and y[e] D[s] of Portland ; may I always have such news of them ! I must say 'twas a damper on my botany w[n] I read w[t] I took for moss, was *no moss* nor no rarity.

M[rs] Bos. *scutter'd* away this morn. *to do nothing.* I'm oblig'd to go to London on y[e] 20th ; w[d] fain have detain'd her till my return ; thought it an agreeable proposition both to her and her daughter ; I might as well have made it to y[e] *winds ;* she's a very *good* woman, but a *very perverse one !*

D[r] Mad[m], I must take leave to desire you to convey my petition to M[rs] Smith,[1] to consider over all her acquaint- ance, if among 'em she *can* find a serv[t] for me, *just like her self :* L—d Suffolk [2] has given a messenger's place to

---

[1] Mrs. Delany's waiting-woman.
[2] Henry Howard, 12th Earl of Suffolk and 5th Earl of Berkshire.

ye husband of my Abigail, and she is eager to be gone; tho' she is not of much use (rather thinks of ornam^{ts}), yet I can't be *quite* wth out a serv^t, and I realy know not where to look for one! I've had such *useless creatures* recom̄ended from *people of rank*, who, I sopose, spoke wth knowledge, that I'll enquire *no more in those quarters*. If it sh^d be in *Mrs Smith's* power to accom̄odate me, I shall be much oblig'd.

The new Earl and Countess[1] have plagu'd all ye western part of this isle; I hope I shall ever have ye grace to stay at home, and ever shall think myself bless'd w^n I can see here such a worthy as d^r Mrs Delany.

The Hon. Mrs. Boscawen to Mrs. Delany.

Glan Villa, 21st Sept. 1776.

My dear madam, I rejoyc'd to hear of the Duchess of Portland's health. I hope the bad weather has not affected her Grace or yourself. I have been reading the new Sylva, or rather only the *new dress* of my good old uncle;[2] I imagine you have done him the honour to look over him. Do you admire the prints, my dear madam? Methinks if *you* had *cut them*, they wou'd have been more exactly the plant they represent. I doubt some of

---

[1] Thomas Villiers, 1st Earl of Clarendon, youngest son of William, 2nd Earl of Jersey. He married, 30th March, 1752, Charlotte, eldest daughter of William Capel, 3rd Earl of Essex, by his first wife, Jane, eldest daughter and coheiress of Henry Hyde, last Earl of Clarendon and Rochester. Lord Cornbury, the only son, having died before his father, the Earldom of Clarendon was given, in June, 1776, to the husband of the eldest daughter of the eldest coheiress of the Hyde estates.

[2] The new edition of Evelyn's "Sylva."

Dr. Hunter's subscribers will grumble at the additional expense, but I have not seen anybody that can tell me whether this edition is acceptable. I know so much (by tradition) of my great-great uncle, the author, that I feel quite interested in this book; there is (I see) a noble list of subscribers. Mrs. Leveson presented hers to Lady Gower, who seem'd to read it with pleasure. I fancy her lady^p is in town just now on the business of moving.

When I return'd hither your dog was one of the first that welcom'd me, but so grown both in height and length, that if he had been lapdog to your lady^p, you wou'd have great reason to complain; for my part, I am satisfy'd that my maids have us'd him well, since he is so much thriven.

Yesterday I heard of a wedding: Sr Gilbert Elliot's youngest dau^r to Mr. Eden,[1] Ld Suffolk's secretary; and, to-day, I was told that Mr. Stanley was to be cofferer again, in the room of Mr. Dyson.

Present my best respects, if you please, to the Duchess, and believe me, with great truth,

Your affectionate faithfull servant,

F. BOSCAWEN.

I must not be so ungratefull as to omit thanking you for Mr. Penant,[2] who entertains me very well sometimes. I will keep him a little longer, and then return him to St. James's Place.

---

[1] Eleanor, youngest daughter of Sir Gilbert Elliot, 1st Earl of Minto, married, in 1776, William Eden, who was, in 1789, created Baron Auckland.

[2] A quarto edition of Pennant's "British Zoology" was in the course of publication in 1776 and 1777; but probably the book alluded to was a volume of his travels in Scotland, published some years previously.

The Dowager-Countess Gower to Mrs. Delany.

Pall Mall, 24th Sept., 76.

I've long experience d^r Mrs Delany's readiness to do me any good, or pleasure. On reading yor letter I ask'd yor serv^t to go wth my message to Mrs Tilt, who went on ye wings of good will; she came, and gave Mrs Burchell so good a character, I desir'd she'd send for her. In ye interim I was solicited to see another, who had serv'd L..y Rockingham,[1] but I concluded she had *too high* ideas *for me,* and so it prov'd, for indeed she was *double refin'd!*

I have this afternoon agreed wth Mrs Burchell, if L..y Cowper gives her ye character she seems to be sure of, and have wrote to her la^p accordingly; this is ye progress of this affair. Must take leave to insert how much I'm oblig'd to Mrs Smith for her zeal to serve me. I hope as long as I live ye magnolias will reward her wth their beauty and their scent. I hope these dry days has taken from ye D^s of P. all rheumatick feelings, y^t health may be as perfect as I wish it. My cook, ye night after I left B. Hill, cut his throat and died on Saturday morn : my being absent, and confined here till Saturday, aggravates this melancholly event. My son has acted most judiciosly in every point; told M^{rs}. Leveson he died of an apoplexy, so no mischeife ensu'd there. No cause is assign'd for the rash *act*; a sober, honest man, and an excellent serv^t, in his profession, and has done better this

---

[1] Anne, daughter and coheiress of Sir Robert Furnese, Bart., Dowager-Countess of Rockingham, married, secondly, Francis, 3rd Baron and 1st Earl of Guilford, being his third wife.

sumer y^n ever. Wee were all much pleas'd wth him, and I thought he was quite easy and hap̃y, and he had much reason so to be; he certainly must be in a ffever and delirium, for he wounded himself in many parts of his body.

Since I've began I can write of nothing else, so will stop short and release you, d^r mad^m, from this painfull subject.

Mrs. Delany to the Viscountess Andover.

Bulstrode, 25th Sept., 1776.

I don't wonder if my dearest Lady Andover at this moment thinks me idle and good for nothing, for not obeying her commands sooner, or what is the same thing to me, her kind wish of my writing soon to her. But the truth is my time has not been quite my own; for as her Grace's *Aurora* does not begin quite as soon as Phœbus's, I have the honour of presiding at the breakfast table, which takes up the time usually devoted to writing; and Bulstrode has had such a succession and variety of visitors, that I am giddy wth the recollection. Perhaps your ladyship will think some part of this paragraph borrow'd from the celebrated *Urn* at Bath: and I do not totally deny the charge.

I have been impatient to give your ladyship an account of our dear friend's health, which I hope I may assure you is good. The Dow^r Marchioness of Lothian and Lady E. Kerr were here from Monday was se'night to last Friday, very entertaining and agreable; beside here have been other inmates, as a Mr. and Mrs. Freeman, a

s 2

Mr. Yate of Cumberland, (a genius in the science of the Papilio, Phalena, Bombex, &c.), and many more personages too numerous to name. Dr. and Mrs. Turton must not be forgot, and for bon bouche, our good Lord Guilford, who seem'd well and happy whilst he was here, but had the mortification on going from hence to Bushy, to find Lord North with a broken arm by a fall from his horse; he writes me word it is set, and I hope it will be attended with no worse consequence. We have had some very good weather, and have not neglected it, tho' the Duchess of Portland has not had a *quiet* enjoyment of it, *which* suits her best; for if there is to be a civil thing done, or said, it comes in the way, for you know it is impossible for her to omit it, and her own precious health must wait for another opportunity; which now she possesses, for we are quite alone, save Mr. Lightfoot, and we are as busy as bees.

I hope I shall soon have the pleasure of hearing all are well at *Elford,* and that your heart is quite easy about Lord Suffolk. The Duchess's most kind compliments with my respects attend on all *there*. If I had time to write this over again, I would not let it appear; but as I have not trust to your gracious acceptance from

Dear madam,

Your ladyship's,

Most affectionate and obed^t hum^{ble} ser^t,

M. DELANY.

The Dss desires me to ask if she did not lend Miss F. Howard a book of MSS. riddles.

Mr. and Mrs. Port and their little family will spend

next winter at Bath; I think I shall feel happy to have them so much nearer. Mr. Bernard Dewes is going to be married to Miss De la Bere;[1] as they marry with reasonable views and prudent schemes, I hope they will be happy.

The Hon. Mrs. Boscawen to Mrs. Delany.

8th Oct., C. H., ? 1776.

Alas! my dear madam, what is it you tell me! Not a word had I heard of the great shock and concern you must have had till I receiv'd your kind letter; very kind indeed to think of me so soon, and of my anxiety for the Duchess and yourself. Is it not very remarkable that I shou'd receive *two* letters from my friend to announce these catastrophes within the space of *three weeks?* Yet so it is, and Lady Gower's servant had as little apparent reason as poor Mr. Cuttle,[2] whose case I really think by your acc^t must have been a sudden frenzy. I have known him in the Duchess's service these ten years at least. What a cheerfull open countenance! but I will not say a word more on this sad subject, after I have express'd my real concern, which I am sure you do not doubt of.

I had the satisfaction to hear of your health by Mr. Cole, who was a most pleasing guest, but tarry'd but a day; Mrs. Cole was with him. They proceeded next morning on their way to Mr. Jenyns's in Cambridge-

---

[1] Anne, eldest daughter of John De la Bere, Esq., of Cheltenham.

[2] Mr. Cuttle was a servant of the Duchess of Portland, who destroyed himself.

shire. Mrs. Walsingham has had a kind and friendly vision of placing me on the south side of Taplin Hill, by way of bringing me into the land of the living, and within reach of that charming society which she often enjoys; but these are Chateaux en Espagne, and I must not hope to be transplanted so agreeably. You are travelling with Mr. Pennant, you say—do you not then want y^r volume again? No! for you are reading that which belongs to her Grace, and *mine* is *yours*; (that sounds very true and friendly, does it not, my dear madam?) but yours shall *not* be mine respecting the white dog, for the naughty cur ran away from us, and we cou'd not find him high nor low for three days. No wonder then, when Mrs. Burrows had got him safe lock'd up, for thither he stroll'd, and they happen'd to know him; but since this elopem^t my coachman never suffers him to run with the chaize, because he is "a great fool," that is the character of your dog not to flatter you; but we shall not publish it. Bless me! what a long article I have made of the foolish dog,[1] and now my letter must be double, and I have no frank. I shall send it to London. You have heard, I suppose, that Sr Gilb. Elliot's [2] eldest son is going to be marry'd to Miss Amyand. She has a very good fortune.

Do you know that Mr. Pennant is at this time (I believe) at Badminton; I have a notion so. After a Welsh tour he had a mind to see a certain manuscript

---

[1] The white dog and his adventures, and Lady Gower's letter of Oct. 9th, 1776, relating to the suicide of the two servants, authenticate the assigned date of this letter.

[2] Gilbert Elliot, 4th Baronet and 1st Earl of Minto, married, Jan. 3, 1777, Anna Maria, eldest daughter of Sir George Amyand, Bart.

(and a curious one it is) wrote (and drawn) by the Secretary of the 1st Duke of Beaufort, who was *Lord President of Wales*; but I shall hear more of this matter. I have had a letter from Mrs. Montagu from Chaillot, very pleasant. Mr. Burrows has one still more entertaining. She thinks she shall return this month. Adieu, my dear madam.

The Dowager-Countess Gower to Mrs. Delany.

Bill Hill, 9th Oct., 76.

I rec̃d yor letter yesterday wth ye similar acc^t of w^t has hapen'd here. I too well know w^t sensasions ye d^r Dutchess must have on this melancholly occasion: shall be thankful for one line to know how you both do ; may it have no ill affect on yours and her health is my earnest wish. Sure there is somthing in ye air y^t causes y^s insanity, for it can't in any light be look'd upon as ye deed of a rational being. I'm much concern'd M^{rs}. Mountagu w^d think of undertaking such a journey as to Melton, 'tis 80 miles more y^n she need to go ; days shorten'd, bad weather probably approaching, waters to pass, and her state of health. I took ye liberty to write my remonstrances to her little secretary ; I wish they might have weight, for I'm realy under apprehensions for her ; it may proceed from low spirits, ye consequence of ye dismal scenes I've had, for till now I had got clear of y^t listlessness and languor I complain'd of w^n you was here, and long before ; it convinc'd me ye disorder must be very potent to feel it, when I had ye hapiness of yor converse. The reflection how much worse this misfortune might have been had any evil hapen'd to those nearer my heart, will, I hope, disipate the impression, and make me thankfull yᵉ shock was no greater.

'Tis early to make any judgmᵗ of Ann Burchell,[1] as hitherto her *behaviour* has been *proper*, and she seems qualified for her office. Yoʳ goodness in endeavouring to accomodate me is an additional obligation to one yᵗ *you*, dʳ madᵐ, have *ever* oblig'd, and who will *ever retain* a just sense of it. My son and Mʳˢ Leveson desire their respects to you and yᵉ Dˢ of P.

———

The Hon. Mrs. Boscawen to Mrs. Delany.

Glan Villa, 14th Oct., 1776.

Shall you think me unreasonable if I send a hue and cry after you, and confess that I think it a long time since I have had the pleasure to hear from you. If I knew that you were quite well I would forego the entertainmᵗ your letters give, and always agree to your going out in this fine weather rather than sit down to yʳ écritoire ; but let me then once possess this bill of health, and then be assur'd that if you propos'd to write on till it became one of those delightfull epistles you so often honour me with, I should only reply, (with seeming ingratitude), "Allez vous promener, madame." To-day we are busy, for all our green-house plants are hous'd, and we pretend to display much taste in ranging them. By and by there will be a semicircle, and the horse-shoe bench in the centre (all surrounded

———

[1] Lady Gower calls her maid by her Christian as well as surname, an example which it would be well if modern ladies followed.

with geranium blossom and balm of Gilead) will be very
warm and pleasant, and fragrant. The principal figure
is a yellow carnation, wch having miss'd its opportunity
to blow, is now making itself and us amends. *How perfectly* you would *represent* it! Au reste, I have not
forgot to collect seeds for Mrs. Port.

Yesterday we went to see Ken Wood, but seeing
Ld Mansfield come home, and being told there was to be
company at dinner, we thought it polite to refrain from
walking out, and only just to take a glance of the very
excellent library, &c., promising ourselves, as indeed the
servants very civilly promised us, we sh^d see ye woods
and gardens at full liberty another time. Not such was
our reception at Lady Di. Beauclerc's on Muswell Hill;
tho' we met her lady^p taking an airing, and that Mr.
Beauclerc was in town, yet they wou'd not admit us to
see the conservatory (wch was all we aspir'd to) without a
ticket. Resistance, you know, always makes one more
obstinate, so Mrs. Leveson has wrote to Sr Joshua
Reynolds to beg *he will obtain* this necessary passport.
She is very well, so is y^r younger cousin. Mr. Leveson
has made a little excursion into Cornwall, and has
visited his *uncle* at Tregothnan, and (with much more
agrément probably) Mr. Pitt at Boconnoc : there he
found L^d and L^y Edgcumbe, but they are now return'd
home, and have got the Duke (if not Dss) of Northumberland and L^d and L^y Algernon Percy. The Dss of
Beaufort is at Monmouth; she express'd much gratitude
to you, dear madam, and Mr. Dewes, and wish'd she
had any chance of meeting the latter while he stay'd in
the county. She was at Gloster in her way to Monmouth, but I believe it was only *en passant* to rest her-

self. The canvass goes on with prodigious success. I am summon'd to repair to the greenhouse. Adieu, my dear madam.

F. B.

I saw Mrs. Chapone one day this week, thought her well and in spirits.

The Hon. Mrs. Boscawen to Mrs. Delany.

Glan Villa, 17th Oct., 1776.

I had the satisfaction to hear from you at Windsor last Thursday. That day if you had taken a long lunette d'approche you wou'd have seen your humble servant sitting at dinner most comfortably with Lady Bute at Luton Hoo; nor could anything exceed her lady[ps] kindness and hospitality towards me. You may be sure I did not réclamer the one or the other, or even mean to let her know I was so near her; my aim was to see that delightfull conservatory *in particular*, and the garden *in general*. As I pass'd the *castle-gate* in my way to the town, we enquired of the porter about seeing the garden, wch he said we might do, and come in there, only keeping the gravel road, w[ch] w[d] lead directly to the garden: it did so, and there I entertain'd myself highly above an hour; the gardener more civil and agreeable than ever I saw one, the conservatory more delightfull. Here I was talking to him of Mrs. Delany, when a serv[t] came from Lady Bute with her most kind commands to dine with her en famille; I obey'd immediately, for dinner hour was very near come. At table was only (beside my

lady and her two dau^{rs}) Mrs. Muir, a widow lady in
deep mourning, and her daughter. Ld Bute was gone
into Hampshire. Our friends at Bulstrode the very
first subject we spoke upon. After dinner Lady Bute
had the goodness to shew me the whole house, and to
invite me most kindly to remain in it that night (with
Miss Sayer, who was with me), but with very true sense
of her goodness and relish for her agreeable company, I
chose rather to proceed to my lodging at the inn because
of setting out early next day for *Wrest*,[1] which I did, and
had fine weather to see (at leisure) those immense gardens, wch contain 150 acres. We spent near three hours
there, having a good little boy that shew'd it us, whom
we made wait as long as ever we pleas'd, giving him
part of the contents of our basket to stay his stomach,
for we din'd in ye gardens ; they are *Versailles* in *some*
places, in *others* a more pleasing English garden, in w^{ch},
however, Mr. Mason cou'd make some improvem^{ts}. The
water very pleasant and beautifull every where, except in
one square *looking-glass* near an immense heavy ugly
building call'd the Pavilion. I long'd to see the house,
fancying I sh^d find pictures—portraits at least ; but as
they told me it was never shown when the family was
there, I wou'd by no means ask to see it, especially as I
heard my Lord was less well that day than he had been
for some time. That I do not say one word of what I
saw at Luton Hoo [2] you will easily understand, for

> " The place *you know*, and all its charms,
>   Which every eye with pleasure warms."

Perhaps you will think this is not the proper season, but

---

[1] Wrest Park, Bedfordshire, the seat of Earl De Grey.
[2] The seat of the Earl of Bute.

if you consider that the exotick plants are all assembled together, and that in the park and woods the lovely beeches are not strip'd but wear a sort of demi-saison, wch is extremely rich and becoming, you will be convinc'd that October is as favourable a time as le mois de Mai, " tant joli mois." To compleat the prosperity of my journey, I found on my return to ye inn the most delightful news of our success at Long Island,[1] so that I had a most agreeable supper, and drank health to the noble brothers.[2] We have had a letter from Capt. Evelyn from the field of battle; he was in ye brigade of light infantry, and took 5 officers prisoners who were sent to observe our motions. He mentions Dr. Boscawen's son being well, for whom we were in great care, being the only child. O! to complete this by good news from N. York, and then peace! Adieu, my dear madam, for here comes the post, wch will never wait a minute, and it rains too hard to send (agreeably) my usual messenger after it. Best respects to the Duchess. Has she any commands to the East Indies?

Ev^r y^rs.

---

[1] Long Island, the scene of Sir Peter Parker and General Clinton's defeat, was retaken by the British forces under General Howe, in conjunction with the fleet under Lord Howe, in the same year, 1776.

[2] Richard, 4th Viscount and 1st Earl Howe, and his brother, General Sir William Howe.

The Hon. Mrs. Boscawen to Mrs. Delany.

Glan Villa, 5th Nov., 1776.

I hope the Duchess and yourself are both in perfect health. I cou'd wish you both to enjoy this good news from America without any alloy of private concern, but I am afraid that the great loss of the Archbishop of York and the affliction of your friend Ld Foley are most sensibly felt by both their friends at Bulstrode. I heard just now, indeed, that his Grace is still alive, but (as L^y Edgcumbe adds) "it is without hope of recovery," which does not materially differ from Mrs. Aislabie's information (wch I thought but too good authority), and indeed great concern express'd for his irreparable loss. Mrs. Aislabie is my neighbour, having a villa at Hendon (that was Ld Northampton's). Lady Edgcumbe I saw in London on Saturday. I went to visit both my sons-in-law; the Duke of Beaufort came to Parlia^t, and Mr. Leveson, on the news of the armament, to offer his service ; it was accepted, and he had the command of the Valiant man-of-war confer'd upon him, the news of which he receiv'd in my room, and *set me* to work immediately to help to raise fishermen *in Cornwall,* and let the pilchards go free. This I did with great alacrity (and one of his lieutenants is order'd to the neighbourhood of *Roscrow,* as well as to Mevagissy), but I hope there will be no French war. God forbid ! for surely we have business enough upon our hands : it is a great comfort to see it in a prosperous way, and wou'd be great pity to obstruct it.

I hear Ld Chatham's illness (the gout in his stomach and head) is thought to be very dangerous by his physi-

cian Dr Addington. I was told, indeed, that he wish'd
to be releas'd, because (he said) if he linger'd much
longer it wou'd entirely destroy the health of dear Lady
Chatham. I know not if this is true, but I know she
has long been a most tender and unweary'd nurse.

A particular friend of Mr. T. Pitts (Mr. Coote the
banker) has thrown himself into the Thames, (alas!
what numberless instances of this cruel insanity!) and
has left a letter to Mr. Pitt, probably recommending his
poor wife and children.

Mrs. Fitzgerald and her child are I hear so totally
délaissée by her wretched husband, afterwards hang'd
(whose fine liveries and equipage you read of in Lady
Stormont's Train,) that Lady Anne Conolly has been
oblig'd to send down a steward into Derbyshire to ac-
quire credit in *her* name for Mrs. Fitzgerald, and to discharge debts there wch hinder'd her being trusted; for it
seems the poor young woman chuses to remain there
rather than come to London, as her mother offers her, to
reside in her house. Is not dear Mrs. Port astonish'd
that there can be such a *père de famille?* so deceitful a
wretch; for you remember, I dare say, telling me how
plausible he appear'd as a neighbour to Ilam. I *prophecy'd
then* how differently he wou'd be thought of ere long.

I purpose to remove whenever I have a daughter in
London, and prudence, I think, counsels one to be there
very early in the next month, if not sooner. Mrs.
Leveson will stay with Lady Gower I dare say as long
as she can, that is, till within a week perhaps of her
lady^{ps} removal. I have had a very kind invitation to
come once more to Bill Hill because it is so much warmer
than this cottage.

The white dog has been quite lost above a week, but I have not so much car'd since you said you meant to give him away. He went away of himself, not being allow'd to go with my chaize since his first elopem^t.

Mrs. Port, of Ilam, to Rousseau.

1776.

MONSIEUR,

Je ne puis me refuser le plaisir que cette occasion me presente, de vous adresser quelques lignes ; d'autant plus que j'y suis portée par deux raisons. La prémière pour servir d'introduction à mon frère, qui désire ardemment connoître une personne qu'il a depuis long-tems connu et admiré dans ses ouvrages : la seconde pour vous marquer ma reconnoissance, de ce que Monsr Bothby m'a appris que vous m'aviez honoré de votre souvenir. Il n'est pas possible de vous exprimer les regrets que je sens de ce que vous avez quitté ce pays ; car sans parler de l'avantage que j'aurois de pouvoir jouir de votre compagnie, et de votre conversation, ce me seroit une grande consolation, ayant quatre petits enfants[1] qui se trouveroient trop heureux de pouvoir profiter de vos sages avis.

Je suis très charmée d'apprendre que vous jouïssez d'une bonne santé : puissiez vous en jouïr long-tems,

------

[1] "*Quatre petits enfants.*"—Georgina Mary Ann, born 1771 ; John, born 1773 ; George Rowe, born 1774 ; and Bernard, Vicar of Ilam, born 17th March, 1776, died Jan. 1854.

accompagnée de toute la félicité que vous communiquez aux autres ; et je ne vois pas de bornes a ce souhait.

Je suis, Monsr

Votre très obligée et très fidéle servante,

MARIE.[1]

Court Dewes, Esq., to Mrs. Delany.

Paris, 6th Nov., 1776.

DEAR MADAM,

I have two very kind and entertaining letters to thank you for, one of ye 1st Oct^r, wch I found waiting for me here at my arrival, the other of the 27th, wch I received the day before yesterday, and cannot but think myself much obliged to you that you have afforded me so much of your time when you have so many valuable uses to employ it in.

I have been in y^r great town about a fortnight ; but, great as it is, I cannot think it above two-thirds as big as London. The streets are narrower and dirtier, but ye people look *gayer* and are better dressed. But I am not going to give you a description of it, it would take a volume. For ye first ten days I was in lodgings at 2 guin^s a week, had my coach and my laquais, besides Edmund, my own valet de chambre. The day after my arrival (wch you will think more incredible) I sat *two hours* to have my hair dressed, and I had 36 papillotes in it, wch I had ye curiosity to count ; but do not imagine f^m y^s that I am going to turn out a fine gentleman at an age when it would be time (as to externals at least) to lay

---

[1] This letter is a specimen of the tone in which ladies then addressed Rousseau who did not at all adopt his opinions, but who were impressed with the idea that he was a superior being.

that character aside. I intend all ye flutter shall pass away as I pass f^m Paris, and fancy you will see me return as *plain* and as *frugal* as ever.

I have already begun a reform, and having seen most of the places worth seeing that are at a distance, I have now laid down my equipage, and shall see ye places that are within a walk on foot; but there being no raised pavement on each side of ye streets, as there is in London, walking is almost as *inconvenient* as it is *unfashionable!*

I am not without hopes of seeing Rousseau, tho' I have not done it yet. As soon as I arriv'd I called at his lodgings, up three pair of stairs, in an unfashionable part of ye town, and mean looking house, making a striking contrast to ye ostentation wth wch his *rival* Voltaire lives in his "chateau" (as he calls it) at Ferney. I was admitted into a little kind of antichamber filled w^th *bird cages*; there I saw Madame Rousseau (late Vasseur); she told me her husband (she repeated "*mon Mari*" 10 *times* I believe in five minutes' conversation) had had a fall, had hurt himself, and could not see anybody, but if I would call in a week's time I might see him. I left my letter, and in about a week after sent to know how he did, and if he was well enough to admit me; but he still continued too ill to receive visits. I fancy he is *really so*, for I do not find that when he is well he is uncommonly difficult of access. As he now has resumed his first occupation, and copies music for hire, esteeming it his duty to evince by his practise ye truth of what he has somewhere said, that "*every one in society ought to have some employment*," I shall call upon him again to-morrow, and then if I do not succeed shall give ye matter up.

I am much obliged to you for your *kind offer* of assistance on my travels, but I assure you I have no occasion to trouble you. Tho' I talk of "ye flutter" I have been making here, my tour has not been an expensive one, nor have I or shall I spend *more* money than I am *abundantly* furnished wth. I received yesterday a joint letter f^m Mr. and Mrs. Port f^m Bath, w^ch, if you write soon, I should be obliged to you if you would thank them for, and say I will answer soon. When I said that they would have advantages for educating their children at Bath, I meant only what is *commonly* called "*education*," what might *more properly* be called *instruction*, and that they w^d more easily find masters than in ye country for useful or ornamental accomplishments ; but if you mean what *alone* deserves ye name of education, and what is too much neglected, ye inspiring them wth happy dispositions, *good habits*, and giving a *right turn* to their understandings, I agree wth you in fearing that Bath may not be ye proper situation for such purposes ; but I have great confidence in their mother's good sense. I only wish she may not find too numerous a family on her hands. *One* spoilt child (their Tissington neighbour) has been ye talk of Paris, where extravagance is no novelty, for his equipage, entertainments, and every species of expence. I wonder how he supports it, as he has not always been fortunate at play. The true reason of his stay is that he cannot pay ye debts he has contracted, and if he does not return till he has paid them, I am afraid his poor wife will continue to lament his absence for some time longer, wch will be doubly irksome to her now she has lost ye family at Ilam. That family will likewise be a great loss to a nearer friend (at Calwich), especially if his *northern* lass continues obdurate ; if she should, and he should not be so deeply smitten as to prevent his turning his thoughts elsewhere, ye sooner he tries his fortune in another quarter ye better, for (except Mr. M.) he has now hardly a neighbour one w^d wish to pass two hours wth. Your account of poor Mr. Cuttle shocked me, but I will not recall ye melancholy scene by reflections on it.

I did not go within 150 miles of Solfaterra, or I sh^d have remembered your pink colour spar.

Bernard I find goes on as he could wish. I write to him by y^s post, and not knowing where he is, direct to London ; if he sh^d not be there, I wish he knew, y^t there is a letter of mine waiting for him at ye Union Coffee House, in wch I have begged of him not to let my absence prevent ye completion of his happiness, as I sh^d be very happy to salute a *second* sister at my return. I shall stay here at least I believe a fortnight longer. If any letter sh^d come after I have left Paris, it will be sent after me. I have hardly left room to beg my humble respects to the Duchess of Portland and to subscribe myself your dutiful and affec.

C. DEWES.

Mr. Frederick Montagu[1] to Mrs. Delany.

Hanover Square, November 8th, 1776.

DEAR MADAM,

I have this moment received your letter, and have the pleasure of informing you that my mother bore

---

[1] Frederick Montagu, of Papplewick, a scion of the Sandwich family ; his mother was Mrs. Montagu " the little," the intimate friend of Lady Bute,

her journey very well. She came to town last Saturday in very tolerable health and spirits, and has had no considerable complaint since. I don't hear that the Archbishop of York[1] is dead, but there are no hopes. The Bp. of Lichfield[2] is instructing his Royal pupil at Kew; Mason is grumbling in Yorkshire; the Duchess of Devonshire carries her plumes *higher than ever;* your friend is in great spirits about the success in America.[3] The Bishops are preparing the Form of Prayer for the fast, and if they are *not careful* Mason will attack their *lawn sleeves!* Mrs. Brough is a great comfort to us. Adieu, in haste. My mother sends her love to you, and we both join in proper comp[s] to the Duchess of Portland and Lady Wallingford.

Yours with the greatest truth,

F. MONTAGUE.

P.S. Lord Guilford[4] is perfectly well at Waldershare,[5] where the Willoughbys[6] are going.

I have opened my letter again to inform you that

Lady Gower, and Mrs. Delany. He was, on his father's side, related to Lady Bute.

[1] Dr. Gilbert, Archbishop of York, died in Nov., 1776.

[2] Dr. Hurd, afterwards Bishop of Worcester, was appointed Preceptor to the Prince of Wales and Duke of York in 1776, on the resignation of Dr. Markham, then Bishop of Chester, and afterwards Archbishop of York.

[3] The Declaration of American Independence was made July 4, 1776. The success here alluded to was gained by General Howe, acting in concert with his brother, Lord Howe, who commanded the British fleet.

[4] Francis North, 1st Earl of Guilford. His first wife was the Lady Lucy Montagu, daughter of George Montagu, Earl of Halifax. Lord North, their eldest son, was Prime Minister from 1770 to 1781, to whom Mr. Frederick Montagu was thus related.

[5] Waldershare Park, Kent, the seat of the Earls of Guilford.

[6] John Peyto Verney, 6th Baron Willoughby, married, in 1761, Lady Louisa North, daughter of Francis, 1st Earl of Guilford.

Mr. North,[1] Lord North's son, is going to be married to *Miss Egerton, the great Cheshire heiress.* Old Sam Egerton gives her *one hundred thousand pounds down.* I don't write in figures, for fear you should think I put an 0 too much.

The Hon. Mrs. Boscawen to Mrs. Delany.

Glan Villa, Wednesday, 20th Nov., 1776.

I have planted all my trees. I cannot put my head out of doors because of the stormy wind and tempest. I have a bit of a leisure morning, and a good frank to dear Mrs. Delany. Why, then, shou'd I not try to amuse her a little? Likely story indeed, that from my dull cottage in a dull morning of November, my pen, duller than both, shou'd produce anything amusing. Well—I give it up; but I shall nevertheless proceed to tell her that Monday I was at Bush Hill, and had a pleasant walk, and still pleasanter conversation, with my agreeable neighbour Mrs. Mellish. We talk'd of you, my dear madam (a favourite subject with both, for some people have particular fancies). Mrs. Mellish gave me the inclos'd letter from Voltaire, for I had never before seen it. Perhaps you have; if not, la voici à votre service. Don't you like his *suspending* his dying agony to write (death is so apt to wait till people have done their business and are at *leisure*); but you see this is near 6 years ago, so it has been a pretty long "*agonie,*" or rather he

---

[1] George Augustus North, afterwards 3rd Earl of Guilford, married, first, in 1785, Maria Frances Mary, daughter of George Hobart, 3rd Earl of Buckinghamshire; and 2nd, in 1796, Susan, daughter of Thomas Coutts, Esq.

has made use of death (as the old man wou'd have done to pick up his sticks) to stand in the stead of speeches and complit[s] to Mr. Fawkes,[1] and at the same time has a mind to appear to be not only "ferme, mais enjoué entre les bras de la mort." [2]

Have you heard, my dear madam, that Hume [3] has left 2 treatises to be publish'd (they are already printed). I saw a letter yesterday to Mrs. Smith of Hadley, wch said they had read them. One was to prove the soul is mortal. Being printed they wou'd have been publish'd during the life of the author (this letter added), had not L[d] Mansfield prevented it by assuring him he *should be prosecuted*. Now he has bequeath'd them to his nephew, with orders that if no bookseller or publisher will undertake to give them to the publick, he, the nephew, shall publish them. What had le genre humain done to Mr. Hume that he shou'd have such a spite against it? I hope L[d] Mansfield will again interpose; for with all desirable freedom left to the Press there is still, I conclude, some legal restraint upon y[e] publication of certain atrocious attacks upon the Establishment, of which Christianity, thank God, as yet makes a part. I saw yesterday a handbill (printed) w[ch] was treason from top to bottom, abusing the K—, "with whom we had no business," quite an expensive superfluity, and proposing a covenant (w[ch] is ready cut and dry'd) to be signed by all those who are of this opinion, and who will join in turning this same Old England *into a republick!* I believe

---

[1] Francis Fawkes, A.M., Rector of Hayes. He published translations of Anacreon, Sappho, Bion, Moschus and Theocritus; and died in 1777.

[2] Voltaire died May 30, 1778.

[3] Hume died in 1776.

we must return to the good old toast of "Church and King," for both seem to be in danger, if we may judge by the fierceness of the attacks made upon them.

Mais—revenons à nos moutons. Is this India paper good for anything to you, my dear madam. It is *real Indian*, I am sure, having found it in a writing-box of ebony, inlaid with ivory, wch was made at Madrass. I have half-a-dozen sheets more if this shou'd be of any use to you.

I purpose to go to Lon^n to-morrow to see Mrs. Leveson, who is encamp'd somewhere between her old house and her new. I sho^d like *to take advantage of her distress* to bring her down here. Her boys remain with their kind "*granmama*." The eldest governs her lady^p with a high hand, I dare-say.

The Rev. Mr. Fawkes, who translated Anacreon and Theocritus, sent the last-mentioned work over as a present to Voltaire, with a letter in French, and received in return the following answer :—

" à Ferney ce 9e Fevrier, 1771.

" MONSIEUR,

" Quoique l'état où je suis me permette à peine de voir les trésors de l'antiquité que vous avez rajeunis, je me hâte de vous remercier, de peur de mourir sans m'être acquitté de ce devoir. J'interromps l'agonie pour vous dire combien je suis sensible à votre mérite, et reconnoissant de vos bontés. Si je m'échappe de ma maladie je vous remercierai plus au long, sinon—je vous prierai de faire l'épitaphe de

" Votre très humble et très obéissant serviteur,

" VOLTAIRE."

The Dowager-Countess Gower to Mrs. Delany.

Bill Hill, 25th Nov., 76.

Dr Mrs Delany congratulates me on Leveson's re-entering employ. I am not one of those y^t rejoice at it, considering all y^t has past. I don't think 'twas his part to offer his service. I am sure he was under *no obligation*; but he had *navy reasons*, quite out of my province, so I remain'd neuter. He and Mrs. Leveson have both left me, she to look after her ffurniture, and he wild after his ship. I'm hap̃y he's fond of his profession, and wth a full confidence y^t Providence is ye same at sea as at land. There's no place exempt from dangers. The two boys left here perfectly well, and my boisterous ffriend as conformable to me and as amiable as ever, but yet utters but few words, wch to me is a matter of wonder. Here I'll stop, least you sho^d think ye nurse is cor̃esponding wth you.

I had my fears ye D^s of Portland's spirits were much affected by acc^{ts} I heard of ye B^p of York.[1] Time has prov'd not so bad as reported; hope by y^s time his recovery is perfected, and y^t ye D^s is quite tranquil, to w^m I desire my most affec^t respects. I heard last post Mrs. Mountagu was very well. I have not heard such good of her a long time; wish I may have conviction of ye truth of it next week, being oblig'd to go to London for a few days.

The North's appear to me to be ffortune's favourite sons. May they make a proper use of it; *madam ex-*

---

[1] Dr. John Gilbert was at that time Archbishop of York. His only child and heiress, Emma, married George, 1st Earl of Mount Edgcumbe.

cepted, all goes to ye aggrandizing of 'em wth out a check. As for Ministerial abuse, I look on that as a tribute that all in power must pay. How many will be disapointed, y^t^ thought their Tomy's worthy this heiress! In y^s^ desert I have nothing to fill a letter wth but self, and w^t^ belongs thereuntoo. Magnolia has not ceas'd to make efforts to charm; ye 2^d^ best has now two bloom as large as a turkey egg, and of a lovely white; but ye weather is too cold for it to venture to expand. It does all it can to please, and I am pleas'd. I don't desire you to think of London till ab^t^ ye 20th of next month, at wch time I shall be much interested in yor movements.

Pray where is to be had ye remedy for ye jaundice? wch Lady Willoughby [1] took. I've a serv^t^ ill of y^t^ disorder.

Since I wrote thus farr, a letter has call'd me to London. Y^e^ affair will keep me there a few days. I cary this.

Mrs. Delany to the Rev. John Dewes, at Calwich.

Bulstrode, 5th Dec., 1776.

Now I have lost my good intelligence out of your neighbourhood, my dear nephew, I must intrude on your retirement to ask y^u^ how you do, but hope you have thoughts of coming among your friends in London, and giving me the pleasure of having my solicitude gratified more fully. Tho' I am a little premature in my congrat^ns^ on Bernard's marriage, it is not unlikely but this

---

[1] Lady Louisa North, sister of the Prime Minister, and daughter of Francis, 1st Earl of Guilford, married John Peyto, 6th Baron Willoughby De Broke, in 1761.

may kiss your hands if not *on,* at least very near the time. He seems to have chosen a young woman who promises to make him happy, and then of course all his friends so, and I hope to congratulate you on the like occasion, when you meet with one worthy of you. I was in hopes of seeing Court to-day, but he is too busy, he writes me word, to leave London yet, and waits also to salute the bride and bridegroom. They are to be at my house, and will take possession some days before I shall be there. They are so good as to excuse me for not being there to receive them, as the Dss of Portland has been much out of order, and staying in this good air is better for her than the fogs of London, so I cannot possibly leave her: but I suppose we shall go the week after next. I had a letter last post from your dear sister, to assure me she was much better of her feverish cold. The children are still ill. I own I was in hopes it would have proved the small-pox, as that is apt to be caught on changing of situation, especially more likely in a place never free from it, after a succession of much company, *philosophers, poets,* and *kings!*

We have lately enjoy'd a very pleasing tranquillity. Our last book (for we work and read by turns) was Mr. Pennant's last tour to Scotland, wch I think entertaining, and must be more so to you, who have explored some of his paths.

We have had some sad interruptions to our pleasure this summer. The astonishing desperate action of Mr. Cuttle, the Dss's butler, hung heavily on us a great while, and the melancholy state of health the Archbishop of York is in, with very little hopes of his recovering. I have no news but what the papers tell you; thankfull for our success in America so far, and hoping a happy conclusion. The Dss of Portland desires her comp^ts to you. Believe me my dear nephew, with every warm wish on ye approaching season and new year,

Ever your affectionate Aunt and humble serv^t,

M. DELANY.

Pray make my compliments to Mr. and Mrs. Mills. I hope they are well and their daughter. How does *Nathan* and *Mary?* remember me kindly to them.

Mrs. Delany to the Viscountess Andover.

Bulstrode, 13th Dec., 1776.

Here I come, my dear Lady Andover, to present to you and your amiable companion a whole possy of *charades,* which I hope will prove worthy of a place at your fireside, by giving you the amusement of leading your brains into a *labyrinth,* (or what you please to call it,) and the satisfaction of gaining the wish'd for exit. On the whole, if they divert you they will do their duty. Their interpretation, shou'd you be at a loss, will not be utter'd till you demand it in person in the by-corner of St. James's Place, and hope that day is not far off, and that when your ladyship and Miss Fanny Howard have eaten your Xtmas pye at Elford, you will finish your Xtmas fare in London. It is impossible to allow you a longer latitude. By this invitation your ladyship will imagine the chaise is at the door, and we are going to set off. I believe that will not be till the latter end of next week, and when it comes I shall be sorry, so luxurious and so selfish am I. And all this while a bride and bride-groom[1] have possession of my house, and wait for my coming to wish them joy; and much joy I wish them.

Tho' I seem *in spirits*, I am not, because our dear friend is *not so*, having this morning receiv'd an account of the Archb[p] of York's death;[2] but it has long been expected, and he was reduced to that state of health that was rather more affecting than the consequence of it; and therefore trust when the natural tribute is paid it will soon be succeeded by those consoling considerations that must be suggested by such a heart and head as our most dear friend is bless'd with.

The Duke of Portland dines here to-day; goes away to-morrow. The light has left me in the lurch, and I can only say every affectionate wish attends Elford from Bulstrode. Pray a word or two soon.

Mrs. Bernard Dewes[3] to Mrs. Viney.

St. James's Place, Dec. 14, 1776.

MY DEAREST MADAM,

Accept my sincerest thanks for your very kind letter, which I received this day. Be assured, my dear madam, that none among the many which I have had on this occasion was more welcome to me than yours. Mr. Dewes's and my best thanks also to your sister for her kind wishes.

---

[1] Mr. Bernard Dewes married Anne, eldest daughter of John De la Bere, Esq.

[2] The Hon. and Rev. Dr. Drummond, Archbishop of York, died Dec. 15th, 1776.

[3] Anne De la Bere (Mrs. Bernard Dewes) was married in this month, Dec. 1776.

We arrived here to dinner on Monday, found Mrs. Delany not returned, on account of the Duchess of Portland's not being quite well; we hope to see her next week. Our present scheme is to stay here about a month, from thence to Bath, to pay a visit to Mr. and Mrs. Port, and then to Welsbourn. Mr. Dewes as well as myself will have the greatest pleasure in waiting on you and Mrs. A. Viney at Gloster. We have heard of another house in Warwickshire, we are to know for a certainty next week whether we can have it or not *ready furnished*. I have many letters to write, therefore, my dear madam, you will excuse my adding more to this than that I am

Your affectionate and

Obliged, humble servant,

A. DEWES.

The Hon. Mrs. Boscawen to Mrs. Delany.

Audley Street, 13th Dec., 1776.

MY DEAR MADAM,

Every day we have fancy'd that Capt Willm Gardiner will arrive from New York with good news from Genl Howe, to whom he is aide-de-camp. Mr. Luke Gardiner, his brother, has been come from Ireland some time in hopes of his arrival; his wife,[1] one of the 3 graces (Montgomerys), I never saw till now; she is by no means equal to Lady Townshend in beauty: and besides waiting for news to write you, I have often waited (in vain)

---

[1] One of the coheiresses of Sir William Montgomery, of Magbie Hill, Bart., wife of Right Hon. Luke Gardiner, who was created Baron Mountjoy, 1789. She was sister of Anne, Marchioness Townshend.

for leisure. Both my daughters in London, and one of
them chiefly in her own apartm^t, find me perpetual,
employment! then in the morning, when the paper is
spread to write to Mrs. Delany, behold 7 grandchildren
in my room: a pretty groupe it was, I assure you.
Cousin John Leveson, who at his first arrival in London
had all his *forest* airs, and was much like. unto a wild
colt, spurning and kicking every one that came near
him, is now much tamer, et se laisse vaincre par la beauté,
et la douceur de ses petites cousines. Mrs. Leveson
was at Caractacus last night, but I don't think she
lik'd it in ye theatre much better than she has always
done in her own closet; indeed, I think 'tis difficult, for
surely 'tis charming to read.

My dear madam, I have been at the Chapel Royal to
celebrate the fast, and have heard (every word of) an
incomparable good sermon by Dr. Porteous. I had
great satisfaction in seeing Lady Weymouth look so
perfectly well: grown fat, surely. Her lady^p went out
of the closet so soon after the service was over that it
was not in my power to ask her (being at the other end
of the closet) if she had any commands for Bulstrode, as
it is just possible she may not write herself to-day. She
will tell you that we are to have no riots in Westm^r ab^t
the election, wch is a *very good hearing*. Ld Mahon,[1]
whom the Opposition would have been glad of, I suppose,
says he spent *too much* last time: Ld Pitt[2] is not of age,

---

[1] Charles Stanhope, who at his father's death, in 1786, became 3rd Earl of
Stanhope. He was distinguished for scientific knowledge and mechanical
talents.

[2] John, eldest son of the great Earl of Chatham, born Sept. 10th, 1757.
He succeeded to the Earldom, 1778.

and Ld Mount Morres[1] is *not to be found !* I think: tant-
y-a that nobody will oppose Ld Petersham.[2] Lady
Harrington[3] has been extremely alerte ; I hear her lady^p
says she "shall spend her Christmas holydays at
Chevely,"[4] having promis'd Ld Granby.[5] The play to be
exhibited at the Town Hall at Henley you know more
of than I can tell you. Mr. Onslow[6] is to be marry'd
next week—and Mr. Elliot[7] (to Miss Amyand) the week
after. Is Mr. Dewes[8] marry'd ? Mrs. Leveson thinks
she saw him with his bride last night at Caractacus, if so
please to accept my compli^{mts}.

---

[1] Hervey Redmond de Montmorency, 2nd Viscount Mountmorres.

[2] Charles Stanhope, who at his father's death, April 1, 1779, became 3rd Earl of Harrington.

[3] Caroline, eldest daughter of Charles Fitzroy, Duke of Grafton, wife of William, 2nd Earl of Harrington, and mother of Lord Petersham.

[4] Chevely Park, Cambridgeshire, a seat of the Duke of Rutland's.

[5] John Manners, Lord Granby, a celebrated General of the British forces in Germany. He died before his father, John, 3rd Duke of Rutland.

[6] The Hon. Thomas Onslow married his first wife, Miss Ellerker, of Risby Park, Dec. 29th, 1776. The year in which this letter was written is ascertained by this fact. He was many years afterwards 2nd Earl Onslow.

[7] Gilbert Elliot, Esq., married, Jan. 3, 1777, Anna Maria, eldest daughter of Sir George Amyand, Bart. He succeeded his father, Sir Gilbert Elliot, as 4th Bart., filled many high offices of the state, and was created Earl of Minto on returning home from his government of Bengal in 1813.

[8] Bernard, 2nd son of John Dewes, of Welsbourn, Esq., married, 1776, to Miss De la Bere.

The Dowager-Countess Gower to Mrs. Delany.

Bill Hill, 15th Dec^r., 76.

I last post read in ye news paper Mr. Bernard Dewes was mañied ; as you last sumer express'd yor *approbation* of his choice, I can't omit my congratulations, interesting myself in whatever concerns you, hoping all consequences from this new allie will be to you an additional hapĩness. I heard Mr. Port was at Bath, not on acc^t of health I hope. I reĉed a letter from ye D^s of P., wch I looked upon as a bill of health wch gave me great satisfaction. I did not see Mr. Mason in all ye days I was in London, he was quite absorb'd in Caractacus, but determin'd to preach to his flock on ye fast day; w^t is very extraordinary, he has recomended *a cook* to me, ye mañer was, " *Delboux to L . . . y Gower !* " This man he was acquainted wth, last year was out of business, and from a motive of charity took him into ye countrey. It was a great and impertinent joke of ye waggs, y^t Mason sh^d have a *man cook!* and now they say he has *fatted him!* All judge for others, few know how to judge for themselves. This pretty story is ye most amusing I'm now worth.   My young people have all left me, and I'm in a most profound retreat.   I guess wee shall soon meet, in health and chearfulness I hope; till y^t day comes, dear madam, adieu.

Mrs. Delany to Mrs. Ann Viney.

St. James's Place, March 1st, 1777.

I have lately been much hurried and ill, which have prevented my writing sooner, and I am uneasy at not having heard lately how you and your sister do. I was taken ill on Ash Wednesday with a very smart attack of fever, but I thank God bleeding and Dr. Turton's prescriptions soon abated my fever, and has left only weakness to struggle with; but the hopes of my dear Mrs. Port's coming kept up my spirits. I expected her, her dear little girl and youngest boy, a lovely child, on the 22nd of last month (Mr. Port not till to day). On the night of the thaw, which was the day before, I was obliged to quit my bed at midnight and go into the room prepared for Mrs. P.; for the melting of the snow penetrated into my room in every part of the ceiling, which is still so damp I dare not return into it, but have put a bed for myself in Mrs. Port's dressing-room; so that my dear guests are sadly crowded: however, friends that delight in one another's company make all matters easy. Tho' I still feel in a maze I am surprisingly well, at least *so happy* with my present company that I don't feel my own infirmities. Mrs. Port desires her best compliments, and mine, to the dear sisters; she is charming well, and Miss Port a most engaging girl.

M. DELANY.

The following riddles were subjoined :—

What a good boy will do when he chooses at school
To remember his blessing and not play the fool.
My second great travellers often have seen,
Now pitched on the sands, and now spread on the green.

Some transient view of the whole you secure
While honours, and riches, and health you procure,
But 'tis virtue alone that will make it *endure*.

My first (bar accidents) you'll find
The property of all mankind,
Yet *many*, who have *more than one*,
With truth may say that they *have none*.
My second's often but a toy,
Sometimes a gift received with joy,
And those who give and take it know
The height of happiness or woe ;
My whole's an ornament the fair
In various shapes and sizes rear.

My first is a lyar, a cheat, a deceiver,
   Yet by mortals will ever be courted,
For those are most blest who most blindly believe her,
   And the wretched by her are supported.
My second is neither so large nor so much ;
   My *tout* is a heart-piercing word,
For if we are *that*, its sad nature is such,
   That no other can comfort afford.

The Countess of Stamford to Mrs. Delany.

Bullstrode, April ye 2nd, 1777.

MY DEAREST FRIEND,

Far from thinking your letter too long, I felt both sorry and obliged to you when I came to the end of it ; *sorry* that it was not as long again, and *very much obliged* to you, who are in the centre of all your friends, for bestowing so much of your *precious time* on me.

Your account of my dear mother made me sincerely happy, and as you were so kind to give me the satisfaction of knowing you *could not* make the excuse of want of health for *not* accompanying her to Mrs. Wilmott's, I flatter myself I shall hear you were of the party, and that you were both well amused.

You can better imagine, my dear Mrs. Delany, than I can describe to you, the tranquillity and peace of mind I enjoy at this moment. The comfort of seeing a daily amendment in my dear children; the reflecting on my dearest mother's *unbounded goodness* and kindness to me; and the indulgence of a thousand pleasing thoughts which this enchanting place recalls to my mind, makes me happier than I can find words to express; for indeed, at times the power of utterance is lost, and its only vent is at the eyes. But this, my friend, I *only* say to *you*, for *modern hearts* are too refined for such *old-fashion'd* sensations.

I have not yet complained of the weather; a proof how thoroughly contented I am in every other respect. Tho' I must own, I feel a little cross with the cold north-east wind. It will not allow this delightful place to disclose all its sweets; tho' little Queen Mab begs me to assure you there are many of *your little favorites* in full bloom; and that the woods in the garden are enamell'd with primroses, violets, &c.

If I don't quit this subject I shall trespass too long on your patience. I will only add the kind love of all your little friends. My lord went to town yesterday to meet our dear boy. I hope you have constant good accounts of Mrs. Port and her family. I must beg you to present my duty to my mother; I do not write to her to-night, but I will to-morrow.

I am, my dearest friend,
Y^{rs} very affectionately,
H. C. STAMFORD.

The Hon. Mrs. Boscawen to Mrs. Delany.

Glan Villa, May 21st, 1777.

Tuesday the 20th, I was treated and regal'd with it at my return from London (yes, from London, and without seeing you); thither we went in the morning thro' torrents of rain, about some mantua-making business of my daughter's : this done it was agreed we should have the pleasure to wait on Mrs. Delany ; and Mrs. Leveson at length call'd on me in her coach for that purpose, nay, we even began to go, when, unluckily for my pleasure, I bethought myself to look what o'clock it was, and discovered, alas ! that the hour was compleatly come to carry us back again : and we submitted returning to the place from whence we came, and thro' the same unrelenting torrents as we came in. Dinner we found impatient, and as to the evening, we spent it by the side of a good, crackling, blazing, wood fire, sticking close to our books, except the short and pleasant interruptions of our bouncing boys, whose tempers are a little try'd by so much confinement; however, y^r friend delights himself with your present, the pretty cane, which is his horse in hand while he rides upon another, and with uplifted hand whips both, and supplies with ideal journies to Bill Hill to "*visu granmama Gower*" the want of shorter excursions upon my gravel-walks, w^{ch}, however, he has obtain'd today to his great satisfaction. My dear madam, believe me, you have no reason to regret being absent from sweet Bulstrode. The keen north-east has never ceas'd to blow, and I know not how it is that I have escap'd getting an ague while I have listen'd to ye nightingale. Every night, at midnight I open my closet window and stand starving to hear 4 or 5 of those wonderfull creatures straining their throats and answering each other; (doubtless they are making lamentations and elegies on the cold, for so keen an air comes to my blue nose while I attend to them that proclaims it not Whitsun holidays, but Christmas). Here I should end, but that I have to boast of some social pleasures (if no rural ones). We have made a visit to Mrs. Mellish, and found her, wch was very agreeable, and we have received one from Mr. and Mrs. Cole, who were so good to come and dine with us; in the afternoon also came Mrs. Smith, and the whole formed a very pleasant conversazione round a good fire. One afternoon we spent at Mrs. Burrows's and this is dedicated to return Mrs. Smith's visit by appointment. Mrs. Walsingham reckons me (I fancy) under some evil influence to have deserted (voluntarily) so much good company, but besides that I always lov'd to be in the country in *spring* (and did not certainly bargain for winter weather), I took my daughter while I could get her, and in the absence of her lord and master; her children, too, were in danger of hoopingcough, so rife in London, and will be benefitted by country air, good milk, &c. We are all well, I thank God, malgre le froid et les frimats; aussi bien cela ne gagne point mon cœur, where you reign, my dear madam, in a very warm corner, and may discern that with great warmth of affection I remain your faithfull and oblig'd servant,

F. Boscawen.

I beg my respects to the lady of the sopha, (certainly I should like a place near her once more) ; y^r cousin sends hers to you.

The Countess Gower to Mrs. Delany, St. James's Place, London.

Bill Hill, 6th June, 77.

I am ashamed I'm two leters in arrear to dear Mrs Delany, who merits other treatment ; I make no *excuses*, having been told they are *generally* lies ; but do assure her it always revives me to see her writing.

The summer is at last come, tho' I can't say it has yet brought such soft agreeable evenings as June used to bring.   I, who am a night walker, have generally felt a chill in the air, and am told there is a frost most mornings.   My fruit has suffered greatly ; nevertheless all around is beautifull ; sorry I am the Dowager Duchess of Portland can't enjoy those at Bulstrode, which always wear the greenest liveries.   I wish Mr Lever health to attend her : he can't have a wish beyond that.   My poor old gardener I believe is a good one, and *a mule* ; thinks ladys know nothing, so has *not* regarded my directions in watering the magnolia, and I don't see the least symptom of one bloom. You reckon me solitary ; I have a great deal of company (such as it is,) and talk more than ever I did in my life, even to be hoarse at the end of ye day.   Excepting the consequences of this sort of exercise, I'm very well, even better than well, if possible, from hearing Leveson is arrived in perfect health at Portsmouth with a prize not very profitable, but a mark he has *not* been *idle*. I ought to congratulate you on your friend's having so large a legacy left him: 'twas from a motive of charity I conclude; indeed he *has* been a beggar a long time. I wish the bequest had come sooner; it might have saved a *tax*! I own I grudge my mite, and so does honest Mason, I dare say, and *growls*, tho' at his favorite retreat. I see among the advertisements a bookseller has wrote him a letter concerning Gray's Poems; but he is above being disturbed at such things. Mrs. Montagu's recovery is surprizing; Papplewick will confirm it, and I hope she will long enjoy health and ease.

Your leaving London seeming to be uncertain, I direct this to St. James's Place, tho' I hope it will not find you there, being persuaded both you and ye Duchess will be better pleased in the shades at Bulstrode, and I am sure better for your healths. That all things may contribute thereunto is the constant desire of y^r most faithfull

M. G.

The Hon. Mrs. Boscawen to Mrs. Delany.

Glan Villa, yᵉ 7th June, 1777.

I cou'd almost chide my dear madam that you did not find one day to eat my brown bread and country fare. You shou'd have been in no danger upon Finchley Common ; we would have reconducted you with our whole body of horse wᶜʰ (having Mrs. Leveson's for recruits) is now considerable : but murmuring is vain. You had a very hot day for your little journey, so much the more delightfull must the shades of Bulstrode appear. The courtiers that day must have suffer'd a little from their loyalty, but as pride feels no pain I hope the high heads and waving streamers for (I think no plumes come there) diverted some and consol'd others. I shall hear a little about it by and by, as I expect my friends Lord and Lady Edgcumbe to dinner, and I thought myself lucky last night in the arrival of a very fine haunch of venison, wᶜʰ, as it had march'd far, will be very good to eat; 'tis the first I have seen, and it is *not* stall fed. Don't you like my telling you my dinner (to wᶜʰ I may add that my own garden produces les pois verds) as well as my guests, but if I did not what wou'd this little corner produce ? Why a great *match*, but that you know ; the Duke of Shandoy's[1] his villa is within a mile, and his future Duchess is resident at another neighbours of mine, viz. Judge

---

[1] James Brydges, 3rd Duke of Chandos, married, first, in 1753, Mary, daughter and heiress of John Nicol, of Southgate, Middlesex, Esq. She died in 1768, leaving no child. He married, secondly, June 21, 1777, Anne Eliza, daughter of Richard Gamon, Esq., and widow of Robert Hope Elletson, Esq. The only child of this marriage was Anne Eliza, who married Richard, Earl Temple.

Welles, whose lady I imagine is exceedingly affairée with this *great event* and *accompanies* Mrs. Elletson to dine with his Grace, and then his Grace *to dine with them!* Methinks this Chandos family delights in puddles—tho' not always so thick as the hostler's sweepings can make it—but, more or less, 'tis always far remov'd from the clear stream of noble or gentle blood. I am very glad you approve of Miss More's Essays, such an *imprimatur* does her and them honour. I believe her to be a worthy and religious woman of exceeding good principles, and then one may hope that whatever she writes may do *some* good ; at least we are sure it can do no harm. She wrote me that she had had the honour of a very polite card from Mrs. Delany, and was *much flatter'd* with her notice, and I remember she added that you was to go out of town the next day; this was towards the end of May I believe.

Adieu, my dear madam. I think I hear the sound of coaches. I will get my packet made up ready for his lordship to frank. Pardon its dullness.

Dr. W. H. Roberts to Mrs. Viney.

Eton College, June 11th, 1777.

I am concerned to hear your account of Mrs. Dewes,[1] nothing can be more amiable than her disposition ; she has married into a family where she is received with the greatest affection. Mrs. Delany, whom I often

---

[1] " *Mrs. Dewes.*"—Anne De la Bere, the wife of Mr. Bernard Dewes, whose early death was the cause of deep sorrow to her own family as well as that of her husband.

visited when I was last in town, speaks of her as if she was her child; I hope that this disorder is but accidental, and that she will live to be as happy as she deserves.

The Hon. Mrs. Boscawen to Mrs. Delany.

Glan Villa, 20th June, 1777.

Indeed, my dear madam, I should have been most extremely uneasy and unhappy, if I had heard of y^r being in St. James's Place, and Dr Turton's charrot at y^r door. I return you, therefore, many thanks for the antidote with which you prepar'd me for news, which wou'd have poison'd my tranquility. If you return'd yesterday to sweet Bulstrode you had not a good day for your journey; but you thought it good, if it restor'd you to her Grace, on whose tender care I rely for y^r being perfectly recovered, else I know we shall have you again in London, which God forbid! the *truth* is, my dear madam, *you* have *too much* (good) blood in your veins, you must, therefore, part with some from time to time, (tho' the elect Duchess of Ch . . . . cannot buy it, which is pity). Do you ever drink new-milk whey of a morning? That which comes out of the dairy at Bulstrode, and from the beautiful snowy cows, must be excellent, and if it agrees with you as a cooling beverage, it must be wholsome and lower that rich blood of yours : C'est mettre de l'eau dans son vin : however, I won't have you take me for your physician nor whey for y^r physick without Dr. Turton's approbation. I hope you had the wisdom to take his particular directions for your *future conduct*, as to whether you *may* eat *anything* for your supper, &c. *If I do,* I dream of treasons, stratagems, and spoils, so I never pretend to more than a china orange or a glass of lemonade. I wish you had better weather, that you might walk out, and make the tour of Elizium. Wensday was fine, and Mrs. Leveson and I had a very pleasant party with Mrs. Aislabie at South Lodge, where there are (dit on) £500 worth of plants. Miss Sharp has sold it, and herself has hir'd the house where Peter Colinson[1] lived, and where he has left *his mark.* I arriv'd at Mrs. Burrows t'other night, just after Mrs. Vesey (who had din'd there) was gone : they thought her much out of spirits at her approaching departure.

Adieu, my dearest madam ; take a vast deal of care of yourself. Ever your faithfull and obliged,

F. B.

The Earl of Guilford to Mrs. Delany.

Wroxton, July y⁰ 9th, 1777.

MADAM,

Having been so long detained in town by bad weather, I could only enquire at the gate after your health, and that of the Duchess of Portland ; and had great satisfaction in learning they were both very good : when most rheumatick people are complaining. You have *so much* agreeable amusement *at home,* that tho' Bulstrode is such a charming place, I have not so much

---

[1] An eminent botanist, and the friend of Linnæus, after whom the genus Collinsonia was named. Peter Collinson was born in 1694, and died in 1768.

compassion for you as for most people in bad weather. I had a very wet journey, and found everything here cold, damp, and dismal, but am, thank God, pure well. The sun shines, and glass rises, and I hope I shall be in a better way to receive you. If you execute my scheme of going by Wroxton to Warwickshire, my horses shall meet you at Hopcrofts Holt, the next stage to Islip, and carry you to Compton or Welsbourn, after you have reposed yourself a little here. I can't say I have succeeded for L^y Wallingford, tho' I zealously wish her success. L^y North has, however, promised to use her endeavours; so that I don't absolutely despair. I beg the favor of you to present my best respects to my Lady Duchess, and believe me with great esteem.

Madam,

Your most obedient,

And obliged humble servant,

GUILFORD.

Wroxton, July ye 9th, 1777.

Mrs. Delany to the Rev. John Dewes, at Calwich.

Bulstrode, 11th July, 1777.

I am much obliged to my dear nephew for his punctuallity, and wish other paymasters were as exact. I think with great pleasure of your meeting altogether, and shou'd be happy to be of the party; but tho', I thank God, I cannot complain of any considerable want of health, considering my great age, I feel every year weakens me, and one or two feverish attacks I have had within these 2 months makes me apprehensive that a long journey, and a great distance from the advice I am used to, wou'd be a hazardous undertaking. I am afraid I shall disappoint my dear friends at Malvern Hall, as I have given them an expectation of my making them a visit and have not yet named my fears to them of such an undertaking ; and indeed, when I mentioned such a scheme to them, I thought I might be able to accomplish it. Don't mention this to them till I do it myself which will be in a post or two.

Most sincerely and affec^t,
M. DELANY.

Mrs. Delany, like other persons of her time (when the treatment of patients was generally to torture by blisters or kill by bleeding), always supposed that the weakness she experienced after such discipline was occasioned by age, instead of being surprised at having survived its effects.

The Hon. Mrs. Boscawen to Mrs. Delany.

Glan Villa, 16th July, 1777.

MY DEAR MADAM,

Just as we were sitting down to dinner arriv'd to our great surprise and satisfaction, the Lady of Bill Hill, where her long residence and profound uninterrupted solitude have had no bad effect upon the spirits, for I never saw them better, or her ladyship more "*chapsey*," to use her own term. She gave us an account of all her proceedings : where she had succeeded, and where fail'd : the character of her gardener, whom she represented most exactly to the life as we knew (for he lived with me at Hatchland Park 20 years) ; that he was no flatterer, for when she asked him, "if he had ever seen so pretty a place as Bill Hill ?" he answered, " *Yes, many;*" he is, nevertheless, rather a favourite, and yet the sweet magnolias do not succeed this year, and, 'tis suspected, thro' his fault, wch I am really sorry for, as my lady is so fond of them ; but what you will really like to hear is, that Lady Gower announced the approaching payment of Mr. Leveson's paternal fortune, with *all the interest* that has accumulated thereon, to *a very considerable amount.* She seem'd very desirous of his return, wch I hope will happen before the end of this month. Her ladyship was also much pleas'd with the "*pretty wretch,*" and commended his looks and his growth ; he rode in upon the stick you gave him.

Mrs. Chapone is at Mrs. Smith's, at Hadley, and both were to have dined with me yesterday, but sent an excuse, Mrs. Smith having had a fall, wch had much alarm'd them : but I have had a good account since from the doctor. You have a *new* neighbour at Chalfont, respectable and amiable personages, whom I honour and love very much, so that I rather envy you. They did look at something this way, and I want them much more than you do.

I hope you want nothing, wch is only another way of saying, I hope your have got health. To hear so much will give sincere pleasure to

Your very affectionate friend and serv^t,

F. BOSCAWEN.

The Dowager-Countess Gower to Mrs. Delany.

Bill Hill, 20th July, 77.

I was haul'd to London 13th inst, so had not dr Mrs D's letter till I found it here last ffriday; wn in town I went to see my dr little Johñy at Colney Hatch; to my great comfort found him perfectly well. Mrs Bos., who is so kind as to let 'em play there ys sumer, told me you had not been perfectly well, wch makes me take ye first post I cd make use of, to enquire if yor disorder is quite gone off.

I cannot allow yor scheme was built on a bad ffounda-tion, nor can't credit you ever built on one of yt sort; ye best are liable to be marr'd and spoil'd; ye pleasure of seeing you here wd be great, but yt wd be marr'd wn I thought yor health might suffer. A magnolia from hence, sure, can't be so ungratefull as not to bloom at Bulstrode. I'm pleas'd wth ye report, and hearing her Grace enjoys un-interupted health gives me true satisfaction.

Mrs Mountagu indulg'd me in allowing somebody to acquaint me she was well after her journey. I fear ye Dean of York[1] will never find a perfect recovery. As to myself my añual cough (as I call it) came as usual ye be-gining of June. I hope it is at ye heigth; for indeed it is very severe, and ys interȓupting my rest harrasses me extreamly. I'm under great concern for L..y Kath. Pelham.[2] To see her amiable daughter lingring out

---

[1] The Rev. Dr. Fountayne, son-in-law of Mrs. Montagu.

[2] Catherine, eldest daughter of John, 2nd Duke of Rutland, married the Right Hon. Henry Pelham, whom she survived. Her eldest daughter, Catherine, married Henry, 9th Earl of Lincoln; she died in 1760, and her husband be-came Duke of Newcastle at her uncle's death. Her second daughter, Frances, who was also a coheiress of Pelham Holles, Duke of Newcastle, married

life in such a tedious, hopeless way is a most deplorable situation; y^t good woman's lot is hard, for as soon as time has worn off ye bitterness of one loss, she feels another: this, I fear, will sink her quite. L . . y Sondes was good in all relations; w^t her ffamily will do wth out her, I cannot form. I sent, ye morn I came here; ye ans^r was, she had a quiet night, but ye ffaculty expect her death every hour. Her Grace of Queensberry[1] departed last ffriday morn! I sent to know if report said true; ye serv^t confirm'd it, y^t after five days' illness she was just dead of a complaint on her breast! There went a *soul* of *whim!* but *no life* of *pleasure!* for tho' all at home was at her devotion, she never seem'd to be sensible of ye hapiness, from her own disposition. An extensive triffling genius, innumerable plans, all productive of disapointm^ts. She had a *great deal* to give; w^m she w^d think worthy I ne'er heard she hinted. L . . y Clarendon is on one of her sumer tours. She did me ye hon^r to notify L . . y Eliz. Capel's[2] intended mariage; why or wherefore I can't imagine, for I'm no way related to ye l . . y. I'm sory for Ld Monson, who is comended by all y^t know him; he seems to me an ill-fated young man. Dow^r. L . . y Monson[3] is unhapy wth his choice.

Adieu, d^r Mad^m, ever yor most faithfull

M. G.

---

the Hon. Lewis Monson, who was created Baron Sondes in 1760, on inheriting the estates of his cousin, Thomas, 3rd and last Earl of Rockingham. Lady Sondes died July 31, 1777, leaving three sons.

[1] Catherine, the celebrated Duchess of Queensberry, whose portrait, in the second volume of this work, is engraved, from a painting from the life by her cousin, Mary Granville (Mrs. Delany).

[2] John, 3rd Lord Monson, married, July 13, 1777, Elizabeth, 4th daughter of William Capel, 4th Earl of Essex.

[3] Theodosia, daughter of John Maddison, Esq., and widow of John, 2nd Baron Monson.

The Earl of Guilford to Mrs. Delany.

Wroxton, July yᵉ 26th, 1777.

MADAM,

I received the honor of your letter, when I had an opportunity of immediately condoling with Lady Willoughby on our mutual disappointments. We had reckon'd *much* upon the pleasure of seeing you, and were endeavouring to make our places put on their best looks for your reception. We had a bright sun, and prosperous hay-making, and flatter'd ourselves we should succeed, till we received your mortifying letter. But the scene immediately changed, and we have had a return of winter. Lady Willoughby thinks herself particularly unlucky in not being able to get into Warwickshire till it was too late for her seeing Mrs. Port. Upon the arrival of fine weather, Lord and Lady Dartmouth resolved upon endeavouring to catch some of it here. They set out for Compton yesterday se'nnight, where I met them, and with Lᵈ and Lʸ Willoughby came back with them hither on Monday; where Mr. William and Mr. Charles Legge also met them. We had laid schemes for all kinds of summer amusements, but have been totally disappointed, the weather having been constantly cold and wet; and they were all obliged to leave me yesterday, very much chagrined. They desired me to assure you and the Dutchess of Portland of their best wishes, and present their compliments. I should have been extreamly happy to have paid my respects at Bulstrode as I came hither, but did not know but her Grace might have had company, and my calling might have been troublesome. As it happen'd, I had been detained in town beyond my time, and was obliged to make as much expedition as I could in my journey; and the weather was so miserably wet and cold, that I think you would not have been glad to see me. If I come directly from Wroxton to London in September, I flatter myself nothing will prevent my having the honor of calling at Bulstrode, but hearing my coming would be inconvenient. I am extreamly sorry to hear her Grace has had another loss from her menagerie. She is so generous to her friends, that she is the last person in the world who deserves the least to be robbed.

I beg the favor of you to present my best respects to my Lady Dutchess: I heartily wish you may both enjoy perfect health in your expeditions; and as much pleasure as your friends cannot fail of receiving from your visits. I have the honor to be, with the most sincere esteem,

Madam,

Your most obedient

And obliged, humble servant,

GUILFORD.

Wroxton, July ye 26th, 1777.

The Hon. Mrs. Boscawen to Mrs. Delany.

Glan Villa, 25th July, 1777.

Your kind letter of the 15th, my dear madam, in the true spirit of its mistress, gratify'd and indulg'd my wishes before they were well utter'd. Mrs. Sandford's visit must have done you good, and her too; as to the fine boys, (especially my old acquaintance,) I suppose they were the happiest mortals the sun shone upon, or rather *the rain fell upon*. My neighbours (in town) the

Pinto's,[1] breakfasted here one day, and liked my tapis verd so well that Mad[e] said they wou'd come again and dine. Monsr added they would bring me *l'Abbé Reynal*[2] if I had any curiosity to see him, or rather hear him: car il n'est question avec lui que d'avoir des oreilles, votre langue peut s'endormir. Well,—this arrangement, you see, saves trouble. Monday last the party came, the Abbé *talk'd incessantly*—even some very good venison did not interrupt the course of his *Anecdotes historiques;* but as the talk was very agreeable, and the histories very curious and pleasant, I was quite sorry when the sun set and the coach was announc'd. I desired Mrs. Chapone to come and drink tea, thinking it would be a treat to her, as it was, and I made Monsr l'Abbé a present of all her books neatly bound. He was to leave London next day, and I have since heard he did so. He must be a very extraordinary man, with a wonderful memory—I think no Englishman (nor even such a prating Englishwoman as I am) can have any idea of talking for 8 hours *successfully* without interruption. One must have *heard and seen it to believe it!* I long'd for a book in w[ch] shou'd be written everything he had said; it seemed to me as if a great deal of it se laisseroit fort bien lire, but perhaps his *tone* and *shrugs* were an essential part. Did you never see him at Mrs. Vesey's?

Adieu, my dearest madam. I do *not* require any condolence for Mr. P. of facetious memory. I wish his

---

[1] The Portuguese Minister and his wife.

[2] William Thomas Francis Raynal, born in 1718, at St. Genies, and educated as a Jesuit; he became a pseudo-philosopher, wrote for the Encyclopædia, and was the author of many historical and political works. He died at Passy in 1796.

widow and child *well*, and I think they will *not* be *less so* for his decease! Entre nous—*another prize* to the Valiant. My best respects wait on the Duchess. Yours ever.

I have often *wonder'd* what there was so *pitifull* in returning to one's country, one's home, one's friends— *far otherwise* deserving that title than such as present themselves of a *Sunday evening in Bolton Row*. Par desœuvrement.

This unfinished Essay on Propriety was written by Mrs. Delany for the future use of her beloved grand-niece, Georgina M. A. Port, then six years old, and when she probably did not expect to live till the child would be old enough to understand it.

Bulstrode, 3rd Aug., 1777.

(In my 78th year.)

Age is the season for giving advice, youth that of receiving it. By *this date* you may see, in *that* article, I am well entitled to the undertaking,—I wish I were so in every article for your sake. To give advice is a delicate task, but if too delicately treated is useless. If the wound you mean to cure is deep it must be probed, and that is painful to the humane surgeon as well as the patient, therefore the best way is to apply proper remedies in time, to prevent so disagreable an operation. So do not, my dear child, be startled at the awful word *advice*, for I only mean to recommend to your intimate acquaintance a lady, who will guard you against the want of it, and likewise from those errors that otherwise might expose you to what is much more irksome than advice—*regret* and *reproach*. This friend I present to your regard, is never presuming, pert, or conceited, but humble, modest, and unaffected, attentive to everything that can improve her understanding or polish her manners. She never takes the place she ought not, or is at a loss to know what belongs to her. She never gives her opinion but from a desire of further information. All her votarys so truly respect, and are so sensible of her value, that they never forsake her. Her name is *Propriety*. To define her exactly is difficult, and the pleasure and honor of her company must be dilligently sought for; and never for one moment neglected, for if once lost she is very rarely regain'd.

There, my dear child, ends my preamble, and I would willingly sketch out a few hints, which my long experience has pointed out to me,—a finished work I am incapable of undertaking. Your dear mama has carefully attended to your childhood, and laid that foundation which alone is worth building upon, by forming your religious principles, which her example, as well as precept, has strongly recommended to you. She has taught you, and will proceed to give you every advantage in her power, and your fondness for her, and gratitude, will, I make no doubt, go hand in hand in making you return these obligations with true respect and tender affection. But a word or two from a by-stander may not be amiss; and such as they are accept them kindly, whether you think them of consequence or not. Mrs. Chapone's Essays on the Improvement of the Mind I hope you will read once a year, till you will have a daughter to read them to you: they speak to the heart, as well as the head, and are as entertaining as useful; and I think I

shall say but few things to you, but what you may find
there better dress'd.

Apropos—this leads me to the article of dress; a most
tender point, for I have given *less offence* in observing on
a *moral failing*, than in setting a cap in *better* order!
The fashion, if you chance to live with the beau monde,
must be complied with; but sense forbids it should be
to any extremity, and, indeed, in my youth it was
reckon'd *very vulgar* to be *extravagantly* in the fashion:
but the fair lady who I hope will be your constant companion, when she finds you are upon the point of being
seduced by her enemies *Vanity* or *Assurance*, will give
you a twitch and save you. In the country nothing is
more absurd than to dress fantastically, and turn the
brains of your humble neighbours; who will pique themselves in apeing *the squire's* daughter! And believe me this
can't be innocently done, as (such an example) will certainly
interfere with their station of life, and make them less
willing to submit to the duties of it. Dress ought always
to be suited to the situation and circumstances of the
person. The *appearance* of great economy, where economy
is required, is *most respectable*, where it is not, it is re-
proachable; tho' *never to be neglected* by the *most opulent*.
The friend at your elbow (Lady Propriety) is the best
frisseur in the world, and the most reasonable. She understands every part of dress to admiration. She will never
suffer you to wear your hat with *one edge* to touch your
nose, and the other edge perpendicularly in the air! with
long streamers dangling like a poor mad woman, who I
remember lived in a hollow-tree and a toad was her companion; she used to beg ribbons to dress herself with,
but yet was *not* so mad as to wear her head-dress *too*

high to go *under the arch* of *her hollow-tree!* Fashions are fluctuating, by the time you wear lappets or a womanly dress it may be less lofty, but whatever it is bear in mind that *moderation* is always genteel. " *Genteel!*" what a pretty word ! But how is it to be described ? The bons vivans would say, it is like a well made dish, composed of every good thing without tasting of any one particularly. I think it is like those few mixtures of sweets, that are pleasant to everybody and offensive to none ; in plain English it is an *ease* and a grace *entirely free from affectation.* If it appears studied it loses its name ! Nature not tortur'd is *always genteel;* children, as soon as they have strength to walk upright are *so,* till *pinch'd* or *tutor'd* indiscreetly they lose that simplicity of nature which they were born with. As you grow up you will be in danger of being hurt by imitation ; but here I hope your sagacious friend will tip you on the shoulder, and prevent any bad consequences. Mimickery is a dangerous snare, and children, who are quick and lively are apt to fall into it ; it is a disgrace to the heart, whatever it may be to the head : I think it is to both ; for it is silly, as well as wicked, to expose the *failings* of those you converse with. I do not mean that you should *shut* your eyes against *them ;* but turn *them* to your own advantage by watchfully *avoiding* what you think so *absurd.* Blemishes and infirmities that are natural, it is cruel to the last degree to ridicule ; they ought to raise your pity, not provoke your laughter. Make it your own case, and be thankful it is not so in reallity. To *see,* and to *expose,* are very different things, and as the generality of the world are too prone to censure we should avoid all occasions of encouraging it.

The Countess Cowper to Mrs. Port, of Ilam.

Wimbledon Park, Aug. 11th, 77.

MY DEAREST MRS. PORT,

I have this moment received your agreable and acceptable letter from Calwich, and am sure that sweet place is now all harmony, and may be enjoyed without *fear* and *trembling*. My best compliments to all the inhabitants. I thought you were to spend ye approaching winter at Bath; tho' I am sure Ilam is more to your taste, even in winter. I am entirely of Madame de Sevigné's opinion, "*un hiver à la campagne n'est pas si affreux que de loin.*" Lord and Lady Spencer are gone with Lord Althorpe[1] a little tour abroad, and propose bringing him back to college in Octo$^{br.}$ Harriot is of the party. I passed a week with them here, before they went, and whilst this place was cleaning I went for a week to Holywell House, and had y^e pleasure of seeing Lady F. Bulkeley every day during my stay there. As y^e dry rot is again in my house at Richmond, till that is set to rights I shall reside here. Miss Jane Vernon spends this month wth me, as Lady Harriot[2] is in waiting at Gunnersbury. My heart aches at present for poor dear William Tollemache,[3] as ye Repulse, of which ship he was 1st lieutenant, has not been heard of since ye 16th of December last, when she was separated from her company by a storm. 'Tis terrible to lose two nephews at

---

[1] Lord Althorp, eldest son of John, 1st Earl Spencer.

[2] Lady Harriet Vernon, wife of Henry Vernon, Esq., and sister of the last Earl of Strafford. She was Lady of the Bedchamber to Princess Amelia.

[3] The Hon. William Tollemache, youngest son of Lionel, 3rd Earl of Dysart, was lost, in the 26th year of his age, in the "Repulse" frigate, in a hurricane, 16th Dec., 1776.

sea! Poor George Tollemache[1] was kill'd by a fall from y[e] main-mast of y[e] Modeste some years ago. The Dean of Ossory's eldest son was 2nd lieutenant on board y[e] Repulse. Gen. Fitz. is gone suddenly into Ireland; he called upon me at St. Alban's as he went; seem'd greatly *hurried*, and hardly sat down, and look'd ill.

Such a July I never remember in my long life! I hope we shall have a fine autumn. My compliments in particular to Mr. Port; I hope all y[r] charming children will continue well, and that y[u] may only receive pleasure from them, but never any pain. Miss Williams is much obliged to y[u] for y[r] remembrance. She is much approved of by all those I wish she shou'd be. Adieu, ma très chère et très aimable amie.

Toujours votre très affectionée

S. G. COWPER.

Y[r] brother John *ought* to be now Dr Dewes, and give his *Reverend* hand in marriage!

Pray call upon poor Henzey.

The Hon. Mrs. Boscawen to Mrs. Delany.

Glan Villa, 19th Aug., 1777.

Having wish'd very much to hear that your hot journey did not disagree with you, my dearest madam, y[r] kind information gave me such real pleasure that, in gratitude, I ought not to have delay'd a moment to thank you for it; but you must know that I have been

---

[1] The Hon. George Tollemache, 3rd son of Lionel, Earl of Dysart, was killed, in the 16th year of his age, by a fall from the mast-head of the "Modeste" man-of-war, in a voyage to Lisbon, Oct., 1760.

in trouble, wch began the very day after I receiv'd y^r welcome letter.

Last Saturday I went to London, met Mrs. Walsingham,[1] and went with her (and little Charlotte[2]) to the Queen's House, where I was highly entertained indeed, as you will easily believe who have seen that delightfull collection of pictures. In the evening we came hither, time enough for a very pleasant walk, partly by moonlight; but next morning, at church, Miss Boyle was taken ill, and all our social pleasure vanish'd. Her poor mother determin'd to take her to London, that she might have the physical people she was accustom'd to. She went accordingly, and I had the mortification to hear next morning that both her physician (Warren) and apothecary were absent, and out of town : she got, however, Sr Noah Thomas, and he said the child wou'd have a scarlet fever and putrid sore throat. Alarm'd and much concern'd at such dreadfull news, I got up this morning before six, and went to my poor friend ; most agreeably surpris'd I was to find her quite compos'd and cheerfull (Mrs. Trevor with her), and the precious child pure well, *no scarlet fever or sore throat* of any kind ! I staid till the physician (so happily mistaken) made his visit, and had the satisfaction to hear him say he had order'd her 5 grains of rhubarb, and 15 of magnesia, by way of *finishing*

---

[1] Charlotte, 2nd daughter and coheiress of Sir Charles Hanbury Williams, by Frances, 2nd daughter and coheiress of Thomas, Earl Coningsby, married, in 1759, the Hon. Robert Boyle Walsingham, fifth son of Henry Boyle, 1st Earl of Shannon. She had two children : Richard, born in 1762, died in 1788 ; and Charlotte, afterwards Baroness de Ros in her own right. Admiral Walsingham was lost on board the "Thunderer" in 1779.

[2] Charlotte Boyle, afterwards Baroness de Ros, married Lord Henry Fitzgerald, younger son of James, 1st Duke of Leinster.

up this unlucky business, if I may so call anything that
by God's blessing is so happily ended : but poor Mrs.
Wals. was in agonies of terror on Monday ; Mrs. Trevor
told me nothing cou'd exceed them. Her plan, of course,
is entirely at an end: from me she was to have gone to
Lord Amherst's,[1] and from thence 'cross the country to
Lord Onslow's[2] to visit their respective lady's, her friends.
Now she will be happy to resettle herself quietly in her
castle, where I hope she will be to-morrow ; but you
may believe, my dear madam, by this long story, that my
mind and time have been much taken up with my
friend's distress. That of poor Lady Aylesford I greatly
commiserate ! perhaps it is the *more* severe for that she
had open'd her heart to joy ! but, alas, how short and
transient the gleam ! Poor Gen[1] Prescot's[3] fate puts me
in mind of an unfortunate Frenchman, Monsieur Hoc-
quart, who was taken 3 times by Admiral Boscawen.[4] I
fear Prescott will not fall into such generous hands.
The taking of Ticonderago, I am very much inclin'd to
believe, but am told there is no certain account of it yet.

---

[1] Jeffery Amherst, Commander-in-Chief of the British Army in North
America from 1758 to 1764, was created Baron Amherst in 1776. In 1796
he was made a Field Marshal.

[2] George, 4th Baron Onslow, and afterwards Earl of Onslow. He married,
in 1753, Henrietta, daughter of Sir John Shelley, Bart.

[3] On the 10th July, 1777, Colonel Barton, with several officers and
volunteers, passed by night from Providence to Rhode Island, eluded the
watchfulness of the ships of war, and succeeded in surprising General Prescott,
who commanded in chief, in his quarters, and brought him and his aide-de-
camp safe to the Continent.

[4] The " English Cyclopædia," in the 1st vol. of the Biography, mentions
that, in the year 1755, Admiral Boscawen fell in with the French naval
squadron, and "captured two 64-gun ships with 1,500 prisoners, including
the French Commander Hoquart, who had twice before ' defeated and
taken prisoner by Boscawen."

Adieu, my dear madam, I hope you do not *work* too hard, tempted by curious materials and *fine originals,*[1] but rather that you enjoy (with some degree of indolence) this tardy summer. Luton and Lady Bute's excellent society are also fine additions to it. If on your return you shou'd come this way, I hope to profit by it. I shall not go to Badminton these ten days, I think. Mrs. Walsingham has so lately receiv'd the pleasure of hearing from the Duchess of Portland, that I do not ask you how her Grace does. I will only wish that you may both meet in the same perfect health. Ever, my dear madam,

Y^r faithfull affectionate serv^t,

F. B.

Mrs. Delany to Mrs. Port, of Ilam.

Bulstrode, 31st Aug., 1777.

I returned here yesterday, and tho' a good deal tired last night, find myself much refresh'd to-day, and happy in our dear Dss's being return'd from Weymouth charming well. She went and made a visit of two days to Mrs. Sandford, at Lyme, and found her and her sons greatly improved in health and looks since their being there so much; that situation, and bathing, agrees with them all. She has got a young clergyman, recommended to her by the famous Dr. Horne of Oxford, a Mr. Rook, who promises to prove a very good tutor to her sons; and Dr. Horne, who she saw at Oxford, approved extreamly of her sons, and the progress they had already made, and

---

[1] Mrs. Delany was then at Luton, and many of her flowers were dated Luton.

Joseph Brown, sc

SARAH CHAPONE.

"The Nut-Brown Maid."

From an original Portrait in oil painted by Mrs Delany,
in the possession of Erskine Douglas Sandford Esq.

may prove of great service to those who are to go to the University. It is the Dr. Horne[1] who ans[d] Hume's Life, and some years ago published an excellent comment on the Psalms. As soon as Lyme grows too cold and dreary Mrs. S. removes to Bath. I know nothing of Mrs. R. ; I heard she was expected at Lady West[d's], at Hammersmith, the latter end of this month. I wrote you word that Lady Car. Stuart[2] was to be married to Mr. Dawson, L[d] Carlow's son ; he came to Luton last Tuesday, and staid till Thursday. He appears like a man of fashion—tall, genteel, not handsome ; *rather serious*, but seems *very sincerely* attached to her. It is *not* a great match, but a very *reasonable one,* as they seem to like one another, and friends on both sides are satisfied. I passed my time very agreably at Luton, and am much obliged to Lord as well as Lady Bute for much attention and kindness. The place is magnificent; the woods, the lawns, the water, and the immense collection of trees, flowers, and shrubs, from *the cedar to the hysop on the wall,* charming, and the weather so constantly fine that I tour'd round the park, or winding thro' a variety of ridings every day for two hours, with Lady Bute, in her little low, easy chaise. But, now and then, a secret recollection would come across my mind of a certain dear society I had *vainly hoped* to partake of, that cast a gloom on all my enjoyments, till a little more recollection soften'd the bitterness of it, by representing how many

---

[1] Dr. George Horne, afterwards Bishop of Norwich, born 1730, died 1792. Besides the well-known Commentary on the Book of Psalms, Bishop Horne wrote many religious works, sermons, &c.

[2] Lady Caroline Stuart married the Hon. John Dawson, afterwards Earl of Portarlington, on the 24th Dec., 1777.

undeserved blessings *I have* enjoy'd, and that I still
enjoy many, at an age when it is natural to expect infirmities that might have rendered me incapable of any
enjoyment. I am happy with y^r good account of your
sister Dewes, and beg my love to her, and thanks for her
very kind letter. I will write to her as soon as she gets
home. I am now very busy with my hortus siccus, to
wch I added, at Luton, twelve rare plants. I am glad you
are so soon to embrace your dear children; may every
year of their lives make them more and more dear to
you, wch cannot be without a grateful return on their side.
I am glad Miss H. Mead is to spend the winter with
you: a cheerful domestick winter will warm you, tho'
your mountains are cover'd with snow: and what can
add more compleatly to that satisfaction than the con-
sciousness of performing our duty to the best of our
power?

Mrs. Delany to Mrs. Port, of Ilam.

Bulstrode, 19th Sept., 1777.

How good and kind you are, my dearest Mary, in
communicating so immediately to me y^r joy and satisfaction in finding your dear, lovely children so well and
so good; pray God bless you in one another, and grant
that their filial gratitude may keep pace with the tender
and judicious attention of their dear parents. I see you
all so happy together, so rationally engaged, that I think
you are *more enviable* than your *great neighbour*: in all
states Providence has thought fit to temper our worldly
happiness with allays of sickness, pain, sorrow; the
greatest and *richest* are so far from being exempted that

they feel them with the added mortification that all *those superior* advantages they possess can't ease a pang; but a submission to the Divine will, the consideration of a *future state*, and an humble, diligent endeavour of attaining *it*, are never-failing cordials and supports, and these, my dearest Mary, are *as much* within your reach (and mine) as in the power of those of the highest rank and largest fortunes; *nay, more*, for *they* may be too much entangled with temptations, and *devour'd* by dissipation, to make use of these all healing blessings,—their passions inflamed, and their judgment blinded.

What delightful weather! Ilam must be enchanting, and the moon *shines on us both*, and listens to our soliloquies in the height of beauty. Last Monday we dined at Kew with the Bishop of Litchfield,[1] who gave us an elegant little dinner, seasoned with his delicate and edifying conversation; the day was very hot, and the dust troublesome, but the inconvenience that attended it would have been a tax willingly paid but our dear Dss was attacked that night with a severe fit of the rheumatism, and has suffer'd a great deal of pain, but I thank God she is much better to-day. Mr. and Mrs. Cole came by appointment on Tuesday for two or three days, wch was rather unlucky; but he is a very entertaining man, of a particular character, and between whiles, when the Duchess was well eno' to see them, he diverted her. Mrs. Cole[2] was sister to the late Sir Anthony Abdy, a very pretty kind of woman; they went away yesterday.

---

[1] "Bishop of Lichfield."—Dr. Hurd.

[2] "Mrs. Cole."—Anne Hester, youngest daughter of Sir William Abdy, and sister of Sir Anthony Thomas Abdy, married Charles Nelson Cole, Esq., of the Middle Temple.

I hope the shock of an earthquake, tho' very slight, that was felt in Cheshire did not affect Staffordshire. Lady Stamford felt it; she was at church, but did not know what it was till she came from church, which I am glad of. I suppose she will soon be confined. The Duke of Glocest' much better. We have been much shock'd with an acc' in the newspaper to day of Lord Harcourt's[1] sad and fatal accident; striving to save a favorite dog from being drowned in a narrow well, fell in and was drowned himself; we have had no account but from the newspaper, but that is so circumstantial I fear it is too true. How I pity all his family! tho' Lord Nuneham[2] is a whimsical man, they say he has great humanity, and lived well with his father. This morning I finished my 400th plant!

The Dowager-Countess Gower to Mrs. Delany.

Bill Hill, 19th Sept., 77.

I was much rejoic'd to see yo' handwriting, d' mad", thinking it long—very long—since I had y' pleasure, concluded rambling was y° hindrance; for tho' I pass for a tardy writer, I had not been guilty of omissions to you, for on my return from London I found a letter

---

[1] "The Right Hon. the Earl of Harcourt died, 16th Aug., 1777, at his seat at Newnham, in Oxfordshire. His lordship had gone out to take his morning's walk in the park, and did not return at his usual hour, was found by his servants in a narrow well, nothing appearing above water but the feet and legs, occasioned (as it is imagined) by his over-reaching himself in order to save the life of his favourite dog, who was found in the well with him, standing on his master's feet."

[2] George Simon Harcourt, Lord Nuneham, succeeded to the Earldom of Harcourt on the death of his father, Simon, 1st Earl of Harcourt.

from you, wch I ans^d ye 20th July, and directed to S^t. James's Place, wch I do sopose you ne'er receiv'd; and if you was not possess'd of a double portion of candour, I must appear a very ungratefull wretch . . . Gooseberries have done their part, and freed me from my añual cough; and please myself wth proposing a morning vissit to Bulstrode, thinking it a vast while since I've seen ye worthy inhabitants. Mrs. Leveson and family din'd wth me in her way to Badminton; boil'd chicks was all I c^d give 'em, here's no lodging to be had. I fear ye days will be too short for me to see my d^r Johny on his return; I wish 'em *safe at home*, I can't like nursseries vissiting. Mrs. Bos : also took a baite here on ye same road; seem'd in good spirits, as she had reason, going to be wth all her children and grandchildren; she has been very kind to mine, to be crowded up wth 'em all this sumer. This alliance you mention will, I hope, increase L . . y Bute's[1] hapiness, 'twas news to me; being at Luton so many days, among such variety of plants, must have greatly enrich'd *yor works*;[2] in my small improvem^{ts} I've several pretty ones I never saw before : I don't think it consistent wth comon sense for an old woman to write or talk in ye future tense, however, for once I will, to say I hope you'l take a review of 'em next year. My magnolia has, and has had many ffowers, tho' not so large, nor contain'd so many leaves as last year, nor ye smell so fragrant; I'm very angry at ye D^{s's} for not blooming. Desire my best respects to her Grace.

---

[1] This alludes to the intended marriage of the Countess of Bute's daughter, Lady Caroline Stuart, with the Honourable John Dawson, which took place Jan. 1, 1778.

[2] The Flora of Mrs. Delany.

I'm much oblig'd to you, d^r mad^m, for yor kind congratulations on Leveson's success; it reads well in ye newspaper, and shows he has kept a good look out, as ye sea-men call it; ye profits will not be considerable.

Mrs. Mountagu I hear has been and is better than for some years; long may it last. *Abuse* is y^e *daily bread* of *party*. The wit of Windsor is, the K . g has made himself so popular there y^t next election he'll be chose wthout oposition,

I pity L . . y Clifford[1] extreamly, having lost ye most amiable child she had, and appear'd healthfull. The tears for L . y Alesford's son, killed in America, are dry'd up wth ye joy of her daughter's mariage.[2]

I'm glad L . y Andover[3] is pleas'd wth it; many events of y^t sort has not hapen'd to her.

You seem in good spirits by yor letter, wch raises those of y^r faithfull

M. G.

I'll direct this to Whitehall.

---

[1] Sophia, 3rd daughter of Samuel Campbell, Esq., of Leitrim, married Edward Southwell, 17th Baron de Clifford. He died Nov. 1, 1777.

[2] Lady Charlotte Finch, daughter of Heneage, 3rd Earl of Aylesford, became the second wife, in 1777, of Henry, 12th Earl of Suffolk, and 5th Earl of Berkshire.

[3] Mary, 2nd daughter of Heneage, 2nd Earl of Aylesford, married William, Lord Andover, who died before his father, the 11th Earl of Suffolk and 4th of Berkshire.

The Hon. Mrs. Boscawen to Mrs. Delany.

Badminton, Monday, 6th Oct., 1777.

Mrs. Leveson took herself away from hence a little rashly on the news of the Valiant's arrival at Portsmouth, whereas a few days wou'd have convinc'd her that in these bustling times the Valiant's captain has no leisure to play with his children or visit his wife; as she is by this time convinced of this, I imagine she will listen to my proposal of returning to her old quarters at Glan Villa, where the red cows and the green grass will be better for the stout boys than their present station in Charles Street, and us two much better together these long evenings than separate. She has let her house in South Street, to Lord Edward Bentinck for 100 guineas a year, and his lordship repairs. She cou'd not sell it, so is mightfuly pleas'd to let it : 'tis a very pleasant habitation for a single gentleman or lady, and has very good offices lately built, and kitchen out of doors. I beg, my dear madam, you will present my respects to the Duchess of Portland, and say I beg her Grace won't think of writing to me; if I hear any news in London, I will write to her Grace.

My séjour here has been very pleasant, owing to the uninterrupted health of my dear daughter and all her lovely tribe; she has *six* here that cannot be exceeded; none, however, beat Lady Harriet,[1] the Duchess of Portland's goddaughter, who at 2 years and two months, makes a trio with her sisters, and in all respects seems

---

[1] Lady Harriet Isabella Somerset, third daughter of Henry, 5th Duke of Beaufort, was born July 9th, 1775. In 1804 she married Col. Mitchell, and died in 1855.

Y 2

fit to keep them company, and converse with them.
Just now, indeed, she has assum'd a higher office, that of
comforter to her little brother, Edward, now weaning; she
calls him "*mine boy*," and is most carefully occupy'd to
amuse him under his misfortunes, charging her *own*
nurse to "take care of mine boy." This is a grandmother's story, my dear madam; but you will forgive
it. I assure you 'tis very pleasant to behold, and singular in so young a child. The weakly one (for the
Duchess of Beaufort has *seven*), is at Brighthelmston,
under the care of Dr. Pepys, for sea-bathing.

Dunkirk is only a single house, but as it is the regular
post-house, they have a post-mark. Adieu, my dear
madam, I shall trespass too much. Accept the Duchess
of Beaufort's best compliments, and my earnest wishes
to receive good news from Bulstrode.

Ever most sincerely and affectionately yours,

F. B.

Pray return my comp^ts to Mrs. Dashwood.

The Dowager-Countess Gower to Mrs. Delany.

Bill Hill, 17th Oct^r., 77.

Doing w^t one likes is certainly ye greatest restorative :
after being at Bullstrode, (as ye song says) my heart was
as light as a feather all day ; and if I hear ye D^s of Portland can enjoy this fine weather, it will continue so : she
has my best wishes, and pray convey my most sincere
respects. I reach'd home in very good time, had but
little rain ; w^n ever 'tis wanted I sh^d go to Bullstrode, for

I don't remember ever having a dry day for y^t expedition. I found yor kind enquiry after me, wch I ought to have rec̃ed last Sunday, was mislaid at ye post-house at Twyford. On search find I'm rich in Naples-ffiggs. I will send 'em on Tuesday next to ye care of Mrs. Marsh at Maidenhead Bridge; if her Grace pleases to send for 'em on Wednesday next I hope she'll receive 'em safe. No news known to yor most faithfull, so adieu.

Mrs. Delany to Mrs. Port, of Ilam.

Bulstrode, 20th Oct., 1777.

MY DEAREST MARY,

Tho' this letter ought to be addressed to my dear nephew, as I have not time to write to both I trust you will, with your best graces, (that is, in the kindest manner), thank him for his kind letter, and assure him I was much obliged to him for it. May all his *searches* answer his labour, and wishes, and turn his *copper* into *gold!* he is too prudent, and too well-acquainted with the danger of trusting to expectation, and throwing away the substance for ye shadow— to run any hazard. Such a *will-o'-the-wisp*, lost our family £2000 a year in Yorkshire, where my grandmother Granville,[1] threw away *that estate* in *hopes of doubling it* by a *copper mine!* Mrs. Dashwood left us last Monday, and we are quite alone; but far from being "*unkit*," as they say in Gloucestershire; for we have abundance of company at our beck. Never less than 30

---

[1] "*My grandmother Granville.*"—Anne, only daughter and heiress of Cuthbert Morley, of Haunby, in the county of York, and wife of Bernard, fourth son of Sir Bevil Granville.

hares sup with us every evening, besides a variety of other guests, fed by the bountiful hand who knows so well how to distribute the gifts of Providence.

I will send you a packet of seeds from Mr. Bromton. Did you sow the feather grass seed, and does it appear yet? I am so *plentifully* supplied with the hothouse here, and from the Queen's garden at Kew, that natural plants have been a good deal laid aside this year, for foreigners, but not less in fav[r]. O! how I long to *show you* the progress I have made! and *will*, and *do*, flatter myself *that* is a happiness I shall be permitted to enjoy. Cherishing that view, I do my best to fill up the time (still spared me) in the best manner I can; and when I hear those friends I love are well and happy, I don't feel so much tired of my journey as I might expect to be.

Lady Walling[d] has been ill, but is well again; she has taken a house in North Park Street, near Mrs. A. Foley's. Mr. Dawson, who is to marry Lady Car. Stuart, is gone to Ireland to finish the settlements, and returns the end of this month.

Last Monday Lady Gower made us a morning visit, and seems quite well and in spirits.

I have desired Mrs. Dashwood to get the *forks* for *my little bird*[1] and Johnny.

How does your agreable friends Mrs. and Miss Joddrel do? Were they sensible of the shock of the earthquake? I heard it was more felt at Manchester than any where.

I enclose you the verses I promised you, and desire you will make Mr. P., or some of your secretarys write

---

[1] "*My little bird*."—Georgina Mary Ann Port. One of these "forks" is in the Editor's possession.

them out, as *I have not time* to copy them. Now I know you smile, and say what can take up so much of A. D.'s time? No children to teach or play with; no house matters to torment her; no books to publish; no politicks to work her brains? All this is true, but *idleness never grew in my soil,* tho' I can't boast of any very useful employments, only such as keep me from being a burthen to my friends, and *banish the spleen*; and therefore, are *as important* for the present use as matters of a higher nature.

Mrs. Delany to Mrs. Port, of Ilam.

Bulstrode, 16th Nov., 1777.

What a shocking end our worthless cousin Tolmache[1] has come to! kill'd (in America) in a duel by Mr. Pennington, as worthless, I suppose, as himself. The cause of the quarrel, *a song.* They could not wreck their vengeance on shipboard, but immediately on their landing fought. Mr. Penn[n] has 7 wounds. What a furious animal is man without principles to check him, when he gives way to y[e] violent sallies of his passions!

I suppose you heard another bro[r] of Lord Dysart's was drown'd some time ago. Surely their poor sisters (if they have feeling hearts) must be saddly shock'd! but as to Lady Bridget, she has no reason to lament this loss, tho' the shocking manner of his death may affect her: his extravagance *would* have ruined her, and before he went last abroad she was obliged to sell three hundred pound a year to pay his debts!

---

[1] Captain the Hon. John Tollemache was killed, in the 25th year of his age, at New York, in a duel, by Mr. Pennington, whose brother was created Lord Muncaster, 1783.

The good news of the defeat of Washington, and taking possession of Philadelphia, is certainly true, tho' no direct account has come from General How, who it is thought waits till the winter campaign is over before he sends his dispatches, unwilling to write till he can give an account of everything that has past.

Last Thursday Miss Thynne[1] was presented at Court for the first time of her appearing, and everybody was charmed with her ; beside her pretty and agreable figure, her total freedom from all manner of affectation, and her *modest gentle manner*, add greatly to her appearance. I wish she had *more* rivals *in that way*.

We are in expectation of a visit from Mr. Montagu and Mr. Mason.

Did I send you an *Ode on Hope?*[2] If not, I will, tho' I am bound not to give a copy, so at yʳ leisure send it back.

The Hon. Mrs. Boscawen to Mrs. Delany.

Glan Villa, yᵉ 25th Nov., 1777.

I did believe, my dearest madam, that a compliment of condolance was but too much due to you for the loss of a worthy friend; and, alas! I can tell you how to repay it in kind, for I too have lost a beloved cousin, and *very very* old friend, a friend of 40 years, for being my cousin germain (the daughter of my uncle, Colˡ Edward Evelyn,) we spent much of our youth together. This was Mrs. Sayer, who was interr'd last Wednesday, to my very great concern (else I should have wrote to

---

[1] " Miss Thynne."—The Hon. Louisa Thynne, eldest daughter of Viscount Weymouth.

[2] Ode to Hope, published in Edinburgh, 1789.

you). Her daughter you have seen with me, I think. *Her* loss is irreparable, for a kinder, pleasanter, more *delightful* mother no poor girl ever lost. My poor friend has had many complaints for some time, but a fund of cheerfulness and never-ceasing good humour made one fancy they were slight ones, so that I never thought myself in danger of losing her till the letter came to my servant wch announc'd that she was given over, and she dy'd the next day. I wou'd have fetch'd away *my poor Fanny*, but she desir'd not to leave her father, nor the house, however melancholy ; and now, the last sad duties performed, they are gone to Mr. Evelyn's, her uncle, in Surry. I assure you a greater private loss can hardly be where there are only two children. But then Lord Clifford,[1] had eight,—tho' he can hardly be said to be a private loss, so perfectly did he understand everything that regarded the public good. Him, too, I have sincerely regretted, having been long and intimately acquainted with him and his sweet wife, who was the happiest of women. I never saw a more affectionate husband, or a more agreeable companion. He dy'd at Avignon. She, poor woman, is return'd, and travell'd 16 hours every day, so that she arriv'd ye 11th day, and of those had spent 21 hours in the vessel between Calais and Dover, during wch time she sat always in ye coach upon the deck. The Duke of Beaufort and Mr. Vernon of Park Place have the great charge of guardian, trustee, and executor, together with Lady Clifford. She lost one son a few months ago, but has still 8 children left! You see, my dear madam, that tho' it is not long since we

---

[1] Hugh, 4th Baron Clifford, d. March, 1732 ; Hugh, 5th Baron, d. (according to Burke) 1783 ?

met, I have had more than one trouble in the time. My good Mrs. Leveson has made me several visits, and my son has staid with me. Next month I purpose to fix in my winter quarters. You seem also to think of them. The weather is really fine. Having a good deal of planting to inspect to-day, I was out a long time, and even in these northern regions it was quite mild. I intended to have told you I was in London at yᵉ meeting of the Parliament to see the Duke of Beaufort, and how I *was astonished* to hear of this *new* edition of the E. of Chatham,[1] but in so doing I must make this scribble more costly, which is not worth its present price. I will only add, therefore, that I heard Lord Hyde[2] was going to be marry'd to Miss Grimstone, wᶜʰ I did *not* believe, but I found Mrs. Walsing. *did*. The lady is not rich.

Adieu, my dearest madam.

Present my best respects.

The Dowager-Countess Gower to Mrs. Delany.

Bill Hill, 28ᵗʰ Novr., 77.

I'm much oblig'd by two letters and a long list of plants, some of wᶜʰ I have my designs upon, and will mark wᵗʰ a ×, but can't contrive to get 'em here safe at present. Next spring I have a conveyance in veiw, and yᵗ will be time enough to ornimᵗ this favourite humble *cot* of mine. All thanks and good wishes to yᵉ

---

[1] During the Parliamentary Session of 1777, Lord Chatham exerted his failing energies to give reiterated warnings on the subject of American affairs.

[2] Lord Hyde became 2nd Earl of Clarendon on his father's death, and died, unmarried, in 1824.

donor, who I hope is free from all rheumatism. Y^e weather is remarkably dry, wch I think suits her; ye winds cutting cold; but w^n I recollect this sort of weather agrees wth her my hatred of 'em abates. I was in London ye beginning of this month; after I return'd heard you was there at ye same time; after news and after thoughts are useless; I was unlucky not to have better intelligence. Mrs. Montagu also came to town soon after I return'd here. I'm inform'd she's not so well since she came to London as she was in ye countrey.

Will Mrs. S. departure make any alteration in y^t quarter? Perhaps it may be news to you (and all I have) y^t L. .y Mary Duncan[1] is arriv'd in England. She has *lost* y^e *Doctor* long since, and *now all* his ffortune, call'd £30,000, from ye negligence of ye managers in fflorida, where he had laid it all out in purchases of land by ye advice of Mr. Geo. Grenville. L. .y M. offer'd ye Doc^{rs} next heir, as he is called, half ye profits if he w^d go and look after it, and he is call'd "*brute*," &c., &c., for refusing; but I acquit him, concluding *Sauny* w^d go where anything was to be got! On L. .y M.'s arrival, L. .y Charlotte[2] held out ye olive-branch, wch L. .y M. rejected. L. .y C. shines in conduct but not in robes; for going to L. .d Thanet's[3] in Kent, she lost her trunk from ye inn, richly laden. Having finish'd the history of the Tufton ffamily, must finish this wth ye sincere repetition of being yor most faithfull,

M. G.

---

[1] Mary, eldest daughter of Sackville, 7th Earl of Thanet, married, Sept. 5th, 1763, Sir William Duncan, M.D. She died in 1806.

[2] Charlotte, second and youngest daughter of Sackville, 7th Earl of Thanet. She died, unmarried, in 1803.

[3] Sackville, 8th Earl of Thanet, brother of Lady Mary Duncan and of Lady Charlotte Tufton.

The Hon. Mrs. Boscawen to Mrs. Delany.

Audley Street, 12th Dec., 1777.

Your last kind letter, my dearest madam, gave me so fair a challenge to write that I shou'd certainly have taken up the gauntlet but for two reasons; the first, that I have had very weak blind eyes, wch having pleaded I think you may dispense with the second, and indeed that is no other than a certain depression of spirits most unfit to produce a chearfull letter, No private concern occasions it, I thank God; but I was received (when I came to Lon^n,) and much surpriz'd indeed with the sad account of public misfortune; it made me very grave, and I have remain'd so, that is dull and heavy ever since. Much anxiety and much grief in families I am acquainted with have taken place since the news of Burgoyne's[1] situation arriv'd; y^r neighbour, Mrs. Dunbar, has lost her nephew, brother to Miss Morgan, who lives with her. He was a very fine youth.

Yesterday I saw Mrs. Montagu, your friend. She was as well as I left her in Nov^r : her eyes entirely free from inflamation, and her spirits and health seemingly good.

Ld Guilford was with her, who looks perfectly well. Lady Gower is still in her *profound solitude.* Mr. Leveson has been in town, and has received the *good lump* of £11,800 for accumulated interest due to him, wch is an undoubted proof that the *principal sum* for wch that

---

[1] General John Burgoyne, commanding the royal forces in Canada, having, with 10,000 men, invaded the American province of New England, was stormed in his camp at Saratoga by the Republican Generals Gates and Arnold, and forced to capitulate, Oct. 7, 1777.

interest proceeds is due to him also. He went yesterday to Portsmouth to see his ships come out of dock, and how long to stay I know not. T'other morning I sat a long hour with my old friend Lady Chatham;[1] we were very glad to see each other after years of absence, though our political creed, as far as I have any, differs widely I suspect. Surprizing as it is my lord is recover'd perfectly. More surprizing it is, (in my opinion) that he wishes once more to guide le Timon de l'etat, so does Ld Shelburne, sous ses auspices, cum multis aliis; but I doubt it is very far from clear that they wou'd do better for us than the powers that are, and therefore I do not imagine they have a majority of good wishes. I know no news; the two new L^ds of the Bedcham^r you will hear before this reaches you—viz., Ld Winchelsea[2] and Ld Aylesford,[3] in ye room of Ld Carmarthen[4] (Chamberlain to the Qu.) and Ld Jersey,[5] who resigns.

Mrs. Vesey, I hear, is delighted with Lucan, so that all the reluctance she express'd (and I believe felt) at going there was *entirely wasted* and *thrown away*. Several letters have been receiv'd from her (I'm *not* sure they are *all decypher'd yet*). I am glad to hear she is well, and well pleased. A Mr. Nicoll, nephew to ye late Sr James Grey, and the gent. I imagine of whom L^y Lothian bo^t her house in Curzon Street, took the liberty

---

[1] Lady Hester Grenville, youngest daughter of Richard Grenville, Esq., and Hester, Countess of Temple, and widow of William Pitt, Earl of Chatham.

[2] George Finch, 8th Earl of Winchelsea

[3] Heneage Finch, 4th Earl of Aylesford, succeeded to the title on the decease of his father, May 9th, 1777.

[4] Francis Godolphin Osborne, afterwards 5th Duke of Leeds. His first wife was Amelia, only child and heiress of Robert D'Arcy, Earl of Holderness and Baron Conyers.

[5] George Bussey Villiers, 4th Earl of Jersey.

to blow out his brains t'other morning at his country house near Hadley; why or wherefore I know not. Adieu, my dearest madam.

Your very affectionate, faithfull,

Obliged servant.

F. BOSCAWEN.

My friend, Miss More, succeeds prodigiously, and Percy[1] is triumphant. There is a *charming* poem call'd "the Justification;" but as *it is* spitefull and venomous, *you* will *not* admit ye serpent.

Mrs. Delany to Mrs. Port, of Ilam.

St. James's Place, 23rd Dec., 1777.

I hear nothing relating to publick affairs that can be depended upon but that Burgoyne was unsuccessful; but I hope good news will come from Philadelphia.

As to marriages, &c., they stand thus: Lady Louisa Leveson to be married to Mr. McDonald[2] of the Temple, a rising genius in the law, a man of merit in other respects; without a fortune, which the lady's will amply supply: Miss Gold, a beauty, to Temple Lutterel;[3] *her* choice *not* altogether so promising of happiness. In a few days Lady Caroline Stuart will make Mr. Dawson a happy man, and I hope he will return the compliment by making her a happy woman! Poor Lady Bute, tho'

---

[1] Hannah More's Tragedy of "Percy" was performed at Drury Lane in the year 1778.

[2] Archibald M'Donald, Esq., M.P. for Hindon, married, 26th Dec., 1777, the Hon. Louisa Leveson Gower, 3rd daughter to Earl Gower.

[3] The Hon. Temple Luttrell (brother of the Duchess of Cumberland), married, in 1778, a daughter of Judge Gould.

satisfied with the match, feels the loss already of so agre-able a companion, and I know how to pity her when I am so selfish as only to think of home, but such thoughts I stifle in the birth, and hope she will have as much reason as I have to be satisfied with the lot of her valu-able child. *Hope* is found—

> "The pain in pleasure still the same,
> *It* seeks that heaven from whence it came."

You may keep it till you have a frank to send it. I am sure it will delight you. It softens all our cares and levels all the difficulties of our meeting, wch when con-venient and practicable will give mutual joy.

I hope you have got your good neighbour home at Calwich to help to keep you warm and cheerful at Xtmas. My love and warmest wishes for your all enjoying the blessings of this blessed season, and many happy new years. You may show the poem to any friend you think worthy of it, but *not* give a copy. It is a *lady's* perform-ance *not* of your acquaintance.

London is eno' to turn the brains of old as well as young. What with Smith's long lists of what is wanted, household accounts during my absence, visits morning, noon, and night, I have hardly time left me to scratch a few lines to my dearest Mary. This moment Lady Bute and Lady Louisa[1] have left me—past three o'clock.

Lady Caroline Stuart was to have been married yester-day morning, and to have gone out of town immediately after the ceremony. Lady Bute was here on Thursday evening, and when she returned home found Lady Car.

---

[1] Lady Louisa Stuart, daughter of John, Earl of Bute, died unmarried, 1851.

so ill that the wedding is put off for some time. She is better to-day; it proved a feverish cold.

Last night I had the *honour* of a visit from the Dss of Bedford;[1] it lasted *full ten minutes,* and long eno'! I did *not dare* to wish her joy of Lady Louisa McDonald's marriage, wch was celebrated on Friday last, much to the discontent of *all* except the partys most concerned. I hope they will be happy; they both have good characters; she is so wise as to despise the idle young men of the present age, and to chuse a companion for real merit.—

> "Let women to superiour fortune born
> For *real virtue,* all temptation scorn."

I think those lines are in the *Brittish Enchanters.*[2] The town is rather empty. Politicians are laying their wise heads together how to attack and how to defend measures at the meeting of Parliament; the *Bon Ton* how to astonish the world with new devises of dress, &c. Lady Weymouth at Ealing. The town has made a match already for Miss Thynne[3]—Lord Aylsford; but I don't hear anything of it from good grounds. *He* must be very deserving to be worthy of *her,* and I don't know *eno'* of him to wish about it.

May many new years be added to my dearest Mary, with heaven's best blessings.

Pray tell me how many plates of plants Mr. Ehret's book has that is in ye study at Ilam.

---

[1] "Duchess of Bedford."—Gertrude, daughter of John, 1st Earl Gower, and wife of John, 4th Duke of Bedford.

[2] "The British Enchanters; or, No Magic like Love," by George, Lord Lansdowne.

[3] Louisa, daughter of Thomas, Viscount Weymouth, 1st Marquis of Bath, married, 18th Nov., 1781, Heneage, 4th Earl of Aylesford.

CHAPTER XXVI.

JANUARY 1778—DECEMBER 1780.

The Countess Cowper to Mrs. Port.

Richmond, Jan. 1st, 1778.

Many happy new years to my dearest Mrs. Port and her family. I am glad y[e] last year is expired, as it has been a very unfortunate one to many families, and in particular to y[e] poor dear Tollemaches ! my heart bleeds for Lady Bridget T.[1] who doated upon her husband, and to lose him in so cruel a manner still adds to y[e] affliction. His Majesty has been very bountifull to the Css Delawar[2] by giving her a pension of £1000 per annum. But nothing can compensate for y[e] loss of a beloved husband. I hope you have now quite recover'd y[r] spirits, and have not your usual *qualms.* I hear y[u] are soon to have another wedding in y[r] family.[3] An agreable sister so near will be delightful.

---

[1] Lady Bridget, daughter of Robert, 1st Earl of Northington, and widow of the Hon. George Fox Lane, married, in 1773, the Hon. John Tollemache, Capt. R.N., who lost his life in a duel with Mr. Pennington, afterwards Lord Muncaster, at New York, 25th Sept., 1777.

[2] Mary, daughter of Lieut.-Gen. Wynyard, married John, 2nd Earl Delawarr, who was appointed, in 1776, Master of the Horse to Queen Charlotte, and died 22nd November, 1777.

[3] " Another wedding."—The marriage of John Dewes (afterwards Granville) to Harriet Joan De la Bere, sister of Mrs. Bernard Dewes.

The Richmond gentlemen gave a ball to ye ladies last Monday and a supper. I thought the rooms wou'd be too hot for me, as it was not at ye Assembly Room but at ye Talbot, so excused myself. Lady M. M.[1] went, and staid supper; she sends her love to y^u, but I believe she has forgot how to write! Mrs. Jeffreys has been dangerously ill, and still keeps house. My neighbours as usual, neither *sick* nor *well*, not plumper. I have had a crying cold, but no flying pains as yet. I sleep in my *cold bath*,[2] and avoid ye fire as much as ever. You see by this tho' I grow *old, not cold*. All well and joyous at Althorpe, till ye birthday, wch will bring them all to town. My best compliments to Mr. Port, and love to all ye little ones, but in particular to my *agreable engaging* god-daughter[3]—(*her mother was so before her*);—she made me not only *like* her, but also *love* her! Miss Williams has but delicate health, apt to catch a cold, but it does not affect her voice, so I hope she is not consumptive. She is a very deserving young woman, and a *great* acquisition to me, as music is my hoby-horse! My compliments to Mrs. Goodwin and Miss Mead. I conclude you have had a merry Xtmas, tho' no *Goody's* as at Welsbourn. Pray take notice of good worthy Henzey whenever you go through Ashborn. I shall write to her very soon. I hope to get this franked, as it is hardly worth postage, tho' I know y^u will think it is, as it comes from *my dear —daughter.*

Y^r ever affectionate,
S. G. COWPER.

---

[1] Lady Mary Mordaunt.
[2] Lady Cowper used to call her bed her " *cold bath.*"
[3] Georgina Mary Anne Port, god-daughter of Countess Cowper.

Mr. Fitz. wou'd have been thrown into prison abroad had not L^r Mary Fitz. distress'd herself to raise £1,200 for him. How he gets any one to trust him is astonishing!

Mrs. Delany to Mrs. Port, of Ilam.

Jan. 3rd, 1778.

[The commencement of this letter is missing.]

I think this sounds a little like a Quaker ; but the .extravagance of the times inclines one rather to go into the other extreme. Every day produces somebody *ruined* and *undone* by their *unaccountable expenses!* I want a magic wand to turn all these spendthrifts (*so little worthy* of the blessings of fortune) into tailors and cobblers, and make them *work hard* for a subsistence ; *so* (says my dear Mary,) "*my A. D. is grown a cross old woman.*"

Lord Onslow[1] who was thought rich (and his lady had no reason to think otherwise) is now declared to be an hundred thousand pound in debt, and they feel so little shame, so little sensible of their folly and dishonesty, that they appear in the midst of all the numerous assemblies and spectacles as gay and as fine as ever.

I have not heard very lately from Malvern, indeed my own fault, but hope they are well. C^t and John *have* heard. *The lover* sets off next week to settle all matters at Cheltenham, *the coach is bespoke!* and he seems in high spirits! Our dear Duchess, I thank God, is pure well again. She and Lady Mansfield and Miss Murrays

---

[1] George, 4th Baron Onslow, who married, in 1753, Henrietta, daughter of Sir John Shelley, Bart. Lord Onslow was created, 19th June, 1801, Viscount Cranley and Earl of Onslow, and died 17th May, 1814.

drink tea here this afternoon. Lady Stamford is very well. Lady Weymouth as usual. No truth in the report of Miss Thynne and Lord Aylsford. Lady Derby[1] was last week at an assembly and ball at Mrs. Onslow's ; staid till five in the morning ; *her* chair not come and no chairmen to be had. But it gave an opportunity to two heroes to show their prowess and gallantry. Lord Lindsey[2] and Mr. Storer[3] undertook the important charge of carrying her home in Mrs. Onslow's chair. In their way they met her own chair coming for her ; but they were too proud of their burden to give it up, and only halted to furnish themselves with her chairmen's straps, that they might finish their task more steadily. So you see the *bon ton* can *transform* themselves without the help of any magical wand! The laugh against Lord Shelburne is turned into pity, on his losing his youngest child, a very fine boy, of an inflamation in his bowels. Mrs. An: Foley[4] came to town from Hasely (where her mother and Miss Foley are) very much alarmed about her eldest girl, who has been very ill with a billious complaint, but is now thought out of danger. The Clanbrasils daily expected. Mrs. Granville confined with the gout. Did I tell you Mr. Pitt[5] had made me a present

---

[1] " Lady Derby."—Elizabeth, only daughter of James, 6th Duke of Hamilton, married, 23rd June, 1774, Edward, 12th Earl of Derby. The Countess of Derby died 14th March, 1797.

[2] Robert, Marquis of Lindsey, eldest son of Peregrine, 3rd Duke of Ancaster.

[3] Anthony Storer, Esq., one of the correspondents of George Selwyn, was appointed one of the Members of the Board of Trade in 1781.

[4] "Mrs. An: Foley."—Elizabeth, daughter and heiress of Boulter Tomlinson, Esq., married, in 1773, Andrew Foley, Esq., third son of Thomas Foley (afterwards Lord Foley).

[5] Thomas Pitt, Esq., of Boconnoc ; he was created Baron Camelford, of Boconnoc, 5th Jan., 1784, and died in 1793.

of my great grandfather's[1] portrait, his lady's, and *his father's*, Sir Bernard Granville, but I am to *leave them back to him*; however, I am *very well pleased* with the company of these ancient gentry.

Ever most tenderly yours,
M. DELANY.

I have not yet had time to range my Ilam curiosities, but I value them extremely. The dear little angels, they are all well and good, and I must be happy.

St. James's Place, 3ᵈ Jan., 1778.

Mrs. Delany to Mrs. Port, of Ilam.

St. James's Place, 10th Jan., 1778.

The fogs have been prodigious, no snow to signify, but so cold I have not yet gone out, even to my good friend Mrs. Montague's little Sunday congregation; hope to do so to-morrow, if my *tremendous* Dss will give me leave; for now Dr. Turton has renounced me, she takes the management of your A. D. on herself, and with Lady Bute, Lady Weymouth, and Mr. Montagu, sat with me all the afternoon yesterday. On Thursday Lady Caroline Dawson[2] (who had been presented that morning) came in her bridal apparel, glittering like the moon in a lympid stream: white and silver, or rather all silver—the prettiest silk I ever saw—and richly trimm'd with silver, festooned and betassel'd, and her lace as fine as if my *enemy* had woven it. I hope she will be happy,

---

[1] Sir Bevil Granville.
[2] Lady Caroline Stuart, fifth daughter of John, Earl of Bute, married, 1st Jan., 1778, the Hon. John Dawson, eldest son of Viscount Carlow.

as she is very deserving. Lady Bute seems happy with the match, which promises well. The match at present *most* talked of is Lord Shelburn[1] to Miss Molesworth, Lady (*illegible*) neice; a fortune of £40,000, and a right to twice as much, but she *is* pretty, quiet, and young, and I believe will be obedient to his nod. I don't wonder you should delight in the musical notes of your little choir, tho' sometimes too powerful, but at a proper distance; but how happy should I be to be stunn'd sometimes with their unanimous strains! I have search'd the town over for old *proverb* cards, but they are not to be found, nor any new ones that you have not got already; but I will venture to throw into your box a pack of *conversation* cards, that are all pictures, and a pack of oracles, that are all *sentiments*; but I won't answer for their delicacy, not having eyes to read all the bad print, so I leave that to your discretion. I have been at as great a loss to get you a few yards of *true* Indian dimity. Your neighbour, Manchester, has brought that manufacture to so great a perfection, that it is difficult to know *which* is *the right*! However, I cut that matter short by sending you four yards, ell-wide, that I had by me, of finer than I can meet with, and I *am sure* it *is* Indian, tho' *not now* as white as Manchester, but will wash of a very good colour. I have got a piece of Nankeen, and propose sending the box next week. My spirits have been a little

---

[1] William, 2nd Earl of Shelburne, who was created, in 1784, Marquis of Lansdowne. He married, first, in 1765, Sophia, daughter of John, Earl Granville; and secondly, in 1779, Louisa, daughter of John Fitzpatrick, Earl of Upper Ossory.

discomposed this morning with a visit from Dr. Foley,[1] now Dean of Worcester; we were *mutually affected!* He asked very kindly after you and your brothers, and your sister-in-law, Dewes, and said he was very well acquainted with her and Miss H. D.,[2] and gave the latter a *very* amiable character. I long for your next letter. It is absolutely so dark that, tho' I write with my spectacles (which I *have never* done before,) I can hardly see to add the best and warmest wishes to dear Ilam.

" *Hope* " arrived safe : what a *charming poem!*

Master Edgcumb's verses to Sr George Baker.

THE HOOPING COUGH. (Believed to be written 1778.)

I happen'd at Harrow to have a bad cold,
By Emanuel quickly the tidings were told;
The carriage was sent for, and when it came down,
We pack'd bag and baggage and went off to town.
When we came home, we *found* all the house in a flurry
And the doc^r (Sr George) arriv'd all in a hurry.
(That doct^r so famous for curing all ills
With his bleedings, his vomits, his purgings and pills;
But for my part I think that his physical stuff
In *all* sorts of complaints does *more harm* than enough.)
Well, Sr George, as I told you came puffing and blowing,
With his looks so profound and his bow wondrous knowing
" How do you do, s^r," (says he,) " I hope you are well,"
" What brings you from Harrow? I beg you will tell."

[1] Dr. Robert Foley, Dean of Worcester, half-brother to Thomas Foley, Esq.
[2] " Miss H. D."—Miss Harriet De la Bere.
[3] Sir George Baker, Physician in Ordinary to the King, and Physician to the Queen. Created a Baronet in 1766, died in 1809.

" Oh, 'tis only a cough, sr, pray don't be afraid,
" But this tutor of mine all this fidget has made ;
" For he *thought* that I *hoop'd*, but I am *sure he is wrong*,
" I do nothing *but* cough, and that all the day long ;
" And I have often heard say (I don't know if 'tis true)
" That *that*, comes by fits, and these fits are but few."
" Come, give me your hand, sir, your pulse I must feel,
" It is quick,—*there is fever*, oh yes ! *a great deal*."
" Then 'twas you, sir, that brought it, you've flurried me quite ;
" I think I shall never recover my fright."
And indeed I was terrified out of my wits,
For he talked so of *coughs*, and of *hoopings*, and *fits*.
I coughed, and he heard it, consider'd a while,
And soon after exclaim'd—" By the sound of this bout
" I think in a hooping at last 'twill turn out ;
" It *may* be, it *may not*, I will not pretend
" To declare what it is, but in that, it *may end*."
This done, he consults for the good of the nation,
Finds fault with the measures of Administration ;
And then he abuses the leaders of faction,
Who to get a good place throw all to distraction ;
And lastly laments the American war,
And thinks that the struggle's been carried too far.
At last to my infinite joy he takes leave,
And stretches his hand out his fee to receive.
Ah ! that's his delight ; if he gets but his fee
Not a fig for his patient, he don't care for me.
But I wonder why any man is such a ninny
As for staying five minutes to give him a guinea.
But, alas ! in this tribe each plague has its brother,
I no sooner lost one than there followed another :
Mr. Powel has heard on't, so he needs must follow ;
" What, (says he,) you're come with a hoop and a hollow ?
" I don't think, mind, you'll hoop, tho' ye Doc^r says yea ;
" You do not hoop now, that I safely may say."
I ask'd him a question—" Mr. Powel, I pray
" May I eat any meat at my dinner to-day ?"
" O no, I think not, mind, I say by no means,
" You should eat nothing now but *pudding and greens*."
And thus it went on, and we never cou'd know,
For the Doc^r says yes ; Mr. Powel says no ;
But the Doc^r was right, tho' we thought he was wrong,
For I did begin hooping before it was long ;
And then he began of all medicines to chuse
What was best, and determined *emetics* to use !

And I needs must be sent, for the change of ye air,
To Salthill and Reading, and I don't know where.
But at last I'm in hopes to be cheerful and gay
For the Doc^r has left us, for ever, to-day ;
So Sir George, Mr. Pow'l, and *foul physick* adieu !
You'll get no more of us, we want no more of you !

SIR GEORGE BAKER'S ANSWER.

If coughing can bring up such verses as these,
Go, hoop o'er again, and with *wit* pay your *fees ;*
Wit, out of abundance, *you* freely *may give*,
And I'll stretch out my hand for't, as long as I live !

Mrs. Delany to Miss Port, of Ilam.

St. James's Place, 22nd Jan., 1778.

MY DEAR CHILD,

I am very much obliged to you for your very
pretty skreen and kind letter, very well written for a first
tryal ; I value both, more as the work of your dear little
fingers than on any other account.   Pray give my love
to your brothers for the *curiosities* they have been so kind
as to send me, and to your mama for the shells, some of
which are the best of the kind I have met with, particularly that which was wrap'd in the bit of brown
paper, which the Duchess D^r of Portland has placed in
her cabinet : the name is *Helix arbustorum*.   *I wish* my
dear bird and I cou'd work together ; I cou'd join my
tears to yours that we are at so great a distance, but as
it is not in our power to meet at present, we must live in
hopes that we shall before it is very long.   It makes me
some amends to hear so good an account of my dearest
G. M. A., and I look upon you as *my deputy* to take
care of your dear and precious mama—to nurse her when

she is sick, to read to her and lull her to sleep when she is not well eno' to *talk*, and when she *is*, to cheer her with your innocent and lively prattle, and, by your own gentle manners, to set an example to your dear brothers not to disturb her with any noise. Nothing can make her so happy as to see you all improving every day, and attentive to all your lessons; and pray talk a great deal of French to her,—I am sure your good Mrs. A. Vrankin will enable and encourage you to do it: pray remember me very kindly to her. I hope you will like your cloak and apron; I did not edge it with fur, wch is much the fashion, as I remembered you had one of that sort, and spring is coming on. I must now pack up the box that conveys this. Your uncles (Court and John) came to town last night, and I expect them every moment.

I desire my kind compliments to Miss H. Mead;[1] I have taken the liberty to send her a fashionable fan, tho' a trifle I am asham'd of. Say everything that's kind to your dear papa and mama, and believe me ever, my dearest child, your affectionate aunt and humble servt,

M. DELANY.

From Mr. Court Dewes to Mr. Bernard Dewes.

Temple, Jan. 24th, 1778.

DEAR BERNARD,

I did not write to you f^m Welsbourn, according to my promise, because I cou'd send you no decisive account of ye matter you interested yourself in. I can now give you such a one as you wish, Mr. Mordaunt

---

[1] Henrietta, second daughter of Captain Joseph Mead, R.N., married, in 1782, Fiennes Sanderson Miller, Esq., of Radway, Warwickshire.

having in a very handsome manner inform'd me that the Chancellor had complimented him wth ye living of Welsbourn, and that he *had*, at *my request*, nominated Mr. Williams. You will easily believe the pleasure y^s has given me, especially as, *instead* of *one*, it will, very probably be a means of procuring us *two* agreeable neighbours, and will be a settlement for W^ms for life. We had a very good journey to town ; found Mrs. Delany in very good spirits, recovered from her illness, though I think she looks thin, and seemingly very *well* pleased wth y^e *treaty* that is going forward! Westminster Hall swarms wth silk gowns, tho' I am told there are several discontented at not having had offers of them—Kenyon,[1] I hear, and Geo. Harding ; it is a true comedy to see Widmore strutting in his. I think I know of no news to entertain you w^th, or, if I did, have I time to write it, as I am going to ye opera to-night wth John, and must seal up my letter y^s morning. He (John) is *very busy in his preparations*. I have not yet got ye parcels for Miss Snow ; when I have I will send *you*. If you have any other commands for me, let me know, and they shall be executed by, dear Bern^d,

Your affectionate br^r,
C. DEWES.

---

[1] Lloyd Kenyon, born at Gredington, in Flintshire, in 1733 ; called to the Bar in 1761, made Attorney-General in 1782, Master of the Rolls in 1784, a Chief Justice of the King's Bench, and elevated to the Peerage, in 1788 ; died April, 1802.

The Rev. John Dewes to the Countess Cowper.

MADAM,

The honour your ladyship has done me by your notice and good wishes demands of me every respect and attention. In this light (besides flattering myself that your ladyship will approve my choice) I take the liberty of acquainting you that I have made my addresses to Miss De la Bere, the next sister to Mrs. Bernard Dewes; that I am very well receiv'd, and things are in such a train that in six weeks or two months I shall have the pleasure and honour of informing you of an event, the prospect of which promises much happiness to myself, and is very well thought of by all my friends; it were improper for me, with my present feelings, to pass any incomiums upon the lady, but when I have the honour and opportunity of presenting her to you, which I hope to have, your discernment *will tell you* what *she is!*

Mrs. Delany has been indispos'd lately, which has prevented her writing, but she is better again.

And I beg, madam, to be consider'd, with the greatest respect, your ladyship's

Most obliged,

And most obedient, humble servant,

J. DEWES.

The Countess Cowper to the Rev. Mr. Dewes, at Mrs. Delany's, St. James's Place, London.

Richmond, Feb. 4th, 78.

S^R,

I congratulate y^u upon·y^r intended marriage, as I make no doubt of its proving an happy union from ye knowledge I have of y^r amiable disposition, and ye character I have heard of ye De la Bere family. I like Mrs. Dewes *extreamly*, and as *I know* y^u have a good taste I do not doubt I shall be as well pleas'd wth your choice, and hope y^u will bring *my new cosin* to spend a day wth me. I am very sorry to hear Mrs. Delany has been indisposed; but hope she will soon be well again, and make her friends happy still for some years. Be so good as to make my best compliments to her, and believe me, S^r,

Your sincere,

Humble servant,

G. C. COWPER.

The Countess Cowper to Mrs. Port, of Ilam.

Richmond, Feb. 22nd, 78.

This is, I think, my dearest Mrs. Port's birthday, and a more amiable object it never produced! Oh! this day twelve years *we passed it together!* But now y^u are " over ye hills and far away!" Lady M. M. and I shall toast you to-day, and wish y^u most ardently many happy returns of it. I hope y^u will produce another fine boy, as you have never a Christian name left for a girl, and I wou'd have *my dear little goddaughter without competitors!* She is *quite* to *my taste!* I have received a very sensible letter from y^r brother John to inform me of his intended marriage, and *I approve* of his choice. I hear her *much commended*, and I hope she will prove not only an agreeable companion to him, but also to you. I heard lately from Mrs. Ravaud. She says you have dropp'd her as a correspondent? *Pray* write to her sometimes. Remember how she *nursed* you here—you know she is *soon hurt*, and has really great merit towards her friends. I thought her broke when I saw her in ye autumn, and fear she will not be long-lived—but I think she *cannot fail* of a *seat* in heaven, tho' she has *not* (as Mrs. Delany and me) a "*steeple*" in her stomach! The *Gen.* is as odd as ever; says that "not even old father Time can lay his hand upon me," but "slips over me without making any impression." My best compliments to Mr. Port, whether *warm* or *cold*. Tell him I think my *warmth* rather encreases, but not my *fat*. I hope he has *not* return'd again to eating *suppers,* as they will spoil his complexion, and I cannot send him any of *my wash* so far! We have been near having another catastrophe in ye Tolle-mache family; as Mrs. T. has narrowly escaped from having her skull fractur'd by her horse throwing her, and kicking her head and face. I hope *her beauty* will not be impair'd; but she is still under surgeon's hands.

I am now in mourning for Lord Shelburne's youngest son, who died almost suddenly by a disorder in his bowels; a very uncommon boy of his age; he was but nine years old, but I own Lord Fitzmaurice was always my favourite, as *he is* like his mother. How many nephews and neices I have had ye misfortune to mourn for! I hope in God that those that yet remain will be spared. My sister and her little grand-daughter are well. Poor

Lady De la Warr[1] I fear will not long outlive her beloved lord; it may be happier for herself. But she will be a terrible loss to her three daughters. Poor Lady Bridget Tollemache has taken a lodging for two months at Hampstead, for change of air, as her son has been ill; but as he is a strong child I hope he will soon get well. London has been very sickly this winter. Putrid sore throats and fevers. The Dss of Devon. is *much quieter* than she was, and is always at home *before* the Duke; and whatever people may say, and, tho' *so much admired,* she has no cicisbio, which is now much y[e] *ton.* Harriot[2] is vastly improved, and almost as tall as her sister. Gen. Fitz. says "she is delicious!" I hope she will not be married before she is compleat twenty; she is only now in her 17th year. Lord Althorpe is at Cambridge, and as *yet* all that is right. Lady M. M. sends her love to y[u], mine to ye little ones. Miss Williams desires her complimen[ts]; she is a very good young woman. Adieu,

Ma chère toute à vous,

S. G. Cowper.

---

[1] Lady Delawarr died 27th Oct., 1784, having survived her husband seven years. Her daughter, Lady Georgiana, married, in 1782, Edward Pery Buckley, Esq., and Lady Matilda married, 18th July, 1793, General Henry Wynyard.

[2] Lady Henrietta Frances Spencer, second daughter of John, Earl Spencer, and sister of Georgiana, Duchess of Devonshire. Lady Henrietta married, 27th Nov., 1780, Frederick, 3rd Earl of Bessborough; and died 11th Nov., 1821.

Mrs. Delany to Mrs. Dewes.

St. James's Place, 31st March, 1778.

I must sincerely congratulate my dear Mrs. John Dewes on her marriage, and hope the union will prove as happy a one to her, as it cannot fail of being to my nephew and all those who wish him the true blessings of life. It is with real pleasure that I salute you by a name so endeared to me already, and which your amiable qualities *will* entitle you to with the rest of your brothers and sisters, that of subscribing myself

My *dear niece,*

Your affec[te] aunt and humble serv[t],

M. DELANY.

I intended writing to Mr. J. D., but beg you will present him wth my thanks for his letter and congratulations, and then I am sure they will be acceptable (wth my love) and y[e] same to y[r] brother and sister De la Bere.

Mrs. Delany to Mrs. Port, of Ilam.

St. James's Place, 9th April, 1778.

I am glad you have seen your bridal neighbours so well and so happy; long may it last! I received the enclosed letter last post, and not having time to say as much for Mrs. Sand[d] as she wishes me to say, send you her own words. The cap I sent (tho' fashionable) I thought *enormous,* but could not wait for another, and was assured y[u] might squêze and *bend* the *wires* to y[r] taste.

I have been very happy wth y^r dear bro^r and sist^r in law. Seeing them well and happy must make me so, and feel sorry at the approach of the day they threaten to leave me, which is next Wednesday.

Bernard is gone to Miss Harrop's benefit ; Lady Willoughby gave Mrs. Dewes a ticket, but she is so prudent, as it will be a vast croud, to excuse herself from going. Mrs. De la Bere is expected in town to-night, and her daughter is gone to meet her and engage her to dine here next Sunday, for to-morrow we dine at Sr John Mordaunt's,[1] and on Saturday at Lord Willoughby's ; these engagements, with my morning occupations, fill up my time pretty well, but I have stolen an hour tho' by candlelight to write to my dearest M. Our morning visitors were Mr. Winnington, Lady Elizabeth Archer,[2] 2 Miss Young's, Lady Ducie,[3] and Mrs. Weddel ; and I expect Lady Andover, Mrs. Dashwood, and our very dear Duchess.

The Dss. of Chandos[4] met a lady of her acquaintance who look'd pale and thin, and her Grace said, " I believe, madam, we are sympathetical."

Lord Chatham's downfall in the House of Lords[5] I

---

[1] Sir John Mordaunt, one of the Grooms of the Bedchamber, M.P. for the county of Warwick, and LL.D. He married Elizabeth, daughter and coheiress of Thomas Prowse, Esq., and died 18th Nov., 1806.

[2] Lady Elizabeth, daughter of George, Earl of Halifax, and widow of Henry Archer, Esq., brother of Thomas, 1st Lord Archer.

[3] "Lady Ducie."—Margaret, daughter of Sir John Ramsden, married, 20th Feb., 1774, Thomas Reynolds, 2nd Baron Ducie.

[4] "The Duchess of Chandos."—Ann Eliza, daughter of Richard Gamon, Esq., and widow of Roger Hope Elletson, Esq., married, secondly, 21st June, 1777, James Brydges, 3rd Duke of Chandos.

[5] William Pitt, Earl of Chatham, who, on rising to answer a speech of the Duke of Richmond's on the American war, fell down in a fit. He died at Hayes, in Kent, 11th May in the same year, aged 70.

2 A

suppose you have had the particulars of in the newspapers. It made a sad uproar, and was *shocking* to the
beholders, but he is now pretty well again, and I am not
sure he will be sorry it happen'd. Adieu.

Mrs. Delany to Mrs. Port, of Ilam.

St. James's Place, 12th May, 1778.

The clock has just struck 8, and I am in minutely expectation of the Dss D. of Portland's chaise to carry me
to breakfast with Mrs. Mary Smith at her little retreat
in Kentish Town.

Yesterday was a day of mortification. When I sat
down to my solitary meal, a note came from Lord Guilford's, where all the party dined that met the Friday
before at Ld Willoughby's, among them y^r brother Court;
the note was from him to say that Lady Dartmouth had
got a ticket for me for the ancient music, and that
Lord Guilford's coach would fetch me at six. But alas,
it would have been imprudent to engage in a *bustle* that
day, so *very unwillingly* I resisted ye temptation; a few
moments after came a message from Whitehall to say
the Dss of Portland desired to see me, and sent her
coach; so I went there for an hour, and had the satisfaction of finding her much better, left her in the company
of her excellent daughters, and prudently return'd home.
Lady Andover arrived at my door just as I did, drank
tea, and staid the evening: at nine Lady Clanbrassil and
Miss Foley came; the latter was to go to Ranelagh at
ten, with her sister Winnington. All returned from

Portsmouth, much pleased with their expedition,[1] but Lady Clan's spirits were not sufficient to be of the party, tho' her lord went.

This morning I breakfasted with my old agreable friend, Mrs. M. Smith, who seems to live a happy rational life, and is always cheerful and edifying. In my return home I call'd on Lady Bute, who goes out of town for the summer to-morrow; *great* is *her* loss to my little circle; she is both amiable and entertaining; but her spirits have been of late saddly agitated, wch I suppose hastens her leaving London.

Lord Piercy[2] has begun a divorce in the Commons, which will secure a false heir being imposed upon, of which they say there is danger; but he will be too late this year to bring it into the House of Lords, so that if he has courage enough to venture again, he must wait till next year.

Yesterday died Lord Chatham; he never recovered his fall in the House of Lords, but I dare say it was a consolation to him, under all sufferings, to think that he died in his calling. Many panegyricks, many aspersions, will be banded backwards and forwards, as *no man* ever was *higher or lower* in his sentiments, and in the estimation of the world; but he *had* undoubtedly great abilities, and he *had* served his country. He would have been a

---

[1] Their Majesties George III. and Queen Charlotte, attended by their suite, went to Portsmouth on Saturday, 2nd May, 1778, and remained there for a week, inspecting the building-yards, the fortifications, store-houses, &c., &c. On Monday, May 4th, the King reviewed the fleet at Spithead, and their Majesties dined, under an awning, on the deck of the " Prince George " (90 guns.)

[2] Hugh, Earl Percy (afterwards 2nd Duke of Northumberland), married, first, 2nd July, 1764, Lady Anne Stuart, third daughter of the Earl of Bute, from whom he was divorced in 1779; and, secondly, 23rd May, 1779, Frances Julia, daughter of Peter Burrell, Esq., and sister of Peter, Lord Gwydir.

truly greater character, had not an unbounded *ambition*, and a *vanity* hardly to be equaled, tarnished his good qualities. What havock do those 2 *great* underminers of virtue make in the human heart! and how much safer and eligible is that state of life that saves us from such destructive temptations!

I forgot to tell you the civilities of y^r *gossips*. Lady Louisa Manners[1] made me a visit and desired me to assure you, you had "made her happy in the favour you did her." And on Saturday morning last I also had a visit from Genl Fitz^{ms}, with a note in his hand wch he desired me not to peruse till he was gone. It contained his five guineas, and I enclose his note.

The Hon. Mrs. Boscawen to Mrs. Delany.

Glan Villa, 22nd June, 1778.

Dear Madam,

I expect Lord and Lady Edgcumbe to dinner, and as they are not early folk, they will be a little roasted upon Highgate Hill. You bid me write, my dear madam, and I do not dispute your commands, else—what can I say from hence but that my roses are *blown*, and my hay is *not mown*. The only news I have heard I cannot believe. It is that the Duchess of Devonshire march'd thro' Islington at the head of the Derbyshire Militia, dress'd in the uniform of that regiment. The regiment, indeed, I saw at Barnet the other day, and it has probably since march'd thro' Islington, but I

---

[1] Lady Louisa Tollemache, grand-daughter to the 1st Earl Granville, married, in 1765, John Manners, of Grantham Grange, Esq. She became Countess of Dysart on the death of her last surviving brother in 1821; and died in 1840, aged 95.

cannot think your beautifull cousin *march'd* at the head of it, comme une autre d'Eon?

The post is come in since I wrote the above, and I have the pleasure to receive your kind letter. I hope to have the still greater one of seeing you as you return. Every day you will find me at dinner time, Thursday excepted, when I am to dine with Mrs. Aislabie, my neighbour, to meet a much older neighbour, the Lady Dowager Onslow.[1]

I am sorry you had any difficulty about horses, and hope there will be none as you return, for I believe all the militia are pass'd that were going to their several encampments.[2] The Duke of Beaufort is on his march to Warley Common. The Duchess I hope to see to-day. She makes a short excursion, and returns to Bad-minton (now solitary) next Friday. How happy poor Mrs. Stewart wou'd be were her beloved husband only on Warley Common or Cox Heath. I hope in God he is not less safe.

Adieu, dear madam. Our postman (agreeable crea-ture!) stands over us threatening while we sign, seal, and deliver. Hastily, therefore, but very sincerely,

Yours ever,

F. BOSCAWEN.

---

[1] The Dowager Lady Onslow.—Mary, daughter of Sir Edmund Elwell, Bart., married, May 16th, 1741, Richard, 3rd Lord Onslow, who died Oct. 9th, 1776.

[2] During the summer and autumn of 1778, encampments were formed at Salisbury; St. Edmundsbury; Coxheath, in Kent; Warley Common, Essex; and Winchester; consisting of regiments of the line and of militia. Walpole, in May, 1778, says—"The Parliament is only to have short adjournments; and our senators, instead of retiring to horse-races (*their* plough), are all turned soldiers, and disciplining militia. Camps everywhere, and the ladies in the uniform of their husbands."

The Hon. Mrs. Boscawen to Mrs. Delany.

Glan Villa, June 27th, 1778.

My Dear Madam,

I have not been in London since the day I wrote
to you last, and that you was so good to send y^r servant
to me. Loud as my call is there, I have had a shriller
one here. Boys who might wait for the darts or bullets
of the French and Spaniards, will meantime throw *potatoes* at one another's head. Lord Worcester had one of
these aim'd at his crown, but turning round to face his
antagonist at the instant, he received it on the ball of
his eye ; and as it is not yet the time of large potatoes,
the bone did not keep it off—it went under it, as into a
cup. I had therefore the mortification to see him arrive
on Saturday with a bandeau like a blind Cupid ; and
tho' upon inspection, not only of myself, but (since) by a
medical person, there is no harm done, thank God, and
this œil poché is already pretty like the other; yet as
there cou'd be no reading for either, I thought it best to
keep him here than confin'd to his room at Westminster,
for they have a decent custom there, that when a boy is
not well enough to go into school, it is concluded he is
not *able* to go out of his house, and *there* he must stay.
Thus you see, my dear madam, I have a young guest to
whom employment and amusement is at one entrance
quite shut out. By Monday it is supposed he may use
his eyes again, and if I shou'd visit my lady in the straw
between this and then, it will be only a flying visit. I
hope you will soon have the satisfaction to hear the
Duchess arriv'd safe and well at Weymouth, and then
you will have the goodness to impart it to me by a few

lines, *unless* the moderate weather shou'd tempt *you to a march* of a few miles.

With truest affection and respect,

My dear madam,

Most faithfully yours,

F. BOSCAWEN.

I have no engagement after Friday next. Monday would be a pretty day to receive the honour and pleasure of y^r company.

The Hon. Mrs. Boscawen to Mrs. Delany.

Glan Villa, 4th July, 78.

I do not make you any apologies, my dear madam, for delaying to acknowledge your kind and most agreeable letter from Luton Park, because I have waited for one from my Cornish steward, in answer to my questions, "Who is Mr. Basset's agent, and where is Mr. Basset himself?" To-day my Cornish letter arrives, and the information is as follows, verbatim, "Mr. Kevill, of Cambourne, near Redruth, is Mr. Bassett's steward. Mr. Bassett himself will be home in a few months : he has money in plenty in his banker's hands, and, I suspect, does not think his debts are in arrear." Thus sayeth Mr. C. Rashleigh, my informant, and I hope by this time the information is unnecessary, and *that all arrears are paid.* I am sure they ought to be.

I have not forgot y^r commands to have *Sensibility,* " *They best can taste it who can feel it most*;" but indeed, my dear madam, 'tis a work de longue haleine, and I have both my dau^{rs} to write to as well as my son, so that when I have dispatch'd a couple of motherly epistles, I am ready to run away, and cannot sit in my closet a moment longer, seeing all the trees wave about and bow their heads, as if fine pleasant breezes waited for me on the bench below; mais, "ce qui est differé n'est pas perdu," and I must become a good deal alter'd before any of your wishes become indifferent to me. Patience then, if you please, and "*Sensibility*" shall *attend* you.

Mrs. Leveson at Bill Hill by this time. I saw her in London yesterday. Also took leave of Lady Edgcumbe, who sets out for her delightfull Mount next Monday.

Publick news or politicks I won't mention; they seem'd to be too melancholy to approach the happy scenes of Bulstrode : and as to private news I was delighted to hear of Ld Suffolk's (probable) recovery, having indeed been very uneasy the past week, and thought of Lady Andover continually. I heard that Sr Geo. Osborne recherche en mariage Lady Heneage Finch,[1] which sounds very likely, as I have been told ce chevalier là is not insensible to pecuniary considerations, and, in obtaining this amiable lady, he may glance at the fortunes of 2 or 3 more; but you will say, perhaps, that the lady herself is alone worthy of preference; indeed I think so. She was always a *great* favourite of mine, but 'tis plain she was *not* his *first* choice, being just as marriageable as she is now when first he enter'd into the holy state!

I expect Mrs. Walsingham every minute (from Cam-

---

[1] Heneage, second daughter of Daniel, 7th Earl of Winchelsea, married, in 1778, Sir George Osborne, of Chicksands, Bart., whose first wife was Elizabeth, daughter and coheiress of John Bannister, Esq.

bridge), and will end this dull epistle with presenting my best respects to the Duchess.

F. B.

The Poem entitled "Sensibility," alluded to in this letter, was the composition of Mrs. Hannah More, addressed to Mrs. Boscawen. The following extracts are taken from the copy given by Mrs. Hannah More herself to the mother of the Editor—

> "Accept, Boscawen! these unpolish'd lays,
> Nor blame too much the verse you cannot praise.
> For you far other bards have wak'd the string;
> Far other bards for you were wont to sing.
> Yet on the gale their parting music steals,
> Yet, your charm'd ear the lov'd impression feels.
> You heard the lyres of Lyttelton and Young;
> And this a Grace, and that a Seraph strung.
> These are no more! But not with these decline
> The Attic chasteness, and the flame divine.
> Still, sad Elfrida's Poet shall complain,
> And either Warton breathe his classic strain,
> Nor fear lest genuine poesy expire
> While tuneful Beattie wakes old Spenser's lyre.
> His sympathetic lay his soul reveals,
> And paints the perfect Bard from what he feels," &c. &c.

The names of Mrs. Delany, Bishop Lowth, Sir Joshua Reynolds, Soame Jenyns, Beilby Porteus, Elizabeth Carter, Hester Chapone, Mrs. Walsingham, Mrs. Barbauld, Garrick, and Dr. Johnson are then enumerated.

Mrs. Delany's name is thus introduced—

> "Delany shines, in worth serenely bright,
> Wisdom's strong ray, and virtue's milder light;
> And she who bless'd the friend, and grac'd the page
> Of Swift, *still lends her lustre to our age:*
> Long, long protract thy light, O star benign!
> Whose *setting* beams with *added brightness shine!*"

And of Mrs. Boscawen, she says—

> "Or you, Boscawen, when you fondly melt
> In raptures none but mothers ever felt,

And view, enamour'd in your beauteous race,
All Leveson's sweetness, and all Beaufort's grace !
Yet think *what dangers* each lov'd child may share,
The youth *if valiant*, and the maid *if fair ?*"

In allusion to Sensibility, the subject of this epistle, Mrs.
Hannah More concludes with these lines—

" 'Tis *this*, tho' Nature's hidden treasures lie,
Bare to the keen inspection of her eye,
Makes *Portland's* face its brightest rapture wear
When her large bounty smooths the bed of care.
'Tis *this* that breathes thro' Sevigné's sweet page,
That nameless grace which soothes a second age.
'Tis *this*, whose charms the soul resistless seize,
And gives Boscawen half her pow'r to please.
Yet, why those terrors ? why that anxious care,
Since *your last hope*[1] the dreadful war *will dare ?*
Why dread that energy of soul which leads
To dang'rous glory by heroic deeds ?
Why tremble lest this ardent soul aspire ?—
You *fear the son* because you *knew the sire.*
Hereditary valour you deplore,
And *dread*, yet *wish*, to find *one hero more !*"

The Dowager-Countess Gower to Mrs. Delany.

Bill Hill, 8th July, 78.

Mrs Delany is always kind to her ffriends, and
never more so y^n in informing those here of her being
well at Bulstrode wth ye good and gracious proprietor.
L..y Gower can't comend herself, having her añual
cough in a great degree; hopes 'tis at its heigth, for
indeed 'tis very troublesome. Mrs Mountagu was not
much fatigued wth her journey hither, has remain'd priⱦy
well since, and, wth in these two days quite jolly.   We

---

[1] Admiral Boscawen's only remaining son was then in America, and at the
battle of Lexington.

admire *Mountaskew*. Mr. T. Pitt says ye owner of y
house deals in angles, from gratitude to ye memory of her
dear spouse. L..y Andover's heart's at ease long before
this, I hope. L..d Suffolk's recovery is wonderfull. I
wish it may last, for her sake.

Mrs Mountagu is yor most faithfull; has got a *little
coach*, wch she's as pleas'd wth as Mas^r Johñy is wth his
hobby. I can't get her to prefer ye post chaize to it.
She has had a letter from M^{rs} ffountayne, wch says M^r
Mountague and her son are perfectly well, both wth 'em
and M^r ffountayne quite recover'd. Mrs M. wants to
indite panegericks on some new walks, but L . . y G.
wants Mrs D. first to come and see if they are worthy.

All here desire their most respectfull complim^{ts} and
best wishes to ye D^s of Portland and yor self for all
health and every hapiness ; none are more sincere than
those from

M. Gower.

Mrs. Delany to the Rev. John Dewes.

Bulstrode, 9th July, 1778.

My dear Nephew,

I have for some weeks past been a sort of ram-
bler in a little compass ; trying my wings for a longer
flight, if my strength will allow me. I left London, 16
of June, for Luton, and staid there till I met the Dss of
Port^d here on the 29th, and had the pleasure of finding
her very well, after an expedition to Dover. This place
is now in its full beauty, and if any situation can bear a
resemblance to Paradise it is this. The *variety* of *creatures* (in perfect agreement) *and vegetables* are a constant
scene of delight and amusement, besides the good taste

in which all the improvem^{ts} are laid out. It has as much magnificence as is necessary, with every elegance and comfort that can be wish'd for, such as everybody must approve and enjoy, and such as are in the power of every rational being, who have *any* possessions, to enjoy—such as I hope my dear nephew and niece will have for many years at Calwich. Happy shou'd I be were I able sometimes to share them with you. I spent my time at Luton very agreably, but *more* of magnificence *than comfort* belongs to that place, except in the very kind and obliging manner I was receiv'd by the owners, who had every consideration for me, to make my situation as easy as possible, and a curious and enquiring mind can't fail of being gratified there, as well as at Bulstrode, wth *every branch* of virtû.

My love to your amiable wife ; the same to Ilam. Lord Guilford came here on Tuesday, and staid till yesterday morning : he has been coaxing me to make him a visit to Wroxton, in my way to Warwickshire ; a *very good bait !* God knows if I shall be able ; I can at pres^t only say I am willing.

Ever y^r affec^{te}
M. DELANY.

Mrs. Delany to Mrs. Port, of Ilam.

Bulstrode, 27th July, 1778.

I am at present, I thank God, very well, but find fatigue of any kind will not do ; but surely I have *great* reason to be thankful for the remaining strength I enjoy at my years, when so many of my cotemporarys are confin'd to their beds or their elbow chairs ? I could wish, if I am so happy as to meet you at Malvern Hall, that there was to be no other company, and that I might have the pleasure of meeting my nephew and neice (J. D's) at Welsbourn, where I propose resting one whole day. I mean it on Mrs. Dewes's account, as it would be less bustle for her. But these are tender points, and we must take them as they happen, I am sure I shall be happy to see them all if I can.

Mrs. Dashwood has been here a week; I intend to try my wings by an excursion of two days to Bill Hill, if she stays here next week. To day Dr. Solander comes, and brings a Mr. Alstromer,[1] a Swedish virtuoso, with him, so we shall be very philosophical; Mr. Lightfoot[2] you may be sure of the party. I am sorry you did not send your little flower, it may come yet; I believe by your description it is a *linaria* or *toad flax*. I suppose Court is gone into Warwickshire, if not tell him I shall immediately pay off Mr. Hammersley's enormous bill, but at any time I had rather be the oppressed than the oppressor! Poor Lady Cork[3] is undone by most inhuman treatment, all she has was seiz'd for debt, and I believe she is at present at Mr. Pointz's. Lady Holland[4] has never recovered a fever she had some time ago, attended

---

[1] Baron C. Alstrœmer, a Swedish botanist, after whom the Alstrœmeria order was named.

[2] The Rev. John Lightfoot, author of the "Flora Scotica," was born at Newent, in Gloucestershire, Dec. 9, 1735. He was one of the most distinguished botanists of his day, and formed a fine herbarium. He drew up, for the Duchess of Portland, a catalogue of the contents of her museum. He died at Uxbridge in 1788.

[3] Edmund, 7th Earl of Cork, married, first, in 1764, Anne, daughter of Kelland Courtenay, Esq., of Pemsford, county Devon.

[4] Stephen, 2nd Lord Holland, married, in 1766, Mary, eldest daughter of John Fitzpatrick, 1st Earl of Upper Ossory. Lady Holland died in 1778.

with a delirium which still continues, and it is fear'd her *son*, a very fine boy, will fall into the dreadful hands of Charles Fox, and then his ruin will be inevitable. These are *melancholly tales*, but a good moral may be drawn from them; *they* teach the dangers of the world, and the necessity of good principles to guard us from its ruin, and to avoid all manner of connextion with those who want virtue and Xtian resolution to do what is right. I can send you no news but what will be old to you; as I suppose you have heard of the match soon to be compleated between Sir George Osborn [1] and Lady Heneage Finch, daughter of the late Lord Winchelsea. She bears a most amiable character; not handsome, but a good fortune. I *hope* she will be happy. I have heard Sir G. O. commended. Lady Charlotte Tufton,[2] who has long been her friend, told Lady H. Finch she had always intended to leave her her jewells as a token of gratitude for the reconciliation she had brought about between her and her nephew Lord Thanet, and was happy she had now so good an opportunity of presenting them to her. Lady H. Finch would not be prevailed upon to accept at present more than a pair of earings and some pins for her hair. It has raised Lady C. Tufton greatly in my esteem, as it proves she is grateful, and generous.

This letter was begun yesterday. Dr. Solander, &c. came as expected, and I am now going to get a botanical lecture and to copy a beautifull flower called *the Stuartia*.

---

[1] Sir George Osborn married, secondly, in 1778, Heneage, daughter of Daniel, 7th Earl of Winchelsea.

[2] Lady Charlotte Tufton was the youngest daughter of Sackville, 7th Earl of Thanet. She was born in Sept. 1728, and died Dec. 12th, 1803. In 1775 her *brother* Sackville was Earl of Thanet; he died 10th April, 1786, and was succeeded by his son Sackville.

Mrs. Delany to Miss Port, of Ilam.

Bulstrode, 27th July, 1778.

I thank you, my dearest *Porty*, for the lines you added to your uncle's letter, and make no doubt of your writing in time as well as you read French. You must avoid scribbling till your hand is settled ; write a line (and not more at a time) two or three times in a day as well as you can, which I think is better than writing three lines at one sitting, as that will not tire your hand or patience ; and by degrees, as you find writing grow more easy, you may double your number. Pray remember me very kindly to Mrs. A. Vrankin, and assure her I am very sorry she should have anything to afflict her ; but the same affection that makes her sorry for her friend will in time reconcile her to her loss when she considers the infirmities that encrease with years, and that she is removed from sorrow and pain to perfect happiness.

My love to your very dear brothers and sister Louisa. I long to see her. Your most affectionate aunt,

M. DELANY.

Mrs. Dashwood is here, and sends her love to you. The Duchess of Portland does you the honour to remember you kindly, as she hears you are "*very good.*" She is glad you have a little sister to delight you, and makes no doubt of your setting her a very good example in every particular, which will make you for her sake, as well as your own, do everything that is praiseworthy.

I enclose you a prayer[1] I am very fond of, and hope you will like it so well as to get it by heart.

The Hon. Mrs. Boscawen to Mrs. Delany.

Glan Villa, 4th Aug., 78.

My dear friend is so little inclin'd to censure or judge harshly of those she honours with her esteem that I am sure she has not once been tempted to say " Mrs. Boscawen is very *ungratefull* not to acknowledge my letter all this while. I don't write such long letters to every-body. She might esteem it a favour, I think." So I do, my dear madam, and a very great one; but it wou'd have been a poor return that I cou'd have made for it, having no one pleasant subject to discourse upon. I have still been harping upon our admiral, and often have been told of *battles* never fought and *victories* never won. Ab^t ten days ago, especially, I was assur'd (and by two Judges of the realm) that we had taken no less than 14 ships of the line; this, tho' I cou'd *not believe*, yet I was disturb'd by it, for half that number wou'd have cost us many lives, as the event has shown; for now the battle is really over, and the extraordinary Gazette come out, it contains nothing but—mischief! killed, so many—wounded, so many. Thank God, the officers have escaped; I imagine therefore the French must have aim'd at the sails and rigging. Doubtless we have done them mischief too; but Mr. Keppel[2] was too noble to talk of

-----

[1] This prayer has not been identified among those left by Mrs. Delany.

[2] Admiral Keppel, being in command of the Channel fleet, encountered the French fleet, commanded by the Comte d'Orvilliers, and an action took place,

damage wch he was not sure he had done; and indeed it seems their whole number is got into Brest, and live to fight another day, and meantime to plague us exceedingly. Thus you see, my dear madam, my head is full of this war, wch I had flatter'd myself we shou'd escape, as we seem'd to pocket the first box on the ear very quietly.

But I will find a pleasanter subject. I am sure the Duchess of Portland's kindness to me is one, and I was very sorry I cou'd not immediately obey commands that were so agreeable; but I hope to find a time, if there be any in the autumn, that is agreeable to her Grace. Mrs. Leveson is a great admirer of your friend Mrs. Montagu; she adds that she is well. Lady Gower is also very well, wch I rejoyce at, and hope to find her so next week.

Mrs. Chapone has dined with me, and I with her at Hadley, from whence she purposes to depart to-morrow, so I will go and bid her good-by this evening. For news, I hear that L^y Ravensworth[1] is reconcil'd to her gr. daugh^r, and has invited her, her husband, and his mother to visit her, having also given her £10,000, and interceded for her to the Duke of Grafton with success. If I were sure I might send you a double lett^r impunément, I wou'd enclose a list of plants to be sold in this country;

July 12, 1778, in which the English had partial success, and the French retired under cover of the night.

[1] Anne, only daughter of Sir Peter Delmé, married Henry Liddell, 1st Baron Ravensworth, in 1735. Their only daughter, Anne, married Lord Euston, afterwards Duke of Grafton, was divorced, and subsequently married the Earl of Upper Ossory. Her only daughter by the first marriage was Georgiana, who married the Rt. Hon. John Smyth, of Heath, in the county of York.

they belong'd to that wretched Mr. Nicol, whose house L^y Lothian[1] has got in Curzon Street. Among these plants is the *new self-moving* plant : the rest have names a foot long, all Latin; I counted 14 letters in one name. It is not likely that you sh^d wish for any of these curious plants at Bulstrode, already provided with them; but if you wish to see the catalogue, please to say so, by return of post; for after Thursday or Friday y^r letters will not reach me here. I think the sale is not yet this fortnight; I cou'd leave orders for purchase. Your faithfull

F. B.

Mrs. Delany to Mrs. Port, of Ilam.

The order in which the King and Queen and Royal Family, with their attendants, went from Windsor to breakfast with the Duchess D^r of Portland at Bulstrode, on Wednesday the 12th of Aug^t, 1778, the Prince of Wales's birthday.

2 Servants on horseback.
The Prince of Wales and Prince Frederick on horseback.
General Budé and Montagu, Riding Master.
2 Footmen and two grooms.
King and Queen in a phaeton and a pair.
2 Servants on horseback.
A post chaise and 4 horses, in which were the Princess Royal, Prince Adolphus, the King's seventh son, and Lady Weymouth.
2 Servants on horseback.
A coach and six horses, in which were Princess Augusta, Princess Elizabeth, Lady Charlotte Finch, the Governess to the Royal children, and Miss Goldsworthy. 2 footmen behind.

---

[1] Elizabeth, only daughter of Chichester Fortescue, Esq., married, in 1763, William John Kerr, 5th Marquis of Lothian. Possibly the Dowager Marchioness might here be meant; she was the Lady Caroline D'Arcy, only daughter of Robert, Earl of Holderness, widow of William Henry, 4th Marquis of Lothian, and mother of the 5th Marquis.

2 Servants on horseback.

A coach and six horses, in which were Prince William, Prince Edward, the Bishop of Litchfield, and Mr. Arnold, Sub-Preceptor. 2 footmen behind.

2 Servants on horseback.

A coach and six horses, in which were Mr. Hotham, Mr. Smelt, Mr. Lake, Mr. Light. 2 Servants behind the coach.

2 Servants on horseback.

A phaeton, in which were the Duke of Montagu and General Fretock.

N.B.—The Duke of Montagu's phaeton went before the last coach and 6. Each coach had a helper besides footmen and grooms, in all 33 servants, and 56 personages.

It is an *easy matter* to play the herald, and give all the good company *their ranks;* but who can tell with justice and propriety gracious and agreeable *manners* of the royal visitors ? Not I, I assure you, tho' I had the honour of being witness to it; but I will tell you all I can recollect, and turn Mrs. Modesty out of doors when I tell my own share of the honours. This is an impertinent paragraph that has cut the thread of my story, and I am in a hurry, having very little time to spare.

Well then, before 12 o'clock the cavalcade drove into the court, the Dss Dow^r of Portland ready on the stone steps at the hall door to receive her royal guests. I was below stairs in my own apartment, not dress'd, and uncertain if I should be thought of. But down came Lady Weymouth (with her pretty eyes sparkling,) with the Queen's commands that I should attend her, which I did. The Queen most graciously came up to me and the 3 princesses. The King and the 2 eldest princes were in the dining-room looking at the pictures, but soon came in, and then they all went in a train thro' the great apartment to the Duchess of Portland's china closet, and with wondering and enquiring eyes admired all her magnificent curiosities. They staid above half an hour, and I took that time to take breath and sit down quietly in the drawing-room; when they returned the Queen sat down, and called me to her to talk about *the chenille work*, praising it much more than it deserv'd, but with a politeness that could not fail of giving pleasure; and, indeed, her manners are most engaging, there is so much dignity and affability blended that it is hard to say whether one's respect or love predominates. The Duchess of Portland brought her Majesty a dish of tea, roles and cakes, which she accepted, but would carry *it* back herself when she had drank her tea, into the gallery, where everything proper for the time of day was prepared, tea, chocolate, &c.; bread-and-butter, roles, cakes, and—on another table all sorts of fruit and ice. When the tea was done with, a cold colation took its place.

The King drank chocolate, the younger part of the company seem'd to take a *good* share of *all* the good things; as all these tables were placed near the drawing-room, the rest of the gallery was free.

The King was all spirits and good humour, extreamly pleased, as well as the Queen, with the place and entertainment, and, above all, you may easily believe wth the lady that had prepared it.

The King asked me if I had added to my book of flowers, and desired he might see it. It was placed on a table before the Queen, who was attended by the Princess Royal and the rest of ye ladies, the King standing and looking over them. I kept my distance, till the Queen called to me to answer some question about a flower, when I came, and the King brought a chair and set it at the table, opposite to the Queen, and graciously took me by the hand and seated me in it, an hon^r I could not receive without some confusion and hesitation; "sit down, sit down," said her Majesty; "it is *not* every body has a chair brought them by a King." It would take a quire of paper to tell you all that past at Bulstrode that morning, and I must carry you on to new scenes and new honours at Windsor. I had an opportunity of saying to the Queen that it "had *long* been my wish to see *all* the royal family." Upon wch she said, "You have not seen them all yet, but if you will come to Windsor Castle with ye Dss of Portland, you *shall* see them *altogether*." The King came up to us, and on her telling him what had passed he confirmed the same, and the next day was named, but that (history) I must deferr to another opportunity; as I can now only tell you that please God to-morrow I go to London, and the Dss goes to Weymouth; on Thursday to Dow^r Lady Gow^{rs}; on Monday the 24th from thence to Wroxton and Compton; to Welsbourn on Monday 31 Aug^t; and from thence the 2nd or 3^d of Sept^r, (if I can then go) to Malvern without giving too much hurry.

Not a word have I heard since the first acc^t of y^r sister (in law) being brought to bed.

St. James's Place.

Tuesday night, just come from Hanover Square, where I found my little friend very tolerably well.

I have had a good acc^t from Malvern, and hope to be there, please God, on the 3rd of Sep^t. Now happy with the hopes of embracing my two dearest Marys.

Mrs. Delany to the Viscountess Andover.

Bulstrode, 14th Aug., 1778.

" Now the hurley-burley's done !"

Their Majesties, his Royal Highness the Prince of
Wales, their R. H.'s, 4 Princes beside, and three Princesses,
Duke of Montagu,[1] Bishop Litchfield,[2] two Gen[ls], five
gentlemen, Lady Weymouth, Lady Charlotte Finch,[3] and
Miss Goldsworthy, and thirty-two serv[ts], all breakfasted
at Bulstrode on Wednesday the 12th of August, 1778,
the Prince of Wales's birthday. So far is *no bad copy*
of a *newspaper paragraph,* but *differs* in one point essentially, it being *literally true !* but I want real eloquence to do justice to their graceful and engaging
manner of accepting the entertainm[t] prepared for them
at Bulstrode, where every thing conspired to do honour
to the Lady of the Manor, who has borne all her tryals so
manfully; but a heart that so truly feels the happiness
it can bestow sustains itself on every occasion.

I outdo the humourous lieutenant, not only in love
with *the King,* but with *the Queen,* and with *all the
Royal family,* for I found myself (thro' their grace
and favour) so perfectly at ease that I did not feel

[1] George Brudenell, 4th Earl of Cardigan, married Lady Mary Montagu,
one of the daughters and coheiresses of John, 2nd Duke of Montagu, and
assumed the name and arms of Montagu; was created Duke of Montagu,
5th Nov., 1766. The Duke was Governor to the Prince of Wales and Prince
Frederic. He died 23rd May, 1790.

[2] Dr. Richard Hurd, Master of the Temple, Bishop of Lichfield from 1774
to 1781, was Preceptor to the Prince of Wales. In 1781 Bishop Hurd was
translated to the see of Worcester, and he died in 1808.

[3] Lady Charlotte Finch, daughter of Thomas Fermor, Earl of Pomfret,
and wife of the Hon. Thomas Finch, brother of Daniel, 7th Earl of Winchelsea.
Lady Charlotte was Governess to the Princesses, daughters of George III.
She died 11th July, 1813, in her 88th year.

the least fluttered, and truly *vanity* is an excellent help-
mate, and *she* was my good friend, and swallow'd all the
food that she met with !

The Royals walk'd thro' the great apartment, admired
everything they saw, the young ones full of observation
and proper questions, some skipping, some whistling, and
delighted above measure ; charm'd with the excellent
breakfast and eat abundantly. To tell you all wou'd be
more than you desire, and wou'd not do unless I was *a
bard,* and could sing their story how—

> " Once on a day the Royal Court
> To Bulstrode fair did all resort," &c., &c.

but there is a sequel that wou'd make an excellent 2nd
part to ye ballad.

I was commanded to attend the Dss of Portland to
Windsor Castle yesterday afternoon, wch I did. Got there
by 6, the hour appointed, and was receiv'd in the low
apartment at ye Castle ; at 7 King and Queen and eleven
of their children walk'd forth, as is their daily rule, to
take a turn on the terrass, and left the Dss of P. and
Lady Weymouth, the Bishop of Litchfield and Mrs.
Delany, till their return. No unpleasant pause in the
concert. In less than half an hour they all came back,
and we were all removed to the Queen's house, the *brilliancy* of which, (after the solemn brown of the Castle,)
almost put out my eyes. A concert of musick 1st, and
then a ball begun by the Prince of Wales, and the Bishop
of Osnaburg dancing a minuet *incomparably well*—then
country dances—then cottillions—then, after viewing
some beautiful tables, clocks, &c., we came home at ten
o'clock chattering over the busyness of the day, and

much pleased, tho' fatigued to the last degree, but both well to-day, and ever dearest Lady Andover and Miss Howard's truly affectionate.　　　　　　　　　M. D.

On Tuesday the Dss of Portl^d setts out for Weymouth, and I for Bill Hill, after a day's halt in London. If I continue well and in the humour I am in I shall, please God, proceed as far as Malvern Hall to see my *new* little niece,[1] and enjoy a nest of nephews and nieces for one week only. A line directed to St. James's Place to inform me of y^r ladyship's health, and to say you forgive this tedious long visit, will greatly add to the happiness of dear Lady Andover's most affectionate,

　　　　　　　　　　　And obedient,

　　　　　　　　　　　　M. Delany.

Mrs. Delany to Mrs. Port, of Ilam.

Bill Hill, 21st August, 1778.

I came here last night about 7; had a good night; Mrs. Boscawen here, and I am very comfortable; a cool room to the north; and propose, please God, to go to Woodstock on Monday, to Wroxton on Tuesday, to

---

[1] Anne, only daughter of Bernard Dewes, Esq., born 1778, married, in January, 1805, George Frederick Stratton, of Tew Park, Esq., and died Jan 20th, 1861; a few days previous to which she wrote the following lines to the Editor on the subject of the present work, being at that time perfectly well—" It will be to me most interesting, as *I recollect so much of her* (Mrs. Delany) *and can bring her to my mind continually.*" This lady inherited much of the beauty of her grandmother, Anne Granville, and a very fine cartoon of her, by Sir Thomas Lawrence, as well as an oil picture, with a Newfoundland dog, by the same master, are in the possession of her nephew, Mr. Granville, at Welsbourn. Anne Dewes (Mrs. Stratton) was the last surviving member of the family who had had *personal* intercourse with Mrs. Delany.

Welsbourn the 31st of this month, to *Malvern Hall*[1] the 3rd of Sept[r], where I shall be happy to see *you all well!* I feel too much affected with the hopes of such a meeting to say more on the subject, but will proceed wth what past at Windsor Castle.

You remember Wednesday 12th of August, the Prince of Wales's birthday, the Royal Family breakfasted at Bulstrode, and appointed the day following for the Duchess Dow[r] of Portland to attend them at Windsor Castle at 6 in the afternoon, and were graciously pleased to command me to come also. The King told me it "should be no fatigue to me. I should have *no stairs* to go up, and a cool room." We went as appointed, and were conducted to the lower private apartment of the castle. In the first large room with great bay windows were the 3 eldest Princess's and the ladies that attend them. We past thro' to the Queen's bedchamber, where she was with Lady Weymouth and Lady Charlotte Finch. She received the Duchess of Portland with gracious smiles, and was so easy and condescending in her manner to me that I felt no perturbation, tho' it is *so long a time* since *I was conversant with Kings and Courts!* The Queen sate down, and not only made the ladies do the same, but had a chair placed for me opposite to her, and commanded me to sit down, asking me at the same time "if it was too much in the air of the door and window?" What dignity such strokes of humanity and *delicate good breeding* add to the highest rank! In that room were the two youngest Princess's, one (Princess Mary) *not three*, the other *not a year* old; both lovely children.

---

[1] Malvern Hall,—then the residence of Mr. and Mrs. Bernard Dewes.

Princess Mary a *delightful* little creature, curtseying and prattling to everybody. She calls the Duchess of Portland "Lady Weymouth's mama." She asked me if I was "another mamma of Lady Weymouth's?" but I must not tell you too much of what was said, but proceed to what *was done*.

A little before seven the King and his *seven sons* came into the room, and after a great deal of gracious conversation the Queen told the Dss of Portland she hoped she would excuse her taking her *usual walk* wth the King and all the Princes and Princesses on Windsor Terrass, "*as the people constantly expected to see them.*" Musick was playing all this time, just under the window, that sounded very sweet and pleasant. The Queen said she "would leave Lady Weymouth, that the Dss might not lose any of her company," and the Queen went and fetch'd the Bishop of Litchfield to be of our party till they came in from their *walk*, which lasted about half an hour. When they return'd, the King, Queen, &c. went into the next room, which was lighted up, and where the musick was playing and the tea ready. I kept back as you may imagine, not advancing but as I was called. Princess Mary was sitting in the first bow window looking at the crowd gathered under it. I stop'd, and she asked me several questions, in which time I was separated from the rest of ye train, and liked my corner so well that I remained there. The Princes and Princess's had a mind to dance. They were permitted to do so, and were a pretty show indeed. I was so pleased with seeing them dance that I forgot I was standing all this time, when the Duke of Montagu came up to me, and drew a chair for me, saying "the King had sent him to desire me to sit down," which I *then* found *I was glad to do*. The Princes between their dances came up and talk'd to me with the greatest politeness and good humour. The King came up to the Prince of Wales, who was standing near me, and said he "thought they had better dance no more to that musick, being composed of hautbois and other wind musick, as he thought it *must be painful* to them to play any longer, and His Majesty was sure the Prince, &c., would be unwilling to hurt them, but at the Queen's house they should have properer musick, and dance as long as they liked." The word was given, and their Majesties, &c., walked to the Queen's house, which is across the great court, and part of Windsor town. The Queen said she had ordered a chaise for the Dss of Portland and me, as she thought that walking might not be agreable. We followed, and were ushered into the house by the gentlemen that were ready at the door. Indeed, the entrance into the first room was eblouissante after coming out of the sombre apartment in Windsor, all furnished with beautiful Indian paper, chairs covered with different embroideries of yᵉ liveliest colors, glasses, tables, sconces, in the best taste, the whole calculated to give the greatest cheerfulness to the place, and it had its effect. The second room we passed through was the music room, where the concert began as soon as we entered. As I was the last in the train, and timid of being too forward, I stop'd in this room, where the King soon came, took me by the hand, and led me into the drawing-room to the Queen. After looking about and admiring the encouragement given to our own manufactures, we went back into the first room and were all seated. The Prince of Wales and Bishop of Osnaburg began the ball, and danced a

minuet better than I ever saw danced. Then the Prince
of Wales danced with the Princess Royal, who has a very
graceful agreable *air*, but *not a good ear*. After that
a country dance the Prince of Wales, Princess Royal,
the Bish^p of Osn. (that is Prince Frederic), Princess
Aug^{ta}, Prince William, Princess Elizabeth. Miss Goldsworthy wth Genl Hotham, and Miss Hamilton and
Genl Bude. At a little after nine it broke up. The
delightful little Princess Mary, who had been spec-
tator all this time, then danced with Prince Adolphus a
dance of their *own composing*, and soon after all were
dispersed. We got into the chaise about ten, and got
home very well by moonlight and chaise lamps, much
pleased with our entertainment, and less fatigued than I
could have imagined.

The following extracts are taken from a letter of Mrs. Delany's
to the Hon. Mrs. Hamilton,[1] in reference to these royal visits.

Mrs. Delany says,—" Mr. Smelt's character sets him above
most men, and does great honour to the king, who calls him his
' *friend*,' and has drawn him out of his solitude (the life he had
chosen) to enjoy his conversation every leisure moment.

" The Queen was in a hat and an Italian nightgown of purple
lutestring trimmed with silver gauze. She is both graceful and
genteel ; the dignity and sweetness of her manners, the perfect
propriety of everything she says or does, satisfies everybody she
honours with her distinction, so much that beauty is not wanting to make her perfectly agreeable, and though age and my
long retirement from Court made me feel timid on being called
to make my appearance, I soon found myself perfectly at
ease."

---

[1] Dorothea, daughter of James Forth, of Redwood, Esq., and widow of the
Hon. and Rev. Francis Hamilton, son of James, 7th Earl of Abercorn.

After an allusion to the King's good humour, and expressing her respect for his character, " so severely tried by his enemies at home as well as abroad," she says that " he was in a uniform of blue and gold, and all his attendants likewise in uniform. The princesses all in frocks." Mrs. Delany took the opportunity, when the royal family had passed on to the great apartments, to remain in the drawing-room, where she sat down ; but the Princess Royal returned to fetch her, saying, " the Queen had missed her in the train." She said that she " obeyed the summons with her best alacrity." The Queen, meeting her half way, and on seeing her hasten her steps, called out, " Though I desired you to come, I did *not* desire you *to run* and fatigue yourself."

Two chairs were placed in the middle of the great drawing-room for the King and Queen. The King placed the Duchess of Portland in his own chair, and walked about himself. Breakfast was prepared in a long gallery that ran the length of the great apartments (suite of eight rooms and three closets). The King and the royal family did not choose to have breakfast brought to the drawing-room, but went to the gallery, where tables were spread with tea, coffee, chocolate, and cakes, fruits and ices, to which succeeded (as if by magic) a cold repast. The Queen remained in the drawing-room, with Mrs. Delany standing at the back of her chair, which was worked in chenilles by Mrs. Delany from nature, of which the Queen expressed great admiration. The Duchess of Portland brought the Queen her breakfast of tea and biscuits on a waiter ; and after she had finished she did not allow the Duchess to carry her cup back to the gallery, but took it herself, and examined all the preparations. The Queen asked Mrs. Delany " why she did *not* appear with the Duchess on her arrival, as she *might have been certain that she would ask for her ?*" Mrs. Delany, in the course of conversation, told the Queen that she " was particularly happy to pay her duty to Her Majesty at that time as it gave her an opportunity of seeing so many of the royal family, an honour of which she hitherto had been deprived by age and retirement." The Queen said she " had not yet seen *all* her children." On which the

King said, "You may put Mrs. Delany into the way of doing that by naming a day for her to drink tea at Windsor Castle." And the following day was appointed.

The Earl of Guilford to Mrs. Delany.

Wroxton, Sept. 1st, 1778.

MADAM,

I was rather mortified at receiving a letter from London, as it seems to put you farther from the execution of your scheme : which I hoped you would have recovered strength to do, before my house filled with company. I am extremely concerned you do not find yourself equal in strength and spirits to the undertaking ; as well as for my own disappointment, which was *very great*. I had got for you two *young beaux*—Ld Lewisham [1] and Mr. Legge, and three sorts of *fine lillies* in full bloom. I hope you will have received the letters directed to your servant in town, one that I had directed to you there having come back to me I can't tell how. I wrote to you also directed Bill Hill near Reading, but possibly that direction may not be right. The letter which came back to me, I meant should have been sent to you to Bill Hill : but as it was chiefly to say my horses should not fail to meet you at Woodstock at the time appointed I shall not trouble you with it. If the weather, having grown so cool, should have given you strength, and courage to undertake your journey ; I fancy by the middle of next week I may have no company left but Lord and Lady Willoughby, and be able to receive you in a quiet

---

[1] George, Lord Lewisham (eldest son of William, 2nd Earl of Dartmouth), born 3rd Oct. 1755.

way, I beg you to accept my best wishes for your speedy,
and perfect recovery, and believe me,

Madam,

Your most obedient, and humble servant,

GUILFORD.

The Hon. Mrs. Boscawen to Mrs. Delany.

St. Clere (Mr. Evelyn's),[1] 15th Sept. 78.

I return you many thanks, my dear madam, for re-
membering your friend at Bounds,[2] who certainly had
some curiosity, (and that not of the impertinent kind,)
to know whether you remain'd where I left you or ven-
tur'd over hills and dales. Your indisposition was unwelcome news to me; but now let us say all is well that
ends well, and e'er you get this, you will, I trust, be
restor'd to your own again. Health attend you, my dear
madam, and here is weather that alone, and of itself,
seems able to restore it where it has been wanting; however, were you to see the open window near wch I sit
you wou'd allow that it cannot be much pleasanter out
of doors (vive Kent for fine prospects). I see at this moment such an amphitheatre spread all around, first gently

------

[1] William Evelyn Glanville, Esq., of St. Clere, Kent, married, first,
Frances, only child and heress of William Glanville, Esq. Of this marriage
Frances, married to the Hon. Edward Boscawen, was the only child, and heiress
to her mother's property. William Evelyn Glanville, Esq., married, secondly,
Bridget, daughter of Hugh Raymond, Esq., and had two sons and a daughter.
The eldest son, William Evelyn, Esq., of St. Clere, married Susan Barret;
the second son, George Raymond Evelyn, Esq., married the Lady Jane
Leslie, daughter of John, 8th Earl of Rothes, who, on the death of her
brother John, the 9th Earl, became in her own right Countess of Rothes.
Her son, George William Evelyn, was the 10th Earl.

[2] Boundes Park, Kent, the property of Sir Charles Hardinge, Bart. (1861).

descending, then as gently rising field above field and
church beyond church, that it is like the map of an estate
laid down before me. I see Knowl;[1] Seven Oak and its
various buildings, Ld Amherst's new house and pillar,
are very conspicuous; Chevening,[2] Ld Stanhope's; Comb
Bank, Westerham; and such a near prospect with villages
and farms, that, indeed, nothing can exceed it except the
prospects of Bounds, wch are delightfull. There I spent 8
days most agreeably. I deliver'd yor kind compliments
to Miss Lambard,[3] who was much pleas'd by yor remembrance, and beg'd me not to forget her respects. The
other young ladies I did not see, but one of them was on
a visit to Mrs. Johnson, (sister to the late Bishop of
Worcester,) who has a house on Mount Ephraim. All
these young ladies have had an irreparable loss! But it
is a pleasure to hear how much they are esteem'd and
well spoken of, and Miss Lambard has in Sr Sydney and
Lady Smythe friends that seem to love her as their
own: indeed, she is very amiable. They hop'd she
wou'd stay with them as long as they remain in the
country.

Yesterday all Kent was attracted to the grand review
at Coxheath; but I went 5 miles another way to see
my old friend, whose wonderful *green* age you have heard
me speak of. Afterwards I went to Chepsted, wch was
much farther, to see Mr. Polhil's, a seat much cry'd up,
and w^{ch} (therefore, perhaps,) did not answer my expectation. I went into the house to see a portrait, (a very
fine one, indeed, of *a very mischievous man*,) Genl

---

[1] Montreal and Knowle, near Seven Oaks, in Kent, seats of the Earl Amherst.
[2] Chevening, the seat of Earl Stanhope.
[3] A sister of Multon Lambard, of Beechmount, Esq., Seven Oaks, Kent.

Ireton,[1] who marry'd a dau[r] of Ol. Cromwell, and from whom Mr. Polhill is lineally descended. It is an original, I know not by what hand (you cou'd tell probably), but very finely painted indeed, and quite alive. There was one also of O. Cromwell, but that seem'd to be a copy. To-morrow I purpose to leave Kent and return to my quiet cottage, where (in ab[t] a week) I have promis'd to visit my dear daur[r] at How-Hatch in Essex, near Warley Camp. Meantime let me have one line, and if it tells me that all is well at Bullstrode, it will be a most delightfull one to

Y[r] very affectionate faithfull friend,

F. B.

Mrs. Montagu (Hill Street) is coming to Tunbridge Hot Well, to drink the waters.

Frederic Montagu, Esq., to Mrs. Delany.

Hanover Square, Sep. 24th, 1778.

Your letter was sent after me into Kent, where I have been upon a visit at Mr. Townshend's. I was young enough to go over to Coxheath, where I was much amused; the view of the camp is very picturesque.

My mother is very well, and much at your service. I go out of town to-morrow for a day or two, and shall be in Nottingshamshire the beginning of next week. Pitt left London the day that you did; "the Virgin" arrived that evening from Luton, and Mrs. Pitt escap'd

---

[1] Henry Ireton, the Parliamentary general and Commander-in-Chief in Ireland, was born in 1610, and died in 1651.

the next morning by break of day. I call'd this morning to enquire after Mrs. Pitt and the children, and had a very good account, but in the midst of my inquiries I was struck with the sign of Mrs. Anne's old coach at the door, upon which I ran immediately away, and *thought* "the Virgin" was at my heels the whole length of Oxford Street.

I rejoice much that you give so good an account of yourself, if you *can* survive the houses of Clarendon, and Forbes nothing will ever hurt you!

Mrs. Ravaud to Mrs. Delany.

Bath, Oct. 1st, 1778.

Returning from our summer's ramble, my d^r A. D., I met your kind epistle, a much more salutary sugar-plumb than what the common people call "*caraway comforts.*" Tho' I grieve for the disappointment you met with this summer, yet as you *are* "*after being*" so well, I don't know but that I rejoice upon the whole; for in general you attend so little to yourself, that 'tis necessary now and then to rouse you with something of the fever kind, and bring you under proper discipline: this I hope will be repairing the house, and renewing the lease. I think we have never mentioned Lady Westmoreland since her death;[1] 'twas not quite unexpected by us, for we found her last year more subject to the complaint of which she died than heretofore; and not being able to take the medicines usually given upon those occasions, we

---

[1] Elizabeth, Dowager Countess of Westmoreland, widow of Thomas, 8th Earl, and daughter of William Swymmer, died 7th August, 1778.

always apprehended it must be fatal; but all this foresight did not prevent our concern, or hinder the regret natural for the loss of so worthy a character and a person who had *long* honour'd Mrs. Shelley and me with her particular regard. *If* friendship, my d^r A. D., was to end with this life, surely true wisdom wou'd prohibit the contracting any.

Mrs. Sanford is at Lyme. We have not heard from her lately; therefore will suppose no news to be, at least, a good sign. Mi. Kitty is come home pure, and N. R. quite at your service, supposing you reasonable, and not requiring her to run about the town, or dance cotillions! Any other method of expressing my regard for my d^r A. D., which she pleases to appoint, will be chearfully embraced by her.

Very affectionate, &c., &c.

M. M. R.

We, that is, *the spinsters,* beg leave to present our respectful compliments to the Dutchess of Portland.

The Hon. Mrs. Boscawen to Mrs. Delany.

How Hatch, near Warley Camp, 15th Oct. 1778.

You are at a loss to know, my dear madam, where your most kind and agreeable epistle wou'd find me ; why—had it marched without *halting* (for I have caught the military stile) it wou'd have found me—in the midst of a battle. Yes, I assure you, and a most tremendous battle I thought it; un feu terrible et continuel, made me wish myself anywhere else; still more do I wish that

2 c 2

nobody lov'd battles more than I do, and then all wou'd
be peace, blessed peace ! which I long for. I have been
in this *warlike neighbourhood* ten days, and am now
returning to my quiet cottage, with the satisfaction of
leaving my dear daughter[1] much better than I found her ;
for, alas ! she has had a most terrible sprain (of the leg
that was broke), and I found her quite helpless upon the
couch, carry'd and lifted about : but now she is able to
walk supported by sticks (and is quite free from pain, I
thank God). We have had fine airings, however, almost
every morning : sometimes I get out, and she remains in
the coach ; but yesterday we both din'd in the Col. of the
Grenadiers' tent (that is his Grace of Beaufort), and we
were entertain'd with the musick of yᵉ 25ᵗʰ Regtᵗ that
us'd to play to her Majesty at Windsor last year ; I have
been at Lᵈ Petre's[2], and seen the magnificent and superb
preparations he has made for the reception of his royal
guests ;[3] but I can hardly afford to our gracious Queen all
that cannonading wᶜʰ I *saw, heard,* and *felt,* last Monday
when the army rehears'd something of that wᶜʰ they are
to perform when the King comes. I hope, however, it
will agree with *her* better than it did with *me* (who am a
coward). The beginning of it was charming, when all

---

[1] The Duchess of Beaufort.

[2] Robert Edward Petre, 9th Baron Petre, married, first, in 1762, Anne,
daughter and coheiress of Philip Howard, of Buckenham, Norfolk, Esqʳ, and
niece of Edward, 9th Duke of Norfolk, at whose decease, in 1777, Lady Petre
became a coheiress of several baronies (still in abeyance in 1859).

[3] " Their Majesties set out on Monday, the 19th October, from the Queen's
house, and arrived that afternoon at Thornden Place, in Essex, the seat of
Lord Petre. On Tuesday the King reviewed the troops encamped at Warley,
and on Wednesday, their Majesties visited Navestock, the seat of Earl Waldegrave, and returned to London that evening." The King and Queen, and their
suite, during their stay at Thornden, were most magnificently entertained by
Lord Petre, at an expense, it is said, of upwards of £12,000.

the army here march'd in battalions by the general, and saluted without firing, the musick playing; but afterwards, when the *horrid cannon* open'd their brazen mouths, and all the troops attack'd or defended, we wou'd have *retreated* if we could; but the light-infantry occupy'd the wood thro' wch we must have pass'd, and kept up a continual fire: in short, I promise myself *never* to be in another battle, and I made it worse by thinking "if such is a *mock* fight, what must a *real* one be?"

Your account of yourself, dear madam, and of the agreeable autumn you have enjoy'd, pleases me much, and I heard too (from L^y Gower) that she found you quite recover'd. Mrs. Leveson is still at Portsmouth; Mr. Leveson is to come in there, (to clean I understand,) and then go out again. He will be able to make a visit to Lady Gower, I sh^d suppose, tho' probably a short one. I was very sorry for L^y Thanet. Were you not surpris'd to hear that Mr. Ed. Foley was going to be marry'd to L^y A. Coventry?[1] Deux vauriens je crois, n'est ce pas? Adieu, dear madam: it is late, for we have had company at supper; Ld Winchelsea was one, who seems a very agreeable man I think.

I hope you have got the Duchess again, and beg my best respects to her Grace.

Faithfully and gratefully yours,
F. Boscawen.

I hope Mrs. Port is well, and poor Mrs. Smith better.

---

[1] The Hon. Edward Foley, second son of Thomas, 1st Lord Foley, married, first, in 1778, Lady Anne Coventry, daughter of George William, 6th Earl of Coventry, from whom he was divorced in 1787. Mr. Foley married, secondly, in 1790, Eliza Maria Foley, daughter and heiress of John Hodgetts, Esq., of Prestwood, and died in 1803.

Frederick Montagu, Esq., to Mrs. Delany.

Papplewick, Oct. 24th, 1778.

MADAM,

I beg that you will send Mason an account of the constant vexations you receive from your *too neighbourly* neighbours : he would recommend some medicine to you, tho' perhaps it might *not* be anodyne. I am convinced that if he was in your situation he would shoot the porcupine and bar up the doors and windows of the house; and if that was not sufficient he would get a *certificate* from Mr. Lightfoot that he *was dead* and decently buried in Uxbridge Church. I most truly pity Anne P. Her situation of mind when I was in London was dreadfull indeed, perhaps worse than that it may be now, if her head is absolutely gone. *The expectation* of what was coming was horrible ! I have the highest respect for Lʸ B., and am afraid that the visit must have been very troublesome to her. I expect to hear every post of the Traveller. I am by no means easy about Lord Dartmouth. I had a letter from him lately in very low spirits. He was going to Bath. Pray remember my most respectful compˢ to the Dutchess of Portland. Have you heard the particulars of the Chandos christening ?¹ While the candles were lighting, the *child expir'd* under a load of lace. However, the Dutchess of C. was determin'd that the ceremony should proceed, and it *did* proceed : the K. and Q. were very

---

¹ Georgina Charlotte, eldest daughter of James, 3rd and last Duke of Chandos (by his 2nd wife, Ann Eliza, daughter of Richard Gamon, Esq.), born September 7th, 1778, and " died the day after she was baptized." Their Majesties in person were sponsors.

gracious, and the Archbishop of Canterbury observed that he "never had christened a more quiet child." You see that we know something in the country!

I am
Y^r very faithfully
And affectionately,
FRED. MONTAGU.

Court Dewes, Esq., to his brother, the Rev. John Dewes.

Welsbourn, Oct. 27th, 1778.

DEAR JOHN,

Your kind letter of ye 9 inst. gave me great pleasure, as it induces me to hope that you do not really think one who has always had ye most sincere regard for you, wch he has endeavour'd to shew by his actions, so much your enemy as you chose to say he was ye last time you were at Welsbourn; and I am happy in having y^s opportunity of attributing all that passed then to ye heat of dispute, and from y^s time forward will neither say or think a word more about it, or ever give you occasion to do so. I am much obliged to you for desiring to see me at Calwich, and were I to consult my own pleasure I should certainly accept your invitation, and having spent several *un*pleasant Novembers at Calwich, come and spend *one pleasant one*, for ye scene is shifted between us and you. Here am I tête à tête wth an old man, and y^e *sports* are fled into Staffordshire; but as I must go to town, after Xmas, I cannot tell how to leave my father before, and I expect my sister-in-law, Dewes, too to be here, while Bern^d is in London, wch will bring it pretty near Xmas. My father is got better, I think, than he has

been since his first illness in the spring, and, as a proof
of it, he desires me to give his love to you and my sister,
and will be very glad to see you whenever it is agreable
to you; so *I hope,* for my sake, you will come as soon
as you can, as I shall go to town about ye middle of
Jan^y.

I do not see any objection to your letting Lord Harcourt[1] have copies of Mr Rousseau's billets, for I think
there is nothing in them that can do either him or Mr.
Granville discredit. I *was* writing to Mrs. Delany when
I received your letter, and as it is a matter of delicacy, of
wch ladies are ye best judges, I asked her opinion, wch I
will let you know when I receive it.

I am very sorry my sister is tormented wth ye toothach.
In ye long experience I have had of that disorder I have
never found but one thing of service to me, and that is,
an oz. of juniper berries boiled in a pint of vinegar till
it comes to half a pint, and to wash ye mouth wth it as
hot as you can bear it; but I have never used it unless
when I was *very bad,* as it is apt to take ye skin off y^e
inside of ye mouth. I think I am almost passed having
ye tooth ach now, and must comfort myself as well as I
can, that what I have *lost* in *beauty* I have got in *ease!*

I did not know of your being at Malvern 'till you
were gone f^m thence. I was there for a day last week,
and much pleased to see that my sister had in a great
measure recover'd her looks and spirits, wch were both
very indifferent when I was there before. I wish I had
any entertainment to send you from hence, but our
uniform life affords none; we go on in ye old way, *read-*

---

[1] George Simon, 2nd Earl Harcourt, who succeeded his father in 1777, and
died in April, 1809.

ing, music, and *walking* in ye morning, and quadrille in ye afternoon.

Make mine and my father's kind love and comp^ts as due, and believe me very sincerely, dear John,

Your affectionate brother,

C. DEWES.

P.S. All our neighbours enquire after you, and desire their comp^ts.

The Hon. Mrs. Boscawen to Mrs. Delany.

Glan Villa, Thursday evening, 28th Oct. 1778.

Your commands shou'd have been instantly obey'd, my dear madam, by the first return of post, if, as I was just sat down to write, I had not been agreeably interrupted by the arrival of Mrs. Dunbar, who was so kind to come thro' much bad weather to visit me this morning, and staid till 2 o'clock; by that time our post is come and gone, wch is almost *one* and the *same motion.*

I hope the honours that awaited you at Windsor Lodge last Monday have agreed with you perfectly well, and then they cou'd not but be pleasant and agreeable. I too have rec^d an honour that was exceedingly so to me, as you will easily believe, when I tell you it was a visit from the Earl of Mansfield.[1] His lord^p and Miss Eliz. Murray[2] were riding this way, and sent word they wou'd alight "if I pleas'd." You may be sure I *pleas'd,*

---

[1] The Hon. William Murray, created Baron Mansfield in 1756, and Earl of Mansfield, 19th October, 1776.

[2] The Hon. Elizabeth Mary Murray, daughter of David, 7th Viscount Stormont, and great-niece of the Earl of Mansfield.

and receiv'd them at the door of my cottage, with uncommon satisfaction; I had a great deal also in hearing of my lady's recovery, to whom (it seems) I ow'd this favour, as my lord was pleas'd to say he came to thank me for the kind concern I had express'd for her dangerous illness. After my illustrious guest had sat some time, and talked of you, dear madam, and walked in my garden, he remounted his palfrey with his fair neice; but they had not been gone long enough to carry them half way to High Gate, when a prodigious heavy shower fell, wch gave me great disturbance. I sent however next day to know how they got home, and Miss E. Murray was so good to write me word they escap'd that heavy rain. She adds, that Lady Mansfield mends very fast, but her lady^{p} is not yet out of her chamber, else you may believe I shou'd have gone myself the next day to acknowledge the honour I had received.

I am very glad you have got my good friends, Mr. and Mrs. Cole, with you, so you will know nothing of what dark and dismal weather we have had to-day; but *we do* (pray tell them with my complim^{ts}), and find our evenings very different from the pleasant ones of last week. They have left an hostage with me (Mrs. Cole's umbrella), so I don't despair of their return. Col. Campbell, whom they met, is going to defend Jamaica.

I cannot lay in Lon^{n} next week, because I believe the, D. and Dss. of B. and 5 children will lodge at my house (their own repairing) in their way to Oxfordsh. There is still an infectious disease in the village of Badminton.

---

[1] In 1779, Georgia was subdued for the time by Commodore Parker and Colonel Campbell.

All well at Bill Hill, and my lady rides every other
day. I am vastly glad y^u like y^r new damsel. Adieu,
my dear madam.

F. B.

The Hon. Mrs. Boscawen to Mrs. Delany.

Glan Villa, 4th Nov. 1778.

This is not a letter, my dear, *honoured* friend, mais un
véritable dépêche, *secret, and very confidential,* and its design and meaning, to know, as I am sure *you* can tell me
very *exactly,* when I shall wait on the Duchess at Bulstrode, most agreeably to her Grace. After this day
se'night, ye 11th, I shall be entirely at her commands to
come the 12th, 13th, 14 (if one may happen to be preferable to the other), and you can tell me also, my dear
madam, whether I shall stay only 2 days, or 3, 4 or 5 ?
for many, besides myself, probably are candidates for her
excellent society. Mr. and Mrs. Cole have given me a
charming account of the days they had the happiness to
spend at Bulstrode. I expect them here by and by.

To return : I shou'd not ask you, at this distance, the
length of my visit, but that I intend to order my family
to remove in my absence, and settle themselves in winter
quarters, w^{ch}, tho' one shou'd suppose was the slightest
of all operations, yet they *always* contrive to make a fuss
with it, and especially desire to know a little beforehand.
As to myself I am naughty, and apt to *fly away* from any
bustle of this kind, having indeed two old servants that
perform it in *due order.* These I shall leave, and bring
with me to Bulstrode a certain *little body* known to Mrs.
Smith by the name of " Bet." I shall have the pleasure

to hear from you by Monday next. Please to direct to Audley Street, as I reckon Mrs. Leveson will be in town that day, and I shall go up to her.

My dear madam, the post arrives, and brings me, alass! from Miss Lambert the sad news of the loss of hers and my excellent friend, *Sir Sydney Smyth*.[1] He was indeed much worn by the diligent and faithfull discharge of the great trusts committed to him, and a continual series of business for near 50 years, his constitution *never strong*, but he had retir'd from that business, and, in his retirement, was so chearfull and happy, that I did not (I own) foresee this misfortune. My poor friend (the happiest wife 45 years that ever was) removes to London to-morrow, and the possibility of her being, in a day or two, willing to see me, her very old friend, makes me add to what I had wrote on the other side, that it shall be the 13th or 14th, if you please, before I go to Bulstrode. I know Lady Smythe has in Miss Lambard a most affectionate (*daughter* I might say); still I shou'd wish to attend her if she will admit me.

I will say no more at present. I hope you are well, dear madam, and the Duchess in perfect health: my respects wait on her Grace.

Most faithfully yours,
F. BOSCAWEN.

Mr. and Mrs. Cole were with me when the post came in, but I did not see the enclosed to my servant till after they were gone; yet by Mrs. Boone I was informed of the loss of my excellent friend, who was quite worn out, so that

---

[1] The Rt. Hon. Sir Sydney Stafford Smythe, died Oct. 30th, 1778.

we ought not to regret that he advanc'd no farther in a state of decay, which might have been very painfull. Now it was little more than his breath failing, and his (very gently) exchanging this life for a better. Yet you wou'd pity his lady if you had ever seen the remarkable state of happiness, comfort, and mutual affection they liv'd in for so many years.

The Hon. Mrs. Boscawen to Mrs. Delany.

Audley Street, Monday, yᵉ 9ᵗʰ Novr, 1778.

My dear Madam,

The privilege of seeing poor Lady Smythe, wᶜʰ I have done twice, brought me to London last week, and now again that I am here, I know you wou'd not chuse that I shou'd go back again without taking a *bit* of Mrs. Leveson, who is come to town to-day with her husband, who has a wound on his head got on board ship in a storm, and comes to show it to a surgeon. I have not seen them yet, but am going to Charles Street. They mean to stay in town until Thursday.

These unforeseen delays, my dear madam, have put back all my little plans at home, bottoms to wind up, &c., so that it is a necessity to take 3 days more; but Tuesday the 17ᵗʰ I promise myself the honour to dine with her Grace, and will be with you by 4, ready drest, wᶜʰ I imagine will be in time.

Charles street. Afternoon.

Mr. and Mrs. Leveson make a very good report of Lady Gower's health, who rides out. Lady Anne Cecil[1]

---

[1] Lady Anne Cecil.—Daughter of James, 5th Earl of Salisbury, and of Lady Anne Tufton, second daughter and coheiress of Thomas, 6th Earl of Thanet.

is at Bill Hill. Mr. Leveson looks thin, but I hope his wound is in a fair way. As they are but just arrived I cannot get any news of them. But here is Mrs. R. Brudenell;[1] yet of her can I get nothing but a report that St. Christopher is taken by the Americans; but such ill news I had rather not believe. That the Mastership of the Horse is to be in commission; but that too wants confirmation. Poor Mrs. Walsingham tells me she is very unwell; and I am afraid very low with the loss of two good friends, Mr. Dunbar (very important to her) and good Sir Sydney, very kind upon all occasions. An aide-de-camp is really come from St. H. Clinton, and they say with good news; God grant it!

Adieu, dear madam. Most truly I am your affectionate servant

F. BOSCAWEN.

The Hon. Mrs. Boscawen to Mrs. Delany.

Audley Street, Dec. 7th, 1778.

No, certainly, my dear madam, I will not suspect you forget me, for that wou'd mortify me extremely, and nobody loves much mortification; on the other hand I hardly expected the favour and great pleasure of a letter from you: as it is for other purposes that George places the great chair, &c., as soon as you have done breakfast!

Lady Anne Cecil married William Strode, Esq. She was niece to Lady Gower.

[1] Mrs. R. Brudenell.—Anne, daughter of Sir Cecil Bisshopp, married, in 1759, the Hon. Robert Brudenell, third son of George, 3rd Earl of Cardigan. Mr. Brudenell died in 1770, leaving a son, Robert, who succeeded as 6th Earl of Cardigan, and a daughter, Charlotte, Maid of Honour to Queen Charlotte.

There I hope you miss'd me! Many plants have been immortaliz'd, I suppose, since I paid my tribute of admiration to them.[1] And of an evening can I expect you to write? One wou'd not leave the drawing-room at Bulstrode and the good company there to write anything whatever; (unless it were *a treaty of peace!*)

I left Bill Hill on Thursday last, and pass'd thro' many waters, wch look'd as if they wou'd also pass thro me! I went, as you will hear, to Mrs. Walsingham, as she had been at the pains to send a special messenger to entreat me. I pass'd one day and 2 evenings with her most agreeably, and I had only one more morning at liberty. I gave her notice that I should vote for a visit to Bulstrode; and she would have seconded me, I perceived, most heartily. It was a storm all the while I staid in her exalted castle; we made a visit to the provost, and he return'd it in the evening, and supp'd with us. Mr. and Mrs. Leveson took a sudden resolution to remove to London (upon advice of his ship coming out of dock). I expect them at dinner by-and-by. He was in hopes to have staid in the country a little longer, but had quite recover'd his health. You will expect much news from London. I will tell you who I have seen: imprimis, Mr. and Mrs. Jennings bro^t me home from chapel yesterday; they are in perfect preservation; then came to visit me Mr. Cole. I din'd with Lord and Lady Edgcumbe, who also enquir'd after you; but your perfect panegyrick was reserved for Mrs. Montagu's circle. There (after seeking Mrs. Vesey in vain at her

---

[1] Alluding to Mrs. Delany's Flora.

own house, I followed her) and found the lady of the
house, and Mr. Smelt :[1] speaking of you, he address'd
to Mrs. Montagu so perfect and so just a panegyrick of
you that I sat by her and enjoy'd it most exceedingly,
ever and anon putting in my little word, wch served as an
encore to make him continue sur nouveaux frais.   Mrs.
Vesey was gone, and there was only Mr. Smelt and
myself.   I wish you had been behind the arras ; but no !
you would have been choked with heat, for Mrs. M. had
had a great deal of company, who had din'd with her,
Bushes, Garricks, &c.   They were all gone before I
arriv'd.   Mrs. Vesey is *in beauty*.   Now for news.   I
have heard that Lady Derby is to be divorc'd[2], and to
marry the D. of Dorset, but surely that is not probable ?
Mr. T. Pitt writes from Pisa in perfect health and
spirits : had din'd at Sr H. Mann's, sitting between Lady
Berkeley and Lady Maynard, was proceeding to Rome
and to Naples for the winter.   I sent to enquire after
Lady Bute yesterday, and would have waited on her, but
the serv^t told mine my lord was not well.   Lord Temple
and his nephew Grenville, who liv'd with him, are
parted, and the latter is coming to live in Bolton Row.
I heard they did not speak ; but what the occasion of
this rupture I did not hear.   One cannot help accusing
the young gent^n of *some ingratitude* I think.   Mrs. Staple-
ton and Miss Grenvilles go to live with Lord Temple in
his room.   The Duke of Ancaster[3] gives much signs of

---

[1] Mr. Smelt was for some years Sub-Preceptor to the Prince of Wales and
Duke of York.

[2] This divorce did not take place.

[3] Robert Bertie, 4th Duke of Ancaster.   He died unmarried, July 8,
1779.

reformation : is gone with his mother[1] and sisters[2] to Grimsthorp,[3] and pays them the utmost attention. Since I wrote ye enclos'd I have heard that Lord Derby announc'd to his lady on Friday last that their divorce was begun in the Commons, wch news threw her into fits. She went as soon as she was able to her bro^rs[4] (who is come alone, leaving his lady in Scotland ;) there the Duke of Dorset[5] waited on Lady D. and Duke Hamilton, and declar'd to both his intentions to marry her as soon as possible. Next day (viz., yesterday,) she had a levee, when she received with a smiling countenance, Lady Essex,[6] Lady Betty Delme,[7] Lady Julia Howard,[8] Lady Melburne,[9] Mrs. Meynell and I think I heard a 6th, but have forgot who it was "Let wealth, let honours, wait the wedded dame; August her deed and sacred be her fame." Thus you see I did not tell you a fib in the first part of my letter, tho' I *really* concluded *I had*. I

---

[1] The mother of the 4th Duke of Ancaster was Mary, daughter of Thomas Panton, Esq., second wife of Peregrine, the 3rd Duke.

[2] The sisters of the 4th Duke of Ancaster were : 1, Priscilla, who married Sir Peter Burrell, 1st Baron Gwyder, and became in her own right Baroness Willoughby D'Eresby ; and 2, Georgiana, who married George, 1st Marquis of Cholmondeley.

[3] Grimsthorpe, Lincolnshire, now (1861) a seat belonging to Lord Willoughby D'Eresby.

[4] Douglas, 8th Duke of Hamilton.

[5] John Frederick Germain, 3rd Duke of Dorset. He did not marry until 1790, and his wife was Arabella, daughter of Sir Charles Cope, Bart.

[6] Harriet, daughter of Col. Bladen, and second wife of William Anne Capel, 4th Earl of Essex.

[7] Lady Elizabeth Howard, eldest daughter, by the second marriage, of Henry Howard, 4th Earl of Carlisle, married, in 1769, Peter Delmé, Esq. After his death she married Captain Charles Garnier.

[8] Lady Juliana Howard, youngest daughter of the 4th Earl of Carlisle, and sister to Lady Elizabeth Delmé.

[9] Elizabeth, only daughter of Sir Ralph Milbanke, Bart., married, in 1769, Peniston Lamb, 1st Viscount Melbourne.

have been visiting poor Lady Smythe! Miss Lambard enquir'd much after you. I hear Lord Bute is better to-day.

Y^r faithful and affectionate servant,

F. Boscawen.

Pray don't omit my compli^{ts} to Mr. Lightfoot on Wednesday.

The Bishop of Exeter is my near neighbour in this street, a house *Mad^e Dalitz* did live in. A prodigious long day expected in the H. of Lords to-day upon the manifesto of the Commissioners. Mr. Jenkinson[1] is Secretary at War.

The Dowager-Countess Gower to Mrs. Delany.

Bill Hill, 10th Dec., 78.

While I had any intercourse wth ye world or anything in it, I often heard of you d^r mad^m and ye D^s of P., and always good news, wch made enquiries un-necessary. Now all have left me and no hope of my curiosity being satisfied any way but this, to ask wⁿ you move to London, to have ye pleasure of knowing wⁿ I shall see you, I hope ab^t Xmas, proposing to be in London at y^t time. You have been releas'd from Chaffont notes, by ye ill habbit of body of one of y^e *poor pusses*, their indulgent mother has *cram'd* 'em till they are a composition of

---

[1] Charles Jenkinson, who succeeded, in 1789, to a family Baronetcy, and was, in 1786, created Baron Hawkesbury, and in 1796, Earl of Liverpool. He commenced his political career as private secretary to John Stuart, Earl of Bute.

gross humors; I know you to be an excellent Xtian, or you w^d rejoice at y^s deliverance. There is no writing we know ye D^s can't decypher, L^y Mary's[1] excepted.

I had a letter from London yesterday full of ruins and divorces, and ye misserable state of Mrs. Ann Pitt,[2] who is now mov'd to one of Doctor Duffell's houses. Mrs. Digby[3] is releas'd; report says Ld. Bute is dangerously ill. The letter was enough to give one ye vapours was I so dispos'd. Y^e storm on Tuesday must have had y^t affect, had Leveson been at sea; I hope they'll all be over before he's order'd out. I don't remember so much tempestuous weather any season as this.

Pray ye most aff^{cte} respects to ye D^s of P. from d^r Mrs. Delany's most faithfull,

M. G.

Mrs. Delany to Mrs. J. Dewes, at Edward Witts's, Esq., Lowerford Park, near Chipping Norton, Oxfordshire.

St. James's Place, 22nd Jan., 1778.

MY DEAR NIECE,

I have long intended myself the pleasure of writing, but a cross fever has engrossed too much of my time ever since I wrote last to my nephew John, who I hope

---

[1] The Hon. John Forbes, Admiral of the Fleet, second son of George, 3rd Earl of Granard, married Lady Mary Capel, daughter of William, 3rd Earl òf Essex. Their children, "the Pusses," were—Catherine, married to William, Earl of Mornington; and Maria, married to John, Earl of Clarendon. From incidental allusions in the course of Lady Gower's and Mrs. Boscawen's letters, Admiral Forbes appears to have resided at Chalfont.

[2] "Mrs. Ann Pitt."—Sister of the great Earl of Chatham. She was Maid of Honour to Queen Caroline, and died, unmarried, in 1781.

[3] The Hon. Mrs. Digby, widow of the Hon. Edward Digby, died in Nov., 1778. She was Charlotte, last surviving child of Sir Stephen Fox, and mother of Edward, 6th Baron Digby, and of Henry, 7th Baron and 1st Earl Digby.

receiv'd that letter. I thank God I am much better, tho'
sensible of being weaker than before my illness, which
indeed, I believe, was much owing to my great agitation
of mind on your dear sister-in-law Port's account, who
bears her *great reverse* of fortune with uncommon fortitude ; but I hope they will sett their affairs in such a train
as may enable them to enjoy what is left. It is truly an
heart-breaking sight to see her suffer so much anxiety.
But this touches me too much and I must say no more ;
for I have other tender subjects to mention, which are
yours and your sister's health. I am quite anxious for y^r
sister Bernard Dewes coming to towne with little Anne ;[1]
it is of the utmost consequence, I shou'd think, to have
the earliest and best advice; I wish it had not been so
long delay'd.

My love to my nephew. I am desired to add the love
of Mr. Court Dewes and Mrs. Port and ye little ones
duty to you both.

Mrs. Delany to Mrs. Port, of Ilam.

1779.

Mrs. Boscawen comes here for a week. Mr. Leveson
returned safe after many perils. Mr. Charles Stuart[2]
still abroad waiting the events of war, separated from
his bride in a fortnight after they married. Both
worthy, amiable, and tenderly attached to each other, and

---

[1] Afterwards Mrs. Stratton ; died Jan., 1861.
[2] Charles Stuart, 4th son of John, Earl of Bute, married, 19th April, 1778,
Louisa, 2nd daughter of Lord Vere Bertie.

besides her terrors for the hazards he runs, and uncertainty of his return, she has been for six months past attending her dying mother, and is ready to lye-in. *Lady Bute* has been her great support, and a wonderful woman *she* is, and bears up under such complicated misfortunes that nothing but true Christian philosophy could support, and added to all her family distresses she has two old friends in a deplorable state—the Dow^r Marchioness of Lothian and Mrs. A. Pitt—on whom she attends every leisure hour she has. I hear Dr Roberts is going to be married to a person that bears a very good *character*; I hope she deserves *it* for the sake of his poor children. I don't recollect her name, but suppose you may hear it. I hope all are well at Cal. my love to them and Mr. P. and all the little ones.

It has just struck into my head that as you purpose letting Ilam you may wish to deposit little knick-knacks, &c., somewhere else, and why not send them to me if you think it convenient? I will take care of them.

I thank God the dear Duchess is pure well, and sends her love to "*our Mary.*" I have good accounts from Hanover Sq^r and from Mrs. Sandford. We made Lady (*illegible*) a visit yesterday morning; it is impossible not to moralize on seeing one who was a beauty so gay, so admired, and so courted by the wits of the age, reduced to be the *companion* of so lowly a (*illegible*). She looked ill and out of spirits.

Have you heard lately from Lady Cowper? Does she know about your affairs? we are irregular correspondents, but constant well wishers to each other. Tho' I write enormous letters to you, writing is not *as easy* to me as it

used to be, but as long as I can scrawl it will be a delight
to me to assure you of my constant tender affection.

M. DELANY.

Lord Dartmouth finds Bath waters agree with him.
His friends are not easy about the state of his health.
What a loss would such a man be both in public and
private life!

It will have appeared in former letters that Mrs. Delany had
been under great anxiety in the course of the year 1778, in consequence of difficulties respecting the affairs of Mr. Port, of Ilam.
In that year Mrs. Port visited her in London, bringing with her
her eldest child—the little girl so especially prized by Mrs. Delany, and called by her " *the sweet bird*,"—whose parents were
persuaded by Mrs. Delany to leave their daughter in her care,
and she actually, at the age of seventy-eight, by her own
earnest desire, took charge of her little grand-niece of seven
years old, with all the warm and active interest which was characteristic of her early youth, and with all the systematic energy of
middle age.   Mrs. Delany's affections seemed to revive and to be
concentrated upon this child, who was then about the age that
her grandmother Ann Granville was when she and her sister
Mary Granville (afterwards Mrs. Delany) were carried off by their
aunt, Lady Stanley, at the period when Lord Lansdowne and his
brother, Colonel Granville, were arrested and sent to the
Tower.

Mrs. Delany to Mrs. Port, of Ilam.

St. James's Place, 27th February, 1779.

Don't imagine I mean to scribble to you every post;
no such thing, for after this letter I shall go on with my

usual weekly journal; but I thought a confirmation of
my continuing well, and that my dear little charge is
everything we can wish her, wou'd not be unwelcome.
The weather has been charming, and we last night bid
the moon tell you some very tender tales, as we looked at
her upon the stairs; and taking it for granted she has
done justice to our love and duty, our regrets and lamentations for the loss of such good and dear company, I
now proceed.

I ended Thursday with grumbling at Mrs. Kinnersley's
nocturnal visit. Friday morning our breakfast was
gulp'd down rather better than the morning before,
(Mary is now at my elbow looking over a drawer of shells
and insists on my adding " her duty," and that " when
she hears *the organ* it always puts her in mind of dear
mama.") At twelve came Mr. Cole with his friend Mr.
Symonds, and afterwards Mr. Martheille, Lady Andover, and Miss F., and Lady Stamford, who came from
Whitehall to *spirit me up* to accept of Lord Exeter's [1]
ticket for his concert, wch I unwillingly assented to. The
morning closed with Court and Mr. Smelt, and the
evening circle was Lady Bute, Mrs. Vesey and Miss
Gregory, Lady Beaulieu, Lord Dartmouth, Lady Stamford, Duchess of Portland till eleven; "*the sweet bird*"
perch'd at my elbow till her usual hour of retirement,
and *not unnoticed!* Yesterday morning I had only Mr.
Montagu, Mr. Mulso, Mrs. Boscawen, Miss Jennings; and
at seven came her Grace's coach to convey me to Lady
Stamford and together we went, and I must own I had

---

[1] Brownlow, 9th Earl of Exeter, who married, in 1749, Letitia, daughter and
heiress of the Hon. Horatio Townshend, and died, s.p., in 1793.

no reason to repent of my bold undertaking ; it was neither hot nor crowded, the musical band choice, not large, Lord Mornington play'd the harps[d], Mr. Hays first violin—an excellent performer ; Miss Harrop sung four songs and a ballad, *as well as* they *cou'd be sung* her voice, manner, and taste pleasing and affecting. I was almost overset w[th] "*Dové Sei*"—tender affections must sympathize wth such kind of harmony and expression ! On the whole I was well, and entertained, slept better than for many nights before. Sunday morning it being very fine I sent G. M. A. to early chapel to St. James's with Mrs. Silvestre,[1] and at eleven I went to my good little friend's conventicle, and found her very ill ; she *had* been blooded the day before, but her cough has continued so bad, and the oppression on her breath, that she was blister'd again yesterday, (Tuesday, 2nd March.) To return to Sunday, Court dined here, and you may guess *the subject* of our conversation ! In the even[g] came Lady Bute, Lady Beaulieu, Lady Cecil Rice[2] and her daughter, &c., and yesterday (after some scruples) I yielded to an invitation, made in a very kind manner, to y[r] daughter to dine and spend the day en famille wth her, and as she is a very tender motherly *discreet woman,* I thought you would have no objection, and the *dear child* was delighted to go ; so after *we* had performed *all our tasks, at two we*

---

[1] "*Mrs. Silvester*" was the person engaged by Mrs. Delany to attend upon her *little* great-niece.

[2] Lady Cecil Rice, the only child of William Talbot, 1st Earl Talbot (who was created Baron Dynevor, 17th Oct. 1780, with remainder to his only child), and wife of George Rice, Esq., of Newton. Lady Cecil Rice had two daughters, Henrietta Cecilia, married, in 1788, to Magens Dorrien Magens, Esq. ; and Maria, married, in 1796, to Admiral John Markham.

sallied out and I took Lady Stamford in my way, who
has added not a little to *her* happiness, by inviting her
to come and dine with her young people, and meet all
the young Thynnes and stay till seven or perhaps till
eight o'clock next Saturday; but I have not yet told her
the day as it is at a distance, and the hope of it is
a spur (en attendant) to *our* industry. I carried her at
three to Mrs. Pott's, and delivered her into her hands,
and then went by appointm^t to dine with Mrs. Montagu,
who was not allow'd to see anybody else, and very ill I
thought her till ab^t an hour before I left her wch was
eight o'clock she then coughed less; I then pick'd up
my little treasure, had many thanks for the trust I had
reposed in them, and came directly home, very impatient indeed for the happy tidings your dear kind
letter brought me. I indulged Mary with reading
it; wch she did wth no small sensibility. I thank God for
your having had so good a journey, and hope you do
not now feel the effects of so great a hurry. Had I *less
delight* in this dear child than I have the thoughts of its
relieving you for some time of an additional care, and
the satisfaction *your partiality* takes in her being some
time longer *with me*, would be sufficient to make her a
most welcome guest. She has walk'd twice in the park;
Mr. Bolton has come every day, is now with her, and I
am in treaty with Mon^r French, L^y Stam^{ds} dancing master,
for one month to teach *us* to *walk* and *curtsey*.

George goes on Thursday; and Lord E. Archer's Jo.
comes in his place.

Mrs. Boscawen has called and comes this even^g; no
Mrs. Lev^n.—Here I was called away by Mrs. Cowper,
(our dear *Mrs. Dashwood's* woman), wth a paper from poor

Mrs. Bristow of little tokens *she* had left to some of her particular friends as follows : " To the Dow^r Duchess of Portland, a Japan dressing-box, any shells she pleases, and two pieces of china.

To Mrs. Delany, the remainder of her shells and two pieces of china.

To Lady Weyth, two pieces of. china.

To Lady Stamford Dss Dow^r of Portland's portrait."

I have been too much affected to add anything more to this letter, but love and best wishes to Ilam from my most dear M.

Yo^r ever affectionate,

M. D.

P.S. When I had recover'd my conference with Mrs. Cowper, the Dss's coach came about two, so I thought I would myself carry Lady Wey, and Lady Stam^d, their legacies, which cost us *all* tears ; but I thought it was best to have so much over. An Irish lady, that called on me to-day, tells me that Miss Caulfield is married to Col^l Lyons at last, a vast match every way for him, who, tho' an agreable man, is an invalid to the last degree, I always thought there was a mutual liking. Adieu.

I took Mary with me, and introduced her to the *seven* Thynnes. She was much pleased wth her morning jaunt ; she wants sadly to write to mama, but Mr. Bolton, who commends her " *coming on*," begs a *little longer* patience. *She* is, *indeed, a jewel !*

In fragments of other letters Mrs. Delany writes as follows:—

"G. M. A. was vastly happy at Lady Stamford's from half an hour after one, till half-past nine, came home with dancing eyes and entertain'd my company with the feats of the day, the whole ended in a ball; and another Ball of Innocents she is invited to at Miss Sharpe's. Take care of your clavicord strings, most happy am I to think you will not neglect y^r playing when time permits, *you are now* almost *the only one* that does justice to y^e *best of musick*. I could write on, but must break off now as a flow^r waits for me."

"G. M. A. does not yet know of her happy destiny for this evening. Mr. Marlheille is to give her this morning her French lecture, and I thought the joy in store might interfere with her attention. She is everybody's delight, no wonder she shou'd wind about my *heart*, attached to it by the double tye of being the child of my dearest Mary, and *I could carry this chain* at least *a link higher*.

"I am to go next Saturday to Lord Exeter's concert, a proof of my being well."

Mrs. Delany to Mrs. Port.

St. James's Place, 6th March, 1779.

I left off last Tuesday. The even^g ended wth an agreable circle, which I believe I mentioned. Wednesday morning I undertook the melancholy office of *delivering* into Lady Weymouth's and Lady Stamford's hands the little friendly tokens of our poor deceased friend. First I went to Lady Wey., she was not at home. I took my dear charge with me and went in as Miss Thynne *was* at home, we found her surrounded by her sisters *at work*, so I introduced G. M. A. to them *all*. From thence we went to Lady Stamford, where I found Lady W. and Lady Bute who looks better. Ld Bute is gone to Luton without any complaint but weakness in his limbs wch air and exercise she hopes will get the better of.

Wednesday evening, Mrs. Leveson, Mrs. Boscawen, Lady Wallingford, Mr. Symonds, and Duchess of Portland. Thur^y:—I spent the day at Whitehall and was to have carried Georgina with me, but I knew it was a particularly busy morning with her Grace so that pleasure is *in petto*. Yesterday Lady Mansfield and her neices, the Dss of P. and her daughters were the sum total (but a rich one) of my circle. G. M. A. made *no insignificant* figure in the piece and receiv'd much commendation with great modesty; her favourite Miss Thynne, was of the party. Poor Lady Andover is, with great reason, more allarm'd than ever at Lord Suffolk. He bore the 2 first days' journey to Bath better than could have been expected but was so ill at the Devises that they thought all wou'd have ended there, however he has got to Bath under Moyes's hands, but fear there are small hopes of his recovery.

Yesterday our dear child took her first dancing lesson of Mr. French, who can give us no other time than half-an-hour after four Mond., Wed., and Fri^y, so I dine at three to be ready for him. I *treated* myself with seeing her *first steps*, which promise to admiration; and her master was delighted to find her so well form'd to his hands, and so ready to take instruction. She curtsy'd, she hopp'd about and beat time, and after a few handings about, repeated the same by herself to the melody of the little Kit, wch he says is uncommon, as he seldom finds them ready eno' for the fiddle till after a month or two's learning in hand : indeed he seems to have a particular good method, and she was much pleased. Here the coach came and I went to Hanover Square, found all there better. Lady Andover and her daughter set out to-morrow for Bath Town : I dread the end of the journey for her. Court dines here to-morrow, and on Monday I dine at Ld Willoughby's to meet Lord and Lady Dart-mouth; does not that speak well for me ? Smith has been bad but is better, and Mrs. Silvestre goes on à merveille. Bolton commends his little schollar and will soon allow her to write to you, which *in her mind* she does hourly, as well as talk of you; I hope notwith-standing her *great sensibillity* of y^r tenderness, wch she truly returns, that she is well pleased, and she most cheerfully performs all her little exercises.

Mrs. Delany to Mrs. Port, of Ilam.

St. James's Place, 16th March, 1779.

We go on charmingly, my dearest Mary; your sweet child, I thank God, perfectly well and as good as you can wish her to be. I dined yesterday at Lord Guilford's; only met the Ladys Dartmouth and Willoughby, their lords were squabbling at the House of Lords, as Mr. Montagu was at the House of C⁹. I was at first coming in shock'd to see Lord Guilf ᵈ look remarkably ill and our dear Lady Wil ʸ of course dejected; he has a very bad cold, it begun with a good deal of fever, it was abated yesterday and he grew still better before I left him; so well that the ladies went to the An. Mus. I made an hour's visit in my way home in Hanover Square. Mr. Fountayne still in a precarious state. The Dean of York and Mrs. Fountayne are expected in town this week, which I am very glad of. I came home at half an hour past eight and who should I find *gracing* my sofa but the Duchess of Portland and Lady Stamford, and G. M. A. *doing the honours* of my drawing-room, much to the satisfaction of all parties! Her writing master comes four times a-week, her dancing master three. She has been a second time to see Mrs. Stainsforth at the Queen's house and found her at home. Miss Hariot Thynne has got the yellow jaundice, which has delayed the promised meeting. Lady Cowper came to town yesterday and called here before I was return'd home in the evening. I sent to her this morning and she comes at eight this evening, stays in town till Friday for Lady

Newhaven's[1] concert. I shall ask her to dine here to-morrow or Thursday.

I am afraid Mr. Bloxam will deprive you of a tenant. I wish that affair was well settl'd. Miss Townshend,[2] Lady Greenwich's daughter, has carried off (for I hear the gentleman was not very willing), a Mr. Wilson, an Irishman that nobody knows by any other character than that of being very forward and very sarcastic. There is no end of vice and folly! Happy is the lot of security where innocence may escape the sad temptations of the *beau monde!* Lady Andover and Miss F. H[d] are so overwhelm'd with sorrow[3] and busyness that nobody but those who are unavoidable have seen them. My dear friend is to go I believe this evening, and I shall be glad when the meeting is over! I believe I told you Lord Suffolk had left his house in Duke Street his plate and jewells to poor Lady Suffolk. Three thousand pound a-year goes with the title, and all the rest (money and estates) to the amount of above £5000 a-year to Lady Andover, and Miss Fanny Howard afterwards. Shou'd Lady Suffolk produce a son, w[ch] I don't think is likely, that of course will alter the pres[t] settlement as far as it regards the estates.

---

[1] Sir William Mayne was created Baron Newhaven in 1776. He mar. in 1758, the Hon. Frances Allen, daughter and coheiress of Joshua, Viscount Allen.

[2] "The Hon. Miss Townshend, daughter of Lady Greenwich and the Hon. Charles Townshend (Chancellor of the Exchequer, 1766 to 1767), and half-sister to the Duke of Buccleuch, married, in March, 1779, Richard Wilson, of Aytone, in Ireland, Esq."

[3] Henry, 12th Earl of Suffolk, died 6th March, 1779. His second wife, Lady Charlotte Finch, daughter of Heneage, Earl of Aylesford, to whom he was married in 1777, gave birth to a son on the 8th of August, 1779, who succeeded as 13th Earl of Suffolk, but died two days afterwards, when the honours reverted to his great-uncle, the Hon. Thomas Howard.

As I was deeply engaged at my work who shou'd walk in but Lady Beaulieu introducing Lady Cecilia Johnston[1] who I have not seen these *twenty years!* and I cou'd then have spared her visit. After two or three fibs and curtseys on both sides; of "I have long wish'd to renew my acquaintance," and, "You flatter me," and so forth—one of my mosaic books was desired and hurried over with a volley of compliments, so ended the visit. I was cross'd as I knew it would curtail my letter, for I can now only add our dear child's best duty and love and the best wishes of my dearest Mary.

Yours ever,

M. D.

Miss Port, of Ilam, to her mother.

St. James's Place, 20th March, 1779.

I was so happy with your letter that I longed to write to dear mamma, but Mr. Bolton was cruel, tho' A. D. is not; I am very happy here. I often think of you, and wish you could now and then step over here just to see how well A. D. and I agree, and that I might kiss my dear mamma and ask her blessing. I have seen a number of fine people, and Lady Cowper all in her jewels, with a rose in the middle of her bows. My A. D. has had a frock made up and 3 caps, which Mrs Silvestre has made. My A. D. insists on my wearing gloves, and she tells me that I am to take rhubarb.—I don't like it,

---

[1] Lady Cecilia Johnstone was the eldest daughter of John, Earl of Delawarr and married General James Johnston.

but I will do it because you desire it. Mr. French is very tall, and makes fine bows, takes a great deal of pains, and says " Bravo," when I do well; the Dss of Portland has brought me from Bulstrode all the flowers you can think of, and she asks me every day how my A. D. does? She is very well, and we walked to Mrs. Kene;[1] saw her pretty girl, who sung surprizingly. We went to Lady C. Finch and Mrs. Fielding's to wish them joy of Mrs. F.'s being bedchamber-woman to the Queen. The Dss of Portland has dined here 3 times, and Lady Cowper once. I have a great deal more to tell my dearest mamma, but can only add my duty and love to Ilam.

From y[r] dutyfull and affectionate daughter,

G. M. A. Port.

Mrs. Delany to Mrs. Port, of Ilam.

St. James's Place, 1st April, 1779.

I hope you are well, my dearest child. I can't help fearing you are too much hurried; take care of damps in your new house, for nothing is more likely to give fevers than such sort of damps; but I depend on Mr. P.'s watchful care of you, and trust that you will be supported by Providence under all tryals; without that hope I should be miserable indeed! I rejoice at the good account of your dear boys and lovely Louisa,[2] who I hope has been wean'd some time : our precious G. M. A.

---

[1] Elizabeth, second daughter of George, Viscount Lewisham, and sister of William, 2nd Earl of Dartmouth, married Whitshed Keene, Esq., M.P.

[2] Louisa Port, born 8th May, 1778. Her godfather and godmothers were, General the Hon. FitzWilliam, Lady Louisa Manners, and Lady Willoughby de Broke.

is pure well.   After my return from a very affecting
visit to Lady Andover, Mary met me at the door,
and made me follow her into the parlour to behold a
compleat set of *young* Nankeen china which she had
just received from the Duchess of Portland : her raptures
were prodigious, and indeed they are *very fine* and pretty
of their kind, not quite so small as for baby things, nor
large eno' for grown ladies, and she insists on my telling
you all this, and that there are twelve teacups and saucers,
6 coffee cups and teapot, sugar dish, milk mug, 2 bread-
and-butter plates, and they have been produced for the
entertainment of all my company every afternoon, and
" Lord Guilford has given her a pocket-book, and Mrs.
Boscawen has given her a smelling-bottle quite in a new
taste, such a onê as she " thinks as you never saw," and
she would have written all this herself and more, but she
is not allow'd to write any more letters yet, and she was
three days writing the last," (this is her dictating.) How
awkwardly I have gone on with my letter, and I now
return to poor Lady Andover, who is involved not only
in much sorrow, but a confusion of busyness.   As it is
thought Lady Suffolk is breeding, I suppose there will
be a suspension of busyness for some time, and her poor
spirits have time to repose.   I think poor Miss Howard
seems as deeply struck as her mother, tho' they both
endeavour to submit with Christian resignation, and *that*
with the help of time, I trust, will give them comfort;
and when they are able to reflect on the little prospect of
happiness there was from his *miserable* state of health, it
will in some measure reconcile them to the event.   They
seem'd to receive a little consolation from my visit ; and
I have promised to dine there to-day.   Yesterday was

the first day that Lady Suffolk and Lady Andover cou'd
bring themselves to meet since their great loss. I am
glad the sad meeting is over. I pity Lady Suffolk
extreamly : she is gentle and affectionate, and young
minds that have *not* been inured to sorrow feel the tooth
of affliction *very sharply ;* but being call'd upon often to
consider the insufficiency of human happiness, leads us to
consider where " only true joy is to be found," and to
bear our present woes as so many guides to our eternal
rest and felicity. My next anxious friends are those in
Hanover Square, where everything is still uncertain, tho'
for a day or two past the medical people have a better
opnion of Mr. Fountayne. I hope they are not mistaken ;
Mrs. Montagu rather better than for some time past.
Our dear Dss is pretty well, and better for having seen
Lady And^{er}, and for an excursion or two to Bulstrode.
Last night I had Mr. and Mrs. Smelt here, and I need
not say *how agreeable !* Her Grace and L^y Weymouth at
past ten bounced in, and Mrs. M. and Miss Gregory.
G. M. A. (no small figure in our circle), she just now says
" pray tell dear mama " that she has " found in the work-
bag you have left two nice plats of hair wch she is sure is
your doing, and begs to know whose hair they are ?"
Her dancing-master delights in her, and you cannot think
how I am amused (for I am *always* by) to see her bound
and frisk about ; still, as I feel the pleasure of her pretty
ways, regretting that I rob you the while. I don't
think she has made a great proficiency with her writing-
master. She has now entered her third month of learning, wch will be eno', as I will make her write every day
2 or 3 lines ; as to *figures,* her father may teach her, and
Mrs. Vrankin her grammar ; another year will make her

2 E 2

attend more to these 2 last, and *not crowd too fast*, but learn perfectly what we are now practising for the present.

The Marchioness of Tweeddale to Mrs. Port, of Ilam.

Ham, April 10th, 1779.

I have deferr'd acknowledging my dear Mrs. Port's agreeable letter of ye 15th of last month, waiting to send her a *few tunes* of my composing, but find she has rec^d them under Mr. Tollemache's cover from Lady Bridget Tollemache, who had them to copy. If they do not amuse her, at least they will remind her of y^e *weak composer* ! I have also set to music some words made on my *dear angels*, which you shall have when I can get them copied; but my compositions come more from *my heart* than my *head* ! I have often inquired after your good aunt, Mrs. Delany; but have never heard from her since you went. You *cou'd not* leave Miss Port in *better* hands. *She* show'd her talents *in you*. It *cheers me* to see under your own hand that you *are* quite happy. A good husband and fine children are ye greatest and most desireable *riches,* and may you never know the loss of them. I have at last got rid of my lawyers. I have for many years past follow'd St. Paul's advice, in suffering onesself to be defrauded, and now (for ye sake of peace and quietness) I have consented to ye selling of *my estate* in Hampshire (as it *is* now *allow'd to be*) and dividing it with my nephew, Thynne Carteret; but as money is so scarce, I fancy we shall not soon get a purchaser. I thank God I am better in health than I could expect,

and my little grandchild has no complaints : she would
be *very glad* to see her cosin Bernard,[1] I must add my
best comp^ts to Mr. Port, and that I am most truly, dear
Mrs. Port,

Your affec^t cosin
And faithful humble serv^t,
F. TWEEDDALE, &c.

Mrs. Delany to Mrs. Port, of Ilam.

St. James's Place, 17th April, 1779.

I am very glad you have settled so well with Mr.
Bloxam, who has behaved so like a gentleman that I hope
he will prove a good neighbour ; but we are both un-
acquainted with Mrs. B., or what sort of children they
may be, but shou'd they not be just such as you would
wish the *proposal* may bring on a greater intimacy
than you wou'd wish to encourage, and lay you under a
particular obligation.

Sunday.

I began this yesterday, and have scribbled it at such a
rate that it is scarcely legible, but I am so busy now
with *rare* specimens from all my botanical friends, and
idle visiters and my little charge must have a share of
my time (tho' not near so much as I wou'd most willingly bestow on her) that it generally drives my writing
to candlelight, which does not suit my age-worn eyes.

---

[1] Bernard Port, of Ilam, born 17th March, 1776 ; his sponsors were the
Hon. Mrs. Elizabeth Granville, Bernard Dewes, Esq., and the Rev. John
Dewes : died Vicar of Ilam, Jan., 1854.

Well, now a word or two *journal wise*. Last Tuesday (I believe I told you so before), I took *my little bird* and Mrs. Pott to Upton in Essex, 10 mile off, to Dr. Fothergill's Garden[1], crammed my tin box with exoticks, overpowered with such variety I knew not what to chuse! G. M. A. delighted, fluttering about like a newborn butterfly, first trying her wings, and then examining and enjoying all the flowers. Thursday she was invited to drink tea at Lady Stamford's. I went to my poor Montagu, still much teiz'd wth her cough and all the family in an anxious state for poor Mr. Fountayne, and I believe with a great deal of reason. On my return home after eight I call'd for the precious charge, who was much pleased with her visit and brought away shells in abundance ; and her collection encreases so fast that you must provide her with a cabinet to keep them, for she promises herself much joy in sorting and entertaining Mr. Beresford with them. To-day *we* are to dine at Mrs. Boscawen's to meet Mrs. Walsingham and *Miss Boyle,* and not a little happy to be so invited, and dinner is order'd at half past three, so for to day adieu. I have been at early prayers and shall make a visit or two in my way to S. Aud. Street.

Monday, 19th.

Home we came at eight after a day agreably spent to all partys ; called for our tea, (the usual supper,) and before it was over in came the Bishop of Exeter[1]. The conversation was wholly engrossed by his lordship and

---

[1] John Fothergill, M.D., was born in Yorkshire, 1712; died 1780. A catalogue of store and green-house plants of his garden at Upton, at the time of his death, was published in 1784.

[2] Dr. John Ross, Bishop of Exeter from 1778 to 1792.

your daughter, to my great entertainment; he has invited *her* to come and *see him*. Lady Gower made her appearance about nine, and finish'd the evening with me. I promised the Dss of Portland to meet her after being at Mrs. Boscawen's, but my heart fail'd me as I knew it would be an assembly of *beaux* and *belle esprits!* This morning Mr. Bloxom brought G. M. A.'s letter; she was gone to take a walk in the park, which she does every morning, and he was in such a violent hurry he wou'd not stay a moment longer than to tell me you were well, that he was going to Ilam in ten days and wou'd call again before he went. I had many questions I wished to ask him, but he wou'd not stay two minutes.

The Bishop of Litchfield[1] made me a visit this morning, and since dinner Mr. French has been with his schollar and gave her a good lesson of steps and beating time; she has six lessons more to come of her second month. Alas! *time flyes fast;* let me know in time before she returns if there is anything particular for her you would have done. I think what you propose of Mr. Port's meeting her at Birmingham, where I will send Mrs. Silvestre with her, will be the best way. To-morrow morning we go airing to the physic-garden at Chelsea.

You have no doubt read and heard much of the shocking affair of Miss Ray for which the miserable wretch was executed yesterday;[2] the horror he seemed to

---

[1] Dr. Richard Hurd, Preceptor to the Prince of Wales, Bishop of Lichfield from 1774 to 1781, when he was translated to Worcester.

[2] Miss Reay was shot by the Rev. Mr. Hackman, as she was coming out of the Covent Garden Theatre, on the 7th of April, 1779, for which offence he was found guilty and executed.

have of his guilt I hope was a sign of sincere penitence.
He desired Lord Sandwich's pardon, without wch he could
not die in peace; Lord S^h sent him word as he "look'd
upon his horrid action as an act of frenzy he forgave it,
that he received the stroke as coming from Providence
wch he ought to submit to, but that he had robb'd him of
all comfort in this world."

Tuesday evening.

We return'd loaded with the spoyls of the Botanical
Garden. G. M. A. was surprized at a live cameleon she
saw in the hot house. At our return I was so happy as
to receive y^r last dear letter. I am sorry for the dear
little B. P., why not give him the juice of clivers or
goose grass, which is wonderfull, pounded with a little
cold water, a small tea cup or about three table spoonfuls
taken every morning.

The herb so much commended by Mrs. Delany, in the above
letter, is thus described by Culpeper in his 'English Physitian,'
pub. 1653:—

"Cleavers is also called aparine, goose-share, goose-grass, and
clavers. It is under the *dominion of the moon;* the juice of the
herb and the seed together helpeth those that are bitten with
an adder, by preserving the heart from the venom. It is familiarly
taken in broth to keep them lean and lank that are apt to grow
fat. The distilled water, drank twice a day, helpeth the yellow
jaundice; and the decoction of the herb in experience is found
to do the same. The juice of the leaves, or they a little bruised
and applied to any bleeding wound, stayeth the bleeding. The
juice is also very good to close up the lips of green wounds, and
the powder of the dried herb strewed thereupon doth the same.
It likewise helpeth ulcers, being boiled with hog's grease. It
healeth all sorts of hard swellings, or kernels in the throat, being
anointed therewith. The juice dropped into the ears taketh away

the pains of them. It is a good remedy in the Spring, eaten, being first chopped sinal and boyled well in water-gruel, it cleans the blood and strengthens the liver, thereby keeping the body in health and fitting it for that change which is coming.

" It groweth by the hedge and ditch sides, and is so troublesome an inhabitant in gardens that it rampeth upon and is ready to choke whatever grows next to it."

Mrs. Delany to Mrs. Port, of Ilam.

St. James's Place, 17th May, 1779.

I must begin my letter with telling you, my dearest M., that the specimen of goose grass or cleavers, that you enclos'd *is* the right sort; it does *not* bear burrs (which are the seed vessels) till after the time of its flowring, and I believe is now in perfection ; and certainly a most extraordinary good remedy for some disorders.

As to our sweet. child I will punctually observe all your directions, but must chide you for *your apology* ; you have done just what I wish'd you to do wch will save me so much trouble. Her uncle will be happy to take the charge of her, and will carry her and George, as you desire, to Malvern Hall, on Tuesday the 25th, and proposes leaving London next Fryday. *I dare not* trust myself just now to say *more* on this tender subject, but *feel my obligation* to you for sparing her *so long to me ;* she truly deserves every attention that can be paid her. With an *excellent* capacity, ready to take instruction ; *healthy,* I thank God, and *sprightly,* tho' delicate in body and mind, and *easily fatigued.* I must at present *force* my pen to another subject.

This morning (for the other side was written at eleven last night) we are going to breakfast with Mrs. M. Smith at Kentish Town, and the Miss Murrays are to meet us. Afterwards call at Dr. Pitcairn's botanical garden, and your brother Court meets us here at dinner.

Mrs. Delany to Miss Port.

St. James's Place, 18th May, 1779.

I thank you, my dear child, for your kind letter, and for the satisfaction you express in having been some time under my care, and willing to come to me again when convenient. I am convinced that every anxious care I have had, and every attention I have paid you, will *not* be forgotten, and if they prove of real advantage to you I shall be happy, and ready to receive my dear delightful companion *again*, when her dear papa and mama can spare her to her

Ever affectionate,

AUNT DELANY.

Think how happy your mama will be to see her dear girl again; and how happy you will be to see her.

John Dewes, of Welsbourn, Esq., to his son, the Rev. John Dewes, at Calwich, near Ashbourn, Derbyshire.

Welsbourn, 18th May, 1779.

DEAR JOHN,

I thank you for yor kind and entertaining letter of the 10th inst, and am very glad to hear that you and Mrs. Dewes are so well; and that she is in so fair a way to help you to an heir to Calwich; as to my health it is but very indifferent, being very weak and low, and very little appetite for any sort of food. I think Mr. Port has been lucky in letting his house, if all ends as well as it begins.

I am glad you have got so much of your *mud* away,[1] and hope you will soon clear away the rest, for it's a teadiouse undertaking, and will be expensive. I am glad Mr. and Mrs. Newdigate are such good neighbours: I think Mr. M. sh^d have known his ffrd's tho^{ts} before he came hither, for I believe he did not expect a better ffortune that what was pposed. The lady looks a little grave upon it, but carrys it off pretty well.

I am sorry poor Nathan has lost his wife; and I think he will not easily meet with such another, and till he does I w^d *not* advise him to marry; wch pray tell him from me. I think you have laid in, or rather laid out, for a fine stock of company for the sumer, so you'l soon have an opportunity of seeing which you like best, that, or the tête à tête you have had for 6 weeks past.

Poor Mrs. Mead, I think, is much in the same state she has been for many months past, so that I doubt she will not soon get over it, if at all. Mrs. Venour is pretty well, but Miss Landor, who came to nurse her, has been very ill, but is on the mending hand. Bernard and his family are coming here for a week, by way of change of air for his little girl after inocculation. Court I expect soon, as term ends this day. I desire my best respects to all wth and ab^t you, and am.

Yo^r m^t aff^t ffa^r,

J. D.

---

[1] The river Dove ran opposite the windows of Calwich, and the mud required removal.

The following Prayer, indorsed by the son to whom the above letter was written, is interesting as composed by the husband of the beautiful and beloved Ann Granville, the brother-in-law of Mary Granville, Mrs. Delany, and the " *best of men* " of Lady Cowper. He was at this period, 1779, eighty-four, and died the following year.

" *Prayers of my dear Father, J. Dewes. Signed J. Granville.*"

O Almighty God that made me, have mercy on me for Christ Jesus sake. Pardon I beseech Thee mine offences, whatever thou hast seen amiss in me now and all the rest of my life, and accept my humble tribute of praise and thanksgiving for Thy mercies vouchsafed me, more especially at this time; for Thy preservation and refreshm^t of me the night past, and for raising me up again to the light of this day; O Lord defend me in the same by Thy mighty power, and grant that this day I fall into no sin neither run into any kind of danger, but that all my doings may be order'd by thy governance to do always that wch is righteous in thy sight, thro' the merritts of Christ Jesus.

Bless me, O L^d, if it be Thy blessed will, with health. *Bless* and prosper me in any business and w^tever I go ab^t more p̃ticularlye (*illegible*).

Nevertheless not as I will but as Thou wilt, Lord grant me patience and resignation to Thy holy will and pleasure, and w^tever my station may be in this world, grant that I may so behave myself in it as finally to obtain an eternall inheritance in the world to come thro' the merritts of C. J.

Bless all my ffr^{ds} p̃ticularlye and grant that I may be a comfort, happiness, and support to them and they to

me. Have mercy, O Lord, upon the whole world, espe-
cialy that part of it whereunto I belong ; grant that we
may be so humbled and reformed that we may be
pardon'd and spared and may be a happy people, and
render Thee thanks and praise for all Thy mercies.

In a more particular manner be mercifull to all those
who suffer under any calamity, affliction, or distress, in
mind, body, or estate; doe Thou in mercy look upon
them, relieve their severall necessities, give them patience
under their sufferings, and in Thy due time a happy
issue out of all their afflictions.

Bless me, Thy unworthy ser^t, by turning me away
from my iniquities and granting me grace and strength
to do good; put into my heart, O Lord, good desires,
and grant me grace and strength to fullfill the same,
that I may be an instrum^t in Thy hands of turning
many to righteousness and may so pass thro' things
temporall as finally to obtain the things eternall in thy
heavenly kingdom, thro' C. J.

Mrs. Delany to Miss Port, of Ilam.

St. James's Place, Friday, May 22nd, 1779.

I can't go to bed till I have written a line or two to my
dear G. M. A. ; and tell her how I have passed *the melancholly day.* I tried to sleep after you left me, but instead
of that followed your steps (in my imagination) till I
thought you were near Salt Hill, I then got up that I
might eat my breakfast much at the same time I thought
you and your dear uncle might be employed the same
way, and hope your breakfast was relished better than

mine! When that was over I wrote a letter, and then
went to my work and finished the flower I began yesterday; but my little handmaid was wanting, to pick up
my papers, to read to me, to hum her tune, and to
prattle to me! I hope the chaise was easy, that the
haymakers were busy, and the May bushes sweet and *full
of birds,* and I don't doubt but you and your uncle were
excellent company to one another.

I dined as I promised with Mrs. Montague, but y^r
friend Mr. Montague was engaged at the House of
Commons, and I saw nothing of him; Mrs. Mon^u pretty
well, and Mr. Fountayne continues to mend. I came
home at nine. The Duchess of Ancaster had been here
just before I came home; and in came Lady Wallingford just as I begun this letter, by this time (past ten
o'clock) I hope my dearest child is fast asleep after
having found her grand papa,[1] her uncle[2] and her aunt,
her cousin Anne,[3] and Mrs. Mead's family, pretty well,
—I wish I could hear *quite* well. My kind compliments
to all, and good night.

Saturday is arrived, and I go on with my letter. I
had a good night, and assure you, my dear child, I am
very well to day and shall be perfectly well when I hear
you and all our friends are so, and that you were not
too much fatigued; it was a very windy day, and almost
blew down the great elm in my garden, and then what
would your *pretty little birds* have done, when they had
lost their green bower, *as well* as the dear little hands, that

---

[1] " *Grandpapa.*"—Mr. Dewes, of Welsbourn.

[2] " *Her uncle.*"—Mr. Bernard Dewes.

[3] " *Her cousin Anne.*"—Anne Dewes (afterwards Mrs. Stratton), only
daughter of Mr. Bernard Dewes and his wife, Anne De la Bere.

used so constantly to crumble food for them? but I sent for the smith and had the tree fastened up with irons and cords, and next year I hope you will see it as flourishing as it is now. A propos, the little parokets told me as well as they could speak that they miss'd you sadly, so does every one in the house, and Smith in particular, who is but very indifferent, and says she " can make me no more gooseberry-fool" since you are not here to eat it! Mrs. Silvester looks *very sad* but goes every day now to dress hair in perfection against she goes to " the *beautiful young lady*," that makes " *such a point of it!*" Pray tell your uncle Bernard I have written the letter his brother and I consulted about; if I get an answer I'll send it him directly. I expect the Grace of Graces every moment, and Lady Bute in the evening, perhaps Mr. Montague, who will wish for you, as well as the rest of the company. I calculate you will receive this the day before you go to Malvern. Writting it in a little hurry, which I cou'd not avoid, must excuse its being so indifferently written. My dearest G. M. A. believe me,

Ever y^r affectionate,
M. DELANY.

Mrs. Delany to Mrs. Port, of Ilam.

Bulstrode, 4th June, 1779.

I left *London* last Wednesday without the least regret. The loss of my little innocent companion, the heat and dust that was almost suffocating, made it an unpleasant *place*; and the circle of friends were dwindling away so that *society was no more!* Judge then, my dearest Mary, how happy I must be in the exchange I have

made? here everything of *art* and *nature* combine to
delight, bestow'd by the most amiable of friends, whose
kindness leaves me no wish, and whose tenderness sooths
every care! I set out at eight, call'd at Brompton
to see my friends there, found them all in comfortable
spirits, Mr. Fountayne certainly much better and *at
present* thought so by the medical faculty. A fresh
air temper'd the heat of the day but nothing could
save us from the dust rous'd by carriages and flocks
of sheep, that obliged me to shut out the friendly
breeze. At half an hour after one I enter'd this fair
domain, which never appear'd in higher beauty. I
had just time to refresh myself, with brushing off the
dust and a dish of tea, settling my drawers and preparing
for my works, when her Grace arrived to compleat the
happiness of the place, but we prudently resolved to content ourselves with the beauties within doors and viewing
what we were to enjoy (please God) the next day.

How I rejoice that you are surrounded with your dear
children. Providence has blessed you with *uncommon*
subjects for the exercise of your maternal judg^t and
tenderness.

Mrs. Delany to Miss Port, of Ilam.

Bulstrode, 6th June, 1779.

I begin a letter to my dearest G. M. A. to-day, tho'
perhaps I may not finish it this post or two, for I am
but just returned from chapel, where Mr. Lightfoot gave
us an excellent sermon ; and had I told him I was going
to write, I am sure would have sent you his kind compli-

ments; and we are to dine early, to take an airing afterwards thro the riding in the wood, where every chirping
bird and lively butterfly will put me in mind of my
dear little child, whose cheerfulness, and good behaviour
enlivened the hours she pass'd with me, and gave me
that satisfaction I must always feel when she is good and
happy. The Friday before I left London, I went to Mr.
Keate's,[1] and was much entertained in their museum;
they were all very sorry you was not of the party,
but when I told them you were so happy as to be with
your dear papa, mama, brothers, and sister, we all agreed
you cou'd not be in a better place, and London was so
hot and dusty that I cou'd not wish you in it. Miss
Keate was sadly disappointed, not knowing you were
gone, and she cut out whilst she stood at my elbow a
figure, which if I can find I will enclose. I have not
yet quite unpacked, but I send you a gold pheasant's
feather, which the Duchess of Portland pick'd up in her
walks yesterday. Mrs. Silvestre went last Tuesday
night to take possession of her new place, and desired to
send her humble service to you and many kind wishes.
Poor Smith was very bad when we came here, but grows
better; she has sent you some butterflies in a round
box, which I hope will come safe with your burreau and
all the rest of the things, and that by this time you have
unpacked them all. The deer, the hares, the pheasants,
the pea fowl, &c. &c., are all well, and bounding, frisking,
and fluttering about, not forgetting the squirels as brisk
and merry as any of them; the park and gardens in

---

[1] George Keate, an English writer, born about 1729; died 1797. He wrote
An Account of the Pelew Islands; Poems and Sketches from Nature, in a
Journey to Margate, &c., &c.

nice order, and when the deer and the mistress of them (who delights in making everything happy about her), is perfectly well, there can be nothing to be wished for but hearing of the health and welfare of absent friends; I thank God her cough is better, and I hope this fine air will cure her soon. She speaks of you most kindly, and sends her best compliments to your mama: she has placed your little tiny rarity in a fine Japan cabinet. Thus far was written last Sunday : Monday we enjoyed in the gardens ; saw the porcupine, who bristled out all his fine quills and is a fine creature ; and the beautiful curlew, whose feathers are of the brightest scarlet, a long slender neck and legs like a crane, and a very long slender bill, this bird is about the size of a large pigeon.

Yesterday the rain prevented our going out, but to *make us amends* Lady Mary Forbes, the Admiral, and 2 daughters spent the afternoon here. My breakfast is ready—then to my work. Everywhere I am to my dearest G. M. A.,

Most truly her affect^{te} Aunt,

M. Delany.

I forgot to tell you that I called at Brompton in my way to Bulstrode, and found Mr. Fountayne much better, and all the family full of hopes of his recovery. Miss Betty charg'd me to give her love to you when I wrote.

I had a letter to-day from Lord Guilford; he tells me all his family are well and he proposes calling here on the 28th of this month for a day or two in his way to Wroxton. Pray make my compliments to Mr. and Mrs. Beresford; I hope she and the little one are quite

well, and be sure to give my love to your uncle and
aunt at Calwich. I hope they are perfectly well and
y^r friends at Malvern Hall when y^u heard.

M. DELAYN.

The following lines were written by Mr. Keate, upon Mrs.
Delany's giving the little daughter mentioned in this letter a
lesson in cutting out a flower from Nature.

LINES BY MR. KEATE.

" With that benevolence which condescends
  To glide its knowledge to the youthful heart,
O'er thee, my child, the good Delany benas,
  Directs thy *scissors*, and reveals her *art*.

Ah! seize the happy moment! she can show
  The mazy path mysterious Nature treads ;
Can steal her varied grace, her varied glow,
  And all the changeful beauties that she spreads.

Then *mark* thy kind instructress, *watch* her hand,
  Her judgement, her inspiring touch attain ;
Thy *scissors* make, *like hers*, a *magic wand* !
  Tho! much I fear thy efforts will be vain.

Failing in this, my child, forbear the strife ;
  Another path to fame by her is shown ;—
Try, by *the pattern* of her *honour'd life*,
  With equal virtue to *cut out thine own*."

The Hon. Mrs. Boscawen to Mrs. Delany.

Glan Villa, 11th June, 1779.

How happy have you made me, my dear friend, by the
delightful account of your own happiness. You are restored to y^r beloved Elisium of Bulstrode, and you see its
noble mistress recovering every day, every hour. I hope
you are perfectly well yourself and in excellent spirits.
Vous narrez, madame, comme Mad^e de Sevigne, so that

all your histories are pictures, and *I see* as plain as can be how her Grace looks afraid if Mr. Kay brings a note upon his waiter, lest it should bring *proposals of ennui.* Then your *race* in the riding made me perfectly tremble for you, and I was as much interested in the victory as Mr. O'Kelly upon Ascot Heath. I would have betted upon your head however, for there is a certain zeal wch generally conquers, and you'll allow it was not wanting on your part: however I was quite refreshed and out of my pain when I saw you safe at home and drinking your tea in quiet; but how was it that the pursuers did *not* follow you quite to head-quarters? You will say perhaps that you made it *very plain* there cou'd be no propriety in such a measure—n'importe, provided my Lady Duchess had not her night's rest disturbed by an *unpleasant* evening, to which she really has a natural aversion, and therefore I hope her Grace will be equally fortunate in all similar perils. I was extremely so in carrying *all* my hay (wch indeed was soon carry'd) before the rain came. Bulstrode Park hill now has a covering of green velvet, nor shall I have any dust during my journey, which begins to-morrow to Bill Hill, and ends, please God, on Monday at Badminton.

Miss J. Young has return'd a visit I made her since I came here, and gives me great hopes of Mr. Fountayne's recovery, which I am heartily rejoiced at. She expects Mrs. Montague at East Barnet as soon as her daughter leaves London, for you know it is supposed that Mr. Fountayne is able to travel into Yorkshire. I saw Mrs. Chapone at Hadley last Wensday. She was only with Mr. Mulso on a dining visit, but means to make them one of residence in a short time; she ask'd much after

you and seemed to doubt whether a letter had not miscarried which she had wrote you on the subject of a
brother in law of Mrs. Carter's. Mrs. Montague has left
Bath, and is at Sandleford in good spirits. Lady Edgecumbe spent the day here last Monday, but I was disappointed of my L$^{d's}$ company by the endless story of
the Greenwich Hospital[1] in the House of Lords, which
however ended that night, little to the honour of the
inveterate prosecutor. I hope you have got the cross-
readings of the Pub. Adv^r to-day, some of them are excellent, though they have lost the charm of novelty; as to
the verses on their Majestie's faults, I am not sure *you*
did *not* write them! We hear of several marriages, viz.,
Lady Hillsboro's son to Mr. Curzon's daughter with
£35,000[2]. Two Miss Langdale's (in their tribe) to Mr.
Clifford[3] and Mr. Butler;[4] Baron Nolken;[5] to *widow Le*

---

[1] On the 11th of March, 1779, the Duke of Richmond brought before the
notice of the House of Lords the subject of the management of Greenwich
Hospital. An inquiry was instituted, and continued to occupy the attention
of the House till the 8th of June, when Earl Bathurst's resolution, that "It is
the opinion of the Committee that the whole of this inquiry appears not to
have been an object fit for Parliamentary deliberation," was carried without a
division. The Duke of Chandos moved "That the thanks of the House be
given to Lord Sandwich for his diligent attention to the affairs of the Hospital,"
which was also carried.

[2] Mary, second wife of Wills, 1st Earl of Hillsborough and 1st Marquis of
Downshire, was the daughter of Lord Stawell, and Baroness Stawell in her own
right. Her first husband was the Rt. Hon. Henry Bilson Legge, a son of
William, 1st Earl of Dartmouth. Her only son, Henry Legge, who after his
mother's death succeeded to her Barony, married Mary, daughter of Viscount
Curzon.

[3] Hugh Edward Henry Clifford, 6th Baron Clifford, of Chudleigh, married,
in 1780, before his father's death, Apollonia, youngest daughter and co-heiress
of Marmaduke, last Lord Langdale of that family.

[4] The Hon. Elizabeth Langdale, daughter of Marmaduke, 5th Baron Langdale, married, in Sept. 1779, Robert Butler, Esq., of Ballyragget, in Ireland.

[5] Baron Nolken, Envoy from Sweden, married, in June, 1779, Mrs. Le Maitre,
widow of the Hon. Mr. Justice Le Maitre.

Maitre. Mad^e Mouflon[1] is better perhaps with one son than two, tho' it should retard a little the *peopling* of the Welsh mountains. Mr. and Mrs. Cole call'd here on Sunday in their way from Judge Ashurst's[2] to London. Adieu, my dearest madam; present my best respects to the Duchess.

John Dewes, of Welsbourn, Esq., to his Eldest Son.

Sat. evening, June 19th, 1779.

DEAR COURT,

  I had yor l^{re} of the 15th ins^t, by which I guess you will not be here before the latter end of next week, a period of time I *never expect to see,* as I grow weaker and weaker every day, and take very little sustinence of any kind. In case of my death before you come hither, (which I think very likely to happen,) I have given Ffrank Dipple[3] directions to take the keys of the two clossets in the little parlour, which I generally carry in my breeches pocket, and keep them till you come, and then deliver them to you; in which two clossets are all other keys belonging to the house, and not deliver them to anybody, nor go into the clossets himself, nor let anybody else till you come, and then to deliver them to you. I have very little money in the house at present. I hope you will find everything in pretty good order, w^{ch}, with

---

 [1] "Muflon."—The Musmon, probably procured by General Paoli for the Duchess of Portland's menagerie. There was then an idea of naturalizing these animals in Wales.

 [2] Sir William Henry Ashurst, Kt., was appointed one of the Puisne Judges of the King's Bench in 1770.

 [3] Old Frank Dipple was his confidential servant, and lived in the family many years after Mr. Dewes's death. He planted a fine oak-tree, now flourishing (1861) at the end of the orchard at Welsbourn.

what I have told you at various times I know will enable you to transact yor affairs with ease and comfort. May the blessing of the Allmighty attend you, to whose providence I humbly recommend you, and am

Yo^r m^t affectionate ff^r,

J. D.

Mr. Dewes did *not* die till the following year, but the above letter is very characteristic of his calm mind and methodical habits.

The Countess Cowper to Mrs. Port, of Ilam.

Richmond, June 22nd, 79.

Many thanks, my dearest Mrs Port, for y^{rs} of the 18th ult., and for y^r kind invitation to y^r new habitation, w^{ch} *were* it a cottage y^u know ye wisest of men said, *a dinner of herbs where love is, is better than a stall'd ox, and hatred therewith.*

If ever I shou'd again travel so far as into Derbyshire, I shall certainly call upon y^u. I had ye satisfaction of seeing Lady Frances Bulkeley's health mend greatly under my roof. She is to make a visit next month to Lady Williams upon Ham Common, and will then pass a few days more wth me. I expect Lady Mary Mordaunt ye end of ye week, for a short time only, as she is to attend her Dutchess (who is now *the Dutchess*) to Scarborough, ye latter end of the summer. Lord and Lady Spencer proposed being at Althorp by ye 20th of Aug^t, and my intention, please God, is to meet them there. But how they will get back I know not! As the Spaniards have joined the French against us, I really think now, nothing less than a miracle can save poor England. In general people seem neither to fear *God* nor man, and y[e] English ladies are grown *quite dare-devils!*

The Dss of Devon cannot be *very* ill, as she danced at y[e] Knights of y[e] Bath's[1] ball till four o'clock in y[e] morning. The young ladies by their manner of living will be soon *old* ones, and no *wash* will ever make them appear well. Lord Spencer has lent his house at S[t] Alban's to poor Lady De la Warr.[2] I fear she will soon lose another grown-up daughter, of a consumption. How her happyness has vanish'd within a very few years! A mother, a beloved husband, and two children grown up, and a third going very fast. God preserve y[r] fine family, but I hope you will not have any encrease. My best compliments to Mr. Port. I conclude you are upon y[e] wing. *" With thee conversing, I forget all time."*

Mrs. Fitz. is just gone, and desired her compliments to y[u] as I told her I was scribbling to y[u]. Poor Mrs. Cowper[3] is at last released. *Tho' sisters-in-law,* we lived in friendship! As I do not doubt y[u] do wth y[rs].

---

[1] "Thirteen Knights of the Bath were installed in Henry VII.'s Chapel at Westminster Abbey, on the 19th of May, 1779. In the evening a grand ball was given by the new Knights, at the King's Theatre in the Haymarket, at which upwards of 1000 of the nobility and gentry were present."

[2] " Lady Delawarr."—Mary, daughter of General Wynyard, married John, 2nd Earl of Delawarr ; and died 27th Oct., 1784. They had two daughters : Georgina, who married, in 1782, Edward Pery Buckley, Esq., and died in 1832 ; and Matilda, married, in 1793, to Gen. Henry Wynyard, and died 1843.

[3] The Hon. Mrs. Cowper, widow of the Hon. Spencer Cowper, Dean of Durham, and daughter of Charles, 2nd Viscount Townshend, died in May, 1779.

Adieu, my dear Mrs. Port. My love to ye little ones, and to yourself *it is unalterable.*

G. C. COWPER.

The Countess of Bute[1] to Mrs. Delany.

Luton Park, July 5th, 1779.

MY DEAR MADAM,

I flatter myself the Duchess and you (who I hope are both in good health) will be glad to hear we are come back from our excursion perfectly well, having had very good travelling weather, which we made good use of. For after staying a few days at our Hampshire cottage,[2] we proceeded to Weymouth for a day, and by going and returning by different roads, traversed great part of Dorsetshire, and almost all the New Forest in Hampshire. My lord has chose a most delightful spot, with not only an extensive sea view, but a very pleasant land prospect. Having the advantage of being very near the Forest, and a rich enclosed country, which I must own I prefer even to the smooth and pleasant downs of Dorsetshire, it is in some respects a perfect contrast to this. The house wou'd stand in half the library, but its small rooms are thoroughly neat and convenient, and being but ten feet high, I had no reason to complain of

---

[1] Mary, only daughter of Edward Wortley Montagu and of the Lady Mary Pierrepont, daughter of Evelyn, 1st Duke of Kingston, married John, 3rd Earl of Bute, who was for more than two years Prime Minister to King George III. Lord Bute died March 10th, 1792 ; Lady Bute died Nov. 13th, 1794.

[2] Sir Egerton Brydges states that " Lord Bute passed the last six or seven years of his life in the most deep and unbroken retirement, principally at a villa which he built on the edge of the cliff at Christchurch, in Hampshire, overlooking the Needles and the Isle of Wight."

the number of stairs to ascend at bed-time. The mild-
ness of the sea air (being due south) makes up for the
want of shelter, there *not* being a *single tree* upon our
territory. The cliff the house stands upon abounds with
fossils, which are to be picked up in plenty after a shower
of rain. I have brought a box full, which have been
gathered by the gardener, and shall be happy if (when
I see you) there are any you have not.

We do not expect any company here, but some of our
children, and *still* flatter ourselves, my dear Mrs. Delany
may be tempted to make this her home while the Duchess is absent from Bulstrode. The flowers have been in
great beauty, tho' I fear this rainy weather will de-
molish many of them; however the conservatory [1] may
afford something to amuse you, and tho' you have a
choice of friends who wou'd be happy with the favour of
your company, there are *none* who wou'd be *more obliged*
to you than this family, and particularly my dear Mrs.
Delany's

Ever faithfull and affectionate,

M. W. Bute.

We all beg our affectionate comp[s] to the Duchess,
despairing that any entreaty cou'd prevail upon her to
do us the honour and real pleasure of coming here.

The friendship which existed between Lord and Lady Bute
and Mrs. Delany was strengthened by the similarity of taste for
botany. Lady Bute alludes in the above letter to the "*flowers*" at

---

[1] Lord Bute's study was botany ; he printed at his own expense a botanical
work, in 9 quarto volumes, of plants appertaining only to England. Only
12 copies were printed, of which the expense amounted to 10,000*l.*

Luton and to " *the conservatory*," as well-known objects of interest to Mrs. Delany. It is a remarkable coincidence that on the *very day* this letter was written, Mrs. Delany recorded her own thoughts and feelings in reference to her Flora upon a sheet of paper placed in the first leaf of that work, which then supplied the place that painting had formerly occupied, but which, after the death of the Dean of Down, she had not continued, from the depressing effect she experienced in the absence of his constant sympathy and pleasure in that art. The tone and tenour of Mrs. Delany's feelings at this period, as expressed in poetry and prose, prove the new-born delight she felt in perfecting her invention when she found that she had still a friend who took as much interest in it as herself. The following lines were written in her own hand, and placed in the first volume of her work—

"PLANTS
Copied after Nature in Paper Mosaick, begun in the year 1774.

Hail to the happy hour ! when fancy led
My pensive mind this flow'ry path to tread ;
And gave me emulation to presume
With timid art to trace fair Nature's bloom :
To view with awe the great Creative power
That shines confess'd in the minutest flower ;
With wonder to pursue the glorious line,
And gratefully adore the Hand Divine !"

"The paper Mosaic work was begun in the 74th year of my age (which I at first only meant as an imitation of an hortus siccus) and as an *employment* and *amusement*, to supply the loss of *those* that had formerly been delightful to me ; but had lost their power of pleasing ; being depriv'd of that friend, whose partial approbation was my pride, and had stampt a value on them.

"Tho' the effect of this work was more than I expected, I thought that a *whim* of my own fancy might fondly beguile my judgment to think better of it than it deserved ; and I shou'd have dropp'd the attempt as vain, had not the Duchess Dowager of Portland look'd on it with favourable eyes. Her approbation was such a sanction to my undertaking, as made it appear of

consequence and gave me courage to go on with confidence
To *her* I owe the spirit of pursuing it with diligence and pleasure.
To *her* I owe more than I dare express, but my heart will ever
feel with the utmost gratitude, and tenderest affection, the honour
and delight I have enjoy'd in her most generous, steady, and
delicate friendship, for above forty years.

" MARY DELANY."

> " ——The same desires, the same ingenious arts
> Delighted both, we own'd and bless'd that power
> That join'd at once, our studies and our hearts."
>
> MASON, Elegy 3rd.

Bulstrode, 5th July, 1779.

On the same page Mrs. Delany had written the following
lines—

> Countless is vegetation's verdant brood
> As are the stars that stud yon cope of heaven ;
> To marshal all her tribes, in order'd file
> Generic or specific, might demand
> His science, wondrous Swede, whose ample mind
> Like ancient Tadmore's philosophic king,
> Stretch'd from the hyssop creeping on the wall
> To Lebanon's proud cedars.
>
> MASON'S 3rd. En. Garⁿ., p. 6.

The Dowager-Countess Gower to Mrs. Delany.

Bill Hill, 11th July, 79.

W^{en} I rec$\bar{e}$d yor letter I was ill and in bed wth y^e
añual hectical complaint I've had many years, but this
attack has been more severe y^n usual, and lasted longer ;
'tis now lessened, but not gone. Mrs Leveson was so
good as to tell you by letter this was y^e cause you did
not hear from me. Last post Mrs Bos. wrote her word
ye Dow. D^s of Portland had been ill, but was better ; I
hope soon to hear she is perfectly well. My ffamily has
left me in order to return wth increase. I had ye rarity

Mr Mason here for some hours; I c^d not profit much by it, being ill, wch think mov'd his compassion to take a *ffence* into his consideration and direct ye collouring wch ans^{rs} all expectation, and I much oblig'd; beyond my own hedge I know nothing of him or Mr Mountagu, my little ffriend passing well, by ye last ans^r I guess gone to Mrs Young.

I had a letter from Chaffont[1] (wch I c^d not read). We club'd to decipher it, in ab^t 3 days made out ye purport of it, wch was to congratulate mě on L . . y Lou. ffitz-patrick's[2] aproaching mariage, a person she knows I scarce know :—*so malapropos!*

I can't help being sorry for poor Tomy,[3] who has been put between 2 stools, and reap'd ye consequences; L . . y Mary says they'll "try at it again;" by grasping at all, they remind one of ye dog in ye ffable. The l . . y mother is a great schemer. I imagine this disapointm^t will keep her at home.

This I hope will find ye Dutch^s of P. perfectly well, wch to hear will be truly satisfactory to yor most faith-full.

---

[1] Chalfont, the residence of Admiral and Lady Mary Forbes.

[2] Lady Louisa Fitzpatrick, daughter of John, Earl of Upper Ossory, married, in July, 1779, William, 2nd Earl of Shelburne, who was created Marquis of Lansdowne in Nov., 1784.

[3] The Hon. Thomas Villiers, who, in 1776, became Lord Hyde, and in 1786, 2nd Earl of Clarendon ; and died, unmarried, in 1824.

Frederick Montagu, Esq., to Mrs. Delany.

Papplewick, July 15th, 1779.

A thousand thanks to you, my dear madam, for your very obliging and entertaining letter, which I should have answered sooner, but that I am but just returned from Yorkshire. I rejoyce much in the good account you give of yourself, and the very good account you give of the Duchess of Portland. The weather is delightful (I am afraid too hot for you,) and this place, if I dared say so, is in high beauty; roses, honeysuckles, and my hay in perfection, and no noxious vapours from politics. Immers'd as you think me in politics, I have been much concerned for Lord Suffolk, *not* for the *Secretary of State* and *Minister*, but for *Lady Andover's son*, whom I sincerely pitied. I was the beginning of this week at Aston.[1] Such a new seat—like a bower in Sr Philip Sydney's Arcadia : woodbines over your head, and minionet at your feet, and the third Book of the Garden upon trees—equal if not superior to the two former. I wished for you there, and I had almost presum'd to say that I wished the Duchess had been there too. Lord and Lady Strafford din'd here, and Lady Strafford[2] told me that Lady Bute had spent a day at Wentworth Castle[3] with her, and that she was in remarkable health and spirits; she added too that she did me the honour to mention me, of which I am not a little proud.

---

[1] The Rev. William Mason, the poet, was Rector of Aston, Yorkshire.

[2] William Wentworth, Earl of Strafford, married Lady Anne Campbell, daughter of John, Duke of Argyll. Lord Strafford died in 1791, when his honours devolved upon his cousin, in whom, eight years afterwards, they became extinct.

[3] Wentworth Castle, near Wakefield, in the county of York, the seat of the Wentworths, Earls of Strafford, now (1861) the property of Earl Fitzwilliam.

My accounts from Bill-Hill are very good. My mother has got a garden chair which suits her extremely. I shall be in town in Septemb^r, and ready to obey your commands and those of the Duchess of Portland, to whom I beg my most respectful compliments. I am with the greatest regard,

Yours most sincerely
FRED. MONTAGU.

Mrs. Delany to Miss Port, of Ilam.

Bulstrode, 1st Aug., 1779.

I shou'd long ago have perform'd my promise of writing to my dearest G.M.A., but have not had time ; but I always think *kindly* and *constantly* of my dear child, and know she does the same by me. Your mama wrote me word that you had spent some days at Calwich; which I am sure was very agreable to you, as well as to your uncle and aunt. Reading will not only make you wise, but good in a serious way; and supply you with infinite entertainment in a pleasant way. Reading will open your mind to every ingenious *art* and *work*, and by observing how amiable a well informed person makes herself and how much esteem'd, it will raise y^r desire of being the same, and make you take pains to deserve as much. I hope you don't neglect your geography, but have got by heart all y^u learnt in London, and go on wth the approbation and assistance of y^r valuable A.V.[1] You see that I look upon you *as still*

---

[1] "A. V."—Mrs. Vrankin, governess to Miss Port.

under my tuition, and it makes me feel at *the moment* as if you were *still* under my roof, wch I must always recollect with pleasure, and with gratitude to your dear mama for having spared you. I hope she is very well; I don't feel the least doubt of your affectionate attention to her, and nothing can contribute more to her health and happiness than seeing you and your dear brothers and sister (to whom I desire my love) perform your tasks well and cheerfully. I think I see *you* encouraging *them* in doing every thing they ought to do; and whispering to them gently to *forbear* doing any thing you think will not please those that claim your obedience as well as kindness. Pray tell me what book you are now reading? and where you have placed your bureau? But as writing a long letter (till your hand is more fix'd) is *not* right; I will be satisfied with any ans^{r} y^{r} mama will please to make for you.

And now I will tell you something of Bulstrode. Poor Smith continues very ill, and I am afraid there is but little chance of her recovery. The dear *Grace of Graces* is much better, and I am, I thank God, very well. I believe the Dss will go to Weymouth next week (you may look in y^{r} map for it), and I propose going to town in my way to Lady Bute's. I shall be sorry to leave this delightfull place; such woods, and groves, and lawns, and terasses not to be described! and all enliven'd with such a variety of animals! hardly to be enumerated: beautiful deer, oxen, cows, sheep of all countrys, bufalos, mouflons, horses, asses; all in their proper places. Then *hares* and *squirrels at every step you take,* so confident of their security that they hardly run away! The great lawn before the house is the nursery of all sorts of pheasants, pea fowl and Guinea fowl, beside interlopers of Bantam pidgeons ; and notwithstanding these numerous *familys* the lawn is kept with as much neatness as the drawing room : such is the diligence of their attendants and the diligent eye of their sovereign lady, who delights in having every thing in the best order, and is herself not only valuable to all that have the happiness of knowing her, but a blessing to *every creature* within her possessions. But what makes her so, my dearest child? *Not* her great fortune,—*not* her high station : but the *goodness of her heart,* the excellence of her principles, the sweetness of her manners, an understanding improved by reading and observation and her *many ingenious pursuits,* which are a constant source of entertainm[t] to herself and those she honours with her conversation. How happy must I be in such a friend! I hope I am not insensible of it, and as a proof, tho' nothing can compensate for her absence, I even wish her *gone* to Weymouth, as everybody says nothing will recover her strength and spirits so soon as that journey, and what adds to her health must add to mine!

T. behaves very well, and I hope will prove a good serv[t]. Mrs. Silvestre is still with Lady Sackville, but I believe will *not* stay long. Mrs. Montagu was pretty well when I heard last ; she is at Miss Julia Yonge's at East Barnet. Lady Stamford and the little lady charming well. Mr. and Mrs. Winnington and Miss Foley are at Cowley by Uxbridge ; I went last Thursday and made them an afternoon's visit ; and the Dss of Portland not being well eno' to go and see them, ask'd them to dinner last Friday, and they were much pleased: and now I think I have tired you. My kindest compliments to your papa and mama, your uncles and aunts, and remember me in a particular manner to your dear A.V.; who I hope enjoys her health.

The dear little Louisa begins to be her pupil, and I *see* her little forefinger pointing at P for *Pa*, and M for *Ma* already; what a delightfull little companion she will be for you! May you long long enjoy the exquisite happiness of true sisterly affection.

I am, my dearest G.M.A.,

Ever your affectionate aunt and humble serv^t,

M. DELANY.

The Dean of York and family are at Melton. I hope Mr. Foun^n bore the journey as well as cou'd be expected. I have not heard since his being there.

The Dowager-Countess Gower to Mrs. Delany.

Burlington Street, 2nd Aug., 79.

Expecting every day ye lawyers w^d call me here, I have put off from time to time writing to d^r Mrs Delany, hoping their call would be whilst you was in town; but yesterday was my earliest sumons, and on my arrival Mrs. Leveson told me you was gone. I hope much for yor health's sake, and y^t you found ye D^s of P. perfectly well; w^n ever her Grace takes a trip to Weymouth you won't forget me, or let *exoticks*, &c., &c., &c., put me out of yor remembrance. I've long wish'd poor Mrs. Simth better health, but am now more anxious ab^t it y^n ever. Sh^d she continue ill, can you think of none y^t can officiate for her?

Wth regret you may sopose I left Bill Hill, wⁿ I tell you I left 13 beautiful flowers on ye magnolia's, most of 'em quite expanded. I've brought to town a layer I took up last May for L. .y Ashburnham;[1] it has one large bloom upon it not quite blown. I wish I c^d have brought her health. She has not been well enough to venture to Sussex wth her ffamily. Thus farr I had wrote on Saturday; was to go where I expected news, deferr'd sealing; wⁿ I came home 'twas too late to add; w^t I heard was very extrodinary, at least to country ears. L. .y Derby[2] is in London, ye gayest person in it; her mother[3] fonder of her yⁿ ever; says ye D. of Argyle has often wrote to desire her to come to Scotland, but she cañot leave L. .y Derby. *Betty Guñing* has a fine spirit! L. .y Leonora Waldegrave[4] has put on weeds for ye late D. of Ancaster. She and her mother[5] say she was to have been mañied to him in two days, if he had not fallen ill.[6] She wrote to ye Dow. Dutchess[7] to acquaint her of this, and to desire her permission to go into mourning; was ans^d she "knew not of such an

---

[1] Elizabeth, daughter and co-heiress of Alderman Crawley, married, June 28, 1756, John, 2nd Earl of Ashburnham.

[2] Elizabeth, only daughter of James, 6th Duke of Hamilton, married, June 23rd, 1774, Edward, 12th Earl of Derby.

[3] The beautiful Gunning, then widow of James, 6th Duke of Hamilton, and wife of John, 5th Duke of Argyll.

[4] Qy. Elizabeth Laura, eldest daughter of James, 2nd Earl Waldegrave.

[5] Maria, illegitimate daughter of the Hon. Sir Edward Walpole, widow of James, 2nd Earl Waldegrave, and afterwards wife of H.R.H. William Henry, Duke of Gloucester.

[6] Robert Bertie, 4th Duke of Ancaster, died unmarried, July 8th, 1779.

[7] Mary, daughter of Thomas Panton, Esq., widow of Peregrine Bertie, 3rd Duke of Ancaster.

intended maȓiage, but she *had her leave* to go into mourning." L. .y Leon. also desir'd a lock of her hair wch she had given his Grace might be return'd, and wth it a lock of his. To write such stuff to ye Dutchess of Ancaster at a time w^n she must be under ye deepest affliction I look upon as ye heigth of cruelty, ye motive vanity, for it can ans^r no other purpose.

This age is full of prodigies. I shall return to my quiet retreat next Wednesday; bless myself y^t I have one, and please myself wth ye hope of seeing you there soon.

The Hon. Mrs. Boscawen to Mrs. Delany.

Glan Villa. Monday night, 2nd Aug., 1779.

It has been a charming day, and the field below my garden has exhibited a busy scene of haymakers, and a gratefull smell of hay. I have only to tell you that we are well all but poor Keeble, who has kept her bed with a violent bilious cholick and obstruction for several days ; but the poor creature is now easier, I thank God, and was up to-day.

Miss Sayer presenting her respects desires also to express much gratitude for your kindness to her. She is retir'd to rest ; but I promis'd I wou'd say a great deal for her. She is indeed very sensible of your goodness to her, and much honour'd by it. We went yesterday to visit Mrs. Mellish, but she was not at home. We have also seen Mrs. Williams, who lamented your departure very much, and the cause still more. She heard from young Mr. Maitland's family that he was going to Scotland to take leave of his friends before he proceeded

to Ireland to his regm^t, and from thence to Quebec.
Mrs. Williams ask'd if Miss Y. was going too, was
answer'd no; that she had been so obliging indeed to say
she "lik'd travelling," but that Mr. W. cou'd not think
of her venturing upon such a journey and voyage! It
seem'd, therefore, doubtful to Mrs. Williams whether
she would now engage in the voyage of matrimony. I
met Miss Young last night as I was going to Mrs.
Mellish's. She seem'd very chearfull.

I rejoyce to hear the Duchess of Portland is well, and
hope my old friend "David Jones" will keep her so.
(I dare say you know that sailors call the sea David
Jones). Good night, my dearest madam. On Saturday
I was prevented writing by the arrival of Mrs. Mostyn
with Lady Mary Kerr,[1] and before they departed came
Mr. and Mrs. Crewe. More good wishes, more affections,
attend you than I can express either morning, noon, or
night. Pray commend me kindly to Mrs. Sandford.
Mrs. Leveson wrote me word of the marriage of an amiable and accomplished lady (whom she was "sure I
wish'd well to,") *as settled*, but *not* to take place till
Septr or October.

You may be sure I have taken care of Mrs. Williams'
letter. I wou'd have carry'd it myself to-day, but that
my g. sons have got my chaise to Westminster. I left
Miss Lambard very well last Friday. She was happy to
hear a good account of your health. I invited my
afflicted cousin, Miss Boone: the loss of her mother I
have much lamented!

---

[1] Lady Mary Kerr, daughter of William, 5th Marquis of Lothian. She
married, 8th Dec., 1788, General the Hon. Frederick St. John, second son of
Frederick, 2nd Viscount Bolingbroke, and died 6th Feb., 1791.

God bless you, my dear friend. Present my best respects to the Duchess, and believe me always most faithfully and affect^ly yours,

F. BOSCAWEN.

Bulstrode, 9th Aug., 1779.

Providence always supports us under all its dispensations, and sends us comfort in the midst of our sorrows; *that* dependence is a never-failing one, and *that* I have experienced in the course of very near 4 score years! and I hope you will do the same with as much cheerfulness of spirit.

I thank God, I am pure well, but much perplexed about Smith, convinced it is quite necessary for me to have a servant that I need not spare when I want her services; and as necessary that she, poor creature, should be free from all care but "*the one thing needful.*"

Smith has lived with me 34 years, and, bating human frailties, wch no one is without, has been a *most excellent servant*, and loves me most sincerely.

There is a person, I believe, you saw (Mrs. Rea) recommended by Mrs. Sandford, who I wanted to be with *G. M. A.* when she was with me, that were she disengaged I should wish to have, and, by all accounts, is just what I want; and I heard she was going to quit her place: so I shall enquire after her, for I am very unwilling to take a perfect stranger about me.

I have got Mary Butcher here; the Dss made me send for her last Thursday to assist Smith to pack up.

Lady Weymouth and her 4 eldest children came here

on Tuesday, and staid till Friday. Many enquiries after my dear little Mary. The enclosed is a *minuet* just arrived *from France*.

You remember Madame de Viry[1] (Miss Speed that was). They were banished for an indiscreet correspondence of Count Viry's, to one of his Terres. No small punishment I believe to my lady, who loved rolling in the great world (she is of an enormous size). But what do you think (they say) is her principal amusement? Why, milking 30 cows *all herself!* Of *old* the *greatest ladies* in their land *fed their sheep* and *milk'd their goats*; but the *bon tons* have other ways of killing old father Time; happy *if* as innocently!

Mrs. Cavendish is dead; has left ye greatest part of her estate to the Duke of Devonshire; that I believe was settled before she died between them. Latimers (in this neighbourhood) and all her curiosities to Lord George Cavendish,[2] the Duke's youngest bro[r]. A snuff-box and a seal or two to the Dr Dss Portlánd, wch were what she had given her.

Poor Mr. Rice's[3] death will be great sorrow to all connected with him; he was a very good man. Lady Cecil Rice and his good mother will be inconsolable; but as I only saw it in the news I have some hope it may not be true.

---

[1] Count Virey, son of the Sardinian Minister in England, married, in 1760, Miss Speed, niece of Lady Cobham. He was afterwards Ambassador in France.

[2] Lord George Augustus Henry Cavendish, third son of William, 4th Duke of Devonshire: born 31st March, 1754; created, in 1831, Earl of Burlington and Baron Cavendish. Latimers now (1861) belongs to his fourth son, Charles, Baron Chesham.

[3] George Rice, Esq., who married Lady Cecil Talbot; died 3rd Aug., 1779.

Lady Suffolk[1] brought to bed of a son.

I am just come to town (Tuesday). Mrs. Leveson and her 3rd son very well; so, I may drink caudle.

Lady Gower, Mrs. Boscawen, Lady Wallingford, Mrs. Vesey in town; so I shall not want company. I am well, tho' low with turning my back to Bulstrode. A thought has just come into my head that if I can bring it about will make me easier about Smith. Mrs. Blackburn (now very infirm) but well eno' to be a comfort to Smith, has a good house in the Haymarket with a very good sort of woman, who has more lodgers. They furnish their own rooms, and provide themselves with food and give £8 a year. If there is a spare room, and Smith will settle in it, I will make her income up to twenty pound a year, and give her things towards furnishing her room. She shall still be my serv[t], and make my caps, and do any work she can s[d] it please God she s[d] grow better; she is very bad, but suffers with great patience.

The Countess of Bute to Mrs. Delany.

Luton Park, Aug. 10th, 1779.

My dear Mrs. Delany is very obliging in her congratulations on Lady Macartney's[2] arrival; which indeed is

---

[1] The widowed Countess of Suffolk was confined of a son on the 8th of Aug., 1778, who died two days afterwards.

[2] Jane, second daughter of the Earl and Countess of Bute, married, Feb. 1st, 1768, Sir George, afterwards Earl, Macartney. She died (his widow) Feb. 28th, 1828. Lady Macartney had apparently been with her husband in the island of Grenada, of which he was appointed Governor in 1775; and on his surrendering himself a prisoner, in July, 1779, to the French under the Count D'Estaing, to have returned alone to England.

a very great happiness for us; and I have the pleasure to see her well, except the fatigue that must attend so long a voyage, with all the disagreable circumstances she has experienced; but she has recovered so much in the short time since her landing, I hope she will soon be quite restored. I am sorry our dear friend has such bad weather for her journey to Weymouth; and much grieved to find there is any doubt of your being able to give us the happiness of seeing you here; but still hope, if it be possible to make it convenient, you will remember how great a favour you would do us. Caroline[1] *is here;* and Lady Macartney is to come; *both* will be *overjoy'd* to see you, as indeed will *the whole family.* I wish extremely I had happened to be in London when you came there; but my stay there was very short, being obliged to go to Laleham to see Lady M. Lowther,[2] who is very much indisposed, in a sort of way that requires great care and attention, having a sort of hectic feavour upon her, that keeps her so weak she is not able to come here. Thus, my dear madam, you see, in a numerous family it is *seldom* one can expect any joy without a considerable drawback. Adieu. I hope to hear from you soon—and am ever

Most sincerely yours,
M. W. BUTE.

---

[1] Caroline, 5th daughter of the Earl and Countess of Bute, m., Dec. 1st, 1777, the Hon. John Dawson, eldest son of Viscount Carlow, and afterwards Earl of Portarlington. She died Jan. 20, 1813.

[2] Mary, eldest daughter of the Earl and Countess of Bute, married Sir James Lowther, Bart., created Earl of Lonsdale in 1784.

The Countess of Bute to Mrs. Delany.

Luton Park, Aug. 17th, 1779.

I am as much disappointed by your want of a servant, my dear Mrs. Delany, as you can be, and am sure *all* my family would be happy to give you every attendance ; but will not say more on the subject, knowing full how disagreeable it is to be without one's own servant. I am the more sorry for this circumstance, from the fineness of the weather, which makes London the more intolerable, and wou'd, I believe, render this place both wholesome and pleasant; however, I *still hope* if you *can* make us happy with your company, you *will* have the goodness to come. I hope the Duchess is reaping benefit from the sea air, which has the property of being cooler in hot weather and milder in cold than any other. I have nothing new to tell you, but must add the kindest comp^s of all here, and beg you to believe me,

Most sincerely and affectionately,

M. W. BUTE.

The Hon. Mrs. Boscawen to Mrs. Delany.

Audley Street, 26th Aug., 1779.

Whether the day produces any news or not, I will not fail to send my dear friend this frank'd cover, as it contains a little word from Mrs. Walsingham, to whom I deliver'd your message, and she wou'd have been *very* glad to have seen you : however, she had got Lady

Amhurst, and afterwards came in Lord Denbigh,[1] his lady being come to visit Lady Blandford,[2] who is now suppos'd to be dying in good earnest. She will not take any remedy or physick whatever, but some wou'd say *that* gives her a *good* chance for *escaping* once more, but for my part I follow good advice, and give a place to the physician, for the Lord hath created him! I had the satisfaction to hear of you, my dear madam, upon the road, and that you had atchiev'd part of your journey; for yesterday evening Mr. and Mrs. Dayrolles made a visit to Mrs. Leveson, and told me they met you at Stanes. Methinks you were lucky, my dear madam, to find Lady Gower alone; I am extremely glad to hear her ladyship is so perfectly well, as Mrs. Dayrolles tells me she is. Please to present my respects to her, and tell her that I am no longer engross'd by our grandson Johnny, but that Mr. Edward has made me sensible of all his charms; the little one[3] promises to be a very fine creature.

My dear madam, Mr. Leveson told us last night that they had cut down the trees at Mount Edgecumbe for an *abbatis*. The Duchess of Portland will lament them, as I do most piteously, the *finest* beeches, the *loveliest old oaks*, that Sir Francis Drake and Sir Walter Raleigh had seen perhaps; and these have their foes, and are now wash'd by the briny wave. O sad; O cruel war! How many French

---

[1] Basil Fielding, 6th Earl of Denbigh, married, April 12th, 1757, Mary, third daughter and coheiress of Sir John Bruce Cotton, Bart.

[2] Maria Catharina, Marchioness of Blandford, died in Sept., 1779, aged 96. She was the daughter of Peter de Yong, and sister to Isabella, Countess of Denbigh, and married, April 25th, 1729, to William, Marquis of Blandford, who died Aug. 24th, 1731.

William Leveson Gower, born in 1779.

and Spanish noblemen have been hospitably and nobly entertain'd at that delightfull place, and how much better a use that is to make of it than to form *batteries* to *blow off their heads!* The Thetis is come in from Lisbon, and spoke with Sr C. Hardy,[1] 20 leagues south of Scilly, the Marlboro' and the Ramilies with the fleet: but your intelligence of the safety of ye Ardent was erroneous I fear.

Adieu, my dear friend; pray let me hear from you soon. I sent to poor Mrs. Montagu this morning. She sends me word she is very poorly, and I sent my young maid to Mrs. Smith, because she was known to her last year at Bulstrode and Bill Hill. She brings word that Mrs. Smith was in bed, so that she cou'd not see her.

Mrs. Leveson is so perfectly well, that I purpose to go out of town next week, perhaps not till after the christening, to see if I can be of use. I have a letter from my son to-day, who has mov'd his camp towards the sea. *All* our coasts *tremble.* How *little* did that *use* to be the case, but " how are the mighty fallen!"

The Valiant is order'd out again immediately, so I do not lose my companions as I was threaten'd. I hope we shall have *more prizes.* I fancy the last will furnish the new house de fond en comble! And I wou'd venture to *give* the Capt. £1000 for his share.

Lady Gower has wrote to us both lately, and seems in very good spirits. My best respects wait on the Duchess. Mrs. L. wou'd say a great deal, if she were not at the bottom of ye garden.

Ever y^r affectionate, faithfull, and obliged,

F. B.

---

[1] Sir Charles Hardy commanded the Channel Fleet in 1779, and died the same year at Spithead.

The Hon. Mrs. Boscawen to Mrs. Delany.

Glan Villa, ye 1st Sept., (*massacre des perdrix*,) 1779.

I hope, my dear madam, you have not suffer'd by the heat of the past four days, but have sat very quiet in your cool north chamber. London was red hot, and I am come hither to breathe a little fresh air; it is much cooler to day, wch is a blessing.

My dear friend, I do not now condole with you on *the loss* of your faithfull servant;[1] that loss is not recent, for in the state she was in, poor woman, her recovery was impossible; indeed, you *had given her up,* nor cou'd wish to prolong her suffering state. She was interr'd last night I find. I think it is the time for these losses. I was complaining to our friend the Dean of Gloster (who came to visit me) of the great one *I had had;* he answer'd it " cou'd not be more irreparable than his," in a housekeeper lately dead of a fever, who had liv'd with him 20 years, and was the worthiest, best, faithfullest servant imaginable, knowing all his ways, all his friends, and providing everything so cleverly, with so much capacity, activity; in short, he is *undone*—as *I am* for poor Sleeve, (whom I see methinks and hear at every corner of this cottage). Friday I purpose to set out for Kent, and beg, dear madam, I may have the pleasure to hear from you. Please to direct to his Grace the Duke of Beaufort, Cox Heath Camp, Kent.

---

[1] Mrs. Smith, who had lived with Mrs. Delany soon after she went to Delville.

Young Lady King [1] was a great fortune, but does *not* certainly belong to the great world, and that is all the information I can give you. I heard no news last night. When there is any, I dare say Mrs. Leveson will take care to inform Lady Gower. I am glad to hear her ladyship is well, and in good spirits; for my part I can tremble like an aspin leaf when I think of invasions, combined fleets; superiority to ours; Ireland especially: but I endeavour to lay hold of ye anchor on which you rest! I hope your dearest Duchess is well. Present my respects to Lady Gower. Accept my best wishes, dear madam, and believe me always most affect^{ly} yours,

F. BOSCAWEN.

The trees cut at Mt. Edgecùmbe are not of any great consequence.

Mrs. Delany to Mrs. Port, of Ilam.

Bill Hill, 2nd Sept., 1779.

MY DEAREST MARY,

I have just receiv'd your letter, and must scratch a few lines from hence, as I am sure you wish to know how I do after the *shock* of losing my old and faithful servant; for such *it was*, tho' expected, and rather to be wished for than not. There is a natural gratitude in the human mind, that makes one for a time recollect the good we have received, and rises above any inconvenience that might have sometimes mixed with many useful qualities; but I find I have suffered for some time past

---

[1] Peter, 6th Lord King, married, Nov. 24, 1774, Charlotte, daughter of Edward Tredcroft, of Horsham, Esq. This Lord King succeeded his father, April 24th, 1779; his mother survived until June, 1784.

more on *her* account than *my own*, for now that her sufferings are over, and I have had some days recollection, I find I am *much relieved*, and more composed than for some months past. Poor Smith was buried last Monday; it was her request to be buried as near as possible to her sister Hawkins. I could not propose to her in her last illness giving up her accounts or keys; and therefore it is necessary for me to go to town before I go to Bulstrode. I shall be glad to have that melancholy work over, that I may shake off as soon as possible the effects of it, and meet my dear friend cheerfully.

I was happy with a letter from Court, with a good acc^t of all my dear nephews and nieces.

Burchel is an excellent attendant as far as I have experienced, and tho' not altogether the servant I want is a very agreable servant. I wrote you word I had engaged Lydia Rea.

The Hon. Mrs. Boscawen to Mrs. Delany.

Sept., 1779.

Yes, indeed, my dear madam, I was anxious to know how you did after y^r melancholy employm^t, but especially I wanted to hear of a restoration to Bulstrode, to friendship, to peace, to everything that can best suit and agree with your mind and body. You were just setting out when you were so kind to write to me. Will not the same kindness dictate 3 lines the day after you arrive? I hope so, and shall look sharp into his Grace's post to-morrow. I promise myself the great pleasure to hear the Duchess of Portland will return in charming

health and spirits after so long a visit to her favourite
" *David Jones* " (so the sailors call the sea), for he is a
good physician, but methinks he was more affairé than
her Grace wou'd have chose, and had certain powerfull
but most unwelcome guests intruded upon him that put
him quite out of countenance, thank God they have retir'd without having done any mischief; but oh, my
dear madam, what a blaze of martial glory *en pure perte*,
at Grenada ![1] How nobly did our fleet behave! and in
hopes of their relief what a noble stand did Ld. Maccartney make. The five ships that cou'd get up fought
like—Englishmen, and so as hardly ever to have been
surpass'd in the glorious annals of our navy; none were
in fault. Adm¹ Byron[2] has not a speck after all our *infamous newspapers*; he and Barrington[3] have never had the
least disagreement, and the latter professes to admire,
respect, and love, his commander. What pity that all
this combining shou'd yet have been ineffectual for want
of the means, and that our enemy shou'd be so much

---

[1] Alluding to the loss of Grenada, one of the Caribbee islands, which was
originally taken by the English from the French in 1762, retaken by the
French in 1779, and restored to the English in 1783. Lord Macartney was
appointed Governor of the island in 1775, and in July, 1779, was obliged to
surrender at discretion to the Count d'Estaing, and was sent as a prisoner to
France.

[2] Admiral the Hon. John Byron, 2nd son of William, 4th Baron Byron.
He was a midshipman on board the " Wager " in Lord Anson's circum-
navigating squadron, and cast away upon a desolate island in the South Seas,
where he went through great hardships for five years. He afterwards distinguished himself in his profession. He married Sophia, daughter of John
Trevannion, of Carhays, Esq., in Cornwall, and died in 1786. Byron, the
poet, was his grandson.

[3] The Hon. Samuel Barrington, Admiral of the White, a distinguished naval
commander, was the fourth son of John, 1st Viscount Barrington, brother of
William, 2nd Viscount ; and of Daines Barrington, the eminent naturalist,
and Shute Barrington, Bishop of Durham. The Admiral died unmarried,
Aug. 16, 1800.

superior in force that were inferior in valour; that Ld Maccartney, so long threaten'd, shou'd have been left so destitute; but, as you say, public cares must be felt in every place, and they proceed too from every quarter. If Ireland shou'd be attack'd; Genl Maxwell is encamp'd with 2 regi^{ts} and one field piece equally à portée of Cork and Waterford and equally able to defend both—*that is neither*, I shou'd suppose! My son is in that camp under no apprehensions, and quite easy. Not so his mother, I have my own share of apprehensions and his too (if indeed any belong to a brave lad of 21[1]). Here we have an extended camp of 11,000 men; 'tis wonderfull to see what the militia are; but I end all this warlike dissertation with heartily joining in your wish for peace—*peace at any rate*. And now, dear madam, there is a call for all letters, and I have hardly time to present my respects to the Duchess or to tell you how much I am y^r

Faithfull and affectionate servant,

F. Boscawen.

The Dss of Beaufort wou'd say a great deal if she knew I were writing to Bulstrode. We have here a friend of Mr. Lightfoot's, Mr. Price, the keeper of the Bodleian Library, a very pleasant guest.

---

[1] George Evelyn Boscawen, 3rd Viscount Falmouth, was born May 6th, 1758. This fact proves the present letter to have been written in 1779. The loss of Granada in 1779, and the calling out of the British Militia in the same year, likewise prove the date.

The Dowager-Countess Gower to Mrs. Delany.

Bill Hill, 8th Sept., 79.

The horses return'd safe and well and brought satisfactory news as farr as Salt Hill, and yesterday ye post
ye intelligable pot hooks. Yo^r morning, I presume, was
pleasantly spent, from ye place its self and ye owner,
w^m, I'm told, has amusing talents, and you w^d not have
felt tir'd had not yor journey ended in St James's Place,
business I hope will dissipate ye affects. I pass'd last
night some time (as usual) in ye double seat, but so un-
couth it seem'd, wanting ye chearfull converse I had been
us'd too. NB. oranges, &c., forgot, unpardonable in me,
who had given my opinion y^t y^e *heigth* of politeness was
attention! you'll never again think me pollish'd in y^e
least degree. Why did you not remind me? The
oranges I've an op̄ortunity of sending I hope before you
leave London ; and tho' I can averr I thought of nothing
but you and yor journey, yet *forgot* my mite to alleviate
it, wonderfull and *innumerable* are ye defects in *human
nature!*

I wish to hear of some amendm^t in poor Mrs. Mountagu's health, for her sake and her ffriends, knowing
'twill add hap̄iness to you, d^r madam, as also to yor
faithfull,

M. G.

The Hon. Mrs. Boscawen to Mrs. Delany.

Hunton, yᵉ 21 Sept., 79.

I was very impatient for my 3 lines, dearest madam, and began to count the days—at length they came with interest, and gave me most sincere pleasure. The good health which the Duchess has broᵗ from Weymᵒ will I hope continue and even increase at Bulstrode. I am very glad my old friend Davy Jones maintains his character with her Grace, he cou'd not have oblig'd me more ! Mrs Leveson tho' likely to hear *most of one side* yet cou'd not fail of good intelligence from the sea. She is now at Bill Hill with my lady, who is in perfect health, and who has return'd to her favourite exercise of riding. Mr. Leveson is gone into Suffolk. From Charles Street I got my intelligence ; that wᶜʰ we have here in camp is reckon'd fort sujet à caution ; and as to the newspapers they are indeed full of absolute falsities. I read this summer a very circumstantial accᵗ of a duel between 2 officers in the Monmonth Fuzileers (wᶜʰ is the D. of Beaufort's Regiᵗ) in wᶜʰ one was kill'd and the other (related to him) almost distracted. I wonder'd my dauʳ had never nam'd such a calamity in her letters, but concluded it was so painfull to her that she avoided speaking of it; however, I cou'd not help (when I came here) asking after the *miserable survivor*, and was agreeably surpriz'd to find the whole a *fiction*, no duel has ever been in the Monmouth, nor quarrel, nor so much as the names of the combatants to be found in the whole corps. Such, and so authentic *are newspapers!*

We have sent you from this camp two candidates for the favour of the freeholders of Bucks. One, viz., Mr.

2 H 2

Tom Grenville,[1] was here as aid-de-camp to General Fraser;[2] and the other, Mr. Hampden,[3] Major to the Bucks militia here encamp'd. I have not seen any advertisem^t on the part of the latter. That of the former is so *fine* that a plain farmer will be at a loss what to make of it I shou'd think.

Indeed I pity Lady Macartney![4] after all her terrors and hair-bredth 'scapes to have such a lasting sorrow and anxiety. Yet I trust her lord is very safe and very politely treated in the hands of the French.[5] *My* intelligence said Granada was shamefully neglected from hence, and it is very true that Ad^l Barrington's powder was bad (as the newspapers mention), for while the balls of the French pierc'd the sides of his ship, his fell short of them, owing to the badness of his powder. A terrible situation! Enfin, I am very much for a bad peace that I hear talk'd of, persuaded that it is at least better than a *bad* war, and *such* we must esteem this where nothing succeeds, for even in the East Indies there has been a defeat (of the Company's forces) not unlike that of Burgoyne. As to Sr Charles Hardy's beating the French,

---

[1] Thomas, second son of the well-known George Grenville, and brother of George, 2nd Earl Temple and 1st Marquis of Buckingham, succeeded that brother in the representation of the county of Bucks in the year 1779.

[2] General Simon Fraser, once a partisan of the Stuarts, and subsequently a distinguished officer in the British army. He served in America and in Portugal. He married Catherine, daughter of John Bristow, Esq., M.P., and died in 1782.

[3] Of Hampden, Bucks.

[4] Lady Jane Stuart, 2nd daughter of the Earl and Countess of Bute, married, Feb. 1st, 1768, Sir George Macartney, afterwards created a Knight of the Bath, a Baron and an Earl.

[5] Alluding to Lord Macartney being then a prisoner of war. He was soon afterwards exchanged, and returned to England.

I own I am *very glad* he did *not try,* for I have always been taught to think that 2 to 1 was fearfull odds.

You see, my dear friend I take to discoursing instead of *informing,* wch is by no means the same thing; but now here is Lady Harriet[1] who says, "Granmama, shall I read my lesson to you?" She is the Duchess of Portland's god-daughter, and one of the finest broad-fac'd lasses I ever saw, with a great rose on each cheek and fine laughing eyes. When she is very good her reward is to come to my room.

Be pleas'd to write to me at your leisure, and direct your next to London or Colne Hatch, where I shall be settled next week,

F. BOSCAWEN.

I am afraid Mrs. Walsingham is not well yet. If you see her be pleased to tell me. The Duchess of Beaufort is much yours; she desires her respectfull compliments to the Duchess. We have been to visit the Duke in his tent this morning, but it was *very cold* and *uncomfortable.*

Mrs. Delany to the Viscountess Andover.

Bulstrode, 9th Oct., 1779.

MY DEAREST MADAM,

I know that dear Lady Andover makes allowances for all my infirmities of body and mind, or I should (at least) take up this whole page in apologies for my long, very long, taciturnity; so, waving what is past, I will lay hold of more recent occurrences, and tell your lady-

---

[1] Lady Harriet Somerset, youngest daughter of Henry, 5th Duke of Beaufort. She married, in 1804, Col. Mitchell, and died 1st June, 1855.

ship what I know will be pleasant and acceptable : in the first place I can give it under my hand, that the Dss D^r of Portland is charming well; and at this moment *charming* with her peculiar address General Paoli, an Italian nobleman *Stat :—(something* I can't recollect); Monsr Gentille, Monsr Poli, Mr. Boswell, who wrote the account of Corsica. They all came clattering here before 12 o'clock (what an undue hour for *her Grace !*[1]) They have devour'd a quantity of breakfast, and now they are all dispatch'd into the garden, &c., conducted by Mr. Yeats and Mr. Lightfoot. Before they sat down to breakfast, who shou'd arrive but Lady Weymouth, four of her daughters, Lord Titchfield, and Master G. Thynne— only for a morning visit; but the Corsican hero and his train stay dinner; and I have stolen down to finish this letter, but perhaps may finish it in London. You may, my dear Lady Andover, very naturally think that so useless a member of society as I am, *might* continue in my chamb^r and be still, knowing my own deficiencies ! I pleaded hard, without success, not to produce myself, but our dear friend will show all her rusty coins, as well as her more polish'd rarities; and I have such a tale to tell you of my exhibition on Wednesday se'night as may well astonish you, considering I am (*as it were*) some years older than I was last year.

A summons came from Windsor to the Dss Dr Portland to come that evening to the Queen's Lodge, and—to "bring Mrs. Delany with her :" the summons was obey'd to a minute, we were there at seven o'clock;

---

[1] "*An undue hour for her Grace.*"—The Duchess of Portland kept very late hours in the latter part of her life. She had two readers, and used to be read to after she was in bed, and did not begin to sleep till morning.

unfortunately, when we stop'd at the Lodge it rain'd
violently, and her Grace (muffled up with her *triple*
drapery) was, on stepping into the door, taken by the
hand by his Majesty (before she could shake off her
involucrums), who laid his commands on the Bishop of
Litchfield to take care of me. Thus honourably conducted we were led into the drawing-room to the Queen;
the ladies with her were Lady Holderness, Lady Weymouth, Lady C. Finch, Lady Boston,[1] Lady Courtown;[2]
and surrounded with her royal offspring. To tell you
all the particulars of their gracious manners, and the
agreableness of the evening, and the delightful and
uncommon scene of *royal domestick* felicity—of the sweet
musick and of *my flirtations*—would be rather too much
for a letter, and must be postpon'd for a winter tale in
S[t]. James's Place, where I hope for the happyness of
seeing my dear Elford friends much and often.

10 Oct.

Here my pen was stop'd, my letter shuffled into
the desk, and blotted, being call'd to the company
above stairs. The *exotics* all return'd from their tour;
such *an uproar of transports* at what they had seen, and
what they heard not to be equall'd but by *Turaco* and
Lory, who set up their throats and join'd in the chorus;
but, to give them their due, they were worthy of the
high and excellent entertainment they receiv'd, and they
seem'd as sensible of the perfections of the soverein of
the place as of her possessions; and we all parted very

---

[1] Christiana, only daughter of Paul Methuen, Esq., married, 15th May, 1775,
Frederick, 2nd Baron Boston.

[2] Mary, daughter and coheiress of Richard Powys, Esq., married, 16th April,
1762, James, 2nd Earl of Courtown.

good friends. At seven o'clock they return'd to London, and the word was given to have all the *comfortable litters* resettled, and we finish'd the even^g with our usual employments.

The Dss's most affectionate compliments to dear Lady Andover and Miss How^d, to whom I beg mine. To-morrow a little busyness carries us to town for a few days. In every place I am, with the truest respect and affection,

Your lady^{ps} most obed^t, hum^{ble} ser^t,

M. DELANY.

If Lady Suffolk is at Elford may I beg my respects.

Mrs. Delany to Miss Port, of Ilam.

Bulstrode, 10th Oct., 1779.

MY DEAR CHILD,

Tho' I have been a great while answering the favour and pleasure of your letter, I assure you it was very acceptable ; the account of your employments, and the satisfaction you take in them, make me very happy ; *nothing* can be obtained *without application,* and with that you may make yourself mistress of every accomplishment *necessary* for you to possess ; and I hope to *see* you *write, hear* you *read, and speak* as well as I wish you to do ; as a good foundation will make everything easy and pleasant to you : and I cannot leave out of *my catalogue of necessaries* that of *working plain work well,* and *when* you have gained these points they will entitle you to accomplishments as opportunity serves, and every gratification of ingenuity you can wish to improve. In my last letter to your dear mama, I began an account of the honours I received at the Queen's Lodge, Windsor, on Wednesday 29th of Sepr (Princess Royal's birthday,) but I don't remember where I left off, and am afraid I may repeat what I have already written; but that must take its chance.

The King met the Duchess Dowr of Portland at the door; he handed the Duchess, and the Bishop of Litchfield handed me, into the drawing-room, where the Queen stood attended by all her royal family, *twelve* in number (the 13th, Prince William Henry, you know, is with the fleet); the ladies there were Lady Holderness, Lady Weymouth, Lady Charlotte Finch, your friend Lady Boston, Lady Courtown; all the gentlemen and ladies belonging to the royal family were in the concert-room, which we passed thro'. The Queen sat down at the upper end of the drawing-room, opposite to the door of the concert-room, which was kept open; the Duchess Dowager of Portland sat on the right side of her Majesty, and the rest of the ladies were seated on each side of her; except *Princess Royal* and Lady C. Finch, as the Queen ordered her Royal Highness to "sit by me and to entertain me, and Lady Charlotte Finch" and I was placed between them.

The Queen was dress'd in an embroider'd lutestring; Princess Royal in deep orange or scarlet, I could not by candlelight distinguish which; Princess Augusta in pink; Princess Elizabeth in blue. These were all in robes without aprons. Princess Mary (a most sweet child) was in cherry-colour'd tabby, with silver leading strings; she is about four years old; she cou'd not remember my name, but, making me a very low curtsey,

she said, " *How do you do, Duchess of Portland's friend;
and how does your little niece do. I wish you had brought
her.*" The King carried about in his arms by turns
Princess Sophia, and the last prince, Octavius; so called
being the 8ᵗʰ son. I never saw more lovely children;
nor a more pleasing sight than the King's fondness for
them, and the Queen's; for they seem to have but *one
mind,* and that is to make everything easy and happy
about them. The King brought in his arms the little
Octavius prince to me, who held out his hand to play
with me, which, on my taking the liberty to kiss, his
M. made him kiss my cheek. We had a charming concert of vocal and instrumental music; but no ladies except
those I have named came into the 2ᵈ drawing-room, nor
any of the gentlemen; they staid in the concert-room.
The King and the rest of the royal family came backwards and forwards, and I can't tell you how gracious
they all were, they talk'd to me a great deal by turns.
When any favourite song was sung, the Queen, attended
by her ladies, went and stood at the door of the concert-
room, and a chair was ordered to be placed at the door
for the Duchess of Portland, when Prince Ernest (about
9 years old) carried a chair so large he could hardly lift
it, and placed it by the Duchess for me to sit by her.
We staid till past 11; came home by a charming moon;
did not sup till past 12, nor in bed till *two*. Now don't
you think, my dearest G. M. A., that A. D. was a great
rake? But the whole affair was so easy and so pleasant
(as I did not stand a quarter of an hour) that I was very
little fatigued, and slept better than usual.

I begun this letter at Bulstrode, and have proceeded
with it in St. James's Place, where I always recollect the

pleasure I had in my dear little girl's company, and everybody remembers her pretty, modest behaviour. A very wise man says that "Praise does a *wise man good*, but a fool *harm;*" it raises in a good mind a desire of being worthy of that praise, but a *simpleton* will think himself good enough, and sit down contented, without taking pains to be either wiser and better. I am come to town to bring Mrs. Anne Burchell, and to take back Mrs. Lydia Ray, who I expect in town this evening. The *Duchess of Portland,* who sends her love to her "sweet little Mary," has some business for two or three days in town; to-morrow we propose breakfasting at Lord Mansfield's, at Kenwood, and, please God, return to Bulstrode on Thursday. *She* desires me to tell you she has found at her grotto some shells, the same as that you gave her, and found on Bunster *a left-handed tooth'd turbo;* but yours is placed in the choice cabinet.

I had a letter yesterday from Lady Sackville, to tell me Mrs. Silvestre did *not suit her;* but if (as she heard I did) I wanted a servant she "might *do for me;*" she has left my neighbourhood and taken a house in Clarges Street.

I hope your dear mama, as I have written so long a letter to you, will take her share of it, and not expect a letter before this day se'night, as I fear it will not be in my power to write sooner; and after the account I have given of *my exploits,* she may conclude I am well.

Lady Spencer has had a bad sprain of her foot, and fancys she has broke her heel. But Mr. Pott says tho' it is a very bad sprain, her heel is not broken; but she *will* go about with a crutch and a stick, though it wou'd be much sooner well if she wou'd be quiet. Lady

Cowper is very well. Lady M. Mordaunt with Lady Tankerville.[1] *My* Mrs. Montague is much better than she has been for some months past. Mr. Fountayne mends slowly. Mr. Mason is at York in residence. The Bishop of Exeter in his diocese. Lord Guildford gone to his house in Kent, expecting Lord and Lady North, their two daughters, and two *eldest sons*, just returned from *their* travels, Lord and Lady Willoughby, and Mrs. Keene. He is like the old patriarch entertaining all his family!

And now, my dear child, it is time to give you a holiday from this lesson.

Believe me ever your most affectionate Aunt.

Pray make my compliments to Mr. and Mrs. Beresford, and to Mrs. Welch, when you see her.

I don't expect you to write to me till your mama and Mrs. Vranken think y[r] hand fix'd enough for it.

Mrs. Delany to Mrs. Port, of Ilam.

Bulstrode, 29th Oct., 1779.

I have so much to tell you, my dearest M., of my late exploits that I must allow myself time for it. But first I must thank you for your satisfactory letter of the 24th. How kindly you gratify me by saying my letters cheer a gloomy moment! But you have a friend *within—rectitude of mind*, that can never fail to console you under all

---

[1] Emma, youngest daughter and coheiress of Sir James Colebrooke, Bart., married, 7th Oct., 1771, Charles, 4th Earl of Tankerville.

events; and that merciful providence that orders all, and *knows whereof we are made*, not only accepts our *endeavours*, but *enables* us to *do our duty*—and how glorious the promised reward!

I am glad you gratified Miss Sparrow, since you were not hurt by it.

I believe I have already told you how well pleased I am so far with Rea; and indeed she promises me much comfort, and seems so happy to be with me, that it adds to my satisfaction.

My dear little George,[1] *indeed I long to see you and all of you!*

And now I must give you my journal.

On Monday last at five o'clock (by their Majesties command) I went with the Dss of Portland to the Queen's Lodge at Windsor; call'd in our way on Mrs. Walsingham, and were at the Lodge precisely at 7; were received in the great drawing room (to which we passed thro' the concert room). When we had made our obeysance, the King sent us all into the drawing room within that (gentlemen and ladies), and shut the door upon us, and said we "must stay there till he opened it." The ladies were the same company that were there the 29th of Sept'. In half an hour or less we were set at liberty, and found ranges of chairs placed behind one another, leaving half of the room next to the concert room free. The King placed the Dss of Port^d in a chair in the first row, directed where the rest of the ladies should sit, and then took me by the hand and placed me by the Bishop of Litchfield and just behind Lady Weymouth in the 3rd row, and

---

[1] "George Port," born Aug., 1774.

then placed himself between the Queen and the Dss D^r of Port^d. The musick play'd a sweet concerto, and then entered the room a Mr. Cary, a famous mimick, and for an hour entertained us excessively, taking off the modern players and singers, and the power he had of changing his voice was surprizing; but part of his merit was lost upon *me*, not being acquainted with several that they say he mimic'd to admiration; but his imitations of the modern singers diverted me very much. When this performance was over, every body stood up, tea was brought, the chairs removed, and a commerce table placed in the middle of the room, and—would you believe it? the *Dss of Portland* made one of the party, which consisted of 8 personages: King, Queen, Prince Frederic (called the Bishop of Osna^s), Dss of Port^d, Lady Weymth, Lady Courtown (neice to the Duke of Montagu), Lady Boston, and Duke of Montagu. Before they sate down, the Queen came up to me most graciously, and said she thought it would be more agreable to me to be in the concert room, and that she would place me there herself. She took me by the hand, and led me into the room, and called to the Bishop of Litchfield and said: "I have brought you an *acceptable* person." I had courage eno' to say it was "impossible I should not be so, having the honour of being *so* introduced," to which her Majesty replied: "It is all your own merit and not at all mine," and then, as if she meant to do me honour, she repeated it again. This would appear *very vain* (and I could not repeat it even to you), but that I wish by it to shew how very polite and amiable *our Queen is*; indeed I had two hours most delightful entertainment; the musick, tho' modern, was excellent in *its kind* and well performed; particularly the first fiddle by Cramer,[1] Abel[2] on the *Viol de Gambo* (tho' I don't like the instrument) and a new hautboy, just come from Germany. The room was full of company, all seated, and I had a comfortable corner. I need not say that one of the most delightful part of the entertainment was the Bishop of Litchfield's conversation, who sate by me all the time, while my vanity was fed between whiles by the notice of the Royal family, who talk'd to me by turns. At eleven we were dismissed, and the Duchess of Portland came off triumphant, with eight guineas in her pocket! We had a fine moon to light us home, and much to recollect and talk of, and were surprized at each other that we were not more fatigued, but I think we were both the better for it.

On Tuesday Mrs. Walsingham and Miss Boyle dined here; on Wednesday Mr. and Mrs. Cole came for a few days, and Lady Weymouth with her six fair daughters and her little son, Master John Thynne, and —. Yesterday morning, as I had just sate down to breakfast with Mr. and Mrs. Cole (her Grace and Lady Weymouth not stirring and the young ones breakfasting by themselves), I was called from breakfast to tell me that the King and the Queen, the Prince of Wales and his brother the Bishop of O., with their attendants, were coming to Bul-

---

[1] William Cramer, born at Mannheim about 1730, was considered the first violinist of his time in Germany. He came to England in 1770, and was nominated chamber-musician to the King, leader of the orchestra at the Opera, and afterwards leader at the Ancient Concerts. He died in 1805.

[2] Charles Frederic Abel, came to England about 1761, and died in London in 1787. Abel performed on several instruments, but chiefly attached himself to the *Viol da Gamba*, now seldom used. He was appointed chamber-musician to Queen Charlotte, and wrote several adagios, overtures, concertos, &c.

strode to breakfast at eleven. It is *now* past ten; but short as the warning was, every body and every thing were ready for their reception, tho' the short warning given was a hint that extraordinary ceremony was to be waved; and altho' magnificence always belongs to Bulstrode, it is not less agreable when under the veil of ease and *abated* ceremony, and I believe their Majesties thought so, as they never appeared more pleased and gracious. They were first all assembled in the drawing room, and Lady Weymouth's being here made every thing easy to the Dss of Portland, and, as usual, I was sent for out of my apartment. The King, &c., in their uniforms blue and gold; his Majesty drove the Queen in an open chaise; unfortunately it was a very bad day, but they inure themselves to *all weathers*. They drank their tea in the gallery; the Queen sate down to my working table, view'd all my implements, looked over a volume of the plants, and made me sit down by her all the time. The Prince of Wales (who brought the chair for me) is a fine youth, with a great deal of civility and address; Prince Frederic is more shy, and I don't think so handsome. The King and the Princes, and I believe the Bishop of Litchfield (whilst the Queen was conversing with the Dss of Portland, of which party I had the honour of having my share) went to the lower apartments, *visited mine*, and frighten'd Rea out of her wits, who cou'd not make her escape, but *locked herself up* in her little room! They walked all over the great apartment, admiring every thing as much as if the first time of seeing them, the day being too wet for walking out of doors; and I believe the King hardly ever sits. They go once a week stag hunting, the King and Princes on horseback, the

Queen in an open chaise, with her lady in waiting; and
the Princess Royal with Miss Goldsworthy, or some of her
other attendant ladies. They say it is a fine show and
a rare object for the country. Did bards exist at this
time, they might give us as good a ballad on the Royal
chase as any of old, and none more worthy to be celebrated, if you consider the *merit* as well as the rank of
the chasers.

Mrs. Delany to Mrs. Anne Viney.

Bulstrode, 31st Oct., 1779.

I am ashamed to be so often put in mind of my promise of sending a specimen of my *paper mosaic*, and was
resolved not to write till I cou'd perform my promise,
wch I fear will not answer your expectations ; I intended
sending it under a frank, which crampt me in the size,
and when I had done it, found it rather too large for such
a conveyance. I have sent you a flower, a piece pack'd
in a little case, by the Glocester coach, or rather should
say shall send it to-morrow by one of the Glocester
coaches that passes over Gerrard's cross; if you and your
sister can judge of the work by so imperfect a specimen,
and approve of it, it will give me great pleasure ; its
novelty recommends it, and allowance must be made for
its being the work of an old woman, nearly ent'ring into
her 80th year ! You would have had my little dog-rose
and jessamine, a week sooner; but that it has been a
week so fill'd with Royal favours that it allowed me no
leisure for any thing else. Last Monday the Queen
desired the Dss Dow^r of Portland to come to her Lodge
at Windsor in the evening, and to bring me with her;

flattering as this distinction was, I felt reluctant to accept of it, as I feared my strength and spirits were not equal to such honours; but the gracious manners of the King and Queen and all the Royal family made it perfectly easy. We had an entertainment there of an extraordinary mimic, who took off with great cleverness the modern players and singers, and afterwards a very well perform'd concert, tho' not the musick I best love,—Cramer the first fiddle, Abel on ye Viol de Gambo and a new hautbois, all excellent in their kind; we did not come home till near 12; and on Thursday the King, Queen, the 2 eldest Princes, and their train breakfasted here, and staid 3 hours, and seemed delighted with the agreable reception they met with. I thank God, the hurry that must attend such engagements, has agreed very well with me, tho' the anxiety I had previously suffered for several weeks, and at last the loss of my poor Smith, had sunk my spirits *very low*. I hope this letter will find you well, and happier in regard to your sister's health; my kind compliments attend her, and if the Dean of Glocester is within your reach, I beg my respects to him; I have lately had the pleasure of talking over his excellent talents and true patriotism with a friend and admirer of the Dean's, Mr. Cole, who with his amiable wife has spent some days here. I like my new servant very much; she is sensible, lively, and attentive, and she reads aloud very well, wch is very comfortable to me. It is time to release you.

M. DELANY.

Mrs. J. Dewes and my godson very well, and at home by this time; and my bro^r (in law) Dewes's life seems *renewed!*

The Countess of Stamford to Mrs. Delany.

Envil, Novr ye 1st, 1779.

It would be a vain attempt to make my dear Mrs. Delany, an *adequate* return for one of the most agreable and entertaining letters I ever read. Let it then, my dearest friend, suffice, that I assure you your most kind intentions were fulfilled in making me most exceedingly happy, and giving me very great amusement. Your account of my dearest mother delighted me, and the recital of your great exploits, &c. &c., astonished, and entertained me beyond measure. When marks of favour are so properly bestowed, it is impossible but they must meet with universal approbation, and you cannot imagine how pleased I am that my dear Mrs. Delany is so particularly and agreably distinguished by their Majesties. Had you not, my dear friend, told me, that you *really* did *see* my mother play at *Commerce*, I should not have creditted so wonderful a piece of news. I am sure I should have doubted my own eyes had I been present. But, it is not improbable, that I should not have been capable of *seeing* at that hour, for my *dormouse disposition* would hardly have permitted me to keep my eyes open ; and what effect a *royal* game at Commerce might have had upon me I cannot say, but *any other* would soon act as an opiate.

From these *great subjects* let me now descend to smaller ones, tho' not of less real consequence, as my dear Mrs. Delany's peace of mind is concerned in them : I mean, your prospect of being well suited in your new servant. I heartily wish you may have got a person to your mind ; for it is a very difficult thing. I speak at present

from experience, tho' I hope, I have got a woman that
will do very well. I like her manner, she is gentle, civil,
and handy, and appears good-tempered, and is *not a fine
lady!* I know you will smile when I tell you, that
when the name of your new servant caught my eye, I
really thought it had been some new curious plant, and
I could not help laughing at the idea. *Lydia Rea* is not
a common name, and I thought it looked *" Linnæan."*
Will you pardon me for trespassing so long on your
time? I cannot, however, release you, till I have added
my lord's best comp[ts] and the children's love ; and beg'd
you to present our duty to my dear mother.

I am, with the truest regard, my dearest friend's

Most obliged and affectionate,

H. C. Stamford.

The Countess Cowper to Mrs. Port, of Ilam.

Richmond, Nov. 5th, 1779.

My dearest Mrs. Port's letters are always most acceptable to me. I am glad to hear y[u] have been amus'd this
summer at Matlock. The winter *amusement* y[u] are in a
way to expect I am sorry for. But all that *is* is right,
and such children as y[rs] are blessings. Y[r] sister in law's
unexpected labour must have occasion'd a great *fuss* at
Welsbourn. I was a calendar month at *dear Althorpe,*
in anxious expectation of Lord and Lady Spencer, but
was at last disappointed of seeing them there. The
newspapers must have informed y[u] how near they were
being taken by two French privateers that chased them
two days and nights! I foretold it wou'd be y[e] case.

But cou'd not prevail in preventing y^e *unnecessary* expedition! But y^u know I had rather people should *go* in good-humour than *stay cloudy,* and life is too short for altercations; at least mine is too far advanced. Had my mind been at ease, I should have enjoy'd Althorp much, the weather proving fine; and I had ye satisfaction to find that my walking days *are not* yet over, tho' my dancing ones are! *I thought of y^u,* &c. &c. &c. Dr. Poyntz came there upon the same *errand.* He is *good,* but *not* entertaining. But we went each our own way, and met in good-humour, at meals. As Lady Spencer soon after her landing unluckily sprain'd her ancle, wch confined her in town, I went from Althorpe to St. James's place, and stay'd a week there, and return'd to my *Palais* on ye 2nd ult. My next door neighbours have both been ill, and look wretchedly, leaner than ever! Mrs. Jeffrey's head is giddy, and keeps house. The Holemans are at Bath—ye youngest, who is not *young,* in a very bad state of health. Poor Lady Jane Scott[1] in a dreadful nervous way at her house at Petersham. In short, the winter begins *tristement.* However, our assembly ye last full moon was very full. We had 170! Our Beaux military bleu's and red's.

Lady Hertford [2] and Lady Eliz. Conway,[3] her daughter, met me from Thames Ditton. She is a fine young woman of y^e *giant* race. My sister and little neice are well.

---

[1] Lady Jane Scott, eldest daughter of Francis, 2nd Duke of Buccleuch, born 1723, died in 1777, unmarried.

[2] The Hon. Isabella Anne Ingram Shepherd, eldest daughter and coheir of Charles Ingram, Viscount Irvine, married, in 1776, Francis, 2nd Marquis of Hertford.

[3] Lady Elizabeth Conway, 5th daughter of Francis, 1st Marquis of Hertford. She died in 1825.

Lord and Lady Spencer are at present at Althorp and Harriot. The Dss of Devon. at camp at Warley wth her caro sposo, and Lord Althorp at Cox-Heath I hear no talk of ye camps being to break up soon; but hope they will not be en-camped the whole winter. My best compliments to Mr. Port and love to ye young ones, and in particular to my *agreable* goddaughter, who is *all propriety!* Lady Mary Mordaunt is now in *office* at Black-Heath, and Lady Frances and Mr. Bulkeley are upon a visit to Dr. Poyntz in Norfolk. Miss Williams's health is much mended, and her conduct good and her voice delightfull. She is greatly improved in her singing by having had some lessons of Mr. Snow, who is a capital musician, a *second* Handel; I tell him I am certain he dropp'd him his *mantle.* He *doats* on his music, and *worships* his *memory.* He is the son of the famous trumpetor Snow, who always was of Mr. Handel's orchestra. I hope you have not laid aside your music, ce seroit dommage! You must not turn a *goody,* tho' that appellation belongs to y^u without ye y. Poor Mrs. Fitzgerald died on ye 22nd ult. in the north of Ireland. *He* was wth her, and has been *quiet* for some time past. Now I imagine he will return to his *old pranks.*

Adieu, ma très chère,

G. S. COWPER.

The Hon. Mrs. Boscawen to Mrs. Delany.

Glan Villa, 10th Nov., (? 1779).

MY DEAR MADAM,

I take this long sheet of paper at y^r cost and charge with little chance, however, of putting anything into it worth reading, much less paying for, if I had not had the honour to pay a visit at Ken Wood last Thursday, and the pleasure to see Lady Mansfield quite recover'd. I met her lady^p, taking the air in her chaize, and she told me that her health had been such that her airing on the preceding day was the *first* she *ever* took *in her life* ! She had been equally a stranger to the most common remedies, such as bark, asses milk, &c., but her late illness I believe, tho' coup d'essai was coup de maitre. She had an excellent physician, she said, and incomparable good nurses. They have now the pleasure to see their cares ended in most perfect success, for my lady has not only recover'd her health but her strength. My Lord was gone to St. James's, it being drawing-room day, and all the family were to remove to Bloom. Sq.[1] as last Monday, which you probably know they did.

And now, my dear madam, I send you pour vous faire ma cour a long history of the Chirimoya,[2] which I beg you will read with the eyes of Mr. Lightfoot, and no other. I think it may be in time promoted to a place in certain invaluable folios.[3] A neighbour of mine, the Rev^d Mr. Neate, had the seed from Spain, gave 2 of them to Clark, the (botanical,) butcher at Barnet, who has given one to Dr. Fothergill,[4] and rais'd a plant with the other. Mr. Neate gave 2 more seeds to Mrs. Lee's gardener at Totteridge, and she has 2 plants : two more

---

[1] Lord Mansfield's house in Bloomsbury Square was burnt down by the mob in 1780; this letter, therefore, must have been written before that date.

[2] The Annona Cherimolia, or Cherimoyer, a species of Custard Apple, is a native of South America. Loudon, in his Encyclopædia of Plants, assigns 1739 as the date of its first cultivation in Britain.

[3] The paper flora of Mrs. Delany.

[4] An eminent physician ; he died in 1780. He was a native of Yorkshire, and his parents were Quakers.

plants I saw to-day in Mr. Neate's green-house, they are fine strait large plants and the leaves large, growing alternate not opposite : but what I saw also to-day was two large seeds, and as I did not steal one I have the satisfaction to think I never shall be guilty of theft ; for it is certain I was strongly tempted. You see, my dear madam, I take for granted that the Chirimoya has not had the honour of being introduc'd to the Duchess and you—a shamefull omission, wch I am ambitious to repair ; but I shall not be at all mortified, if you answer, " My dear friend, I have drawn his picture, and hope to eat his delicious fruit." I hope you will, but then we must prevent the maccaronis from making nosegays, as the ladies of Cuba do, of the flowers ; Cuba, I sh^{d} have told you, is his *native place*, and Ulloa [1] the author of this description. I must now yield to the fragrant Chirimoya, and take my leave with best respects to the Duchess.

The Chirimoya.

" The Chirimoya is universally allow'd to be the most delicious of any known fruit either of India or Europe ; the dimensions are various, being from one to five inches in diameter, its figure is perfectly round, being flatted near the stalk, where it forms a kind of navel; but all the other parts are nearly circular. It is cover'd with a thin soft shell, but adhering so closely to the pulp, as not to be separated without a knife. The outward coat during its growth is of a dark green, but on attaining its full maturity becomes somewhat lighter. This coat is

---

[1] Don Antonio Ulloa, author of " Travels " and a physico-historical work on South America. Died 1795.

variegated with prominent veins, forming a kind of net-work all over it. The pulp is white intermix'd with several almost imperceptible fibres concentring in the core, which extends from the hollow of the excrescence to the opposite side, as they have their origin near the former, so in that part they are larger, and more distinct. The flesh contains a large quantity of juice, resembling honey, and its taste sweet mix'd with a gentle acid : but of a most exquisite flavour. The seeds are found in several parts of the flesh, and are about 7 lines in length and three or four in breadth. They are also somewhat flat, and situated longitudinally. The tree is high and tufted, the stem large and round, but with some inequalities, full of elliptic leaves terminating in a point. The length is about three inches and a half. But what is remarkable in this tree, is, that it every year sheds and renews its leaves. The blossom, in which is the embryo of the fruit, differs very little from the leaves in colour, which is a darkish green. But when arriv'd to its full maturity is of a yellowish green. It is a caper in figure, but something larger, and compos'd of four petals. It is far from being beautiful ; but this deficiency is abundantly supplied by its incomparable fragrancy. This tree is observ'd to be very parsimonious in its blossoms, producing such only as wou'd ripen *into fruit ; did not* the extravagant passion of the ladies, for the excellence of the odour, induce them to purchase the blossoms at any rate."

The description was wrote originally in Spanish.

The Earl of Guilford to Mrs. Delany.

Waldershare, Nov. 15th, 1779.

MADAM,

Nothing can be more obliging than your congratulation on the return of my grandsons. I am truly sensible of your goodness, and take the earliest opportunity of acknowledging it. I shall not fail to communicate to Lord and Lady North their share of it. By the indulgence of the Duchess of Portland, I passed two most agreeable days at Bulstrode, and it brought me good luck, for I have, since then, passed a great deal of happy time at Waldershare. Lord and Lady Willoughby and their eldest girl follow'd me very soon after I came hither, and staid with me about a month, and during the time Lady Drake, Lady North and her three daughters, her two eldest sons, and Mr. Brydone[1] who travelled with them, staid with me near three weeks, and Lord North made us three visits of two days each; and every bed in my house was full. This account will be almost enough to make the Duchess of Portland giddy, and so would such a large party have made me, (tho' I had the greatest pleasure imaginable in their company) had I not been in unusual good health and spirits. Your politeness makes you say very handsome things of my grandsons; and I flatter myself they may in time come to deserve them. I own I was much pleased, thinking I observed many things in which they seem to be improved, and none in which they appear to have been hurt, by their travels. But they are very young, and will have to contend with

---

[1] Patrick Brydone, a Scotchman, author of " Travels into Sicily and Malta." Died 1819.

many strong temptations. But, thank God, their natural dispositions are good, and I hope they will be enabled to withstand them. I was so happy as to have my whole party go from hence in perfect health, notwithstanding we were frequently allarmed with accounts of sickness and deaths in our neighbourhood. Tho' the season has been delightfull, I believe it has been unhealthy in most parts of the kingdom. I hope the cold weather coming will quite recover my Lady Dutchess, who I am extreamly concerned to hear has suffer'd so much by a cold. I doubly lament her Grace's not having been able to obey her Majesty's summons, as I am sure the disappointment will have been very disagreeable to both partys. The Queen, with the *greatest* natural affability and good nature *I ever saw*, has an exceeding *solid good judgment*, and delights in society, which she finds to be *not only* entertaining, but *profitable* to her. I feel *myself doubly* interested in the honours *you* have received, and I shall be much pleased with having an account of them, when we meet. I hope to be in London about the end of this month. Be assured my best respects and most ardent good wishes always attend the ladies at Bulstrode ; and that I have the honour to be, with great truth,

Madam,

Your most obedient and obliged

Humble servant,

GUILFORD.

L^d and L^y Willoughby left me on Friday ; but I will convey to them your kind compliments.

The Hon. Mrs. Boscawen to Mrs. Delany.

Glan Villa, 16th Nov., 1779.

A friend to the author you certainly are, my dearest madam, or you wou'd not prefer her history to that of Don Ulloa, nor the subject of an old wither'd little shrub at Glan villa, to that of the fine, rare beautiful plant the Chirimoyo. Well ; but you do, and there's no accounting for taste (yet Mrs. Delany is reckon'd to have a *pretty* good one). Are you not afraid then of making me vain, and consequently unworthy of your partiality ? for you see I am giving entire credit to your preference and sitting down immediately to tell you that remainder of my history wch you chide me for omitting; but first let me thank you for your good news, and express how sincerely I rejoyce in it. I hope the *winter* wch has visited us since Sunday has made no alteration in the good state of the Duchess's health, but that it is perfect and yours too, my dear madam, en depit de la neige et des frimats, but I believe you was a good deal May surpris'd t'other morning to see the green velvet under your window cover'd with snow ; or was it peculiar to these northern regions ? I am about to quit them and repair to the warmer climate of Bill Hill, where I hope to partake my lady's coffee on Thursday next, having long had the kindest invitations from her lady^{p} as well as pressing exhortations from those to whom she is so hospitable, including little John. Else,—'tis almost time to put oneself into winter quarters, where I purpose to settle the first week of next month. Meantime I made two visits last week to Audley Street; one to see Lady Smythe on her arrival, and one to visit the Dss of Beaufort and her family, who spent last Friday at my house in her way to Oxfordshire, the village of Badminton being still afflicted by an infectious fever. The camp of Coxheath is not yet broke up, nor has the Duke of Beaufort remov'd his war-horse, but I trust in God there will be no call for his Grace to return and mount him. I have a letter to-day from our fleet, dated " *Terrible*," at Torbay, 10th Nov[r], since which I'm sure we have had a *terrible* gale of wind, not to say storm ; but I hope they remained in Torbay, of w[ch], however, no newspaper has yet satisfy'd me.

You ask me what I read, my dear madam ? something very pleasant I assure you, viz., " Dr. Johnson's[1] Prefaces to the Lives, &c., of the Poets." I hope you will get them, w[ch], however, is not easy because they are not to be bought unless you buy *also* a *perfect litter* of poets *in fillagree* (that is very small print, whereas one already possesses said poets in large letter), therefore I cou'd not possibly give ten guineas for this smaller edition ; but a friend of mine, to whom Dr. Johnson presented them, was so kind to lend them to me, and I was so much pleas'd with them, that I am not at all sure I have not told you this story already ; if so you must forgive me, and say to yourself, " 'Tis my own fault ; I wou'd set her a chattering, and like her parrot she repeats the same tale." Au reste, madame, I hear no news from London but that Mr. Wilkes is to be *Chamberlain of the City*,—an appoint[mt] of *peculiar propriety*, as that officer is it seems entrusted with the *orphan's money !* I have not seen

---

[1] Prefaces, Biographical and Critical, to the Works of the English Poets, by Samuel Johnson. Published in 1779.

my friends of Cary Street, only heard from them and rece^d an invitation to dine with them as I pass thro' London, but I disdain'd the proposal being determin'd to dine with *a Duke* that day, viz., *"good Duke Humphry."*[1] You will therefore wish me a good supper at Bill Hill, and I will *remember* to bespeak some roasted potatoes. All hands there will be so glad to hear of the health and happiness of Bulstrode, that I hope y^u will favour me with a letter and always believe me yours.

The Dowager-Countess Gower to Mrs. Delany.

Bill Hill, 17th Nov^r., 79.

Having had op̄ortunities of hearing good news of all at Bulstrode, was content wthout making enquiry of d^r Mrs. Delany, and taking up a mom^t of her time, wch is always well spent. One of my informers was Miss Jeñings, who was so obliging, wth her mother to come here soon after her return, full of ye charms and delights she met wth. Sure no season ever was so plea-sant. I sat out on ye 13th ins^t in a favourite bench till six o'clock, so extrordinary soft an evening ought to be mark'd in my almanack; a suďen change has insu'd, it snow'd yesterday, and I'm wasting by ye fire to day. This change I hope has not affected you nor ye D^s, who have always my best wishes and respects.

Our good little ffreind last acc^t of herself was, she was pritty well. What storms she has weather'd! surprising

---

[1] "Dining with Duke Humfrey." This saying is still used respecting persons who inquire, "Where shall I dine?" or who have lost, or do not expect to have any dinner.

to think on. Mr. ffountayne she has not mention'd lately, by wch I conclude no alteration for ye worse. I'm told many are in London, I hope some of her acquaintance among 'em, her son must soon arrive.

Your neighbours, fame says, have been at one of ye camps, I sopose to show *ye pusses* to ye martial men, that ffamily abounding wth schemers. A mother and daughters going to a camp,——'twoud be more becoming to imitate ye chaste goddess and hunt in ye woods at ——

Mr. Le Grand lately had a letter, or rather a collection of pothooks, ye cheife occurence made out, was, ye Mackoy had *bit her leg* in a violent manner. As I wish to be entertaining I've inserted this news! It must make you laugh. Leveson is in London. Mrs. L——n much yor h^{ble} serv^t. None more faithfully so than,

M. G.

———

[Part of a letter.]

From Mrs. Rea (waiting-woman to Mrs. Delany) to Miss Port, of Ilam.

Bulstrode, Dec^{ber} 1779.

Your dear aunte is very well and in good spirits, her eyes not worse, tho' not well enough to write yet; but was much pleased with your letter. A Saturday morning the Queen, Princess Royal, Princis Agusta, and Princess Sophia came here to make a visit to the Dss of Portland; they came at one o'clock and staid till three, and when they whent away the Queen came up to Mrs. Delany and put a packet into her hand, and said, in a most gracious manner, she hoped Mrs. Delany would look at that sometimes and remember her. When your

aunt opened it it was a *most beautiful* pocket case, the
outside white sattin work'd with gold, and ornamen^d
with gold spangles; the inside—but it is impossible for
me to describe it, it is so elegant; it is lined with pink
sattin, and contains a knife, sizsars, pencle, rule, compas,
bodkin, and more than I can say; but it is all gold and
mother of pearl. At one end there was a little letter
case that contained a letter directed to Mrs. Delany,
written in the Queen's own hand, which she will send a
copy of to your mama, the first time she writes to her.
Sunday morning the Dss of Portland received a note
from Miss Hambleton, to let her know the King and
Queen intended her a visit in the evening, between six
and seven o'clock; at which hour they came with the
Prince of Wales and three of the princesses, Lady Courtown and Miss Hambleton, and the gentlemen in waite-
ing to the Prince of Wales. I wish you had been here,
to have seen the sight; their attendance caried flam-
beaus before them, and they made a very grand show in
the park; her Grace had the house lighted up in a most
magnificent manner; the chandelier in the grate hall
has not been lighted before for *twenty years.* Their
entertainment was tea, coffee, ices, and fruite. They
was all dressed in blue taby, with white sattin puckerd
peticotes, with a blue border, and their heads quite low.
They was all admiration at the lighting up of the
house, and the elegance of everything about them. The
Queen set on the sofa in the drawing and the Dss
of Portland by her; the King took Mrs. Delany by the
hand and seated her by himself, and placed a screen
before her, that the fire might not hurt her eyes; the
rest of the company walk'd about the rooms. The

Princess Agusta plaid on the harpsichorde, and the Prince of Wales sung to her. They all seemed very happy and well pleased with their entertainment. They lookd over Mrs. Delany's nine vol. of flowers ; they whent away about half after ten. My mistress was not in the least fatigued; but highly delighted with the gracious manners of the King and Queen; has had a good night and is very well to-day. Wee leave this sweet place on Fryday. I hope you wil excuse this, as it is not wrote as well as I could wish. I am very busy packin up. I return many thanks for your letter; it was a very pretty one; every body liked it. I think you are very much improved in your writing. I beg my duty to your mama.

L. REA.

The above letter is a good specimen of the letter of a sensible waiting-woman of that period, who wrote what she was desired to communicate in her own way, and did not waste words in phrases which meant nothing.

Mrs. Delany to Mrs. Port, of Ilam.

St. James's Place, 9th Dec., 1779.

The day is so dark I can hardly see, yet I would fain give you some acc^t of Lord Littleton's sad end ; so wicked a wretch hardly breathed, heightened by his having had extraordinary parts, which he so basely has abused—a good figure, rank, and a great fortune. What an honour might he have been to his family and country ! Hagley is within a few miles of Mrs. Amphlet's, a widow with a son and two daughters. She was aunt, or rather,

I believe, cousin german, to the *good* Lord Lytelton, this wretch's father. The late lord visited there often as a neighbour and a relation. One day, in the course of this summer, he dined there, and feigned himself so ill that he must lye there all night; unfortunately, Mrs. Amphlett was taken very ill in the night, and confined to her bed some days; during which time the diabolical scheme was laid. Lord L. returned to Hagley in 2 or 3 days, and the day after the eldest Miss Amphlet told her mother she must go to enquire after my lord's health. She went, whether with the *mother's* consent I can't tell, but at that time she had no suspicion about them.

A message was sent back that her daughter was so happy where she was she would not return. Every means was made use of by the poor mother to get her back to no purpose; and after a series of more circumstances than I can relate, the youngest daughter was inveigled to join their wicked society, and left her mother dying of a broken heart; she is now happily released; and I believe died before Lord Lytelton, who certainly had a remarkable dream of seeing *a bird turned into a woman, who gave him warning of his approaching end*; he told his dream to several people he was limited *to* 3 *days*; on the morning of the 3rd day he told several of his acquaintance, being then in town, that the time was near expired, and seemed *un*apprehensive of any further consequence; carried the two miserable girls and another woman belonging to his society to spend some days at a villa near London; eat a hearty dinner and supper in a flow of spirits; complained of a pain in his stomach, which lasted but a little while before he expired at once. What *a scene of horror* if his sad associates had any sense or conscience! He has died rich, and left £500 a piece to these undone girls; the chief of his fortune to his sister, Lady Valencia. Hagley—

[End of this letter missing.]

The Hon. Mrs. Boscawen to Mrs. Delany.

20th Dec., 1779.

You say nobody tells you news, my dear madam; I love to tell good news. How glad I am, then, to tell you that d'Estaign *is beat.* Yes, indeed, thank God! and wounded (you prophecy'd yesterday he shou'd be reserv'd for such a fate). He attempted to storm Prevost's redoubt; was repulsed; and 1500 Frenchmen slain, and many rebels—of the latter 50 officers. Gen. Clinton's[1] aid-de-camp is come. The event happen'd on the 8th Oct[r].

You see I do not ask you how you do. No, I learn'd this morning in Hanover Sq[r] (Monday at 2 o'clock), and I rejoyce therefore. Sup up this cordial.

The following letter was begun by Mrs. Hamilton (Dorothea Forth), widow of the Hon. and Rev. Francis Hamilton, 9th son of James, 6th Earl of Abercorn, and finished by her daughter, Frances Hamilton.

Summer Hill, Dec. 29th, 1779.

Every good Wish, that is allways in Season, to my Dear Friend, to whom I write in this awkward way, be-

---

[1] Sir Henry Clinton, K.B., Commander of the British land forces in America, nephew of Francis Fiennes Clinton, 6th Earl of Lincoln.

cause I know not how to stop when writing to her, &
cannot go on——

Dear Madam, I will no longer defer thanking you for
your very kind & pleasing Letter; & taking Advantage
of your obliging Invitation to me to continue our Correspondence. I wish I cou'd, with Truth, make my
Letter more satisfactory to you, by saying that there is
any considerable Amendment in my Mother's Health;
but I think she has, at least, lost no ground, since I
wrote last, & is better in Spirits & in some other respects,
than she was three weeks ago : Her Rest & her Appetite,
continue good, & her Thirst & some other symptoms of
her disorder are, since that, rather abated; but her Weakness, & her Indolence are very great; & one Alteration
since, that grieves me much, is her having, (from Difficulties in moving & some others) almost entirely left off
going abroad, even to an intimate friend, or to take the
Air, which Mrs Lyon has often in vain sollicited her to
do : This Circumstance is distressful to me, on many accounts, but chiefly so from my apprehensions that other
Disorders may come on, for Want of Exercise, and her
Weakness increase the faster, from her not exerting the
Strength she has left.   For this last I have the Doctor's
Authority, who continues his visits; tho' he has not
lately made any change in her Medicines or Regimen;
He seems to think her rather better than she was two
or three Weeks ago. The only Time, for six weeks past,
that she has gone out, was last Friday (Christmass Day)
to the Sacrament Service at St Georges Church, Which
agreed so well with her that I cannot but hope she will
be encouraged by that again to gratify her Friends, &
me by using a little Exercise abroad; & going among

them sometimes. It is a Hope I am very unwilling to
give up. We have for these three weeks past, been in a
state of much Suspense & anxiety about my Dear M^{rs}
Lyon, in every thing relating to whom my Mother is
extremely interested. Her Husband, who was quartered
above 80 Miles from Dublin, fell ill of a dangerous epi-
demical Fever, which hurried her down there from her
Father, who was better than usual just when she went;
But a week after Doc^r Caulfield grew ill & died in a few
days; so that his Daughter, who had set out for Dublin
(leaving her husband ill) as soon as she heard of her
Father's danger, was met about half way by an Express
with an Account of his death, & return'd back to Coll.
Lyon, whose Fever was grown less dangerous, but turn'd
to an intermitting one. Thank God, her Health was
not affected, tho' her Mind was a good deal so, particularly by the distressful Circumstancs of this Event. I
heard last from her yesterday, when we had the satisfaction of finding that she continues well, & that Coll.
Lyon is so much better, that they hope if he continues
to amend, to be soon in Town. I am sure you will feel
for her situation. It seems hard that *such* a Daughter
after so many years of dutiful attendance on both
Parents shou'd be obliged to be absent from her Father,
at last, at such a time. But her being, even in that
absence, doing right & in the way of her Duty, must on
reflection, be a Comfort to one of her just way of thinking. Your Hamilton Friends are now pretty well, &
enquire affectionately after you. Mr S. Hamilton is gone
to England upon particular business of State, *very cre-
ditable* to *him* to be employ'd in & that I hope he will
execute so as to be useful to this country. We are here

shewing our Joy for the indulgence the Government has
granted us, by great publick Rejoicings ; & will hereafter
shew our Gratitude, by a peaceable & loyal behaviour, I
hope ; if Incendiaries will be quiet.

It gives me great satisfaction to hear of Mrs Sandford's
situation : & very great to hear that your Health continues good. But how much greater a Blessing is such
a state of Mind as yours is, still warm to the truest
Pleasures this World can afford, & exulting in the Expectation of Those that are infinitely beyond them. May
I profit, as I ought, by such Examples, in a *Friend & a
Mother*, who so convincingly prove that old Age is *not*
distressful, nor the nearer View of Death terrible to those
whose Lives have been truly good !

The Hon. Mrs. Hamilton, who commenced the above letter,
was the person so often alluded to as unrivalled in painting
flowers and insects from Nature.

Mrs. Delany to the Rev. John Dewes.

St. James's Place, 8th Jan., 1780.

Last post I was not very well able to write, having
been much affected by the distress of the Dean of York's [1]
family ; Mr. Fountayne, their only son, a most promising
young man of 21 years of age, died this day was se'night,
and a greater loss no parent can sustain ; and my good
friend, Mrs. Montague, has been dangerously ill ; Providence graciously supports her, she is better in health,

---

[1] Thomas Charles, eldest son of the Rev. Dr. Fountayne, Dean of York, by
his third wife, Anne, only daughter of Charles Montagu, Esq., died 1st Jan.,
1780.

and tho' sorely grieved, is resign'd; I go to her as much as I can, as Mr. Montague is still at York, comforting his mournfull friends, and, I am sure, wants comfort himself, as his heart was set on this worthy nephew; his death was occasioned by a fall from his horse in hunting, two years ago; he received an inward fatal stroke, beyond art to cure. I tell you this melancholy tale, my dear nephew, to account for my not being in very good spirits, tho' otherwise I thank God in good health.

May every blessing that can make life desirable attend you both. Surely nobody can boast of a more worthy and dear circle of nephews and nieces than

Your ever affectionate
M. DELANY.

Kind compliments to Miss Mead.

From Mrs. Delany to the Hon. Mary Hamilton, Maid of Honour to Queen Charlotte.

[Written on a card.]

Mrs. Delany presents her compliments to Miss Hamilton, and hopes that Dr. Turton has done her the justice to say how much she shall esteem the favour of a visit from Miss Ham^{on}, and were she able, she wou'd acknowledge it in person. Mrs. Delany flatters herself with the hopes of seeing Miss Hamilton this morning at any hour most agreable and convenient to her between eleven and two.

Tuesday morning, 11th Jan., 1780.

I shall be impatient to hear again from Ilam how my
dearest Mary's cold does; am sorry for all the sufferers;
but hope this change of weather will melt away all complaints with the ice. You assure me, my precious
child, that you are very careful of yourself; I depend on
your kind and attentive nurses, Mr. Port, Miss Land^r,
&c., more than on your own care; for I know your
attentions to the little ones and family affairs will sometimes make you forget your own *infinite consequence;*
and let me add *that* must be your chief consideration.
You overrate my poor little tokens; poor little specimens of what I wish were in my power to do! but every
year brings some new expense, and clips the wings of
beneficence; the last year was an expensive one, and my
lawyer's merciless bill is unpaid. Court thinks the
demand on me for Smith's funeral I *ought* not pay, as
she left *so much money;* but I fear I have made it unavoidable, by giving the exe^{tr} reason to think I would;
but I will not do more than honestly I ought to do;
this is by way of excuse for the poverty of your Xmas
boxes. Most impatient am I for the day and hour of *my
dearest bird's* flying into my nest, where she will be
received and cherished with love and maternal affection.
I had a letter last night from y^r bro^r Court to say he
proposed dining with me and delivering up his charge
next Saturday. As to your question about *the name,* I
really think you should call it (if it proves a boy) after
one of its gdfoathers. I don't know whether your bro^r
John mentioned to you the purport of my last letter, I

wish he may show it to you, and ask your opinion; as I am apt to think it agrees with mine; but I thought it right not to mention it to any body *but himself* till he had determined the point; if he agrees with me, and he has another son, I shou'd suppose he would *undoubtedly* call it *Bevil*; but do as you like; if your mind is set upon it I shall be satisfied. My poor Mrs. Montague is but indifferently; her pulse still feverish; occasion'd not only by her cold, but the sorrow on her mind; for tho' she is reconciled to the stroke on her own account, she feels for the more near and lasting affliction of her children deprived of such a blessing. Mr. Fred. Montagu, who has undergone the melancholy meritorious task of comforting the family at the Deanery, I believe will be in town to-morrow or Thursday; I shall hope when that sad meeting is over she will be better. Mr. Sackville Hamilton[1] calls on me as often as his consequential negotiations between Ireland and England will allow; I hope it will prove as profitable as it is honourable. He is the same good humour'd well-bred man as ever; and talks of you and your family in an obliging manner, much pleased that he shall be acquainted with y^r daughter, and talks of his wife and fireside with true affection and parental delight. I have asked him to dine here next Sunday, to begin the acquaintance. And now I must have done, having more letters to scribble. My love and kind complim^{ts} to Ilam in particular, to Miss Lander; and depend upon her kind and usual indulgence when you must not write. Ever with ye tenderest love

Your own M. DELANY.

---

[1] Mr. Sackville Hamilton, Secretary of State for Ireland, married Arabella, daughter of the Rev. Dr. Berkeley.

Do you chuse Mary shou'd dine at to, owr stay till my usual hour, wch is half an hour after 3 when alone? *be sincere*; and what sort of supper do you chuse for her? and her hour of going to bed? I depend upon her telling me all your rules exactly. I am sorry I mistook ab^t y^r *antient wake*, but will send it the first opportunity.

The Countess Cowper to Mrs. Port, of Ilam.

Richmond, Feby. 22^d, 1780.

Is it possible that two apprenticeships have past since my dearest *Miss Dewes* celebrated her birth day here? The word *never* I will blot out of my calendar. How happy I am to hear that you have had so favourable a lying-in. I hope this will find you in good spirits, as spring is coming on; and in ye summer I conclude y^n will take a *trip* into Warwickshire, as change of air and place is necessary for both health and spirits. I have not yet been in town, so I have not yet seen y^r sweet girl; but propose going to S^t. James's Place for a few days next week, and Mrs. Delany will be my first visit. There is at present so little *sense* and so much *nonsense* in London, that I am tired to death of it, and am almost ready to say " *Man* delights not me, nor *woman* neither!" but my dear Mrs. Port's company wou'd be as agreeable to me *as ever*, and we should not think ye longest day in the year *long* if we pass'd it together! nor want cards to fill up our time! Y^u are *young* and I am *old*, and *yet* we *think alike!* Lord

Spencer has had ye gout in one foot since he came to town, and Lady Spencer a sore throat; but they are, thank God, both well again. Many old people have died at Richmond this winter, and some young ones. My neighbours are still in their old house, tho' their new one is ready for them. We seldom meet, as their house is *too hot* for me, and mine *not hot enough* for them. My two grand-daughters made me a morning visit last week. The Dss looks well. Harriot[1] has both *handsome* and *ugly days*. Lord Althorp[2] *never* handsome, but always agreable, and a fine young man, and well-behaved in every respect; but does not seem inclined yet to engage in matrimony. I wish he wou'd! all the young men of quality are military mad. Politicks run so *high* that I fear it will bring on a civil warr. God grant it may not. Tis nothing but *hurly burly* at present. What a scene of horror at Althorp![3] 'Twas cruel at a friend's house! Dr. Young, in his Night Thoughts, says, Suicide is the madness of ye heart. How dreadfully common it is grown! 'Tis for want of that only sheet anchor religion, wch you, my dear, possess; and those that have that *treasure* that faileth not can never *sink*! may y^u at least double ye years y^u have

---

[1] Lady Henrietta Frances Spencer, youngest daughter of John, Earl Spencer, married, 27th Nov., 1780, Frederick, Viscount Duncannon, who succeeded as 3rd Earl of Bessborough, on the death of his father, 11th March, 1793.

[2] George John, Viscount Althorp, who succeeded his father as 2nd Earl Spencer in 1783.

[3] Mr. Hans Stanley (grandson of Sir Hans Sloane), in a sudden fit of frenzy, went out of the house at Althorp, in Jan., 1780, and cut his throat in the public road. He was found alive, but died before the company could be fetched from the house.

already seen ; and may all *sorrows* keep far from y^u is ye ardent prayer of y^r ever affectionate

G. C. COWPER.

My best compliments to Mr. Port and the Dewes's. All is *placid* at Calwich I hope now. My love to y^e *group* of little ones. Have y^u Dr. Dodd's thoughts in prison ?[1] I think y^u would like them. A. D. is *more rigid* than you and I. I own I both blamed and pitied him. His brother is ye reader at Richmond Church ; but he does not read like Mr. Marsh. Where is he ? Remember me to poor, good Henzey whenever y^u go through Ashbourne.

Mrs. Delany to Mrs. Port, of Ilam.

St. James's Place, 2nd March, 1780.

Ever delighted to receive a good account of my dearest Mary ; but more particularly so when confirm'd by her own dear hand ; and I proposed writing you a long letter in ans^r to yours of the 24th this post, but so many dabs of business succeeding one another, and so many kind visitors, have devour'd my morning that I can only make a flying meal, and leave my full repast for another day. Our dear G. M. A. pure well ; had a good lesson of French from Mr. Marlheille last Tuesday, but before the lesson

---

[1] Dr. William Dodd, born in 1729, was struck off the list of King's chaplains for offering a bribe to the Lady of the Lord Chancellor to procure him the living of St. George's, Hanover Square. He was afterwards tried for forgery, convicted, and executed at Tyburn. He wrote several works: "Sermons," "Poems," "Thoughts in Prison," &c.

was finished Lady Cowper stop'd at my door. She is in
town for three or 4 days, yesterday was so kind as to
eat a boyled chick with me and your daughter, thinks
her much grown and improved; she, herself is still the
Glastenbury rose, and has her usual good humour and
kindness, you may think *who* was the chief topic of our
conversation.

Tuesday evening I had an agreeable party—Mrs.
Boscawen, the Bishop of Chester, and Mrs. Porteus; she
is alter'd (they say) as to beauty, he is a very agreeable
man; they enquired much after you; Mr. Soames
Jenyngs and my constant friend our inestimable Dss,
who is pretty well. Y^r letter to Lord Clan^e kind and
proper; 'tis franked and gone. One of my visiters this
morning brought such good news that I must forgive
the interruption: that beside the brave news confirm'd of
Admiral Rodney,[1] there is a certain account of General
Parker's[2] having taken and sunk nineteen French ships,
and frigates out of 23, and an Admiral whose name
I don't recollect has taken 3 more; these successes
I hope will soon procure peace. The Spaniards seem
now aware what a dupe they have been to France. The
Spanish Admiral after having struck to our brave Rodney, on delivering his sword, said, he "hoped he should
never draw it again but in alliance with Great Britain."
The news has been celebrated in my house with minuets,
cottilions, and country dances, performed by Miss Port

---

[1] On the 8th of Jan., 1780, Admiral Sir George Rodney, while on the
passage to relieve Gibraltar, captured the whole of a Spanish convoy bound to
Cadiz with stores and provisions; and on the 16th of Jan. he defeated the
Spanish squadron off Cape St. Vincent.

[2] Admiral Sir Hyde Parker was Commander-in-Chief of the British fleet in
the action off St. Lucia in 1780.

and Mrs. Rea! We are now in order to receive Lady Gower, &c., who is now at my door.

M. DELANY.

Mary begun yesterday morning to dance with y⁰ young Thynnes.

Mrs. Delany to Mrs. Port, of Ilam.

St. James's Place, 14th March, 1780.

I was unhappy, my dearest Mary, not to answer your letter and send you the draft last post, but an inundation of visiters and impertinences robbed me of the opportunity; and for fear of not having time eno' to write as much as I wished to do to-day, I began a letter yesterday, and wrote two pages, when alas! I pour'd the ink over it, instead of the sand, and must begin again, tho' your daughter has such an opinion of your cleverness and eyesight, that "she is sure you cou'd read it" thro' its black cloud; however, I *will not set her* an *example* of *laziness* or of being satisfied to send you a letter in such a dishabille.

I enclose you the letters to the little Beresfords; and pray tell them it was my fault entirely that they did not kiss their hands sooner, and now it is without the consent of her master, who desires she may be kept from scribbling a year or two and she will write a very good hand, but Mr. Bolton is not against her writing when anybody can look over her. *Indeed* she *has* a capacity *worth cultivating*; and when she is more advanced in the *most useful parts of education*, her lively parts will easily lead her to those accomplishments which are of *less consequence*, tho' they add an agreeable polish to the whole. She is now

sitting by me casting up sums ag^t Mr. Bolton comes, with
as much importance, as a clerk in the Secretary's office.
I find no difficulty with her about any of her studies,
except what regards French, I can seldom prevail on her
to speak it, tho' she is ready enough to answer me
when I ask her a question; but it is only constant
practise that can make that easy, but she reads it in-
telligibly and understands what she reads, and Mr.
Marlheille says she is improved already by his lessons;
but hopes whens he is at home that Mrs. Vrankin
will keep her to speaking constantly. Mr. French says
" *Bravo*," it is pleasant to see her step and bound like
a little fawn, and he leads her about ye minuet step,
as you desired. She is charming well and does her dear
mama credit in every way.

We went by appointment, last Thursday morning at
eleven o'clock, to St. James's House to Miss Hamilton,[1]
(one of the ladies belonging to ye young Princess's,) and
there we found a circle of superior spirits, feeding their
own mortal part with an excellent breakfast, and feasting
their hearers with the *flow of sense!* Mr. and Mrs.
Smelt, Mrs. Carter, and Mrs. Chapone! After an hour's
agreable repast on the *latter*, we crossed the court and
made a visit to Mrs. Fielding. Lady Charlotte Finch[2]
has been in the country (and is there still) for her health
she is better. I believe her spirits have been much hurt,

---

[1] Miss Mary Hamilton, daughter of Charles Hamilton, Esq., and grand-
daughter of Lord Archibald Hamilton. She married, in 1785, John Dicken-
son, Esq.

[2] George, eldest son of the Hon. William Finch and Lady Charlotte Finch,
succeeded, in 1769, to the Earldom of Winchelsea, on the death of his uncle.
He died unmarried, 2nd Aug., 1826.

by Lord Winchelsea's whim of going to America; she rather wished him to marry and settle, and avoid that *ruinous dissipation* the young men of the age are involved in.

Last night I had a 2ᵈ visit'from the Bishop of Chester, wᶜʰ, being a volunteer, flattered me very much. I had no body beside but *the Grace of my* sopha and Lady and Miss North. My little girl keeps her place on her little stool at my elbow, with some little piece of work or knotting (never unobserved I assure you) till nine, then gives me a kiss, makes a low curtsey (to the company) and exits. I hope by this time Bernard is quite determined to take Hagley, for, by all accounts, it is a most eligible and delightful situation; and Lord and Lady Wescote[1] very good sort of people (she was a Bristow and cousin-german to our dear Mrs. Dashwood), and much inclined to accommodate them in the civilest and most obliging manner. Mrs. Boscawen has represented your broʳ and sister-in-law in so just a light to Lᵈ Wescote (who is her intimate friend) that he wishes *extreamly* to have them his tenants, so I hope no obstacle will arise. I am glad you and Mr. Port think of sending John to school; you do not say where, but I hope you have a reasonable and good one within your reach, that you may have the satisfaction of seeing how he goes on, and in holyday time go on with him at home wᵗʰ those instructions of religion and good manners which are too often neglected at schools.

---

[1] William Henry, 5th son of Sir Thomas Lyttelton, created Baron Westcote, 31st July, 1776; succeeded to the baronetcy on the death of his nephew, Thomas, 2nd Lord Lyttelton, and was created a Peer by the same title in 1794. His second wife, whom he married in 1774, was Caroline, daughter of John Bristow, of Quiddenham, Esq.

Mrs. Delany to Mrs. Port, of Ilam.

St. James's Place, 21st March, 1780.

I hope my last letter and draft on Gosling for L^y Clanbrassil's christning money has arrived safe.

I thank God we are very well and y^r dear and precious child gone with Rea this morn^g to take a walk in the Green Park, before Mr. Marlheille comes; his hours are from 12 to 2, and tho' it seems to be the study *least* agreable to her, I hope it will be of use in making her understand the language and give her some notion of the *present mode* of pronouncing it; should it produce no other good effect, the attention required will be of use and Mrs. Vrankin's usual solicitude to improve her will become more easy. She longs to write to her mama, and she must be indulged in that as a reward when she has performed her task well with Mr. Bolton. In every respect she is a most amiable child.

To-morrow Dr. Burrows (Mrs. Chapone's friend) comes to talk to me about the Charter School, where he has a son; and as he is a man of excellent true Xtian principles as well as a man of learning and superiour genius, his countenance and advice may be of signal service to the dear boy.

Last Friday morning I had a hurley burley visit from *the Marchioness,*[1] just as my own breakfast was over, with her vegetables in her pocket to compose her tea (sage, baume, and ground ivy). After twenty fiddle faddles that worried my man Josiah almost as much as they

---

[1] " *The Marchioness.*"—Qy. Tweeddale.

worried me, two toasts round the loaf, neither too thick nor too thin, too hard or too soft, were made; then in walked my neighbouring Countess,[1] and she had a secret to impart; unfortunately my bedchamber and the back parlour had been washed, and my G.M.A. was busy in the fore parlour with her master; so I was obliged to decamp and *retire* to the schoolroom (not a disagreable repose for half an hour). When the parley was ended, I had a volley of excuses; all which I could have excused; and when I considered the kindness of one of the partys to my dearest M., I forgave all the clatter. I think her very well and in very good spirits, and she spoke of you with great regard. I told you of Lady Cowper's being in town; I have some thoughts of taking her god-daughter to make her a visit some day next week. Rea is *astonished* at her working so well. Last night Lady Jerningham was here with *her harper*, who played and sung very agreably, to the great entertainment of G.M.A., and it made her a little rake. Lady Stamford has inoculated Lady Louisa[2] and two of her younger sons.

I hope Bernard has had his final answer from Ld Wescote. I feel impatient to have him in possession of so desirable a place, and I shall be happy to have his amiable wife gratified in a place she likes so well. How fortunate have the two brothers been in being blessed with *such valuable wives!* Indeed, I think I may say the good fortune has been mutual.

Lord North has had a noble triumph over his envious

---

[1] " *My neighbouring Countess*"—Lady Cowper.

[2] Lady Louisa Grey, 3rd daughter of the Earl of Stamford. She died, unmarried, in Feb., 1830.

and base accusers,[1] and trust he will maintain his ground.

This evening I expect Bishop of Chester and Mrs. Porteus, Bishop of Exeter, and Mr. and Mrs. Smelt, with our excellent Dss whose kindest wishes attend you. Lady Dr Gower was here last night. She desired y^r daughter to make her compliments to you and to know if you collected old seals for a poor woman?

Mrs. Delany to Mrs. Port, of Ilam.

St. James's Place, 28th March, 1780.

Well now for our ball. Did I not write you word that Dr. Burrows had taken a fancy to our dear child's sweet countenance, and invited her to dance with his children, nephews and nieces? I found myself stout eno' yesterday to go and introduce her to the tripping tribe of young dancers. At six we set forward, and were some of the first. Their number was to have been 12 couple, but was rather more. I saw the ball begun, and G.M.A. dance down one dance like *any fairy*, and worthy of a more practised partner than came to her share. However she looked *so well* and *so happy* that I left her, quite satisfied. The Mistress Burrows' are very good sort of people, and tho' ranked among the female *geniuses*, *not* unmindful of *necessary attentions!* and they were

---

[1] On the 20th of March, 1780, the Ministers gained a majority of fifty-three in the debate on the King's household; and the same evening Temple Luttrell, one of the brothers of the Duchess of Cumberland, brought a charge against Lord North of buying a borough, which he thought he had himself bought. He made his own corrupt practices very clear, but could prove nothing against Lord North, and the accusation was voted " frivolous."

delighted and *much obliged* by my trusting such a charge
with them.   She had nothing but simple cake and warm
milk and water.   I beg'd she might have no negus or
lemonade, as one is *too strong* and the other *too cold* for
children.   I sent Rea for her in the Dss's coach *at* 9
o'clock.   She came home before my circle was broke up,
and entertained them all with the entertainment she had
enjoyed, and assured me she could have danced 2 hours
longer.   She slept near 10 hours, and is vastly well, and
at this very time diligent with Mr. Marlheille ; and another engagement is ready for her this evening.   I had
last night a card from Lady Sackville, who now lives in
Clarges-street, to desire Miss Port might meet her
grand-daughters, Lord Thanet's children, at her house
at 6, and stay till half past 8.

To-morrow the Dss of Port^d, Mrs. Boscawen, and Mrs.
Chapone dine with me, and Mr. Montagu has desired to
be of the party, and we are so gracious as to admit him.

Last Saturday morning L^y Cecelia Johnson made me
a visit—a strange rattle ! her daughter I understood
afterwards was all the while in the coach at my door, and
Sr John Ramsden [1] at the coach-door *flirting* wth her *all
the time* (*that's* no new affair).   Lady Cecelia talked of her
and seem'd to wish her well disposed of, and brag'd of
her own prudence in *never having let her keep company
wth girls !*   I made some complim^t about her fearing she
would not long remain under her care, wch she seem'd
to doubt—when behold, this young lady, so delicately
train'd, eloped on Sunday morning with a young Aid-de-

---

[1] Sir John Ramsden succeeded his father in the baronetcy, 10th April, 1769.
He married, 7th July, 1787, the Hon. Louisa Susan Ingram, youngest daughter
and coheiress of Charles, Viscount Irvine, and died in 1839.

camp of Gen¹ Johnson's worth nothing, a brother of Mr. Pelham's,—I forget his name.

I have been interrupted by Mrs. Carter and Miss Sharp.

Mrs. Delany to Mrs. Port, of Ilam.

St. James's Place, 11th April, 1780.

I am afraid you will not think my little charge as much improved in her writing as you might expect, but improved she *certainly* is, and *few* girls of her age write *so well*, and she has so many other things to attend to that we cannot make writing our chief object; and her application is full as much as can be expected from a child of her lively parts. I think her spirits much greater than they were last year; I believe Rea being young, and cheerful, and very fond of her, is an agreable circumstance to her as well as to me, and they have *every day* a good *game of romps*, wch I wink at, as *youthful spirits must have a vent.* Her quickness of observation is often surprizing, and a very little encouragement would make her an excellent mimick—a quality wch encouraged might give a turn of acrimony to her natural sweetness of disposition; I, therefore, check it, and tell her (which she understands very well,) that those painters who deal in *Caracatura*, never produce anything that is *beautiful.* There never was a temper more easily managed; and, indeed, you have laid so excellent a foundation, that there is no doubt of her proving a substantial blessing and comfort to you.

I think *your* academy promises very well. I shall long to hear from you after your tour, and hope you will find everything in regard to the dear boys' new situation perfectly satisfactory to you and Mr. Port: no scheme in life can be without some objections, but if the good preponderates we must rest content and trust in Providence for a blessing on our best purposes.

Lady Cecelia J. is not at all to be pitied. She encouraged her daughter in *all her flirtations*, which were *many*, and knew of this engagement, wch the parents encouraged, expecting a legacy for the young man, *which* turning into another channel, they then forbad any farther intercourse; too late; and the young lady not valuing a censure on the forwardness of her conduct, walk'd off with her lover. However, all parties are now reconciled.

The following letter appears to have been written in answer to a note addressed to Mrs. Delany by her little grand-niece, while under her roof.

Mrs. Delany to Miss Port, of Ilam.

St. James's Place, May 7th, 1780.

Every testimony, my dear child, of your *affection* and *respect* for me is welcome, and I trust will never be separated; for if you love me not only for the kindness, you think I have for you, (and wish to show you on every occasion,) but for the attention, the advice, and anxiety you daily experience, I am satisfied that my tenderness, and cares are well bestowed, and that you will fulfill your promises of doing everything on your part, that can tend to make you amiable and valuable, and add to the happiness of your most affectionate aunt,

M. DELANY.

Mrs. Delany to Mrs. Port, of Ilam.

St. James's Place, 11th May, 1780.

I am but just returned from a pleasant tour this morning with y^r dear child and her playfellow Rea. We went to Lee's at Hammersmith, in search of flowers, but only met with a *crinum*, a sort of Pancratium; from thence returned to Kensington, bought cheesecakes, buns, &c. a whole 18 pennyworth; from thence to a lane that leads to Brompton, bought nosegays; and are now came home hungry as hawks, dinner ready, and we must dress.

Dinner over, Miss Black engaged with her young pupil.

Your letter from Nottingham very satisfactory, and I hope the school will answer all your wishes.

I am to add from G. M. A. with my *own compliments her's*, to your amiable neighbours at the Vicaridge; she will be happy to take lessons of Geography from him; indeed, they are uncommon, and valuable neighbours, and I again congratulate you on such an acquisition. I enjoy the flourishing state of health of your dear nursery. I hope ye little Dewes's will improve in strength, as they grow older, such tender little branches are sensitive of every blast; but care and attention revives many a drooping plant.

Court went out of town this morning, and proposes coming to town again this day se'night. I miss him very much. *Three* fine ladies *picked him up* here last Thursday, and carried him off to ye Ant^t Music.

Last Tuesday Mr George Montagu [1] died, he had been

---

[1] George Montagu, of Roel, Esq., in the county of Gloucester, son of Brigadier-General Edward Montagu, and grand-nephew of the 1st Earl of Halifax of the Montagu family. He died 10th May, 1780.

ill a great while ; beside his sister, his nearest relation is
Mr. Fred. Montagu, and I hope he will inherit what he
does not leave his sister; the will was to be opened to-
day, but I know no particulars yet.

The chief conversation of the town, is now about the
miserable persecuted Lady Cork.[1]   I believe there never
was a train of such villany and malice, as has been and
is still practised against her.   After bribing all her
servants to accuse her in vain, they gained a man who
she employed to write music out for her to make an
affidavit against her ; and proceeded against her accordingly ; and the cause was to have been tried to-morrow
or next day, and all Lady Cork's friends, which are numerous, were resolved to appear to support her character,
w[ch] has been blameless.   But the lawyers L[d] Cork had
engaged, I suppose, found they could not make out their
accusation, and the seduced man has recanted, and has
left them in the lurch.   So the cause is drop'd for the
present on L[d] Cork's side.   But not so on Lady Cork's ;
she is supported by Lord Sandwich, and able council,
and I hope will have it in her power to expose such a
wicked scene as perhaps never was before plann'd.

---

[1] Anne, daughter of Kelland Courtenay, Esq., married, in 1764, Edmund,
7th Earl of Cork.

Mrs. Delany to Mrs. Port, of Ilam.

St. James's Place, 17th May, 1780.

I have this day received your letter and kind remembrance of the 14th of May[1] (old stile) ; most sensible am I of your tenderness on the occasion. Were I fit for the great change w[ch] my time of life may daily expect, I trust those that love me best would rejoyce in so blessed a change for *me*, before the severe infirmities of extream old age make me a pitiable object : but I thank God at present I have no reason to regret my long stay in this world, having, amidst many sorrows, enjoy'd many blessings! and I trust I shall be sustained to the end of my course by that *mighty hand* that called me to this state of tryal; my demerits are great, but I rely on *his* infinite mercy.

I had a visit this morning from Mrs. Chapone and her friend Mrs. Smith and they have run away with *my child* to dinner, promising to return her between 7 and 8. The house is a *desert* without her, a stillness and void that is quite uncomfortable! How unreasonable a lamentation, who have deprived her dear mother of her sweet looks and her sprightly, sensible prattle for almost 5 months! but you'll forgive me.

The dear child is full of glee with the expectation of seeing the King and Queen and all the royal family on the 4th or 5th of June, the King's birthday. Mrs. Stainforth has desired me to send her to her at one o'clock on that day, and she will place her where she will see and be seen very plainly. At present her little head is full

---

[1] Mrs. Delany's birthday.

of an invitation *she* has given to the Dss of Portland,
and to the Bishop of Litchfield and Mr. Montague to
dine here on my *real* birthday, the 25th. I am to have
nothing to do with it! She and Rea are to settle the
dinner; and she has written to her uncle Court to be
sure to be in town by that day, to assist her to entertain
the company. Don't imagine I am spoyling your child,
and making her conceited; far be that from me; and it
is a point I have been very watchful about. Her *extraordinary* quickness and apprehension, with the *great*
approbation she meets with, requires some balance, and
tho' I readily give into any indulgence that may prove
an advantage to her, I am steady in keeping her to those
employments that are necessary for her; and tho' she will
sometimes endeavour to play *them* off or postpone them,
I insist on their being done, as I am sure it has been
your own method, or she *could* not be the *delightful
creature she is!* Tomorrow morning (Thursday being
the only whole holyday in the week) we go to Kentish
Town to breakfast with Mrs. Mary Smith, where Miss
Murrays are to meet us.

Lady Cork's persecution subsides for a while. As soon
as Lord Cork drops his iniquitous cause, w^{ch}, as he has
no real grounds to go on, he must soon, L^y Cork will
sue him, and has wherewithal to expose a wretched
scene of malice and villany.

The Dowager-Countess Gower to Mrs. Delany.

Bill Hill, 21st May, 80.

The news of yor health yor well known hand brought
me, was ye most joyfull I c^d have; hope nothing will

hap̃en to disturb or inter̃upt it. Bill Hill is pleasant, and begins to look pretty, and its best garment is putting on; but still yᵉ winds feel more like March yⁿ May.

Yʳ letter first inform'd me of G. Mountagu's death. It makes me hapỹ his remembring his Couzin ffred;[1] I ap̃rehended a branch not so worthy wᵈ have had yᵉ greatest share; our little ffreind must be very hapỹ to see her son so easy in his ffortune; I wish it may contribute to her health; yᵉ newspaper says yᵉ legacy is only for his life; so I, like yᵉ rest of yᵉ living, find fault, and think it defective.

I think I'm a gainer by yᵉ blunder wᶜʰ detain'd yoʳ letter; wᵗ I lost in time was amply made up wᵗʰ yᵉ addition. I think Mrs. Vesey herself an odd compound, so wonder not at her assembly; odities are yᵉ ffashion. I forgot yᵉ man's *name* yᵗ us'd *to read at houses,* and just before I left London took in yᵉ whole town in a subscription, and gave 'em nothing for it; I *always* imagin'd him *a spy!*

Now this man *wᵗʰ tails,* I conclude is in yᵉ same stile. I'm too old to taste these delights; *feel glad* I'm at so great a distance as almost to be *out of hearing.*

A few days ago I went to make my congratulations on Mr. Neville's[2] intended mar̃iage wᵗʰ Miss Kath. Gren-ville: yᵉ whole ffamily seem'd so hapỹ in yᵉ prosspect of it, yᵗ yᵉ vissit rais'd my spirits (wᶜʰ a country vissit seldom does), and I hear yᵉ Grenville ffamily are equally

---

[1] Horace Walpole says that Mr. George Montagu left 500*l.* a year to Mr. Frederic Montagu.

[2] Richard Aldworth Neville, Esq., of Billingbere, afterwards 2nd Baron Braybrooke, married, in May, 1780, Catherine, youngest daughter of the Rt. Hon. George Grenville.

pleas'd. Mr. Neville, sen[r], never stirring from Billing-bear, L . d and L . y Temple,[1] &c., have all been there; cross'd y[e] country to Stowe, where they are to be maried.

Adieu for y[s] time. Ever faithfully yo[rs].

Mrs. Delany to Mrs. Port, of Ilam.

St. James's Place, 24th May, 1780.
Wed. morning.

I think I must begin this letter with my exploits which *have been* and *are* to be. Last night I was at Mrs. Walsingham's concert on her opening her new house, or rather to celebrate her daughter's[2] birthday, now eleven years old, and tho' remarkably grown this *last* year, tho' very little taller than our Georgina; she is an amiable and ingenious girl.

The concert was splendid; rows above rows of fine ladies with *towering tops*. Not having been much used to see so many together I must own I could not help con-sidering them with some astonishment, and lamenting that so absurd, inconven[t], and unbecoming a fashion should last so long, for though every year has produced some alteration, the *enormity* continues, and one of the most beautiful ornaments of nature, fine hair, is entirely disguised; it appears to me just as ridiculous as if Mr. Port was to fell all his fine hanging woods and feathered hills, and instead of all the beautiful hues of various native greens, should plant only *Scotch firrs* and *brambles!*

---

[1] George, 2nd Earl Temple (brother to the bride elect), was created Marquis of Buckingham in 1784. He married Mary, only child and heiress of Earl Nugent.

[2] Miss Boyle, afterwards (in her own right) Baroness de Ros.

This is a subject as delicate to treat of as politics,
so I don't venture at it in conversation, but give it vent
here by way of digression.

The Dss D[r] of Portland carried me to Mrs. Wal[s] at a
little before 8 ; I had a comfortable seat on a sofa by
her Grace and Lady Bute, and *we* were the only *flat
caps* in the room! The musick was charming; Miss
Harrop sang in perfection some of Handel's fine opera
songs. I staid till near eleven, and was less fatigued
than I expected.

This morning I am going to see my good little friend.
The Dss, Lady Bute, and Mrs. Boscawen come to me in
the evening. I believe I told you that Georgina had invited company for to-morrow, 25th; and it would divert
you to see how busy she is in giving her directions to
Rea, and they are both *as serious together* as you or I
could be!

On Friday morning I am to go to hear Paccherotti[1]
sing at L[y] Edgecumb's in a quiet way, which will suit
me very much, and I have long wished to hear him.
(Afternoon). I found Mrs. Montagu rather better, but
far from well. After Geor[as] dancing was over we visited
the doors of some of our cousins; came home, dressed
and dined, but alas! I was saddly mortified when I
heard the loved knock of the Post to find by your letters
from Calwich so indifferent an account of my dear niece,
(Mrs. J. D.,) and shall be anxious till I hear again; but
I am sure, if my wishes will avail, you and her dear

---

1 Gasparo Pacchiarotti, born about 1750, a celebrated singer, who came first
to England in 1778. He returned again in 1780, and continued principal
singer at the Opera till the commemoration of Handel in 1784, when he again
went to Italy and lived in retirement at Padua.

husband are recompensed for your kind solicitude about
her by seeing her quite well again. I am not at all
surprized at your brother's tender attention to her, as I
know his good disposition and her amiableness and merit.
Next Saturday, if the weather proves tolerably fair, we
go to breakfast with Lady Tweeddale, and dine with *our*
Countess. Court has promised to be here by dinner on
Thursday, that is, to-morrow.

Did I tell you the Dss of Portland wrote a card in
Georgina's name, to invite the Bishop of Litchfield; and
his answ[r] was, "*he would come from Kew on purpose to
obey the summons of so innocent, so fair, and so virtuous a
young lady as Miss Port.*"

I can't express the satisfaction you have given me on
Miss Sparrow's account, and I am heartily glad on Mr.
Port's account that so good a plan is settled for her.

I am just returned from the exhibition; I took Mary
with me, and she was, she said, *more* delighted "than if
it had been a puppet show;"[1] she is now *deeply* engaged
in settling *her desert!*

I have made her up a pink lutestring for the King's
b. day; as perhaps some of the Royal Family may spy
her out when she is peeping at them. I *have* tried her
hair up, but her forehead is now too bald, tho' it will not
appear so another year with a little management of
shaving the young hair. She has a very easy, good air,
and a fine chest. The coat maker advises girts to be
fastened on y[e] top of the stays, and crossed over the
shoulder blades and fastened before, w[ch] will not appear,

---

[1] This taste for the fine arts, particularly painting and sculpture, continued
through life.

being under her slip, to keep her back flat for a year or so, but I *would not* have it *done* without your approbation. Tho' *I don't turn up her hair* I don't *suffer it* to make a dowdy of her by *covering her forehead,* but only a little thin shade about *an inch* over it, which looks becoming and natural.

After this week I shall be monstrous busy, as I am under a necessity of whitewashing, new papering, and painting my draw^g room ; and I have delay'd in hopes of a more conven^t time, but can do it no longer; and removing pictures, books, and China, &c., &c., will find me a good deal of busyness.

I have received a most elegant copy of verses this morning from Mrs. Walsingham. I will write them out for you; but they are far above the deserts of y^r ever affectionate

M. DELANY.

FROM MRS. WALSINGHAM TO MRS. DELANY,

ON HER 80TH BIRTH DAY.

Urg'd by my *hopes*, checkt by my *fears*,
I scarce dare wish you *many* years !
But that your years may happy prove
Agrees with reason as with love ;
With *reason*, that a mind *so pure*,
Stands on the verge of life secure ;
Whether with heartfelt satisfaction,
Reviewing many a generous action,
You trace a life, which *best can tell*
To women, *how* they *may excell ;*
Or looking on with *hope* elate,
Beyond this life's uncertain date,
You with triumphant joy descry
Those blest abodes prepar'd on high !
For spirits perfect and refin'd,
There only you can equals find !
O ! could you leave to those below,
(As once a prophet did, we know,)

Some *mantle blest* that might impart
Some of your virtues to their heart ;
Some of yʳ judgement to their mind
And deck them with yʳ taste refin'd ;
How would *I strive* that robe to share,
For the dear object of my care ;[1]
Nor rob fair Portia[2] of her due,
Believe me, there's *enough for two!*

The Dowager-Countess Gower to Mrs. Delany.

Bill Hill, 4 June, 80.

Not to aꝑear ungratefull, I must thank dear Mʳˢ. Delany for all her kind attentions to me; and propose to her, since yᵉ Dˢ of Portland does not move to Bulstrode this ffortnight, why can't you pass it here? and go from hence thither wⁿ ever her Grace aꝑoints; 'twou'd be more conducive to health yⁿ continuing in London this hot weather. My chaize lies idle; may bring you and yᵉ *little Porte*, &c., here, and carry you to meet yᵉ Dˢ wⁿ ever she calls. You wᵈ make me very haꝑy in so doing.

Mr. M.[3] wrote to me; I'm incapable of giving consolatory sentimᵗˢ equal to wᵗ the reflection of his own conduct has power to give, and referr'd him to it; *that* will be a comfort to him as long as he lives. The haꝑiness my *valuable ffriend* felt from yᵉ affection of her children cañied her thro' a painfull life wᵗʰ chearfulness and content. I'll dwell no longer on this subject; 'tis too melancholly for you. Adieu.

---

[1] Her daughter, Miss Boyle.
[2] Miss Port.
[3] Frederick Montagu, Esq., the son of Lady Gower's and Mrs. Delany's friend, Mrs. Montagu, then recently dead.

The Countess Cowper to Mrs. Port, of Ilam.

Richmond, June 7th, 80.

MY DEAREST MRS. PORT,

I shou'd sooner have acknowledged y^r last agre-able letter; but I have had smarting feet, wch I call my gout, and Lord Spencer being really laid up wth gout at Bath has made me not feel in a humour for writing. He will now, I hope, be soon well. Mrs. Delany is surprisingly so. She breakfasted with my sister at Ham, and dined wth me on Saturday last. My pretty agreable god-daughter and Mr. Court Dewes were of y^t party—*She is delightful!* Mr. C. D. looks thin. I am very glad to hear that y^r *sisters* (in law) are so agre-able to y^u, and so sensible of y^r merit. Y^u must and will prosper I am sure, and be happy in ye long run. But our *longest run* in this changeable world is but short when compared to eternity, where all your virtues will be amply rewarded. Lady Frances Bulkeley is still with me, and desires her love to you, and all y^r Rich-mond *friends* enquire after you. I am sure y^u will be glad to hear that Miss Hay has got happily over ye small-pox. My sister was taken by surprise. Mr. Hay order'd his surgeon to go to Ham wth what was *requisite* in his pocket and inoculate Miss Hay.[1] My sister cou'd not risk refusing it being done, but declared she washed

---

[1] "*Miss Hay.*"—Lady Frances Hay, daughter of Frances Carteret, Marchioness of Tweeddale, married Captain Hay, of the Guards, and "*Miss Hay*" must have been their daughter. The marriage of Lady Frances Hay is not mentioned in Burke, nor the birth of any child of John, 4th Marquis of Tweeddale, except that of George, 5th Marquis.

her hands of it; but it has proved a lucky event. Dreadful riots in London.[1] God knows how it will end. My best compliments to Mr. Port and yᵉ Dewes's. We have had some very hot days, and now it is turned cold again. You may think yourself happy to be so far from London at present, where everything is in yᵉ utmost confusion. All yᵉ soldiers far and near are order'd to town to *guard the Bank*. I fear England is really now undone; we do not deserve yᵉ interposition of Providence; and nothing else can save this wicked, ungrateful nation, so unworthy and unthankfull for so many blessings heap'd upon it, *but all my hope is fix'd and grounded in yᵉ great, yᵉ living Lord.* I fear this gloomy epistle will sink yʳ spirits, wᶜʰ I do not wish to do, but, on yᵉ contrary, raise them as much as in my power. "The *spirit* is willing, but yᵉ *flesh* is weak." The Dss of Devon. has, I fear, got yᵉ hooping cough. She did not go to yᵉ birth-day. My love to the little ones; and be assured, my dearest Mrs. Port, of

My unalterable affection.

G. C. COWPER.

Mrs. Delany to Mrs. Port, of Ilam.

Whitehall, 8th June, 1780.

My dearest Mary may by this time have had an account of the melancholly situation of London, and her

---

[2] The "No Popery" riots are here referred to, when Lord George Gordon, M.P. for Luggershall, assembled an immense mob and marched down to Westminster with a petition for the repeal of the Catholic Relief Bill, passed 1780. The petition was rejected by 192 to 6. Frightful riots followed, which extended to Bath, Bristol, &c. Lord George was tried for High Treason, acquitted of treasonable intentions, but died, in 1793, in Newgate, where he was imprisoned for political offences.

fears may be allarm'd for her particular friends, all of whom, I thank God, are safe and well, and the Dss Dow^r of Portland, myself and dear little girl are going directly to Bulstrode. But as it is satisfactory to know particulars that may be depended upon, I will tell you as much as I can recollect.

Yesterday my poor (*now happy*) friend[1] was buried at Audley Chapel, her good son gone to Windsor for some days.

On Tuesday last, the 6th of this month, the tumult was so desperate, of which you will be informed in the newspapers, that nobody knew how desperately it might end. Lady Weymouth was so terrified for the Dss of Portland, as a disturbance was expected in Privy Garden, that she intreated her to lye that night at Lady Stamford's in Charles Street, wch she did after spending the evening with me; and yesterday she dined with me, and being assured that all things were quiet at Whitehall, and likely to continue so more than any place in London, she resolved to return home last night. Poor Lady Weymouth is not at all well, my lord obliged to stay in town some time, and she can't leave him; she sent all her children yesterday evening to Ealing, and had the goodness to send to desire me to go with them, and carry Georgina with me, but I *could not* do that, having many things to settle, as the Dss was determined to go to day to Bulstrode, and she *insisted* on my coming home with her, and bringing the child with me, as some houses in St. James's Place and Street *were threatened*; and here at Whitehall I have begun my letter, and can

---

[1] Mrs. Montagu.

assure you, tho' I got very little sleep, I am this morning surprizingly well, notwithstanding many shocking
agitations, which the universal distress must occasion.
The dear innocent child (that slept with me as sound as
if all was peace) is perfectly well, and the joy of going
to Bulstrode, and of meeting her dearest mamā at Welsbourne, gets the better of her apprehensions, wch now
and then check the pleasant prospect for a moment.
We have just breakfasted in the bow window. Rea
gone home to pack up our things, and as soon as I can
get some acc^{t} of the Dss of Portland I shall go to
St. James's Place to finish the packing, and set off for
Bulstrode about five in the evening. Court is to meet
me in St. James's Place, and next post will let you
know for a certainty what day he can pick up Georgina
at Bulstrode, to carry her on to Welsbourn. Lord Bute
(and Lady Bute) are gone out of town ; but I fear there
will be *as little mercy* shown to *his* house as to *Lord
Mansfield's* in Bloomsbury Square! Thank God, *he* and
his family are safe and well, but *his house* with everything in it *is burnt to the ground!* and Kenwood would
have met the same fate had not the militia saved it
yesterday.

You will consider when you receive this letter, that
your child and I are safe with our dearest friend at Bulstrode, and under the shadow of the Almighty, who I
trust will protect and deliver us from our enemies.

" During the London riots of 1780, several houses were plun-
dered and destroyed by the mob ; one party of whom went to
the house of the Earl of Mansfield, in Bloomsbury Square, to
which they set fire and consumed it. They began by breaking
down the doors and windows, and flung the furniture into the

street, where large fires were made to destroy it. They then proceeded to his lordship's law library, and destroyed some thousand volumes, with many manuscripts, mortgages, papers, and other deeds. The rich wardrobe of wearing apparel and some fine pictures were also burned. The mob afterwards pulled the house down and destroyed the outhouses and stables, and in a short time the whole was consumed. Lord and Lady Mansfield made their escape through a back door, a few minutes before the rioters broke in and took possession of the house."

Among the reminiscences of Mrs. Delany's niece, who was with her at the time, was having heard of a chimney sweeper being observed dancing before the bonfire in one of Lady Mansfield's hoops.

Cowper has commemorated these riots in two short poems, one beginning,

> " So then the Vandals of our isle,"

and the other,

> " When wit and genius meet their doom," &c.

Horace Walpole also speaks with horror of the atrocities that were committed at that time, but could not resist giving the following ludicrous description in a letter to Lady Ossory, on the 3rd of June.—" The Duke of Gloucester had reached the House with the utmost difficulty ; and found it sunk from the temple of dignity to an asylum of lamentable objects. There were the Lords Hillsborough, Stormont, Townshend, without their bags, and with their hair dishevelled about their ears, and Lord Willoughby without his periwig, and Lord Mansfield, whose glasses had been broken, quivering on the woolsack like an aspen. Lord Ashburnham had been torn out of his chariot, the Bishop of Lincoln ill-treated, the Duke of Northumberland had lost his watch in the holy hurly burly, and Mr. Mackenzie his snuff-box and spectacles. Alarm came that the mob had thrown down Lord Boston and were trampling him to death, which they almost did. They had *diswigged* Lord Bathurst on his answering them stoutly, and told him he was 'the pope' and 'an old woman;' thus splitting Pope Joan into two.   Lord Hillsborough, on being taxed with negligence, affirmed that the Cabinet had the day before empowered Lord North to take precautions ; but two justices that were called, denied having received any orders. Colonel Heywood, a very stout man, and luckily a very cool one, told me he had thrice been collared as he went by the Duke's order to inquire what was doing in the other House ; but though he was not suffered to pass he reasoned the mob into releasing him ;—yet, he said, he never saw so serious an appearance and such determined countenances."

The Hon. Mrs. Boscawen to Mrs. Delany.

Colny Hatch.   Saturday, 10th June, 1780.

Your very kind letter, my dear friend, (kind, indeed, to think of me in the midst of such troubles,) did not reach me till last night by being directed to *Barnet*, wch is general post, whereas our nasty post is the penny. So that the direction is simply to Colny Hatch, Middle-sex.[1] God be praised, you are safe and well.   I hope e'er this reaches you the Duchess and yourself will be able to *enjoy* her delightfull Bulstrode, tho' there must always be sad remembrance of dear friends that have suffer'd.   Oh, ungratefull country, so to reward a life of toil spent in its service !   Lord and Lady Mansfield are seldom long out of my head.   I sent a servant to Mrs. Ramsey, and had the satisfaction to hear that they were *unhurt* at least, but *alass !*   I will, however, say no more on this sad subject.

---

[1] In the Postal districts of Mr. Rowland Hill, "Colney Hatch, *Herts*, N." is the description of this place, which is still reckoned with "London and its environs." (1859.)

This country is full of *refugees*. Mrs. Chapone is at
Mr. Burrow's, and I saw her last night. Mr. and Mrs.
Cole at Mr. J. Baker's at Enfield Chace Gate, they fled
on Wensday night like Lot out of Sodom, the fire
raining upon their heads. Dr. Munro's[1] family are at
Mrs. Smith's at Hadley, they fled from a friend's house,
wch was between two others that were burning, I am not
sure where. We saw all this conflagration on Wensday
night from our garret windows. Judge what we felt
not knowing where it was or who were suffering till the
next day. Lady Edgcumbe fled on Wensday night to
Harrow, but why do I write on, for I perceive I cannot
change the subject? Accept then, once more, my dear
madam, my heartiest thanks for your kindness in writing
to me; you will see how well it was bestow'd by an
anxious enquiry I sent to Mr. Kay. God bless you, and
keep you in health. My best respects wait on the Duchess.

Ever your affectionate faithfull, and

Much obliged serv^t,

F. BOSCAWEN.

The Hon. Mrs. Boscawen to Mrs. Delany.

Glan Villa, ye 15th June, 1780.

I return my most sincere thanks to my kind friend
for the satisfaction of receiving a letter from Bulstrode.
Thank God, you were *quiet* and safe! Happy as usual
I must not expect you to be, while y^r mind dwells so

---

1 John Monro, M.D., an eminent physician. He was born at Greenwich in
1715, and succeeded his father in the charge of the Bridewell and Bethlem
Hospitals. He died in 1791.

much among your suffering friends, and that is so natural that, indeed, I know not how it can be otherwise. Lord Mansfield was at Westmins[r] Hall yesterday (last day of term). Mr. Cole, who din'd her, saw his lord[p], and thought he did not look quite so well as usual: that is too probable, indeed, tho' I am assur'd both my lord and lady are well. What Englishman could see him attend the Courts in West[r] Hall yesterday without blushing for their ungratefull country, which will never again see such a magistrate, and has but too plainly prov'd she does not deserve such a one. It reminds one of the Chancellor Clarendon, who was almost kill'd by an English mob, after being traduc'd and banish'd by an ungratefull parliament. Yet we *cannot* look into the historical registers of past times for a precedent to *these* we now explore. No; *these* stand *quite alone* I think, and will hardly be credited by posterity! You may believe we talk'd them over yesterday, when I tell you that Mr. and Mrs. Jenyns, Mr. and Mrs. Cole came and din'd at my cottage, and spent the day so much more peaceably than those w[ch] have lately pass'd, (for Mr. and Mrs. Jenyns fled one night to the inn at Cranford Bridge,) that I think they were all in spirits, and Mr. Jenyns said many pleasant things in his singular manner, tho' at the bottom of the heart every one must feel a *weight of care* for England, and the *sad wickedness* of Englishmen! As you observe it is only the infantine race that are happy, so that one wou'd say to them, as y[r] friend Mason does—"Stay pitying Time! Prolong their day of bliss!"[1] Pray turn to these sweet lines in

---

[1] Mason's "English Garden," book ii., line 454.

the 2ᵈ book of Gardens; the 2ᵈ I think it is, I'm sure not the last. By this time your sweet niece ¹ is *recall'd*, and you feel her loss! God bless and prosper her wherever she goes! She is, I doubt not *as good* as she is *sensible*, so that she cannot but be happy in many respects, since much of happiness goes surely with a *good heart* and a *good head*, for *folly* and *wickedness* tend always to misery. I am insensibly got into a sermon—the Psalms of last Sunday, I hope you notic'd they were, indeed, proper Psalms for the 2ᵈ Sunday in June 1780! I wish, dear madam, I *cou'd* tell you anything of Lady Jerningham? But Lady Edgcumbe fled to Harrow on the dreadfull Wensday. She has wrote to me from thence; but I have not heard of her return.

If Mr. Kay is come to you pray thank him de ma part for so immediately complying with my request. Will you allow me to make one for another letter, just to tell me how the Duchess and you do! Present my best respects to her Grace, and believe me ever faithfully and most affectionately

Yours,

F. B.

The Earl of Guilford to Mrs. Delany.

London, June 19th, 1780.

Madam,

Your obliging letter hints a permission to me to trouble you now and then with a little true intelligence, for which I am *much obliged* to you, as well as for giving

---

¹ Georgina Mary Ann Port.

me the satisfaction of hearing my Lady Dutchess and you are pretty well after your allarms; you will be glad to hear all has been very quiet to-day; and the two Houses of Parliament have unanimously agreed on loyal addresses. Lord Mansfield made a *very fine* speech in the House of Lords. The D. of Richmond found fault with some words he apprehended to have been in the King's speech, or the address; but they were *not there*! The D. of Manchester desired to know if the cities of London and Westminster were under military law? but it was explained to him that they were not. In the House of Commons Mr. Burke was very explicit in his approbation of the measures which had been taken. Mr. Fox said they *were right* when taken, but reserved to himself the examining whether the military becoming so necessary, might not have been prevented? As to my family, after whom you are so good as to enquire: Lady North has miscarried some days ago, but is pure well. The Bishop set out for Hartlebury pretty well. Lady Willoughby returned from Marshgate much better of her cold. The Dartmouths very well. I scratch this whilst the bell is ringing. I beg the favor of you to present my best respects to my Lady Dutchess, and believe me,

Madam,

Your most obedient

And obliged, humble servant

GUILFORD.

I am, thank God, pretty well. The D. of Cumberland has a levee to-morrow, but not the D. of Gloucester.

Among the MS. of this period, the following verses were found, written by the learned Cambrian, Sir W. Jones, after Lord G. Gordon's riots. It was composed in *one hour* for a society called the Druids, to which Sir W. Jones belonged, and who, during the summer circuit at Cardigan, were accustomed to meet and dine in a romantic situation on the banks of the river Teifi.

1780.

What means all this frensy, what mad men are they
  Who broil and are broil'd for a shade in religion?
Since all sage inspirers one doctrine convey
  From Numa's wild nymph to sly Mohamed's pigeon.
    Then Druids arise,
    Teach the world to be wise,
And the grape's rosy blood for your sacrifice pour,
    Th' immortals invoke,
    And under this oak
Kneel, kneel to the Goddess whom all men adore.

By various high titles this Goddess is nam'd,
  At Ephesus Dian, in Syria Astarte,
In *New* Rome 'tis Mary, Heaven's Regent proclaim'd,
  In *Old* Rome 'twas Venus, the buxom and hearty.
    But crown'd and enthron'd
    Her Godhead is own'd
In desert, in valley, on mountain, on shore,
    Then join our gay crew,
    Turk, Roman and Jew,
And kneel to the Goddess, whom all men adore.

When sallow Parsees, in vain Anquetil's rant,
  Repeat the strange lessons of false Zoroaster,
Or hymn ruddy Mithra's in rapturous cant
  As their surest preserver from every disaster,
    They worship but one,
    Warm and round as the sun,
Which Persia's rich kings on their diadems wore;
    The circle they prize
    Had long left the skies,
And they kneel to the Goddess whom all men adore

When dark visag'd Bramins obsequiously bow
  To the rock whence old Ganges redundantly gushes,
They feign that they bend to the form of a cow,
  And save by this fiction the fair maiden's blushes;

But from Sanscritan Vedes
The discov'ry proceeds
That her aid, whom we honor, e'en Bramin implores;
Like us wildly they dance,
Like us lightly advance,
And kneel to the Goddess whom all men adore.

You have heard of the mysteries hallow'd in Greece,
And shewn to th' elect in the groves of Eleusis,
Our learned, about them, have cackled like geese,
But their learning vain pomp or mere idle abuse is:
Th' initiate were told,
In verses of gold,
Mad Jove and rough Neptune to worship no more;
But with love and with truth
To frolic thro' youth,
And kneel to the Goddess whom all men adore.

Say why to sweet Araby pilgrims repair,
And troop in full caravans yearly to Mecca?
Their mosque is like ours, and no altar is there
Save that which the Patriarch bless'd in Rebecca;
The Koran for you,
Ye Mussulmen true,
Has of nymphs with black eyes and black tresses a store:
Then sink to the ground,
Tho' turban'd and gown'd,
And kneel to the Goddess whom all men adore.

See, Teifi, with joy see our mystical rite
On steep woody marge after ages renewed;
Here once Taliesin thou heard'st with delight,
But what was his voice to the voice of our Druid?
Each year will we greet
Thy shady retreat,
And sing to the Naiads our exquisite lore;
Sweet echo shall laugh
Whilst brimmers we quaff,
And kneel to the Goddess whom all men adore.

Our mystery, Druids, 'tis time to reveal,
And remove the thin gauze which our discipline covers;
Far hence ye profane, whose cold hearts are of steel,
But listen devoutly ye passionate lovers.
Ye zephyrs be dumb,
Cease ye blue flies to hum,

Ye waves kiss the brink of old Teifi no more;
But each to his fair
Waft a sigh or a prayer,
And kneel to the Goddess whom all men adore.

The young oak is an emblem

[The rest is missing.]

The Hon. Mrs. Boscawen to Mrs. Delany.

C. H.   Wensday, 20th June, 1780.

This roasting day makes me think of you, my dearest madam, and wish to know how you do. Yesterday (being Tuesday again) I was thinking too that you might possibly arrive. Before night I had reason to rejoyce you did not. Miss Julia Yonge came to make me a visit at 6 o'clock; while we were drinking our tea the thunder began to roll without ceasing, and the ebony clouds to be parted by continual lightning. You may be sure I exercis'd so much hospitality towards her as to persuade her to take up her lodgings here, wch she accepted, tho' *sans nightcap,* &c. We did the best we cou'd for her, and she is just gone in her open chaise and ponies, wch she drives herself. The storm ceas'd last night about 8 o'clock, and I have not heard of any mischief it has done I thank God.

When shall I see you, my dearest madam. Perhaps you will say "There is no quiet this hot weather like sitting quietly in my elbow chair, and in my north room." May all weathers agree with my dear friend! to know that they so do will be a very great satisfaction to her

Very affectionate servant,

F. BOSCAWEN.

Mrs. Delany to Miss Port, of Ilam.

Bulstrode, 23rd June, 1780.

Yes! my dear child, I *will* write to you and thank you for your very kind letter, which I received, and read at the Grotto yesterday, just after breakfast, and made every allowance you cou'd wish for the haste you wrote in. Much obliged by your taking the first opportunity of writing to me, well assured that you will attend to every thing that can improve you in body and mind, which will not only make you amiable, but valuable to the friends you love so dearly. You are happy, my dear child, to be again under the protection and direction of your dear mama; it reconciles me to your absence, tho' I must own I *miss you so much* that I will not yet trust myself to talk on the subject, but say a word or two (by way of parenthesis) to your dear brother.

(I thank you, my dear little George, for the few lines in "sister's" letter. I am glad you like y^r frock; she will tell you how often we talked of you, and how happy it would make y^r affectionate A D. to see you.)

I wrote to you the day after you left Bulstrode, and directed it to Welsbourne, not being sure that you would leave it as soon as you did. Lady Bute and Lady Louisa[1] came here last Wednesday, and go away to day as soon as they have breakfasted; they were sorry you was gone. Mrs. Boscawen is pretty well, and so are the family at Kenwood, tho' nobody has yet recovered their last sad terrors; but the good news of our compleat victory

---

[1] Lady Louisa Stuart, born August 15, 1757, died August, 1851.

at Charles Town[1] seems to revive all our spirits. I know you love a little bit of politics.

This letter was began yesterday morning at Bulstrode, but we came to town at 6 o'clock to Whitehall, where I lay last night, and I thank God more tranquill than on that sad Wednesday night, which I believe you will never forget; but great reason we have to be thankful that no more mischief was done by such wicked associates.

I write this in St. James's Place, where I am come to see how the new painting of my drawing room comes on, and Mr. Bolton has been here, and has brought the enclosed multiplication table.

I am so hurried I can write no more. Lord Guilford, Lord Dartmouth, and Mr. Montague have been here. I can't write to your dear mama this post; but I trust you will say everything that's kind and proper to her. Believe me, my dearest G. M. A.,

Most affectionately yours,

M. DELANY.

The Duchess of Portland sends her love to you.

The Hon. Mrs. Boscawen to Mrs. Delany.

Glan Villa, ye 6th July, 1780.

MY DEAR MADAM,

London is still so full, that we who have guinguettes in the neighbourhood get more custom than usual. I have had L^y Edgcumbe twice; our friends the Coles ditto, and several other visitors. It was impossible

---

[1] June 15th, 1780, arrived an account of the surrender of Charleston to Sir Henry Clinton.

not to be in some care for the Duchess's early attendance
in Westm^r Hall, wch I knew the preceeding evening by
Mrs. Walsingham, who was here; but I did not know
what was to follow—y^r visit at Ken Wood; yet you describe it so well, my dear madam, that I'm sure *I felt it!*
The approach to it—*the sight of it*—alas! that such pleasures shou'd be *so* turn'd to pain.   But there is nothing
one can say on this sad subject that does not fall short
of one's own sensibility concerning it, and, as you observe, one must be quite marble (like the *insensible neighbour*) not to be deeply impress'd.   Lady Mansfield *does
indeed* look ill.   My dear madam, I think I shou'd have
gone to the top of Highgate Hill and there sat, to have
had a glimpse of you as you return'd, cou'd I have known
the time.   I cou'd not hope you wou'd come here and
honour me with a visit, as that must have detain'd you
a day longer in London, and y^r immediate return to
Bulstrode was necessary to refresh y^r spirits after such a
tryal.

Yesterday I went to Lon^n for the first time since I
left it (*trembling*) on that dreadfull Wensday.   Of course
my friends there wou'd show me both camps.   It was
hot, and yet windy, so I got the tooth ach; but I got,
too, some good news, thank God, that the *whole province* of S. Carolina *had submitted*, and that N. Carolina
also was sending their deputies to the frontiers to meet
Ld Cornwallis on the *same errand*.[1]   God grant us peace!
If my old friend Admiral Geary,[2] who is pursuing the

---

[1] Alluding to the reduction of Charlestown, in South Carolina, by Sir
Henry Clinton and Admiral Arbuthnot, and the favourable position of Lord
Cornwallis.

[2] Admiral Francis Geary was appointed to the command of the grand fleet

French fleet, can but *bring home a good part of it*, surely we may hope for that blessing. I do not find the report of Mr. Walsingham's[1] captures is true, but Monsr de Pinto[2] told me it was likely that Admiral Rodney[3] wou'd fall in with a Spanish squadron inferior to himself; cet excellence là and my neighbor Paoli[4] are to take their ride hither to-morrow. If they bring me any good news, I will try to tell it you before the newspapers.

My visitors yesterday were full of the mariage declaré

on the death of Sir Charles Hardy in 1780 ; and was created a Baronet, 17th Aug., 1782. Sir Francis died, 7th Feb., 1796.

[1] The Hon. Robert Boyle Walsingham was lost in Oct., 1779, on board the "Thunderer" man-of-war, of which he was Commander, in a hurricane in the West Indies.

[2] The Portuguese Ambassador.

[3] Admiral Rodney defeated the Spanish fleet near Cape St. Vincent, Jan. 16th, 1780 ; but news, in those days, travelled slowly.

[4] The Corsicans having revolted against the Genoese, after a long and arduous struggle proclaimed Pasquale de Paoli, in the year 1755, Captain-General of the Corsicans. During twelve years he successfully resisted the efforts of the Genoese, and, with the exception of a few blockaded garrisons, drove them all out of the island. He formed a Legislative Assembly, established a University, settled an Ecclesiastical Hierarchy, and ruled the State with great prudence and skill, under the title of General of the Kingdom and Chief of the Supreme Magistracy of Corsica. The Genoese gave up their claims upon the sovereignty of Corsica to France in the year 1768. Paoli in vain appealed to Europe against the contract, and in vain won two signal victories over the invading French army ; he and the people were finally vanquished in 1769. Paoli withdrew to Leghorn, and thence to England, where he resided until the year 1789, when Mirabeau having moved in the National Assembly the recall of the Corsican patriots, Paoli went to Paris, and was appointed by Louis XVI. his Lieut.-General and Commandant in Corsica. He returned to Corsica, and was welcomed with enthusiasm. Shocked at the atrocities of the French National Convention, he placed the island under the protection of the English, and drove out the French garrisons. It was expected that he would have been appointed Viceroy, but Sir Gilbert Elliot was sent out to execute that office. To avoid dissensions, Paoli withdrew, recommending his countrymen to continue firm in their allegiance to the British crown. He accepted a pension from government, and died in England in the year 1807.

of Ld Egremont and L^y Maria Waldegrave.[1] To *that* I am very indifferent, but far otherwise to the Dss of Ancaster's[2] hopes of recovering both her children, wch I heard with great satisfaction.

I called at L^y Bute's door to inquire after her, and was assur'd that her lady^p and L^y Louisa were perfectly well, and out of town.

Mrs. Leveson writes me (from Lymington) that all Lady Dr Gower's law affairs are settl'd (that is compromis'd), and all law at an end; that *they lose* £30,100 of what was the strict due of principal and interest, but Mr. Leveson's part is deficient only £5000. My lady's all the rest. Very vexatious! yet upon the whole Mrs. L. seems to think it happy to end the lawsuit with the approbation of my lady and in her lifetime. Mrs. Leveson and she have made an excursion to Clarendon Park to visit Col. Bathurst and his lady, who is my cousin-german. Before I end this very dull epistle (pray remember the poor toothach), I must acquaint her Grace that I have been to see a church built and adorn'd by the magnificent Duke of Chandos,[3] à sa maniere—that is, with most superb paintings and immense monuments. The person

---

[1] This marriage did not take place. Charlotte Maria, second daughter of James, 2nd Earl of Waldegrave, married, Nov. 16, 1784, George, 4th Duke of Grafton.

[2] Mary, Duchess of Ancaster, widow of Peregrine Bertie, the 3rd Duke, lost her son Robert, the 4th Duke, July 8th, 1779. Her two remaining children were Lady Priscilla and Lady Georgiana Bertie.

[3] John Brydges, 9th Baron Chandos, 1st Duke of Chandos, Marquis and Earl of Caernarvon and Viscount Wilton. Having acquired the estate of Cannons with his first wife, Mary, last surviving daughter of Sir Thomas Lake, he erected there a stately palace. "The gilding was executed by the famous Pargotti, and the hall painted by Paolucci." The household and maintenance of this splendid residence were proportionate in expense and grandeur. At the Duke's death, the building was pulled down and

who shew'd it, and who seem'd very intelligent, told me the paintings alone cost £9000. I can easily believe it: they were Scripture historys, and, tho' much damag'd in the colouring, display'd good drawing; but all this is to say that having heard the Duchess of Portland speak highly of Cassandra, Dss of Chandos of the Willoughby[1] family, I beg'd the curate to procure me a copy of her inscription, which I have got accordingly, and will send to Bulstrode if the Duchess pleases. I have just rec͠ed a letter from my son at Kilkenny, where they have had great rejoycings on the taking of Charles Town, so I hope they are all loyal. The old seat of the Ormond family is just above the town, and *he groans* over the fine timber and immense old trees that are *laid low there!* and is astonish'd beyond measure at the owner's *being able* so to spoil the magnificence of this ancient seat.

F. B.

In the "Tour through Ireland by two English Gentlemen," published in 1748, is the following account of Kilkenny Castle:—
"The usual residence of the Ormond family was at the Castle of Kilkenny; the inside of which shows all the marks of the greatest magnificence, though almost in ruins. The apartments are indeed not well disposed, as there is little or no hall; but they are in themselves extremely fine. Painting, carving, gilding, and stucco, have exerted their several arts here. Among others,

---

the materials sold. The marble staircase was bought for Chesterfield House, May Fair; the stone obelisks with copper lamps, which lighted the approach from the Edgeware Road, were bought for Wanstead House.

[1] The second wife of John, 1st Duke of Chandos, surnamed "the magnificent," was Cassandra, daughter of Francis Willoughby, and sister of Thomas Willoughby, Lord Middleton. His third wife was Lydia Catherine Van Hatten, widow of Sir Thomas Davall. This Duke died at Cannons, Aug. 9, 1744, and was succeeded by his only surviving son, Henry Brydges, the 2nd Duke.

there is a fine dining-room of a circular form; the tapestry is gone here, the fretwork ceiling dropping to pieces, and the fine chimney-piece serves only to make us regret the loss of the other ornaments. The staircases *are grand* and well adorned in fresco. The principal bed-chamber, with a beautiful octagonal closet, has been the finest I ever saw: the floors of oak, inlaid with great judgment. Over this whole wing runs a gallery above 100 feet long and 30 broad. There are six large casement windows on one side, with a noble one at the end, which commands a fine prospect of the river and adjacent country. This stately room was once hung with fine paintings; and here were exhibited balls, masques, and other entertainments of that kind, with all the regularity and magnificence of a royal court. The many offices here show what the older inhabitants of the city assured us, that while this was the residence of that illustrious family there was no officer wanting here that was to be met with in the palaces of sovereign princes.

"The walls of this city were built in 1382, as it is said, at the expense of one nobleman of the Ormond family; but I cannot find any record of his name. I believe they might be repaired at that time; for it is certain the town was *immured* long before that date. I have read of gates in the year 1209, and gates without walls could be of but little use."

The Earl of Guilford to Mrs. Delany.

Wroxton, July 8th, 1780.

MADAM,

I have too strong a sence of my kind reception, and the great indulgence shown me at Bulstrode, to delay a moment making my warmest acknowledgments. My Lady Duchess and you have been exceedingly kind and charitable to a superannuated deaf invalid, and I hope you will be rewarded for it. The weather has been very favourable for my journey, and I rested pretty well

at Tetsworth. I met Lord Le Despencer [1] near Beacons
Field, and simply concluded him either going to London
or to dine out. I was taken with a curiosity just to
look into his garden, and in the afternoon went boldly
up to the house, and sent a servant to desire leave of the
gardener for me just to look into the garden, when the
answer was he had not dared to do it without telling my
lord I was there, and his lordship was coming out to
meet me. At this I was thunderstruck, and concluded
I should be fatigued to death, but there was no remedy,
and my lord immediately appear'd in an open portico,
and began to show me his curiositys. He was but just
risen from table, and the hour very inconvenient. He
pressed me to drink tea, which I in my confusion accepted.
This brought down Mrs. Parker (*Barker*, or *Darker*) in
an elegant deshabille, whom it had *not* been *at all* my
intention to visit, and I thought the water a *great while
before it boiled*, but both she and my lord overwhelmed
me with politeness! Nothing could appear more con-
jugal; whenever she meant to speak of my lord, she used
the term "*we*," or "*us*." She had got into the middle
of the mob when they were burning S[r] John Fielding's
house, and the description of her fears furnished a great
deal of conversation. When I order'd my carriage my
lord sent it to a garden door, and was to show me a
great deal in walking to it. To this I made a *violent
resistance*, but with no effect. My lord said it was all

---

[1] Sir Francis Dashwood succeeded, on the death of his uncle John,
Earl of Westmoreland, in 1762, to the Barony of Le Despencer in right of
his mother. He married Sarah, daughter and heiress of Thomas Gould,
Esq., and widow of Sir Richard Ellys, Bart., but died, *s. p.*, 11th Dec.,
1781.

down hill, and he walked it every day, so we hobbled out, and I was to admire everything as I passed, which I did very awkwardly, looking upon it as probably the last walk I should ever take. But with labour and sorrow I arrived at my carriage, much *rejoiced* to put an end to a visit *the most* inconvenient and troublesome, both to the visitor and visited, that ever was made! My lord had been so polite as to conduct me to the door of my carriage, when we both seemed to have had enough, and I was in pain to think how he would ever get up the hill again. The place is pretty, but very whimsical. My *distress* was at the time *serious*, but now it is over, and I am alive, I give you leave to laugh at it. I am ashamed to see what a long history I have of this expedition. 'Tis time I should repeat my thanks, and beg you to present my best respects to the Dutchess of Portland. Believe me,

Madam, your most obedient,

And obliged humble servant,

GUILFORD.

I left a travelling watch at Bulstrode, which can at any time be left with my porter at London, for I don't want it.

Mrs. Delany to Miss Port, of Ilam.

Bulstrode, 9th July, 1780.

I am always happy my dear child to receive any mark of your attention and kindness and thank you for your letter which I receiv'd this morning with one enclosed to the DUCHESS DOWAGER OF PORTLAND. Remember when you write to persons for whom you have a particular respect, that *abbreviations* are *not* respectful ; and I must beg you to be *more attentive* when you write, for my credit is concerned as well as your own, and your dear mama is not well eno' and has too many fatigues to go thro' to be able to direct you in an exercise wch indeed is in your own power to do well, and in which you have been so fully instructed. You know, my dear little pupil, that it was the condition of our correspondence that I should criticize y^r letters and I am sure you will take it as kindly as I mean it.

I believe all you say of your little companions, and should indeed be happy to see George as well as the rest of the groupe all very dear to me and am obliged to George for wishing to see me.

I don't doubt but you will do everything in your power to make your dear papa and mama happy, and nothing can make them more so than seeing you properly behaved in every respect. Don't neglect " *Mrs. Propriety*," who we used to talk of so frequently, and I promise you the better you are acquainted with her the better you will like her. I hope your dear mama will recover fast, and that Matlock will perfectly restore her health ; your tender care and attention to her, which I am sure will not be wanting, will greatly contribute towards it. Thus far I had written before I saw your letter to the Dss, which, tho' better written than mine, is carelessly done, but she accepts it with her usual kindness, and desires her love to her " little whisperer." She is, thank God, very well, we spent the whole afternoon on the south terrass, which is beautiful beyond expression. I walk every morning before breakfast. Rea was happy with your kind remembrance. We are going on with Mr. Goldsmith, and Dr. Blair's sermons ; and I work as usual, but *wanting* my little assistant, yet perfectly happy to have her where her *first duty* calls and where she must add to the happiness of so many I love.

I expect Mr. Lightfoot to breakfast in my dressing-room. Breakfast is to be prepared in the gallery for y[r] friend Gen[l] Paoli, Mons[r] Gentilli, Mons[r] Le Comte Cavalli, and Mr. Yeats, who are expected at 12 and are to dine here and Mr. Montagu.

I enclose y[r] feathers and the French verses, and hope you practise repeating them and the French Morning and Evening Hymn, Mr. Marlheille gave you.

[*In another handwriting.*]

Mr. Montagu, who franks y[r] letter, sends his love to you. He is going into Nottingham[e].

Mrs. Delany to Mrs. Port, of Ilam.

Bul[de], 7th Augt., 1780.

I was happy with your last letter from Matlock, and hope you will still find an encrease of strength and health, that you may enjoy your blessings at home; an affectionate husband and amiable promising children are consolations that must mitigate the common sorrows of life, and minister happiness on every trying occasion. There is a tender point w[ch] I have been unwilling to name, w[ch] is our dear Lady Cowper's ill state of health, but I suppose *you* have known it some time, and she bears it with her usual resolution and fortitude; Lady M. Mordaunt is now with her. The marriage of L[y] Har[t] Spencer[1] to Lord Duncannon, son to Lord Besborough, must give her great satisfaction; as beside rank

---

[1] Lady Harriet Spencer was married, 27th Nov., 1780, to William Viscount Duncannon.

and fortune he is a most worthy amiable man, and I believe by all accounts she is a *very valuable* young woman, and I hope will have the good sense not to fall into those giddy errors wh^ch have hurt her sister, who I also hope is now sensible of those errors. *I believe* she *never* meant to do wrong, but pleasure and flattery and violent youthful spirits plunged her into danger before she was aware of the bad consequences.

Lord Egremont's[1] shameful behaviour to Lady Mary Walgrave is still the subject of conversation; no reason can be asin'd, as the young lady was unexceptionable by all I can hear, but the dominion he is under of a great lady (L^y M-l-b-e) who has long endeavoured to prevent any other engagem^t and it is suspected she has *forbid the banns.*

Adieu, my dearest child; take care of yourself and let me know you are well and I shall be well and happy. I had a kind letter from y^r sister-in-law, B. D. with a very good account of all; how thankful ought we to be for the many blessings we enjoy which no body, no accident of life, can rob us of; the reflection of *doing our duty,* the wonders and beauties of the creation, the love of our real friends as long as we are permitted the enjoyment of their *society*; and when it is the will of heaven *that* should cease, the consideration that all tryals are sent to refine us for a blessed state, where only true (that is permanent) joys are to be found.

You see wth what difficulty I cease writing and much would it be lengthened could I say how affect^ly,

I am y^rs,
M. DELANY.

---

[1] George O'Brien, 3rd Earl of Egremont, born 18th Dec., 1751; died unmarried, Nov., 1837.

Mrs. Delany to Mrs. Port, of Ilam.

Bulstrode, 18th Aug., 1780.

How unexpected and *how great* is the loss of our most dear and amiable Mrs Bernard Dewes! but it is the will of heaven, to which we must submit; and she *was so angelic*, we cannot doubt of her present blessed state! My cares are divided among you. The poor disconsolate husband in the first place, and then the parents; indeed the branches of sorrow that attend this fatal stroke are many, but I trust not insupportable, when we consider the hand that gave the *blow*; well assured that his mercy to all his creatures, orders everything for the best; let us rest on that confidence, and not mourn like those *who have no hope.*

I know, my dearest child, the tender share you take in this sad scene. I know your health is not yet well established, yet I know your pious sentiments and Xtian resolutions; on *that* I depend for your not only doing right by yourself, y^r husband, and dear children, but in being a support and comfort to those whose loss in this event is *so much greater* than *yours.* I must think aloud to my dear Mary or I should not have written so much on this subject; it is a relief to my own feelings, which are truly very great. Your bro^r John was so good and considerate as to enclose the sad account in a letter to the Dss of Portland, who told it me with her usual tenderness, and was greatly affected by it herself.

Surely *she* (Mrs. B. D.) must have been farther gone than she imagined, as the child lived 3 hours? I am anxious to hear from them again—her poor sisters!—how I pity them! indeed at present I can think of nothing else. I thank God I am well in health, and if I hear you are so, and that all my distress'd friends feel that composure of mind I wish them, it will be a great consolation to me. Adieu, my dearest child; I must write to y^r bro^{rs}. I wrote yesterday to our poor disconsolate Bern^d, pray God support him! I think I wish he was at Welsbourne for tho' he may go from one awful scene to another the *natural* dissolution that attends old age[1] will make a very little addition to the anguish he now feels and the society of his excellent bro^r and change of scene I should hope would be some consolation to both.

The Dss's most kind and condoling compliments attend you.

Be very careful of y^r health; don't hurry and fatigue yourself when you can possibly avoid it; when the mind has been greatly agitated nothing will recover it like tranquillity.

Mrs. Delany was very much attached to Mrs. Bernard Dewes, who seems to have deserved and obtained the respect and affection of all who ever knew her.

The Dowager-Countess Gower to Mrs. Delany.

Bill Hill, 23rd Aug., 80.

Mrs. Leveson ans^d yor kind enquiries after my health, so thought it needless to interrupt you wth a dull letter of thanks.

Now think it time to remind you have a faithfull well wisher here, who has pleas'd herself wth ye hopes of seeing you, it has been a cordial in ye midst of her languor ye ague has left, wth other complicated incidents in this troublesome world.

The letter you mention I never rec^{e}d, no wonder w^n

----

[1] The failing health of his father, Mr. Dewes, of Welsbourn.

ye time it was wrote is consider'd. My illness and various things had prevented my seeing Mrs. Jeñings and her daughter before last week, both enquir'd much after you. I gave Miss great hopes of meeting you here, she longs for more instructions, believe you'l find her an apt scholar.

I *hear* a melancholly acc^t of poor L . . y Cowper, she was so *regular* and *temperate*, her complaint is a matter of wonder to me ! her grand-daughter[1] is soon to be hañily mañied, at least one may presume so, from ye general character L . . d Duncannon has, but her vain mother[2] is *not* pleas'd, or *pretends* she is not, and I sopose nothing but ye P— of W—, or a Duke w^d content her !

All my young people are at pres^t much taken up wth ye Reading races, I wish 'em well diverted, and all health and hañiness to ye inhabitants of Bulstrode.

The Duchess of Devonshire[3] to Mrs. Port, of Ilam.

DEAR MADAM,   Wimbledon, Aug. 23rd, 1780.

You will not be surprised to hear of the melancholy event of Lady Cowper's[4] death, as my uncle

---

[1] Lady Henrietta, d. of John, 1st Earl Spencer, m., Nov. 27, 1780, Frederick, Lord Duncannon, afterwards 3rd Earl of Bessborough.

[2] Margaret Georgina, daughter of the Rt. Hon. Stephen Poyntz, m. John, 1st Earl Spencer. Their 3 children were : George John, 2nd Earl Spencer ; Georgina, Duchess of Devonshire, and Henrietta Frances, Countess of Bessborough.

[3] " *The Duchess of Devonshire.*"—Lady Georgina Spencer, daughter of John, 1st Earl Spencer.

[4] Georgina Caroline, dau. of John, Earl Granville. Her 1st husband was John Spencer, father to the 1st Earl Spencer. Her 2nd husband was William Clavering, 2nd Earl Cowper. Lady Cowper d. Aug. 21st, 1780. Lady Cowper used to speak of having " *the gout*," which made Lady Gower express her surprise, as Lady Cowper was so temperate.

Poyntz told me he *had* acquainted you with her situation, a situation of such a *dreadful* kind as to cause those who lov'd her rather to rejoice than grieve to hear of her release.

My mother[1] desires me to return you a letter that came to Richmond after Lady Cowper's death. She has been much hurried, but wou'd have written herself if I had not.

> I am, dear madam,
> Your obedient, humble servant,
> G. DEVONSHIRE.

Mrs. Delany to Mrs. Port, of Ilam.

Bulstrode, 25th Aug., 1780.

Too well I know how my dearest Mary would be affected by the surprizing and truly to be lamented event in our family, and we sympathize too sincerely with all those that were related or acquainted with that *angelic creature*; but, as Mr. Bryant said to me, " her innocence and virtue, that make her so great a loss to her family, makes her a fitter inhabitant for heaven than for this world:" these considerations have their weight, which in time will mitigate a sorrow that can never be quite extinguished. O how I pity poor Bernard! Court wrote me word he bore it more calmly than he expected; it was a satisfaction to me to hear he had left Cheltenham, for tho' he removed to a solemn scene,[2] it was what

---

[1] " *My mother.*"—Margaret Georgina, Countess Spencer, daughter of Rt. Hon. Stephen Poyntz.

[2] " *Solemn scene.*"—His father, Mr. Dewes's, last illness.

must give a little turn sometimes to his heart-felt loss ;
and the *expected* event *there* is attended with every
circumstance to mitigate the tender feelings which on
such an occasion are natural ; I don't know *how* to mention our loss at Richmond, which, notwithstanding the
much greater distress of our recent loss, I know, by the
concern I am sensible of, will *add to yours!* and all these
are sad tryals which in the progress of life must attend
us. What a happiness that we have a Comforter whose
never failing Providence will support us under all tryals !
and I have that confidence, my dearest child, in the
rectitude of your mind, that I am sure you will do everything you can to bear up under these dispensations ; and
ye love you have for y^r family and friends will make you
consider your own consequence, and among the number
that of y^r ever affec^te

M. DELANY.

I am *indeed* well *in health.*

Mrs. Delany to Mrs. Port, of Ilam.

Bulstrode, 28th Aug., 1780.

I want to answer the later part of your letter, wch I have
just received, concerning Lady Mary Mordaunt, who came
to me a few days before I left London, to consult with me
what she should do about writing to you again ; I found
it was our dear Lady Cowper's *request* that she should
not say anything ail'd her but a rheumatick fever, and
she made her (as I understood) *read* the letter *to her.*
She said to me she thought that it would give you an

allarm of ye danger our dear friend was in; but I *thought not*, which made me write rather more explicitly to you, and your having been so ill made us all more cautious how we allarmed you; and, indeed, it proceeded *more rapidly* than I expected! I realy believe you have no reason to apprehend any wrong representation, and that *her love* (Lady Cowper's) and her confidence in *yours, lasted to the end.* Lady Spencer's conduct towards L^r^ C. has raised her much in my esteem ; she could not leave Lord Spencer all day, whose health continues very indifferent, but when he was gone to bed at 12 o'clock her chaise was ready at the door, and she went *constantly* at that hour *every night* from *Wimbleton to Richmond;* and after seeing every proper care was taken, went to bed there for 2 or *three hours,* and then returned to Wimble^n^ ! The last week our dear friend felt neither pain or uneasiness, but slept most of the time; I have not seen any body to tell me any more particulars, when I do I will communicate them, for it is a consolation to know the particulars relating to *such* a friend, and rather sooths than aggravates what one feels, but *calm* all suspicious thoughts, my dearest child, for they *must always aggravate,* and I *am sure* there is no real foundation for them ; I cannot but fear for y^r^ suffering in your health from *such a succession* of affecting events; and yet I blame myself for distrusting y^r^ fortitude under tryals that human nature cannot avoid, and are the order of Prvoidence.

My being able to write so much I think is a proof, notwithstanding the great shock I have suffer'd, that my health and nerves have not materialy suffer'd.

Our dear Dss is (she says) *very well,* but *will not* go

to Weymouth ; she says she *" can't leave me,"* and hopes
you will be satisfied wth her care ; indeed, it is beyond all
expression, and the only earthly support I could receive
at a time when I am so anxious for you and poor Bern^d,
and indeed *all of you,* and unable to go to you !

It is evident that Lady Cowper concealed her danger from
Mrs. Port, but the latter was tormented with the idea that Lady
Cowper must have thought her changed, as she was not alarmed,
and did not go to her.

Lady Cowper left numbers of fine snuff-boxes and jewels to
Lord and Lady Spencer and other relations and connections,
specifying the history of many of them, and among others one
that belonged to the Queen of Bohemia, given by her to Prince
Rupert, and by him to his mistress, who pawned it, and it was
redeemed by the Duchess of Marlborough ; also a box with the
freedom of the City of Cork given to her father, Earl Granville.

She left to her god-daughter, Mary Dewes (Mrs. Port of Ilam),
two silver sauce-boats that belonged to Lord Worsley, and two
silver wrought waiters with frames and cups fastened to them.
There is a long declaration from Lady Mary Mordaunt about
the erasure of a legacy to her god-daughter, Caroline Pilkington,
daughter of Colonel Chudleigh.

Mrs. Delany to Mrs. Port, of Ilam.

Bulstrode, 2nd Sept., 1780.

I cannot, my dearest Mary, condole wth you on the
change of scene at Welsbourn ;[1] and I know your *filial
piety* and great *sensibility* will aid you to consider the

------

[1] Mr. Dewes died Aug. 30th, 1780, aged 86.

happiness (we have reason to suppose) he now enjoys ; and that your own conduct towards him was *unblameable*.

I am glad to find your bro^r Dewes and Bern^d are going to Hagley, a change of scene will do them both good ; and since it has pleased God to deprive Bernard of his greatest earthly blessing, I feel some satisfaction in *her* *not* having been with him at Hagley, and hope that he will like to settle there, as it may draw him on to those sort of rational amusements that are best fitted, not only to calm, but exalt the mind.

I am glad the Dss of Devonshire did what was proper towards you ; and y^r not receiving an account from L^y M. M. or Miss W^{ms}, I suppose might be owing to their knowing it was to be done by a properer hand ; the letter that was returned to you must have come to Rich^d at the time of their greatest distress, and our dear (now happy) friend lay above a week in a constant doze, *senseless*, but *easy!* so that *great allowance* must be made. I had no ans^r to my last letters of enquiry, and only receiv'd the account in a letter from *Lady Spencer* ; I wrote you word *how well* she had behaved between her husband and her mother !

I trust a little time will tranquilize y^r dear spirits : your consequence to the darlings that surround you, and your love to Mr. Port will assist you in the good work of taking care of your health, and enable you to enjoy the blessings preserv'd to you ; *adversity* is the touch stone of *true virtue*. What a treasure do you possess in 3 *such bro^{rs}*! it is an *honour* as well as *a delight* to be ally'd to so much goodness ; and I reflect on their tenderness for you, and their readiness to show you every consolatory mark of kindness, with the utmost satisfaction. I dare not reflect on my own inability, which at this time prevents my coming to you, my dearest Mary; I must, and trust I am, thankful to be able at my years to keep up a correspondence that is so soothing to us both. It is impossible for me to tell you in how very kind a manner our dear, inestimable Dss has *felt all your sorrows,* and how constantly you are the tender subject of our conversation; greatly relying on your fortitude; but we agree that a week or ten days spent at Matlock before ye weather changes might be of great use to you, and ought not to be neglected.

I *like* the name of Georgi *Anna*,[1] and I shall be glad when y^u think proper to hear from her.

Mrs. Delany to Miss Port, of Ilam.

Sept. 21, 1780.

It is always a pleasure to me to receive a letter from my dear Georgi-ANNA, and am much obliged to her for that I received last post, made doubly welcome by your assurance that your most dear mama is so much better. I can assure you I am so. I hear the box from Ilam is come to St. James's Place safe. I believe I shall soon go to town for a day or two, and shall then have the

---

[1] " *Georgi Anna.*"—It has before been mentioned that the name of Miss Port, of Ilam, was *Georgina Mary Ann*, after her godmother, Countess Cowper (who died at this period), her great aunt, Mary Granville (Mrs. Delany), and her grandmother, Ann Granville (Mrs. Dewes); and that she was called sometimes by one, sometimes by another of these names, according to the partiality of the different members of the family for her namesakes. The last sentence in the above letter, no doubt, referred to her mother's wish that she should habitually be called by a name that would remind her of Lady Cowper, and Mrs. Delany intimated, by the way she wrote that name, that she wished to perpetuate the memory of her grandmother also, who, in their early days, she called "*Anna.*"

pleasure of opening it. The Dss of Portland has been so good to me that she has shar'd the concern I have been under, and it has *very much* affected her spirits; but I thank God she is now well. I made your *grateful* and *respectful* compliments to her Grace for the *honour* of her most kind letter. She desires me to send her love to you, and she has added many like companions to the little shell known as " *Miss Port's shell*." Mr. Agnew, her gardener, seems to understand shells almost as well as plants, and supplies her with *land* and *river shells*.

I began this letter some days ago, but franks being of no use till next Thursday, I delay my letter. I wish by the delay I could add to its value by making it more entertaining. We have not been at Windsor Lodge ; when the Queen sent about a month ago to the Dss of Portland to spend the evening, and did me the honour to command my attendance too, as we were neither of us well eno' to obey the summons, and since that the weather has been bad, and the Queen too near the time of her lying-in to be encumber'd with any company but those about her. As soon as she is brought to bed we go to town to enquire at St. James's Palace after her Majesty, and have our names set down among the en-quirers, and drink caudle and eat cake, and I will let you know what passes. I have done some rare flowers, and the Dss has been very busy, and Mr. Lightfoot (who always desires his compliments) ranging the birds' nests and eggs in their proper cabinet.[1] We air in the chaise or walk, according to the weather. Lord Ed^d Ben-

---

[1] The Duchess D. of Portland had a fine collection of the nests of various birds with their eggs.

tick has been here some days, and has given me a store
of franks ; but they don't pass till to-morrow, which has
delayed this letter.   Since I receiv'd yours I have receiv'd one from your dear mama from Matlock ; and as I
send you so long a letter, and depend upon y^r saying a
thousand kind things from me to her, I shall not write
again this post or two.   Another letter just received
from your dear mama, who I find was then returned from
Matlock, and preparing for her journey to Welsbourn,
where, I suppose, this will kiss your hands, if the time
of going there is not alter'd, and I shall enclose this to
your uncle Dewes.   How goes on French, geography,
and arithmetic ?   You tell me nothing of the dear little
Louisa, who I wish I could see, as well as her brother
George, &c., &c.   Lord Mansfield is expected here for a
few days, and on Sunday Mr. and Mrs. Cole came for a
week.   A rabbit has had the presumption to find his
way to the hare's supper, and made one of the circle the
night before last ; but orders are given for his execution
or *banishment* at least.   15 little partridges in a covey
roost (if it may be so called) are under the wall by the
path going to the Grotto.   Mouflons and all their fellow-
subjects are quite well, but how can they be otherwise
under the protection of such a sovereign as belongs to
this place?   My love and best wishes I put into your hands,
or rather mouth, to present in due proportions to all the
dear friends you are with, and believe me, dear child,

Your ever affect^{te} M. Delany.

Rea desires you to accept her respects.   She is very
well, and very good.

Bulstrode, Septr 1780.—I hope you will never write
such a blundering letter till you *are past fourscore*.

Frederic Montagu, Esq., to Mrs. Delany.

Papplewick, Oct. 10, 1780.

MY DEAR MADAM,

Many thanks to you for your letter. I began to grow impatient, and wish'd much to know about your health. I was setting out for Wroxton when the dissolution of Parliament put an end to all schemes and prospects. Lord Guilford has some thoughts of visiting you at Bulstrode this month in his way to London; but if he comes you must give him *fires* and *coarse* sheets. He is so attentive to other people, that he *deserves* this attention himself. I have a cold and a bad cough; but as I caught them at Nottingham in recommending Lord E. Bentinck to the country, I must not mind suffering in a good cause. I have spent a few days lately at Wentworth with the Weddells. Mrs. Weddell and I talk'd of you. Mason is at the height of all human felicity in having drove Mr. Lascelles out of his seat for Yorkshire; but what you will care more for is that he is translating Fresnoy's[1] Art of Painting, and he is finishing his Garden. We are going together to Lord John Cavendish in Northamptonshire. He calls here next Thursday.

You will pity them at Melton when I tell you that the Dean's grandson, Master Tatton,[2] a very clever lad

---

[1] Charles Alphonse du Fresnoy, born 1611, a celebrated French poet and painter. He wrote a poem on Painting which was first translated by Dryden; but Mason's translation, published in 1782, was rendered more valuable by notes of Sir Joshua Reynolds.

[2] Wm. Tatton, of Withenshaw, Esq., inherited the estates of his mother's family and took the surname of Egerton after her death, July, 1780. Mr. Tatton m., 1773, Frances Maria, eldest daughter of Dr. Fountayne, Dean of York, and by her had two sons and one daughter, viz., William, b. 1774, d. 1799; Thomas, d. 1778; Frances Maria, d. 1781.

of about 6 years old, and heir to the immense estate of Egerton, is, I am afraid, dying there. It will hurt them very much, and they have had their full share of sorrow. I rejoice to hear that the Dutchess of Portland is now very well, and beg my respectfull comp^s to her Grace.

I am, your most faithfull
And ob^t humble servant,
FRED. MONTAGU.

Mrs. Delany to Mrs. Viney.

Bulstrode, 16th Oct., 1780.

I believe it is long since I wrote to my dear friends at Glocester, and wish to hear from them. I am as well as can be expected, or rather better. Years and sorrow have bow'd me down, but I am thankful for many blessings I still enjoy. I have just received an account of the death of Mrs. Hamilton[1] of Summer Hill, whose painting of flowers and fine work you have, I believe, often admired; but they were the least of her praise. Her happiness must be my consolation. This has been a year of *great mortality* amongst my intimates and friends. Alas! how fleeting are earthly joys? Happy if such strokes make us aspire as we ought to do to that state of joy that will be permanent in all states. Believe me, my dear friends,

Y^r affec^te,
M. DELANY.

All well, I thank God, at Welsbourn.

In the course of twelve months Mrs. Delany had lost her intimate friend, Mrs. Montagu (mother of Mr. Frederic Montagu,

---

[1] The Hon. Mrs. Hamilton, widow of Francis, son of James, 6th Earl of Abercorn.

of Papplewick) ; her niece (by marriage), Anne De la Bere, (Mrs. Bernard Dewes) ; her cousin (Georgina Carteret), Lady Cowper, her brother-in-law, Mr. Dewes, of Welsbourn, and lastly her old friend, endeared to her throughout her many happy years' residence at Delville, Dorothea Forth, Mrs. Hamilton, to whose death she alludes in the present letter.

The Hon. Mrs. Boscawen to Mrs. Delany.

Glan Villa, 20th Oct., 1780.

I remember a good old custom at my good old aunt's, that when she had entertain'd her friends incomparably well (which she was very apt to do), they wou'd take glass in hand when the feast was over and say, " Madam, a cup of thanks." This, then, my dear madam, is my " cup of thanks " for the entertainm^t you have been pleas'd to supply me with, and upon which I have feasted. Nay, I have had a dessert, too, wch I did not expect nor guess that I was to be regal'd from the *Garden.* Now to drop my allegory and take to my book. I must tell you that I mean to restore it safely to the custody of Mary Butcher, by the trusty hand of Ld Worcester's servant, next Monday, so that if you want it you will find it at home. It has amus'd me very much, as all Mr. Walpole's writings do. In his occasional mention of one of your illustrious friends, long since dead, I was sorry to be put in mind of another illustrious and much more amiable one still living. I must quote the passage, and then you will understand me. He says of Swift, that "insolent under the mask of independence, and not content with domineering over her (Qu. Caroline's) politicks, she abandon'd him to his ill-humour, and to *the vexation of that misguided and disappointed ambition that*

perverted and preyed upon his excellent genius."   It is only
the part I have mark'd with lines that I apply to that
excellent genius (Mason), your living friend, for I'm sure
I do not know that he has any ill-humour (besides that
wch factious politicks necessarily give), much less that he
is insolent or domineering : but I had rather not have
been involuntarily reminded of him by any such marks.
Better to have waited till the same observations on gardening, wch Mr. Walpole makes in prose, reviv'd in my
memory his sweet poetry! And now, my dear madam,
I must make one criticism on Mr. Walpole. Why that
poor imitation of Voltaire in the beginning of his treatise
on gardening? Why the "*good man* Noah," and an
affectation of libertinism qui est ce me semble fort de-
placé? Better not have deviated so wide from Milton,
whom so much and so justly he admires.

And now, my dear madam, to change my subject
most entirely, I must tell you that our camp broke up
this morning, and I'm told it was very pretty to see the
officers and men pay their adieu to their beloved General
(for much beloved he was); but as all this pass'd before
9 this morning, I saw nothing of it. You would have
heard a great deal of good musick, but her Grace will be
on my side, and not wonder that I renounc'd a sight
that was calculated for the *larks!* After I have made a
panegyrick on our late General (and I was one of his
admirers), I shou'd tell you 'twas Genl Fawcett; but if
he wou'd but have betray'd a little *lazyness* this morning, I shou'd have counted it in the number of his perfections.

                                             F. B.

Mrs. Delany to Mrs. Port, of Ilam.

Bulstrode, 29th Oct., 1780.

Did I not write you word that Mr. Lightfoot was going to be married? the day Monday was se'night; but did I tell you of his sad disappointment? if I did, forgive this repetition, the failure of old age. On Sunday evening that was to have been the eve of his wedding-day, he was seized with a nervous fever, and for some days thought to be in great danger, but is now so much better that he performed his duty at the chapel here on Friday.

Monday.

I had a kind letter from Mrs. Dewes.[1] I hope Buxton has been of great service to her, and that health and happiness, as far as this world will allow, will attend the dear society; I must not, at my great age, repine at not being able to make one of it, but recollect the many blessings I *have* enjoyed, and am still permitted to enjoy. Unreasonable expectations create disappointm[ts], and are productive of many sorrows. Last Thursday the Dss of Portland and I went a visiting to Windsor: first to Lady Courtown[2]—not at home; then to Mrs. Walsingham—ditto; then to Mrs. Egerton, and found her and her daughters, like the picture of industry, all employed. Mr. Egerton's *not* being in Parliament *this year* is a great loss to me and my correspondents.

Tuesday.

To town we came yesterday. On my arrival I re-

---

[1] Harriet Joan De la Bere, wife of the Rev. John Dewes.

[2] Mary, daughter and coheiress of Richard Powys, Esq., married, 16th April, 1762, James, 2nd Earl of Courtown.

ceived the pleasure of y^{rs} and Bernard's letter, for which accept my thanks. Your dear little ones will rejoyce, to cling about you and tell all their little tales in your absence, and make a pleasant buz about your ears. Long may you bless each other! no pleasures are equal to those that are mix'd with our duties.

I suppose the 2nd week in January will bring me the *much wished-for happiness*; impatient as I am for the time I don't name an earlier day, as I have some little household matters to adjust and would have no embarras when you come. If Court comes to town at his usual time (the 20th of Jan^y) I do not know but that your nearest way would be first to Welsbourne and then to come altogether. The Dss P. and Lady Wey. (who is come for ye R. Xtning [1]) dine with me to-day.

The Dowager-Countess Gower to Mrs. Delany.

Bill Hill, 3rd Nov., 80.

I have long wish'd for that interruption, d^r Mrs D. writes of, and have it under yor hand y^t you w^d obey my commands (as you term it), wch were, to hear now and then you and ye D. D^s of Portland were well. I sh^d have claim'd yor promise repeatedly, had not Mrs. Boscawen made up yor deficiencies, and frequently given good acc^{ts} of both you and her Grace, wch were very satisfactory.

As you have no news when in ye purlieus of St. James's you can expect none from this retreat, but per-

---

[1] "The young Prince was christened on the 31st of Oct., 1780, by the name of Alfred. He was born on the 22nd Sept., and died in 1782."

haps a little history of L..y Craven[1] may amuse a mom[t]. She sent to acquaint a distant relation of hers in this neighbourhood she w[d] make 'em a vissit for a few days, and nam'd y[e] day. Y[e] gentleman is old and sickly, and keeps very early hours. At ten he went to bed, his wife sat up till twelve; then she went to rest. Mr. Le Grand waited for her another hour (who was only a vissitor there), but no lady came, and he retired. Ab[t] 2 o'clock she arriv'd, *driving herself* in a little chaize, and her maid, and put y[e] sober ffamily into a huricane! Y[e] next day she read her works, describ'd the theatre she's building at her house near Newbery, and then took herself away!

If I was her relation I sh[d] solicit her l..d to confine her! What odities there are roving ab[t]! heaven guard me from 'em! I beg my best respects to y[e] D. D[s] of Portland. Mr. and Mrs. Leveson are return'd, desire their complim[ts] to you and her Grace.

Mrs. Delany to Mrs. Port, of Ilam.

Bulstrode, 3rd Nov., 1780.

Here we came last Wednesday, and return to-morrow. Our dear Duchess brought a bad cold with her, and I a little one; but the good air, good fires, and tranquillity of Buls[de] have nursed them away. Miss Jennings, who I believe I have mentioned to you as a sensible, agreable, and ingenious woman, a pupil of mine

---

[1] Elizabeth, daughter of Augustus, 4th Earl Berkeley, wife of William, 6th Baron Craven, who, in 1791, married Christian Frederick, Margrave of Brandenburgh Anspach.

in the paper mosaic work (and the *only one* I have *hopes* of), came here last Thursday, but went away this morning. We have also seen Mr. Lightfoot, but the weather and other interruptions have prevented our visiting the bride. He looks very happy. I made all your compliments, and have promised to return his with his best acknowledgments. I have just received a letter from Mrs. Boscawen, and must transcribe a paragraph : " *Mademoiselle Chudliegh, Hervey, Kinston, Bristol, Wartz* ; is *now Princesse de Radzivil, and may be Queen of Poland, really married to him. The Prince of Radzivil is a grandee of Poland, and has it in contemplation to be King there at the next general election,* which will make a curious finishing to the edifice of her extraordinary fortune." I wish she would write her own memoirs faithfully, they would exceed all that the folly and madness of the world have produced before them, and might well be styled " *extravaganzas.*" Future ages will hardly give credit to such a narrative.

I received, my dearest Mary, your last dear letter the day of my arrival here. I am glad you are determined to bring your man, it will be most convenient to us both. Don't have any scruple about bringing your own chaize, I will take care of a place for it. I beseech you not to load yourself with anything more than what your post-chaise seat will contain, but send your trunks and boxes by the car[r] the week before you come : I insist upon it. Your deep mourning, I suppose, lasts till the end of Feb[y], so that you will not want any great change of raiment.

You may send up G. M. A's coloured coat, as should you be willing to leave her behind till June, *her* mourning will *be out* at the end of 3 q^{rs} of the year mourning. Perhaps rules are altered, but I speak of ancient days.

S^t. J. P., Tuesday morning.

Yester^y we came to town at 3, the Dss dined wth me; Master Sandford, by her appointment, met us. He is a fine, sensible, natural boy, and very civil, and seems in very good health. He flatters himself with the hope of seeing you and his playfellows. My little circle last night, beside her Grace, was Lady Jerningham and Mrs. Boscawen. Just now Lord Willoughby has called upon me; he and all his family are well; not yet fixed in town; inquired kindly after you. I have more letters to write, so, très chère, adieu.

Ever most affect^{ly} your own
A. DELANY.

I enclose a pair of gloves for G. M. A., let me know if they fit. The day for coming to town is fixed (please God) for ye 18th, and any day after that day month (the 18th Jan^y) most happy shall I be to receive my most dear M. and her precious children; but it must depend on the weather and y^r convenience, and I will not suppose any appointed time, to avoid disappointment, for any time will be *convenient* to me, and that *most* which will be so to you. I hope Mr. Port is quite well. *Pen.* (and *even* her high head) will be welcome.

The following letter was indorsed by Miss Hamilton— "Written by Mrs. Delany in her 81st year."

Mrs. Delany to Miss Hamilton,[1] *St. James's Palace.*

St. James's Place, 7th Nov., 1780

The kindness of your heart, my dear madam, is truly gratified, and *I* am more *obliged* to you than I can express; nor can I find words to show how gratefully sensible I am of the high honour the Queen has done me by bestowing on me a lock of her beautiful hair; so precious a gift is indeed inestimable!

I am entirely at a loss to know in what manner to pay my duty and humble acknowledgments, and must rest on that most kind attention and affectionate regard which procured me such a treasure to set me in such a light as may make me appear not entirely unworthy of it. I shou'd have given myself the pleasure of waiting on you this morning, but my weakness and the weather will not permit me; but if Miss Hamilton cou'd call in St. James's Place it will add to the happiness of her

      Most obliged, obed^t, and,

        Give me leave to say, affectionate,

            MARY DELANY.

I shall be at home all the evening, and return to-morrow to Bulstrode.

---

[1] Mary Hamilton, daughter of Charles, son of Lord Archibald Hamilton.

Mrs. Delany to Mrs. Port, of Ilam.

St. James's Place, 8th Nov., 1780.

Just on my return to Bulstrode, I must tell my dearest Mary that I am happy to know you are safe at Ilam, and your fair flock about you,—*a treasure*, and tho' it may cost you some anxiety to protect and turn to the best advantage, it will I trust prove a blessing to you beyond all compare of honour and riches : to train up beings for eternal happiness is the noblest work of mortals, and I make no doubt of your being assisted and supported by that good Providence to whom all hearts are open.

When I came to town on Monday I found a note wth a lock of hair from Miss Hamilton of St James's Palace, (Georgi Anna knows who I mean, *a friend of hers*,) wch I transcribe verbatim, as I cannot part with the original : it may *appear vain*, tho' gratitude is the motive, and also I know you take pleasure in what does me honour.

" St. James's, Nov. 6th, 1780.

" Tho' I wished very much, my dear madam, to have had the pleasure of giving you with my own hand the enclosed, I cannot bring myself to postpone the satisfaction you will have, in having in your possession a lock of her Majesty's hair, wch she herself gave me this morning to present you ; it undoubtedly marks *her* esteem and regard for you, likewise permit *me to add* it proves my affection in having emboldened me to make ye request, and my attention to your wishes in procuring it. There may be *vanity* in *marking this out*, but surely it is allowable *if* it procures me the satisfaction of having obliged Mrs. Delany ?"

I write in a hurry, but was unwilling to lose a post in informing you that the Queen has in the most gracious manner set down one of y^r sons in her list for the Charter House, as she was told I wished to place one of my little nephews there : you must let me know which you determine on. I own I wish to have it *George* ; and as he and his bro^r are too young for immediate admittance there is time to consider about ye eldest, and if George's name and age, (both which must be presented to the Queen,) is sent immediately, we may find some other means should it prove on consideration desirable for John ; and when I am so happy as to see you, we may talk about it ; but I at present think on many accounts it will be best to name George, and his *very name* may be an advantage to *him*. How I long to see the dear little fellow !

This must be secret, and I beg that neither you nor Mr. P. will mention it to *any* of your children, and only to y^r bro^{rs}, with a restriction not to speak of it.

Mr. Lightfoot much better, so is Mr. Montagu, and Lord Dartmouth, and Ld North, who have all been ill.

Miss B. Fountain [1] to be married soon after Xtmas to Mr. Wilson, a very good and agreable match. Lord Spencer better, the wedding going on apace ; when Lady Har^t is married to Lord Duncannon, I suppose you will congrat. L^d and L^y Spencer and the Dss of Devonshire. Lady Will^y very well at Marsh Gate.

---

[1] Elizabeth, second daughter of the Rev. Dr. Fountayne, Dean of York, by his third wife, Anne, only daughter of Charles Montagu, Esq., married, in 1781, Richard Wilson, Esq., eldest son of Dr. Christopher Wilson, Bishop of Bristol. Mr. Frederic Montagu was uncle to Mrs. Wilson.

Mrs. Delany to Mrs. Frances Hamilton.[1]

Bulstrode, Nov. 17th, 1780.

I am infinitely obliged to you, my dear Mrs. Frances Hamilton, for your most kind attention to me in your last most cordial letter; and don't know which endears you most to me, your filial tenderness, or your fortitude[2] and rectitude of mind, which will not only prove your greatest consolation, but an example worthy of imitation to all that know you.

I am most happy that Lady Drogheda was[3] in Ireland at the time you wanted extraordinary consolation, and her excellent mind and heart could not fail of giving it to one so sensible of her great merit. I hope my next letter from you will be from Moore Abbey, and that you will be so good, as to present my best compliments to Lady Drogheda. She was so obliging when in London, to do me the honour of calling upon me, and greatly have I regretted, (though I claim no title to it,) not having a greater intimacy with one so qualified to delight and improve those she converses with. You judged very right in not leaving your own house immediately; and when you return to it, I make no doubt, but that those tender recollections, which at first increased your sorrow, will then pour balm into your wounds; as those virtues

---

[1] This and some other letters to Mrs. Frances Hamilton were published the early part of this century (1800), but had a very limited circulation, and have long been out of print.

[2] "Fortitude" on the death of her mother, *the* Mrs. *Francis* Hamilton, to whom a previous letter was addressed, the widow of the Hon. Francis Hamilton, son of James, 6th Earl of Abercorn.

[3] Ann, daughter of Francis, 1st Marquis of Hertford.

which made *her* so dear and valuable to her friends, could not be rewarded in this world.

I thank God, the Duchess of Portland is well, and charges me with her best compliments to you. Every scrap of ingenuity produced and bestowed by our late unequalled friend [1] is treasured up most carefully : if a duplicate of a *flower* or *insect* comes to your hands, when you are indulging your attention with them, *may I beg it*, if a more worthy suppliant has not been before me ? Tho' after the many tokens I have been indulged with from that dear and most valuable hand, I fear this will appear avaricious : be it so, but avarice is the vice of age !

And now, as I know *you* take pleasure in what gives *me* pleasure, and does me honour, I must tell you of our amiable and gracious Queen's politeness, and (I may presume to add) kindness to me. She was told I had wished for a lock of her hair ; and she sent me one with her own royal fingers : she *heard*, (for she was *not asked* for either,) that I wished to have one of Mrs. Port's [2] boys in the Charter-house, and she gave her commands that one of my little nephews should be set down in her list : you will easily believe I was anxious to make my proper acknowledgements, and under some difficulty how to do it, as I am unable to pay my duty in the drawing-room. When fortunately an agreeable opportunity came in my way. Last Saturday, the 11th of this month, about one o'clock, as I was sitting at work at my paper mosaic, in my working dress, and all my papers littered about me,

---

[1] The Hon. Mrs. Hamilton was unrivalled in painting flowers and insects.
[2] Mrs. Delany's niece.

and the Duchess Dowager of Portland *very intent* at
another table, making a catalogue to a huge folio of portrait prints, the groom of the chambers announced " the
Queen and Princess Royal," who were just driven into
the court : I retired to change my dress, and wait for a
summons, should her Majesty send me her commands.
The Duchess kept her station to receive her Royal visitors, and I was soon sent for, which gave me the opportunity I so much had wished, and my acknowledgements
were most graciously accepted. The Queen staid till
past three, and left us, (though no strangers to her ex-
cellences,) in admiration of her *good sense,* her affability
blended *with dignity,* and her entertaining conversation.
So *much propriety,* so *excellent a heart,* such *true religious
principles,* give a lustre to her royalty that crown and
sceptre alone cannot bestow. I tell you, my dear madam, these particulars, that you may partake of that
admiration which I know your good heart will feel and
enjoy. At the moment you are struck with her superiority, you *love* her as a friend, which is *very rare,*
though I have long experienced this happy union, in the
person for whose sake I have received so many honours.

We went to the Queen's Lodge to enquire after
her Majesty the day after she had been here; which
we did after church-time. Windsor is but eight miles
from hence; I set the Duchess of Portland down at
the Queen's Lodge, and went on in *her* chaise to Mrs.
Walsingham, in the Castle, a sincere admirer of Lady
Drogheda, and who desired me to convey her best compliments, which I put into your hands. I had not been
ten minutes there, when your *very ingenious and agreeable*

cousin, Miss Hamilton,[1] (to whom I am greatly obliged,) came in haste from the Queen, to bring me into her presence, a command I willingly obeyed. Nobody was with the Queen but the Duchess Dowager of Portland. She graciously made me sit down just before her, and a *three hours'* conversation confirmed all I have already said: from thence we went to dine with Mrs. Walsingham, spent a very agreeable day, and came home, by the light of a bright moon, about 8 o'clock. I need say nothing of my health, after such exploits, but I wish you to say a great deal of affectionate and grateful regards to my friends in Ireland, and to believe me

Ever affectionately yours,
M. DELANY.

Mrs. Delany to Mrs. Port, of Ilam.

S^t. James's P., 25th Nov., 1780.

The bad weather has kept us in town all this week, but the Dss of Portland proposes returning to Bulstrode next Wednesday.

I think nothing new has happened since I wrote last, in which I believe I mentioned Miss Hamilton's coming to me on Monday last from the Queen for *George Rowe*

---

[1] "Agreeable cousin, Miss Hamilton."—Mary, daughter of Charles Hamilton, son of Lord Archibald Hamilton, who married Jane, daughter of James, 6th Earl of Abercorn. Lady Jane Hamilton's brother, the Hon. and Rev. Francis Hamilton, married Dorothea Forth, to whose daughter this letter is addressed. Miss Mary Hamilton's *father* was, therefore, first cousin of Mrs. Frances Hamilton, daughter of the Hon. Mrs. Francis Hamilton (Dorothea Forth).

Port's name, &c., now enrolled in the Royal list. I
have seen no body else except Lady Bute, Mr. Montagu
and our beloved Dss, who I thank God is very well. I
have left all my works behind me, and indeed had I not,
the darkness of the days will not permit me to do anyhing
but knot and settle old letters, wch is my present employment; I am searching for some letters of Mrs. Hamilton's (Granby Row) which I can't find. Did I lend them
you among some others of my correspondents? If I did,
bring them with you, and bring the little enamelled
heads I gave you, after Rosalba, as the Dss of Portland
wants to see them.

I am glad you went to Calwich; my greatest satisfaction is thinking of your all being happy in one another's love. Do me justice to all. My poor Bernard
was better last time I saw him, but his feeling heart
will at times get the better of his fortitude, wch indeed is
as great as can be expected.

George Tassener has lost his good Lady Donegal and
his place. He is an honest, sober, good servant, tho'
rough and unpollished. I wish any body would make
a demand for Mary Butcher. She has tired me out with
her temper. But alas, she has no outward charms to
attract, tho' *she thinks* the shoemaker that attends her
is *not* insensible. I doubt it is false fire! I have in my
possession for you from Lord Spencer 2 silver salvers for
chocolate cups, 2 silver sauce boats, and 4 China chocolate cups.

The Hon. Mrs. Boscawen to Mrs. Delany.

Bill Hill, Nov. 27th, 1780.

Yes, my dear madam, I am at Bill Hill, where I have receiv'd the honour and favour of a most kind invitation to Bulstrode: but I have business in London next week (thither I mean to repair on Friday), and by another week I shou'd hope Bulstrode wou'd be transferr'd to Whitehall? This I shall learn when you come next to St. James's Place; I imagine you are now there. *What* honours you have receiv'd I know not, but I know you merit *all* that *can be confer'd,* and therefore I shou'd not suspect you to be *borne away* by them, an effect wch they seldom have on those who really deserve them; I am impatient to hear the particulars, that is to have a conference with you myself, and I promise myself that pleasure for next week, viz. Tuesday ye 5th, in the afternoon; I will hold myself engag'd to you, unless you forbid me. Your noble friend here is in perfect health and at this moment *gone out on horseback* I believe! One frosty day she said if it was market-day at Wokingham she would walk over and see the humours of it. As it was not market-day, I had no need to˙resist the proposal, but I'm sure I cou'd not have comply'd with it, whereas her lady^p seem'd to consider it meerly as "*taking a walk.*" Indeed she is charming well, and vastly kind and good to me, as usual; for she was pleas'd to invite my son to meet me, and he obey'd her obliging summons and is here. On Saturday se'night in Oxfordshire he was witness to the sad scene of Ld Deerhunt's[1] misery, w^{ch}

---

[1] George William Coventry, born in 1758, and succeeded his father, in 1809, as 7th Earl of Coventry. His mother was one of the beautiful Gunnings. She died in 1760.

was such that he call'd out: " Will no one knock me on the head?" It was a sort of bravado to shew how high a leap his horse cou'd take, for the hounds were not running nor the horsemen pursuing. All was at a stand, wch gave this unfortunate young man leisure to attempt impossibilities: he had leap'd over hedges to and fro with success, but at last attempted a very high white rail, the boundary of a riding in Ditchley Wood. He was carry'd to Woodstock in a most dreadfull condition. There his father came to him.

I had a letter yesterday from Ld Worcester, who remains perfectly well at school. I had the satisfaction to see him so before I parted with him from Glan Villa. Mrs. Leveson gives me notice of an airing, and the chaize is ready, so I finish abruptly.

F. BOSCAWEN.

Mrs. Delany to Miss Hamilton.

Nov. 29th, 1780.

I understood, my dear madam, that you intended to send for the locket[1] yesterday, but as that did not happen, I fear I mistook and was to send it to you, which I now do, knowing in whose hands I *trust* the *precious deposite*, but as I go out of town at 12 this morning, I suppose it can *hardly* be returned by that time?

I hope, my dear Miss Hamilton, you will have the indulgence to excuse my *not* sending the paper the

---

[1] This locket with the Queen's hair is set in pearls, and the Queen's Crown and Cypher on the back. It was probably to have the latter added that the Queen desired it to be intrusted to Miss Hamilton.

Duchess of P. shew'd you; it was produced by the fulness of grateful spirits, and it was never meant to have been seen but by her Grace—(and oh! sad to tell!) she betrayed me. I am struck with the apprehension that they may appear too presumptuous and impertinent; and you will see the propriety of suppressing it, and I flatter myself you will forgive

Your most obliged and obed^t

M. DELANY.

Mrs. Delany to Miss Hamilton, at the Queen's Lodge, Windsor.

Bulstrode, Sunday morning.
10th Dec., 1780.

MY DEAR MADAM,

When I had the pleasure of seeing you last in St. James's Place you thought it not unlikely that Bulstrode wou'd be honour'd by a Royal visit, but I am very sorry to tell you that the Dss D^r of Port^d is very much indispos'd with a cold, and confin'd to her bed and chamber. I hope, tho' her cold oppresses her very much at present, that by her submitting to a little care, slops, and warm nursing, they may prove as efficacious as our good friend Dr. Turton's advice, tho' that I esteem excellent; I shall, you may believe, my dear Miss Hamilton, be an attentive deputy, feeling as *I* do the consequence of *such* a friend. The Duchess of P. has not mentioned to Lady Weymouth or Lady Stamf^d her not being well; as she hopes her cold will soon grow better, she wou'd not, at such a distance, give them the uneasiness of knowing she is not quite well.

My dear Madam, you will soon perceive why I write

all this—I cannot but wish the hon^r you mention'd may *not* at this time have *been intended,* as that would lessen the great mortification of being obliged to *give a word to the wise* wch may check an honour and happiness so highly valued by the Dss D^r of Portland; I dare not presume to name my own sensibillity on the occasion : this is all *entre nous*; I have not said any thing of it to the Duchess; she had but an indifferent night, but lyes quiet now ; but I hope if her cold mends enough for her Grace to go to town, as she proposes, to have the great satisfaction of seeing you next week in St. James's Place —in every place

Dear Miss Hamilton's

Most obliged and most faithful, humble serv^t,

M. DELANY.

Mrs. Delany to Miss Hamilton.

St. James's Place, 27th Dec., 1780.

Don't think me ungratefull, my dear Miss Hamilton, for not acknowledging the very kind fav^r of y^r note. I can give you too substantial a reason—that I *was not able* to write, tho' truly sensible of y^r obliging attention. When you can call, I shall now be happy to see you, and you will much oblige

Y^r faithful, hum^{bl} serv^t,

M. DELANY.

I hope Mrs. Goldsworthy is better; I don't send to her, as I think it would be troublesome.

The Duchess of Portland is better.

Dr. Turton has forbid my seeing more than two friends in a day, and still limits me to particulars.

How I am flatter'd with her Majesty's gracious approbation of my—" *works !*" for after such an honour I must not give them any degrading epithet.

As Mrs. Delany here alludes especially to Queen Charlotte's approbation of her " *Works*," and as the Queen had long before and often seen her Flora, and continually sent flowers from Kew as studies for Mrs. Delany to copy to add to the collection, it is very probable that it was at this time (Dec., 1780) that Queen Charlotte made her choice of the twenty plar
and which might then have been offered for h

END OF THE SECOND VOLUME.

(SECOND SERIES.)

LONDON: PRINTED BY W. CLOWES AND SONS, STAMFORD STREET.